I0881171

Sayyid Qutb

Modern Intellectual and Political History of the Middle East
Fred H. Lawson, *Series Editor*

Select Titles in Modern Intellectual and Political History of the Middle East

The Autocratic Parliament: Power and Legitimacy in Egypt, 1866–2011
Irene Weipert-Fenner

Hakibbutz Ha'artzi, Mapam, and the Demise of the Israeli Labor Movement
Tal Elmaliach

Iran's Experiment with Parliamentary Governance: The Second Majles, 1909–1911
Mangol Bayat

National Symbols in Modern Iran: Identity, Ethnicity, and Collective Memory
Menahem Merhavy

Ottoman Rule of Law and the Modern Political Trial: The Yıldız Case
Avi Rubin

Shaykh Yūsuf al-Qaraḍāwī: Spiritual Mentor of Wasaṭī Salafism
Sagi Polka

Watermelon Democracy: Egypt's Turbulent Transition
Joshua Stacher

Why Alliances Fail: Islamist and Leftist Coalitions in North Africa
Matt Buehler

For a full list of titles in this series, visit https://press.syr.edu/supressbook-series/modern-intellectual-and-political-history-of-the-middle-east/.

Sayyid Qutb

An Intellectual Biography

Giedrė Šabasevičiūtė

Syracuse University Press

First Edition 2021

21 22 23 24 25 26 6 5 4 3 2 1

∞ The paper used in this publication meets the minimum requirements of the American National Standard for Information Sciences—Permanence of Paper for Printed Library Materials, ANSI Z39.48-1992.

For a listing of books published and distributed by Syracuse University Press, visit https://press.syr.edu.

ISBN: 978-0-8156-3742-4 (hardcover)
978-0-8156-3728-8 (paperback)
978-0-8156-5529-9 (e-book)

Library of Congress Cataloging-in-Publication Data

Names: Šabasevičiūtė, Giedrė, author.

Title: Sayyid Qutb : an intellectual biography / Giedrė Šabasevičiūtė.

Description: First. | Syracuse : Syracuse University Press, 2021. | Series: Modern intellectual and political history of the Middle East | Includes bibliographical references and index. | Summary: "Standing at the crossroads of biography and intellectual history, this book seeks to trace the debates on literature between writers, Muslim scholars, and Islamists in Egypt between 1900 and 1960. To understand these debates, it follows the intellectual career of Egyptian writer and late-life Islamist, Sayyid Qutb"— Provided by publisher.

Identifiers: LCCN 2021007880 (print) | LCCN 2021007881 (ebook) | ISBN 9780815637424 (hardback) | ISBN 9780815637288 (paperback) | ISBN 9780815655299 (ebook)

Subjects: LCSH: Quṭb, Sayyid, 1906–1966. | Muslim scholars—Egypt—Biography. | Authors, Arab—Egypt—Biography. | Islam—20th century.

Classification: LCC BP80.Q86 S23 2021 (print) | LCC BP80.Q86 (ebook) | DDC 320.55/7092 [B]—dc23

LC record available at https://lccn.loc.gov/2021007880

LC ebook record available at https://lccn.loc.gov/2021007881

Manufactured in the United States of America

To My Parents

Contents

Illustrations

Acknowledgments

The research for this book started ten years ago as a project for a master's thesis in École des hautes études en sciences sociales in Paris. During the time it took to develop into a PhD dissertation, and then into a book, this research traveled through the different intellectual inquiries, scholarly practices, academic cultures, and languages of the countries in which I lived. This book is a patchwork of these, the most prominent of which are the French school of sociology, Anglo-American scholarship in intellectual history, and the Egyptian tradition of literary writing. In many regards, this book is the result of a strenuous effort to reconcile these different intellectual cultures, each with its specific inquiries, methodologies, and notions of truth.

One of the theses of this book is that ideas come into being through mutual interactions with the surrounding community. I need to mention and thank those who helped me to develop mine. First of all, I wish to thank Hamit Bozarslan, who agreed to supervise my master's thesis and PhD dissertation at a time when I hardly spoke French or knew anything about sociology. He was the first one to draw my attention to the parallels of thought between Sayyid Qutb and Marxist intellectuals, and the importance of the post–World War II anticolonial activism in understanding Qutb's life. My four years of fieldwork in Egypt were funded by a two-year doctoral scholarship accorded to me by the CEDEJ in Cairo. Secondly, my writing of this book was made possible by a five-year postdoctoral fellowship at the Oriental Institute of the Czech Academy of Sciences in Prague. I was lucky to have Ondřej Beránek and Jan Zouplna as, respectively, the director of the institute and the Middle Eastern department, who provided all the necessary support for the writing of this book and were patient during its multiple rewritings. My colleagues at the Oriental Institute followed the daily trials of the writing process. I would like to thank especially Nobuko Toyosawa for sharing her experience of writing and publishing, Kevin Schwartz for brainstorming suitable book titles, and Stefano Taglia for putting me in touch with the publisher. This book benefited from conversions with a number of people who all cannot be mentioned here. A special credit goes to Aymon Kreil, Shaaban Yusuf, Lucie Ryzova, Samuli Schielke, Raphael Cormack, Bettina Gräf, Ifdal Elsaket, Angela Giordani, Yoav Di-Capua, Naima Bouras, Gaétan du Roi, Walter Armbrust, Marie Vannetzel, Clément Steuer, Anwar Mugith, Hussam ʻAql, and all my interlocutors who agreed to share their memories of Sayyid Qutb, the majority of whom are not among us anymore. I would like to thank the staff of the Egyptian National Library and the Dominican Institute for Oriental Studies (IDEO) in Cairo, for whom I certainly became a familiar face during the long years of my research. Some of my colleagues and friends have read and commented on draft chapters of this book. My special thanks is addressed to Ebru Akcasu for suggesting improvements of the first chapter, and especially to Muhammad Addakhakhny, who read the entire manuscript hours before its final submission, verified the translation, and challenged me on some of its conclusions. All the translations in this book have been revised and polished with his generous help. I am particularly grateful to Youssef Faltas, who was the first audience for all the ideas of this book and patiently discussed them with me. This book would not have come into fruition without his long-term intellectual companionship and constant encouragement.

Sayyid Qutb

Introduction

The Return of the Ghost

In May 1954 the Egyptian intellectual Sayyid Qutb published a short essay on literature in the inaugural issue of the *Majallat al-Ikhwan al-Muslimin*. Laconically titled "The Method of Literature," the essay aimed to open a field of production and criticism of specifically Islamist literature (*al-adab al-islāmī*).[1] Qutb provided two basic guidelines as conditions for this type of literature to qualify as such. First, and most important, it had to be an honest reflection of the artist's emotive interactions with Islam, which the artist had adopted as his exclusive epistemology. Second, "Islamist literature was a guiding art [*al-fann al-muwājih*]," as he defined it, meaning that it must aim to improve both the material and spiritual living conditions of human society.[2] The notion of Islam-inspired literature was partly an outcome of Qutb's earlier reflections on the relationship between aesthetics and religion, which grew out of his studies on Qur'anic aesthetics in the late 1940s. There, he concluded that art and religion were bound to each other as "branches" (*ṣinwān*), since they both originated from the same realm of human cognition: affect (*wijdān*). Arguing against the widely held position that the arts and religion stood in opposition to each other, Qutb maintained that, in reality, the arts served religion by sharpening human senses and opening them up to the reception of God's message.[3]

Reduced to a single essay, Qutb's engagements with literature after joining the Muslim Brotherhood in 1953 might appear insignificant for Egypt's intellectual history. However, this essay was indeed significant for a substantial proportion of Egyptian intellectuals. Its publication in 1954 launched an intensive debate in the pages of the *Majallat al-Ikhwan al-Muslimin*, where writers grappled for three months with the meaning of *al-adab al-islāmī*, debating whether it referred to literature produced by populations who had received Islamic revelation, or if it was a brand new project to be implemented.[4] The essay was equally important to Qutb himself, who added it to subsequent revisions of his earlier works, such as the third edition of his major book on literary criticism, *al-Naqd al-Adabi: Usuluhu wa Manahijuhu* (Literary Criticism: Its Foundations and Methods, 1960), and the fifth edition of his best-selling opus on social justice, *al-'Adala al-Ijtima'iyya fi-l-Islam* (Social Justice in Islam, 1958).[5] The Islamist perspective on literature was not lost on Qutb's followers either. In the early 1960s, his younger brother Muhammad took the claim of the primordial connection between art and religion as the starting point for his book *Manhaj al-Fann al-Islami* (The Method of Islamist Arts). There, he suggested a sweeping theory of Islamist aesthetics and provided guidelines for artistic expression for those willing to follow the Islamic way of life.[6] The book was fully endorsed and recommended by Sayyid Qutb in his legendary opus *Ma'alim fi-l-Tariq*.[7] Written in prison and published in Cairo in 1964, this was his last book before his execution for conspiracy under Nasser's regime in 1966. The further development of this type of literature, however, had to wait for another decade, when the end of Islamist repression in Arab countries in the 1970s gave it new life. The creation of the International League of Islamic literature in 1981 in Lucknow, India, provided the initiative of exploring Islamist aesthetics within an institutional setting. Although the founding of the International League responded to different needs than Qutb's initial essay, it relied on the Qutb's concept of "Islamic epistemology" (*al-taṣawwur al-islāmī*) as the main criteria for distinguishing Islamist literature from its secular versions.[8]

This historical episode poses a new set of questions with which to approach Egypt's intellectual history in general, and Qutb's biography in particular. Qutb's ambition to elaborate a specifically religious aesthetics, and its relevance to the Islamist movement before the latter was crushed by Nasser's regime in the 1950s and 1960s, indicates that reforming literary imagery along Islamist lines was part of the movement's agenda for change. Yet Islamist engagements with literature are largely absent from global narratives on Egyptian—and, more largely, Arab literature. Instead, these narratives traditionally present Islamism as the nemesis of literature, aesthetics, and the arts. Reproduced implicitly through the refusal to recognize as literature creative works produced in the framework of Islamism, literature's incompatibility with Islamism is reasserted *en force* during confrontations between self-defined secular and religious intellectuals.[9] While the association of literature with Marxist political commitment would not raise eyebrows, literature produced within the circles of Islamic activism gets constructed as an anomaly. Passions surrounding the idea of associating Islam and literature stem from the fact that the latter represents more than itself. Attached to the values of freedom of speech, rationalism, and creative genius, literature is at the heart of the representation of Egypt's intellectual history as torn between secularism and Islamism. This account, which largely follows the older Nahda narrative of the struggle between modernity and tradition, resulted in granting the right of representing Egypt's national history to a handful of modernist writers. With doyen of Arab letters Taha Husayn selected as the most eminent representative of this era, these writers reproduce the discourse of literature as opposed to religious oppression and tradition. Recently, a series of works have complicated this modernist narrative by shedding light on social groups that have been denied presence in Egypt's national history on the grounds of ignorance or illiteracy.[10]

Sayyid Qutb: An Intellectual Biography explores the historical conditions in which the idea of literature as contrary to Islamism emerged in colonial and postcolonial Egypt. To understand these developments, the book follows the intellectual journey of the Egyptian literati-turned-Islamist Sayyid Qutb. Born in 1906 and executed in 1966, Qutb's lifetime spans the historical period covered here, which includes the birth of modern national culture during the interwar period, the subordination of this culture to the post–World War II project of national liberation, and the ambition of the postcolonial Nasserist state to create a new Arab subject. Qutb is commonly considered to have crossed the boundary between literature and Islamism. Born in a village in Upper Egypt, he left for Cairo in the 1920s, where he established himself as a fairly well-known poet and literary critic. During the first four decades of his life, he wrote a wealth of poems, three books on literary criticism, two novels, an autobiography, and two studies on Qur'anic aesthetics. Working as a teacher and a government clerk, he regularly contributed essays to Cairo's bustling intellectual press. By the late 1940s, his intellectual journey took a somewhat different turn. Swept away by the rising tide of anticolonial movements after World War II, Qutb committed himself to politics and in the early 1950s joined the Islamist organization of the Muslim Brotherhood. In parallel with this self-reinvention, Qutb shifted his attention from literary criticism to the advocacy of an Islamic social and political order. Arrested in 1954 as a member of the forbidden organization of the Muslim Brotherhood, Qutb spent the last decade of his life in prison. There, he wrote and rewrote his monumental oeuvre, a commentary of the Qur'an, *Fi Zilal al-Qur'an*. Parts of this text were published in his infamous book *Ma'alim fi-l-Tariq*, which provided the supporting evidence for his execution in 1966.

While it cannot be denied that Qutb's transition to Islamism marked a significant shift in his career, the idea that this shift implied an absolute break from his past is questionable. Rather than providing evidence for literature's incompatibility with Islamism, Qutb's story opens new avenues of exploration: What concretely signified "literature" from which he had allegedly departed? Was it the production of texts recognized as literature, such as fiction, poetry, and criticism? Or was it Egypt's literary community, to which Qutb was tied by bonds of friendship? Or did literature, for Qutb, have a more encompassing meaning, such as an aesthetic approach to the world? Qutb's essay on Islamist literature published in the Muslim Brotherhood's periodical in 1954 (cited at the beginning of this introduction) suggests that he continued to reflect on literature after joining the organization. This essay provides the starting point for the exploration of the various ways his literary past guided his intellectual calling and shaped his Islamist project.

Sayyid Qutb is not an ordinary figure in Egypt's history. Despite being executed in 1966, his presence powerfully haunts the country's political life. Today in Egypt, the mere mention of Qutb's name elicits electrified reactions. "Why Qutb?!" I was asked repeatedly by my interlocutors, who were suspicious that my research might be hiding some sort of political agenda. "Sayyid Qutb is not *adib*, but a terrorist!" strongly affirmed a high-ranking official in the Ministry of Culture, terrified at the idea of associating Qutb's name with the prestigious label of literati. In Egypt—and, to a lesser degree, elsewhere—the mere reference to Qutb has the capacity to conjure up images of terror, bloodshed, and destruction. Certainly, this is due to the manipulation of his image in the decades-long confrontation between the Muslim Brotherhood and the Egyptian state; his name is a reference point through which the Islamist organization can be discredited both culturally and politically. Culturally, Qutb's assumed departure from literature after joining the Brotherhood is cited as evidence of the organization's impermeability to culture.[11] Politically, his book *Maʿalim fi-l-Tariq*, which provided inspiration for the jihadist movements that ravaged the Arab region after his execution, is used as an argument against the Brotherhood's political participation. At each crackdown on Islamists, Qutb returns from his grave in order to "rule Egypt from his tomb."[12]

Yet the political manipulation of Qutb's image does not tell the whole story. Its haunting quality refers to the moral anger invested in people's attitude to the Muslim Brotherhood. As Samuli Schielke has pointed out, one needs to take seriously the emotion of moral hatred as a shadow side of the labor of love that people had been cultivating for decades for the attributes of the Egyptian nation (e.g., the flag, the military, or the leader).[13] Qutb and the Brotherhood are not considered to be part of Egypt's national community both past and present; they have been effectively excommunicated following a series of crackdowns on the Islamist organization. As Walter Armbrust has noted in his analysis of the anti-Brotherhood discourse that surged during the 2013 Rabaʿa massacre, the national excommunication of an adversary is needed in order to deprive it from the "grievability" to which only martyrs are entitled and to open the path to its extermination.[14]

The tracking of Qutb's traces in Egypt's intellectual history confirms his excommunicated status: Qutb is largely absent in literary histories, anthologies, or memoirs of his contemporaries, including those who belonged to his inner circle, an absence usually justified by the mediocrity of his literary output.[15] As a sign of the Brotherhood's status as an excommunicated organization, popular histories typically portray the Brotherhood and by extension Qutb as part of trends and forces foreign to Egypt like Wahabism and Western imperialism,[16] and as the embodiment of moral vices considered alien to the normative Egyptian character like opportunism, national treason, and eccentric sexual behavior.[17] Qutb's name is profoundly rooted in the affective realm of history, formed as a consequence of the duty of love for Egypt. In the eyes of many, the hatred—defined as righteous and ethical—toward the Brotherhood disqualifies Qutb from the historical justice debate.

Qutb's historical absence as an intellectual and his contemporary presence as a ghost determined this book's focus and methodology. This study aims to reverse Qutb's excommunication and to reintegrate him into the archive of Egypt's intellectual history. The task begins with his "liberation" from another archive in which he is usually enclosed: Islamism. Qutb's life has generated a wealth of academic interest; a number of scholars have located his thought in Egypt's political history, used social movement theory to understand it, and examined his biography in relation to local intellectual traditions and reformist discourses.[18] However, despite the variety of approaches, these works converge in reading Qutb's biographical breaks in terms of primarily ideological conversion from variously defined secularism to Islamism.[19] This perspective, which tends to accord to notions of secularism and Islamism an ahistorical essence, stems from a privileged focus on Qutb's "thought" and "beliefs," implicitly viewed as having transformative power in his life.

This book takes a different direction: it situates Qutb in a social history of intellectuals in which the "social" is given the same weight as "texts." Instead of ideas, it takes as its unit of analysis the shifting intellectual circles to which Qutb belonged during his life. His networks provide the microsociological point of access to Egypt's intellectual history, which, during his lifetime, underwent three significant generational reshufflings: the emergence of the generation of modern literati (*jīl al-udabā'*) following World War I; the birth of the second cohort of aspiring writers during the interwar period; and the rise of the post–World II committed intellectuals who would dominate the postcolonial Arab scene during the 1960s. Marked by a strong culture of apprenticeship, these generations were animated by their very specific rivalries. As a member of the middle interwar cohort, Qutb became entangled in the complex ties of discipleship and mentorship to his elders and juniors, benefiting from their respective intellectual climates to forge his own original vision to literature and Islam. What Qutb did was less of a "shift of orientation" than an overstepping of a boundary that was essentially political: he consciously dissociated himself from the generation of his mentors, which by the end of World War II had lost its intellectual credibility and was actively disowned by the postcolonial generation of intellectuals that considered his Islamist outlook a threat to the project of the postcolonial Arab state.

Although focusing on Qutb, this book is not just a tale with one protagonist. Its narrative weaves together three themes: the story of Qutb's conversion; the social history of modern Egyptian literature, based on a generational understanding of literary institutions and creative practices; and a broader history of the emergence of modern national culture in Egypt in which the state played an equal part with literary figures in colliding with and colluding over the definition of an authentic national culture of postcolonial Egypt. The remainder of the introduction will focus on the method that allowed me to weave these themes together, and the ways this study might contribute to convey the discussion on secularity and literature in Arab societies to a more ethnographic direction.

Metaphysical Drive and Shifting Circles of Sociability

Instead of thinking of Qutb's life in terms of a rupture, this book examines his literary and Islamist experiences from the perspective of a biographical continuity. A number of scholars have noted the continuing threads that cut across the different stages of Qutb's life. John Calvert has emphasized the significance of Qutb's emotive engagement with the world, which fueled his passionate commitment to Islam.[20] Sherif Yunis, who has written perhaps the most extensive biography of Qutb, attributes Qutb's Islamization to his Romantic subjectivity (*al-dhāt al-rūmāntīkīyya*), inherited from his literary training.[21] For his part, 'Ali Shalash has remarked on the salience of Qutb's "existential anxiety," which dissipated once he recovered his faith in God.[22]

This book departs from a conviction that more fundamental conclusions could be drawn from these observations. More specifically, it considers Qutb's Islamist project as a reconfigured version of his Romantic literary ethos following multiple readjustments of his intellectual track, which corresponded to his shifting intellectual worlds. The key moment in this transition was the turmoil in which Egypt's intellectuals found themselves after World War II. Following the war, Egypt, like many parts of the colonized world, was swept away by the rising tide of decolonization. Before it resulted in the 1952 military coup that ended the monarchy and laid the foundations for the postcolonial Nasser's state, the movement was experienced as the revolutionary quest for freedom on all fronts, political, economic, or ontological.[23] Many intellectuals readjusted their agendas according to the new requirement to bring their practice closer to sociopolitical struggles, while others observed the change with anxiety.[24] The latter category comprised some of the eminent representatives of the *udabā'* generation, who struggled to come to terms with what they viewed as the "onslaught of materialism" threatening to destroy the values they had been defending all their lives—namely, democracy, education, and individual freedom. These luminaries confronted the "onslaught" differently: the publicist and politician Muhammad Husayn Haykal emphasized the spiritual basis of civilizations, the poet 'Abbas al-'Aqqad strove to convince his readership of the significance of geniuses in his *'Abqariyyat* series, and doyen Taha Husayn tirelessly defended the elitist understanding of culture based on the notion of art for art's sake.

Sayyid Qutb was one of those who readjusted their intellectual practice according to the needs of the postcolonial epoch. Following World War II, he dramatically dissociated himself from a political establishment widely accused of being complicit with colonialism. With this change, Qutb came to see a whole set of policies established since the 1919 revolution to achieve independence—such as elections and diplomacy—as a mere ploy to maintain the colonial status quo. Instead, Qutb swiftly morphed into a committed intellectual who set out to raise popular awareness through fiery articles in the press, activism, and the promotion of street action such as sit-ins, demonstrations, and popular resistance against the British.

But while the political shift was smooth, the intellectual one was less so. In his post–World War II writings, Qutb appears torn between appreciation and criticism of left-wing movements. On the one hand, he admired the left for its revolutionary potential to transform society and motivate humans to act, but on the other he condemned it as limited to the satisfaction of purely material needs. While agreeing with the generation of his mentors such as Haykal, al-'Aqqad, and Husayn, regarding the spiritual basis of civilizations, the significance of geniuses, and the superiority of highbrow art, Qutb strongly denounced the colonial underpinnings of their intellectual practice. A few years after the war, Qutb found himself out of tune in regard to both the generation of his mentors, with whom he disagreed politically, and the rising intellectual guard whom he accused of being blind to the spiritual needs of the postcolonial society. In such conditions, Islamism appeared as a viable solution for reconciling these conflicting demands. As a social movement, it provided a framework for Qutb's political activism while its religious dimension allowed him to connect this-worldly struggles to the higher spiritual aims of humankind. Islamism offered a way to combine Qutb's political activism with his metaphysical drive.

Before the ideological, the tension between the metaphysical drive and this-worldly political commitment is deeply sociological—that is, produced by Qutb's multiple intellectual experiences. This book analyzes his "conversion" by combining two sociological concepts. The first is an "existential problem," suggested by French sociologist Bernard Lahire to grasp literary subjectivities and the way they manifest themselves in writing.[25] The second is "circles of sociability," which provides the microsociological lenses to observe how broader generational shifts in Egypt's culture affected Qutb's intimate intellectual networks. While the notion of "existential problem" provides an access point to the author's interiority, the focus on his practices of sociability allows us to observe how this interiority is shaped, challenged, and modified through intellectual encounters. The combination of concepts leads to multiple sites of observation of Qutb's intellectual track through the combined study of his texts and his shifting intellectual networks.

Qutb's existential problem can be seen in a particular theme that cuts across his entire intellectual oeuvre: his concern over the finitude of human life. The majority of his writings—spanning his Romantic poetry, literary criticism, gothic prose, and studies of the Qur'an—are animated by his persistent curiosity about the metaphysical. His fascination with human fragility in his Romantic poetry, the origin of inspiration in his theory of aesthetics, the psychoanalytical notion of the "unconscious" (*lā-shuʿūr*), the secret of affective power of the Qur'an, and the capacity of Islam to activate extraordinary human powers—all of these themes testify of Qutb's continuous attempt to spot the zones of intersection between the physical and metaphysical worlds.

This quest is rooted in Qutb's particular perspective, shaped by his training in Romantic poetry. He perceived human existence as composed of its two levels: a material world apprehensible through reason, and a spiritual realm accessible via imagination. The distinction between emotion and reason runs through all of Qutb's writings, including his theory of literary aesthetics and his political project of Islam. In his aesthetic theory, published between 1932 and 1947, Qutb spoke of inspiration as the channel through which humans accessed the fragmentary knowledge of the world. His decision to embark on the studies of the Qur'an, the text against which he aimed to challenge his aesthetic model from the late 1930s onward, led him to slightly revise his theory. He arrived at the conclusion that would serve as the basis for his theory of Islamist aesthetics: the poet's inspiration and the Qur'an referred, in fact, to the same truth. In his later political writings, Qutb completed the association between the metaphysical and the divine and transferred the criterion of validity of knowledge from the poet's interiority to the texts and history of Islam. But, even in his late Islamist writings, the importance of the metaphysical was preserved. Qutb claimed that genuine Islam can be accessed only though praxis, which activates the unimaginable wells of human powers that lay beyond willpower. Qutb's entire intellectual oeuvre is driven by his desire to connect to the invisible reality, *ghayb*, either through poetic inspiration or obedience to God's commandments.

As Bernard Lahire defines it, the "existential problem" refers to a set of questions, anxieties, and curiosities that revolve around one essential theme. This nagging question is the origin of artistic inspiration, which takes possession of an author and instills in him the irresistible drive to write. The process of artistic creation acts as a powerful outlet to express this anxiety, contributing to the author's sense of self-fulfillment.[26] Lahire's "existential problem" is a revised version of Pierre Bourdieu's concept of habitus, a sort of "incorporated past" manifesting itself as acquired dispositions to see, feel, and act.[27] Notoriously, individuals cannot change their habitus during their lives, which continues to inform in imperceptible ways their artistic tastes, intellectual interests, and life choices. Still, throughout one's lifetime, that habitus is continuously exposed to new ways of seeing, feeling, and acting, and, under the pressure of major biographical turns, is likely to be modified through the incorporation of new dispositions that are compatible with the acquired ones. By moving across different sites of intellectual practice, intellectuals are constantly exposed to new inquiries, themes, and requirements of genre, which contribute to channel their existential anxiety into new avenues of expression. At the same time, these new avenues adjust the existential problem according to its dominant questions, reshaping it in significant ways.[28]

In Qutb's case, the anticolonial moment after World War II largely disqualified his existential problem designed to understand human existence through art. The ambition to raise humankind to infinite metaphysical heights shaped by Romantic poetry did not fit easily with the postwar urgency to end social and political oppression of the finite world. The ivory tower intellectual who contemplated the universe far away from a suffering society did not correspond to the new notion of intellectual work that demanded full commitment to its struggles. Additionally, Qutb's spiritual ethos was misunderstood by the movements that spearheaded the anticolonial struggle—specifically, the Left and its artistic avatars, or realism and committed literature. These were the conditions that shaped Qutb's cognitive predisposition to embrace the Islamist alternative once he was introduced to it. To paraphrase a famous dictum, Islamism was for Qutb the continuation of literature by other means: the aim remained the same—the spiritual sublimation of humankind—while the means shifted from poetry to the creation of Islamic society.

The understanding of Qutb's metaphysical drive as his existential problem raises two questions. First, how is this existential anxiety shaped? Second, what form does it take in writing? These two questions bring us to the importance of various contexts that allowed or disallowed Qutb's metaphysical quest to thrive. Most of Qutb's biographers have stressed the significance of context in understanding his biographical shifts.[29] But the context defined for this purpose, I would like to argue, has been always too broad. There is no doubt that the watershed events of Egypt's national history—the modernization, the two world wars, the 1919 revolution, the 1952 military coup, and the repeated attempts to eradicate Islamist movements—all left traces on Qutb's cognitive world. Yet, in the absence of supplementary tools allowing to bridge the global and the particular, the description of Egypt's national context in which an individual reality takes place is no more than a juxtaposition of two levels of observation.[30] To give the notion of context all its efficiency, it is necessary to show how these events were mediated through a singular experience of an individual life.

This book suggests connecting the national history and a biography by introducing a "middle" scale of observation: the circles of sociability. The literary circles of sociability comprise an essential institution in Egypt's intellectual life, both past and present. As the next section will demonstrate, in interwar Egypt literary circles provided the most immediate access to the country's intellectual life. Acting as meeting points between intellectuals, where they formed bonds and exchanged books and ideas, these circles played a critical role in forging intellectual curiosities, transmitting tricks of literary craft, providing recognition, and, more generally, steering intellectuals into one or another cultural direction. They functioned as islands of autonomy in the larger field of cultural production, where new literary notions could be improvised and tested and later disseminated to wider publics through print.

An approach focused on sociabilities is particularly fitting for studying Qutb's intellectual life. Qutb was not the type of intellectual to spend days in solitude, attempting to solve some theoretical riddle. Rather, he preferred the clamor of intellectual gatherings and literary confrontations. During his lifetime, Qutb had been seen in the most vibrant spots of Egypt's interwar cultural life, such as the legendary Hilmiyya café, the Apollo Poet Society, the salon organized by the famous poet al-ʿAqqad, the weekly gatherings held in the headquarters of *al-Risala* magazine, the meetings in Misr Library, among many other professional clubs and associations. He also held his own salon in his house in Cairo's suburb of Helwan. Qutb tried a variety of genres, reflecting his endless pursuit for the new; he experimented in poetry, the novel, the autobiography, privileging above all the least time-consuming mode of intellectual intervention—the journal essay. It is perhaps not a coincidence that Qutb's most accomplished work, his Qur'anic interpretation *Fi Zilal al-Qur'an*, was written in prison, where he was isolated from Cairo's bustling intellectual life. Qutb's taste for conviviality is reflected in his leaning toward collective writing. He coauthored books with his sisters Amina and Hamida, with famous Egypt's intellectuals—the novelist 'Abd al-Hamid al-Sahhar and the psychologist Yusuf Murad—and he worked so closely with his brother Muhammad that it is difficult to differentiate their thinking.

Qutb's sociable nature allows us to understand why he became a literary critic. Criticism is the quintessential form of convivial exchange in the press, since it allows one to keep in touch with other people's work. Qutb's passing interest in different fields of knowledge is sometimes cited as evidence of his failure.[31] It is true that Qutb did not start aesthetic revolutions that might have reserved him a place among Egypt's literary "giants." However, such a view is predicated on a particular vision of literature. If we focus exclusively on Qutb's literary production, we might conclude that he did not advance literature in significant ways. But perhaps his significance lay in the backstage of literary production, such as writing criticism, editing periodicals, and providing mentorship to young writers. Perhaps he was similar to hundreds of other writers who formed Egypt's intellectual fabric, and if not for his late Islamist fame he might have sunk into history's oblivion. My interest is precisely to shed light on one of those hundreds, to understand how he arrived in a place where no one expected him to arrive.

This book follows Qutb's biographical turns through his three main "worldly moments" defined by a particular network, a specific mode of intellectual practice, and the nature of social bonds. The first moment consists of Qutb's discipleship to the famous poet 'Abbas al-'Aqqad and his friendship with a circle of Romantic poets formed in the mid-1930s during his studies at the Dar al-'Ulum College. Fascinated with the poetry of al-'Aqqad, the circle provided the first support group for Qutb's literary experiments and accompanied his forays in the press. Together with this circle, Qutb transitioned to the Apollo Poet Society founded in 1932, but broke off when his solidarities with young poets clashed with his loyalty to al-'Aqqad.

Qutb's second "worldly moment" was shaped by the rise of anticolonial activism following World War II, and the accompanying criticism of the interwar colonial culture. It consisted of a constellation of ideologically fluid groups involved in different strands of activism against the monarchy, such as the Publishing Committee of University Graduates, founded in 1942, where Qutb met the future celebrity Naguib Mahfuz; the Dar al-'Ulum association involved in the protest movement against the Ministry of Instruction; and extraparliamentary political movements such as communism, Young Egypt, and the Muslim Brotherhood. It is by remaining in communication with these activist groups that Qutb completed his "conversion" from an ivory-tower intellectual to a revolutionary writer committed to bringing down the monarchy. With some changes in membership, Qutb's network followed him in his postwar individual projects, which would gradually acquire Islamist undertones, such as his established periodicals *al-'Alam al-'Arabi* (1947), *al-Fikr al-Jadid* (1948), and *Majallat al-Ikhwan al-Muslimin* (1954). Qutb's circle, formed at this crucial historical point, provides the clear indication that, beyond the rivalries of the leadership, Islamist and secularist divide was significantly blurred by the common struggle against the colonial generation. It is precisely this postwar intellectual fluidity that facilitated Qutb's transition to the Muslim Brotherhood.

The third and last moment consists of Qutb's gradual integration into the Muslim Brotherhood, which followed three stages: first, insertion into the organization's editorial universe from 1951 onward, which allowed Qutb to become one of the lead writers in the Brotherhood's press; second, integration into the official structure of the organization in 1953, when he was assigned official responsibilities; and, third, the prison years between 1954 and 1964, during which the shared experience of repression and incarceration forged strong links of affection, brotherhood, and solidarity. Each of these "worldly moments" were connected to one or several spaces of socialization, which provided the grounds for intellectual immersion into collectively formed countercultures. These moments allow us to closely observe Qutb's ideological "conversion" in relation to his shifting intellectual worlds, composed of different networks, cultural practices, and ideas. It also reveals that, rather than being the work of an isolated intellectual, these shifts were the result of collective efforts to redefine culture according to postcolonial needs.

Is Literature Secular? Literature, Islam, and *Nadwa* Culture

Here, I would like to expand on the sociability-based approach, to show how it can allow us to access literary worlds more fully beyond the Islamist and secularist divide. For a long period, Arab literature had been the hostage of the modernization paradigm, which tended to assimilate it with the effects of Western modernity. Various avatars of the original binary between the West and Islam, such as the modern and traditional, progressive and conservative, secular and religious, informed the readings of Arab literature, reproducing the discourse disseminated by the cosmopolitan fringes of Arab societies.[32] A related approach has been to study Arab literature through aesthetic categories examined via the texts of famous writers.[33] Although informative for the study of literary content, this approach has resulted in locking literary worlds into published canonical texts, condemning to invisibility those authors and texts that escaped canonization.

Recently, the modernist approach was challenged by two academic traditions, each pulling Arab intellectual history in opposite directions. Inspired by Michel Foucault's inquiry into power and subject formation and Edward Said's critique of Orientalism, the first tradition set out to show how Western imperialism forged subjectivities in European colonies or peripheries by implanting sets of beliefs, norms, and practices that profoundly transformed the subjected populations. As its main site of observation, this research agenda has focused on those social objects that were responsible for executing power in controlled territories like state institutions, and on the discourses of the populations that were the closest to the imperial center, like cosmopolitan elites.[34]

More recently, this tradition has been enriched by a new research agenda aiming to investigate Arab literature from the perspective of secularism as it was redefined by Talal Asad. Thinking of secularism not as the separation of politics from religion but as a worldview that enclosed the literary within a set of sensibilities, imaginaries, interpretative frames, or "embedded philosophies,"[35] this research program has significantly contributed to exposing the modernist bias in recognizing certain texts and practices as literary and others as not.[36] The second approach consisted of the so-called "material turn," which aimed to complicate the reading of Arab intellectual history beyond the focus on texts alone. Instead, it approached intellectual production as deeply embedded in social worlds, consisting of social practices, material objects, and concrete social needs. By shedding light on practices and populations that had often been eclipsed by a focus on the loudest reformist discourses, this research program drew attention to the processes of translation, adaptation, and adjustment to which normative orders were subjected in practice.[37]

This book follows the "material" approach to Arab intellectual history with an interrogation pertaining to the "secular turn": How might Qutb's biography contribute to the academic discussion on secularity and literature in Arab societies? Could Qutb's project of Islamist literature be considered the attempted excavation of the literary from the domain of the secular? In the sense that it resulted from Qutb's act of merging the metaphysical with the divine, it could. Yet, as a trend that has originated within the Islamist movement, deeply attuned to secular forms of being such as modern education, practices of media consumption, and forms of political and associational life characteristic of civil society, Qutb's Islamist literature might as well be a product of secularism.[38] As Gregory Starrett has noted, the concept of secularism is inherently contradictory, as it tends to collapse different genealogies of secularism.[39] Different sites of observation might lead to situating the beginnings of secularism at separate historical points, precluding the possibility of having a unified discussion on where secularism exactly begins and ends.[40] While highly productive for thinking of global forces of history and for the in-depth study of situated worldviews, the concept of secularism is less so in spotting the zones of intersection where the secular collides or colludes with the nonsecular.[41]

More specifically, Qutb's aesthetic project challenges the claim that literature as it emerged on the cusp of the modern age in Egypt was secular. His conception of poetry defies a number of features that are identified as the effects of secularism, such as the precedence of the visual over the sonic, silence over sound, free verse over measured rhythms.[42] Rather, he placed poetry in the nexus of knowledge and sound, considering that poems communicated knowledge through the imagination stirred by sound. He did not splinter the aesthetic domain from other realms of existence; rather, for him, poetry contained the truth of the world. At the same time, he fully embraced the Romantic notion of poetry that relocated the source of inspiration from the social realm to the author's interiority. While his intellectual mindset was deeply shaped by modern sciences and European Romanticism, it was also influenced by other local and nonsecular traditions such as Sufism that Qutb combined in his own original way. To be sure, everyone claimed to be modern and sought to dissociate themselves from practices deemed backward, such as Sufi poetry or the preprint practice of mentorship. Yet it did not prevent them from adopting these cultural practices and molding them according to modern forms.

For example, Qutb never credited Sufi metaphysics with having popularized the notion of "oneness of existence" (*waḥdat al-wujūd*), which he adopted as the bedrock of his intellectual project; instead, he defined it as part of the intuitive truth that each poet holds deep in his heart. This poses the question of whether the modern forms of intellectual life had the determining power in shaping subjectivities, or if it is individuals who manipulated them, infused them with different contents, and subverted them for their own purposes. This question is important to ask, since the remnants of the nonsecular seem to so profoundly shape individual worldviews and trajectories. For Qutb, the nonsecular nexus between sound and knowledge provided the thread that connected his different intellectual experiences and indirectly steered him in the direction of Islamism. As Samuli Schielke has noted, to understand how the secular and the nonsecular organize social imaginaries and practices, additional attention should be paid to specific social milieus and their means of differentiation that mark certain texts as either secular or not.[43]

To see how the notions of secular and nonsecular are articulated in concrete social contexts, this book suggests approaching intellectual life through the institution of a literary club (*nadwa*). In colonial and postcolonial Egypt, intellectual production is embedded in a dynamic culture of social exchange organized around coffeehouses, the headquarters of periodicals, publishing houses, literary salons, and a number of other locations for formal or informal gatherings. The significance of these exchanges is attested to by the large body of literature dedicated to document the worldly dimension of Egypt's intellectual life: literature of rumors, tributes, lampoons, autobiographies, collections of literary feuds, and other texts addressing communities of peers. These texts are rife with accounts of writers spending their time in *nadwa*. As author of children's literature Muhammad Sa'id al-'Aryan described the getaways of his mentor Mustafa Sadiq al-Rafi'i' in Cairo:

> Al-Rafi'i did not have a more favorite *nadwa* at his arrival to Cairo than the headquarters of *al-Muqtataf.* Later, after he got in touch with *al-Risala*, he started frequenting another *nadwa*. He would spent his time between the doctor's Shakhashiri's clinics in Fumm al-Khalidj, the headquarters of *al-Balagh* where he met 'Abd al-Qadir Hamza and al-Mazni, and *al-Risala* where he visited al-Zayat.[44]

In Egypt, *nadwa* might take various shapes, ranging from a simple gathering in a café to exchange news and rumors to formal reunions where texts are read and discussed in the presence of the audience. It is a place where writers form bonds, exchange books, and can come into disagreement. These encounters might lead to the formation of a more intimate network of friends, known as *shilla* (pl. *shilal*). *Shilla* refers to an informal grouping of half a dozen or so individuals who meet on a regular basis. Defined by solidarities based on education, profession, or neighborhood sociability, *shilla* constitutes the most immediate context of socialization in all sectors of social life.[45] But, in literature, the solidarities of *shilla* might assume a particular form: aesthetic affinities turn ordinary circles of friendship into literary schools, coteries, and generations.[46]

The observation of Egypt's intellectual life through the lenses of *nadwa* allows us to make three sets of arguments. First, the modern forms of society did not wipe out the old, but reinvested them with new, modern meanings. Scholars have noted the transformation of public life that print technology had produced in Egypt, instituting new forms of authority and inculcating new norms of social behavior.[47] They also stressed, however, the degree to which modern forms of solidarity overlapped with older ones, creating a fragile consensus based on shared notions of community.[48] A similar suggestion could be made regarding social relations in literature. In Egypt as elsewhere, intellectual life has depended on different sets of social relations, such as the system of courtly patronage in the arts, the practice of private tutoring, or the symbiotic relation with a sheikh posited as the condition of a proper transmission of sciences.[49] People met in informal gatherings, recited poetry, read books out loud, and developed their writings through discussions in multiple sites of convivial exchange, such as private salons (*majālis*), coffeehouses, or mosques.[50] With the advent of printing, these forms of convivial exchange did not disappear, but became new modes of interaction collectively defined as modern: *majālis* were replaced by modern salons, publishing houses, and associations; courtly patronage by the practice of dedication; and the poetry of panegyrics and lampoons by critique and literary feuds. Adapting these forms to modern times transformed them; salons allowed the presence of women (and were held by them), critique was subject to the requirements of literary criticism, and literary feuds were bound by the rules of polite exchange.[51] Yet not all authors considered themselves defined by these rules and shaped them according to their own personal idiosyncrasies.[52]

The formative influence of premodern social forms is particularly salient in the case of the practice of mentorship. In many regards, mentorship reproduced the preprint pattern of knowledge transmission organized in the symbiotic relationship between a sheikh and a disciple. But, under the influence of Romanticism, the modern age introduced a new mode of intellectual authority with which the traditional one had to be reconciled: the condition of artistic genius and originality. Since then, the tension between the requirement of deference to senior authority and the urge to rebel has been an ongoing feature of Egypt's intellectual life. It resulted in the troubled transition from the intellectual authority embodied in master's personal genius to the authority of abstracted intellectual order no longer invested in human life.[53]

Partly, the observed centrality of embodied authority in Egypt's intellectual life is due to the specific historical focus of this book: the beginnings of literary modernity in Egypt. Taha Husayn, ʻAbbas al-ʻAqqad, Tawfiq al-Hakim, and other members of "the *udabā'* generation" not only created a new intellectual order, but also established themselves as semi-institutions who distributed literary recognition. This particular historical circumstance fused their symbolic status as the prophets of modernity with their existence as humans embedded in social relations. For many writers who followed them into the literary scene, inserting themselves into the lineage of these "giants" meant adopting not only their aesthetic style but also access to modernity, and perhaps the only imaginable way to be an *adib*. Often they received from their teachers a certain school of thought as well as their lifestyle, friends, and enemies.

The suggestion of the centrality of embodied authority in literature could also be extended to later periods, as evidenced by the unwithering popularity of tribute literature. Conceived as biographies of eminent writers authored by their friends and disciples, tribute literature aims at paying respect to mentors, but also stresses the author's proximity to an influential writer. Part of a practice that Walter Armbrust defines as *isnād*—borrowing the classical term of Islamic religious science referring to a chain of authoritative voices that allow to trace the origins of a *hadīth*—these writings serve to insert their producers into the lineage of celebrated authors that provided a connection to the origins of literary modernity.[54] And since writers often received from their teachers not only a certain "school of thought," but also friends and enemies, the practice of tribute helped to root intellectual fault lines deep into history.

The emphasis on embodied authority brings us to the second argument: in setting the limits of literature, the affective realm matters. *Nadwa* mediated the reception of literature by infusing it with emotional warmth, upon which this institution was based. Kinship, peer solidarities of *shilla*, discipleship, mentorship, and other configurations that tied writers together affected the direction in which the limits of literature were pushed. Writing about his initial steps into the world of literature, the poet ʻAbbas al-ʻAqqad recalled his regular trips from his hometown Aswan, located in southern Egypt, to Cairo, the city of knowledge and modernity:

> Trips to Cairo were occasions to search for books that were not brought to the province by the ambulant vendors. . . . The book I looked for directed me to *al-Muqtataf* located at the entry of ʿAbd al-ʿAziz Street, since it was there that the book was printed in Cairo. . . . But the main goal of the visit was to meet Dr. Yaʿqub Sarruf, the philosopher of the modern age.[55]

During the first decade of the twentieth century, before bookshops appeared in the most remote corners of Egypt, access to knowledge was mediated by persons, such as the founder of the influential periodical of science *al-Muqtataf*, Yaʿqub Sarruf. At the turn of the century, editors of periodicals carried out most intellectual activities: they printed and sold books, promoted them in their periodicals, and received guests in journal offices, which were next door to the press as well as to their personal lodgings. Soon the situation was inverted, and it was print that mediated human relationships. The critic ʿAbbas Khidr was offended when his friend Muhammad al-ʿAryan offered him his book without a special dedication; he started suspecting him of arrogance and a lack of consideration.[56] Taha Husayn felt "heavily indebted" to a peer writer when he took too long to write a review of the book that the latter had offered to him.[57] Naguib Mahfuz's excitement upon sending dedicated copies of his novel *Radubis* to "the giants" vanished when he found them on sale in a bookstore.[58]

Dedications, book reviews, prefaces, literary battles, and other modes of intellectual exchange in print were thus constitutive of social relationships. Analyzed here as moments of clarity, when affiliations, bonds of solidarity, friendships, and enmities were made visible, these modes of exchange provided an opportunity to demonstrate one's loyalty to a mentor, to position oneself as someone's disciple, to defend a friend, or to settle a score with a long-term opponent. They also revealed relationships between allies and foes, or mentors and disciples, and allowed writers to bolster their reputations by publicly revealing the details of relationships gone sour. With the help of the press, which encouraged polemics to increase its commercial profit, printed exchange had become by the interwar period a routine practice of intellectual bonding. In a certain way, it was a performance that served both to reveal existing intellectual divisions and to redistribute positions of power.

Lastly, the focus on *nadwa* allows us to nuance the determining effects of disciplinary discourses and practices disseminated by modern apparatuses of power. Differently from contexts defined by a more institutionalized culture of intellectual transmission, in interwar Egypt men of letters often developed themselves outside the disciplinary power of educational institutions. As Lucie Ryzova has demonstrated in her work on the emergence of middle-class culture in interwar Egypt, the *efendiyya* class was produced as much by modern schools as by the process of self-formation, or *takwīn*, in which the activities of going to cinema, hanging out with friends in cafés, or simply strolling in the streets occupied a central role.[59] The peer sociabilities of *shilla* acted as "pockets of autonomy," in which young aspiring writers could innovate independently from social control exerted by various disciplinary structures.[60] Indeed, a closer look into the most famous literary collectives of the interwar period, such as the Apollo Poet Society and the Diwan School, reveal that, beyond the surface of aesthetic claims, these were *shilal* of friends who, when not writing poetry, attended Sufi festivals and hanged out in cafés.[61]

As a result, normative orders of literature disseminated from above reached Egyptian intellectuals in a necessarily translated form. Young efendis shaped their worldviews in an intellectual mishmash of Egypt's interwar culture, which was characterized by the productive blending of different sources of knowledge.[62] In this culture, *nadwa* acted as a filter and space of bricolage. Picked up during late evening conversations, and from translated or Arab books passed around, ideas circulated among various readers and passed through multiple layers of discourse. Filtered as much through collective as individual interpretative frameworks, they were open for synthesis that largely outdid the discursive limits between modernity and tradition, or the secular and nonsecular. As the most authoritative classifier of social order in the studied period, the taxonomy of modernity was used in public confrontations, condemning the losing side to the realm of tradition. The stability of these fault lines depended not only on doctrinal positions, but, importantly, on the solidity of intellectual networks based on the mutual exchange of favors, grounded in spaces of socialization, and perpetuated across history through the practice of tribute.

Sources and Overview of Chapters

During the long periods spent researching this book, I experimented with different types of sources, aiming to build an archive of worldly intellectual life in colonial and early postcolonial Egypt. The research started with me reading all the periodicals of highbrow intellectual culture that were available in Cairo's local libraries. Some of them, such as the weekly *al-Risala,* were the object of in-depth study, while for others I consulted lists of contributors, tables of content, sections dedicated to literary news, and book reviews. The next stage was defined by my immersion in all types of literary rumor literature that I came across in Cairo: for example, autobiographies, memoirs, tributes, lampoons, and collections of literary feuds. In parallel, I conducted individual interviews with writers, intellectuals, and activists of both left-wing and Muslim Brotherhood backgrounds, who either had known Qutb personally or observed his rise as a public intellectual after World War II.

Adjusting lenses on Sayyid Qutb, I juxtaposed different printed materials in order to trace the shifts in his circles of sociability. His exchanges in the press, such as reviews, literary feuds, private and public correspondence, and all the "textual noise" produced as a result of intellectual socialization, provided the threads of his networks that could be followed further. Qutb's activity of criticism allowed me to trace his shifting interest from one group of authors to another, suggesting a possible encounter. Since "a printed book is not merely a source of ideas and images, but a carrier of social relationships," I devoted close attention to prefaces and dedications written for Qutb and by him.[63] His edited periodicals—*al-'Alam al-'Arabi* (1947), *al-Fikr al-Jadid* (1948), and the *Majallat al-Ikhwan al-Muslimin* (1954)—were particularly informative of intellectuals who surrounded him during the critical years of his transition to Islamism. The different editions of some of Qutb's books indicated the publishing houses with which he was associated. Their records allowed me to track his gradual integration into the Brotherhood's editorial universe.

The effort to access Qutb's life through his networks was dictated by the particular conditions in which I conducted my research in Cairo: the years of the unfolding Egyptian Revolution of 2011. The extreme political polarization between the state and the Brotherhood that started in 2013 significantly enhanced Qutb's presence as a ghost capable of unleashing violence. As a result, the reconstruction of Qutb's social intellectual life is inevitably partial and fragmentary. Gleaned from different materials, the empirical data contains gaps that the release of new archives on Qutb, such as his correspondence or his personal library, could hopefully fill. Yet the fragmentary nature of source material does not invalidate the purpose of this book, which is to study Qutb in relation to the communities of which he was a part.

This story of Qutb's intellectual journey spans six chapters. The book neither follows a strictly biographical account of his life, nor structures the narrative according to watershed events in national Egypt's history. Instead, each chapter locates Qutb's biographical moments within the larger intellectual debates on literature and Islam. These historical moments are the controversies of the 1920s that crystallized the contours of literature and Islam as autonomous fields of intellectual practice; the attempts to redefine Islam as the sphere of inquiry based on rational thought and freethinking in the 1930s; the anticolonial moment in the postwar period that popularized Islam as a viable political position for Egypt's postcolonial future; the birth of the Islamist literature during the 1950s; the election of Islam as part of the postcolonial culture in the 1960s under the shadow of all-powerful Nasser's state; and Qutb's trial and excommunication from Egypt's intellectual history following his arrest and execution in 1966. Each of these moments contributed to the shaping of Qutb's intellectual life—his literary beginnings, interest in the studies of the Qur'an, transition to revolutionary politics, birth of Islamist literature, and his excommunication.

Chapter 1, "Becoming an *Adib*," opens with Qutb's statement of the illegitimacy of religious arguments in matters of literature. Expressed in a debate conducted for his mentor al-'Aqqad, this position echoes the autonomy of literature established as a norm since the controversies of the 1920s. The chapter then proceeds to explore how this position emerged and how Qutb came to embrace it. Focusing on Qutb's ascent to literary recognition, it situates him in the context of a long-lasting intellectual war waged between a circle of reformist movement, the Salafiyya Bookstore and Publishing House, and Taha Husayn's circle, associated with the newly founded Egyptian University. This chapter views the birth of literary modernity as the outcome of a profound social conflict, pointing to the importance of nonideological factors for the production of ideological positions.

If chapter 1 focuses on Qutb's intellectual sociabilities, chapter 2, "Our Own Brand of Modernity," delves into his intellectual formation. By locating Qutb's thought at the confluence of various intellectual influences, such as psychology, modern science, Sufism, and Romantic poetry, it traces the development of his literary vision and prophecy-bound mission to understand existence. It also explores the formation of Qutb's understanding of religion as an emotional experience in the shadow of the larger surge of interest in Islamic heritage on the part of modernist writers during the interwar.

Chapter 3, "Bringing the Social Back In," focuses on the critical moments of Qutb's intellectual life: transition from institutional political participation to revolutionary politics, departure from Romantic poetry to socially responsible forms of writing, and commitment to Islamic activism. By locating his biographical turns within the context of the postwar aspiration to decolonize culture, the chapter focuses on the way these changes affected his intellectual relationships—namely, his widely publicized break from the established old-guard literati followed by his increasing proximity to young intellectuals. By analyzing Qutb's involvement in postwar intellectual activism in the years between the end of World War II and 1952 Free Officers' Revolution, it traces his gradual integration into the orbit of the Muslim Brotherhood.

Chapter 4, "Literature in the Margins," explores the birth of a specifically Islamist aesthetic by jointly analyzing the writings by Sayyid Qutb and his brother Muhammad. Since the brothers ventured into the topic as part of their activism in the Muslim Brotherhood, the chapter locates their endeavor in the historical perspective of various engagements with literature on the part of intellectuals associated with the Islamist associational scene. Through the examination of their positions on literature in relation to the generational dynamics within the Islamist scene, it explores the process through which Islamist literature shifted from being simply a literature produced by balanced reformers to a literature defined by specific Islamist aesthetics.

Chapter 5, "Faith and State," focuses on Qutb's prison years, stretching from his imprisonment in 1954 to the publication of his major prison work *Ma'alim fi-l-Tariq* in 1964. The chapter situates Qutb's prison texts within the efforts to create a postcolonial culture in Nasser's Egypt as it transitioned from the anticolonial moment to the Arab state. Mirroring the gradual refocusing of anticolonial politics on the survival of the Arab state, Qutb's legendary work *Ma'alim fi-l-Tariq* epitomizes this transition. It also promotes another version of a decolonized Arab self that is anchored in Islam and defined against the intervention of the oppressive Nasser's state.

Chapter 6, "The People against Sayyid Qutb," focuses on the media campaign unleashed against Sayyid Qutb following the exposure of his links to an Islamist network known as the "1965 Organization." The chapter analyses Qutb's public trial as a schismogenetic moment resulting in Qutb's—and, more broadly, the Muslim Brotherhood's—excommunication from Egypt's intellectual history. By republishing the anti-Brotherhood propaganda produced in 1965, the moment of Qutb's excommunication can be endlessly replayed in Egyptian politics as a reminder of the Brotherhood's violent past. Represented as either quintessential martyr or an icon of absolute evil, Qutb is turned into a ghost that repeatedly haunts Egypt's present.

1

Becoming an *Adib*

"Religion . . . Religion . . . Say it a hundred times. We are not, thanks to God, intimidated by these empty exclamations. We have studied and understood religion more than you." This is how Sayyid Qutb responded to the accusations of blasphemy aimed at him in a literary battle in 1938. Rebuffing the intention of his opponent, Muhammad al-Ghamrawi, to turn a literary debate into a religious confrontation, Qutb stressed the illegitimacy of religious arguments in literature and ascribed religion and the arts to distinct spheres of human activity. While the role of Islam, Qutb claimed, was to enhance social cohesion by reforming individual ethics, literature dealt exclusively with the mysteries of the human soul. To think otherwise, and to invoke Islam in matters that laid outside its purview, was a strategy of "the weak and frail ones, who were swept by the tide and did not have the means of swimming."[1] This "tide" referred to the wealth of knowledge that had swept across Egypt during the first decades of the twentieth century, while "the means of swimming" meant the ability to master it.

Within the broader sociopolitical condition of the time, this literary battle could be read as a classical example of the secularization of literature facilitated by the Western colonial domination in Egypt. However, such a view should not prevent us from seeing the diversity of conflicts that these secularized notions of literature helped to disguise. The debate between Qutb and al-Ghamrawi was not about Islam, nor was it, at least initially, about literature. It started as a confrontation centered on a group of people. The battle began with Qutb's intervention into a posthumous literary biography that another writer, Muhammad al-'Aryan, was publishing on his late literary mentor, the poet Mustafa Said al-Rafi'i. Conceived as a tribute to his teacher, al-ʿAryan's essay focused on al-Rafiʿi's personal life, writings, and literary feuds, for which he was famous. Qutb stormed this serene narrative after feeling that al-ʿAryan's account bore prejudice against ʿAbbas al-ʿAqqad, al-Rafiʿi's decades-long rival and the poet whom Qutb had adopted as his own mentor. Gradually, other protagonists joined in, and the debate took a serious turn with the intervention of Rafiʿi's old friend Muhammad al-Ghamrawi. A scholar of both natural and religious sciences, al-Ghamrawi attributed the debate to the old intellectual conflict between Westernizers and supporters of Islam. According to his classification, al-Rafiʿi stood at the vanguard of the partisans of Islam, while Qutb was guilty of spreading Westernized notions of literature.[2]

This chapter explores how these positions emerged in literary debates in colonial Egypt. It argues that the battle between "the new" and "the old" in literature was not only an ideological disagreement on the ways to reform culture; it was also an outcome of a profound generational conflict, which accompanied the demise of the Nahda scholars to the benefit of new intellectual groups, who are known, today, as the founders of modern literature. This generational transition cannot be understood without taking into account a specific intellectual culture organized around the institution of mentorship. While the founders of Egypt's literary modernity, or the *udabāʾ* generation, broke off from their intellectual mentors to be able to reinvent intellectual culture, they founded their practice on the same type of authority against which they had revolted in their youth: the kind deeply anchored in their personal genius.

Qutb's literary taste and intellectual positions should be understood in the framework of his discipleship to a prominent member of the *udabāʾ* generation, the poet ʿAbbas al-ʿAqqad. From al-ʿAqqad, Qutb inherited not only the notions of literature but also his allies and foes. The unrealized transition from embodied authority to the authority of abstract literary order no longer invested in social life came to form a defining feature of Egypt's literary field: the impossibility to reinvent literature without having to mount an open rebellion against one's teachers. As we are going to see throughout this book, this specificity of Egypt's literary trajectory will lead Qutb to dramatically break off from the literary establishment following World War II.

This chapter charts the literary beginnings of Qutb by situating him in the longer generational history. Focusing on different forms of sociability that held writers both together and apart, it argues that the uneasy relationship between Islam and literature often rested on a troubled relationship between two intellectual groups. It analyzes the emergence of literary modernity from the vantage point of two intellectual circles to which al-ʿAqqad and al-Ghamrawi were close: first, the circle of Taha Husayn, composed of a handful of intellectuals who were loosely connected to the Egyptian University, Liberal Constitutionalist Party and its organ *al-Siyasa*; and, second, an important hub of Muslim reform, the Salafiyya Bookstore and Publishing House. Aesthetic choices and intellectual positions often went hand in hand with the adoption of their advocates as intellectual mentors and teachers. The story of Qutb's literary initiation under the guidance of al-ʿAqqad provides insight into the inner workings of Egypt's literary community at that time and their capacity to define possible career tracks.

Cairo Beckons

Sayyid Qutb was born in 1906 in an Upper Egyptian village, Musha, at a time when multiple changes were turning Egypt into a modern colonial state. As in other cases where nation-states emerged from empires, these changes were fueled by the state's need for centralization, which, in Egypt's case, can be traced back to the first decades of the nineteenth century. The modern schooling system, inwardly expanding bureaucracy, and proliferated technologies of print were rapidly transforming identities, practices, and intellectual culture. These alterations originated in Cairo, Egypt's capital, which, throughout the nineteenth century, evolved from a provincial Ottoman capital into one of its most dynamic cities. For centuries, Cairo had been a center of attraction of Muslim students coming to study at the prestigious Azhar University. But, during the last decades of the century, Egypt's capital became the destination of another type of population, who chose it as a refuge from the stifling intellectual atmosphere of Ottoman cities, which fell under the sultan Abdülhamid's control. Reformist intellectuals, merchants, and political activists headed to Cairo to found publishing houses, periodicals, and underground organizations and to devise solutions preventing the cracking Ottoman empire from falling into the hands of Western imperialism. Cairo's status as the city of intellectual refuge created an atmosphere of permissiveness, which radiated far beyond its city limits.

These developments reached Qutb's remote village slowly but steadily. They manifested themselves primarily in the changing forms of politics. Qutb came from a relatively well-off landowning family. As part of the local learned elite, his father was involved in anti-British activism, which, by the turn of the century, had acquired a new structure: the National Party, directed by the charismatic lawyer Mustafa Kamil. As a committee member, Qutb's father subscribed to the party's daily newspaper and regularly hosted local supporters in his home. In his autobiography *Tifl min al-Qariyya* (A Child from a Village), written in 1946, Qutb retrospectively records the mood of secrecy, shut doors, and whispers that pervaded his house during World War I, stirring his young imagination. By degrees, he was allowed to take part in these gatherings and even solicited to read the newspaper aloud to the assembled men.[3]

In parallel, Qutb witnessed the growing inflow of periodicals, magazines, translated books, and people to his village, which came either from Cairo or the provincial capital Asiyut. The ambulant vendor's collection of ancient folk epics and devotional books that he regularly brought to Musha to sell expanded to include detectives and thrillers translated from English.[4] Students from Cairo would come to deliver sermons that were, to Qutb's astonishment, "of their own creation" and not "derived from books."[5] When, in 1912, Qutb reached the age of schooling, a modern primary school had already been founded in his village, and its headmaster and teachers provided another channel to modern intellectual culture. Not only did they change his perception that poetry was a feature of the early inhabitants of the Arabian Peninsula, but they also informed him of the existence of contemporary and living Arab poets, such as the immensely popular neoclassical authors Ahmad Shawqi and Hafiz Ibrahim.[6] Impressed with Qutb's Arabic skills, the school's headmaster passed him two recent books, one a book of history authored by renowned historian and anti-British activist Muhammad Bek Khudari, the other a collection of patriotic poetry by Thabit al-Jurjawi, a poet close to the nationalist movement of Mustafa Kamil. Enthralled with these books, Qutb collected blank sheets of paper and copied them.[7]

Cairo's effervescent modernity reached Qutb's village both in the shape of intellectual culture and as a new set of aspirations. The importance of education and its associated forms of literacy, new practices of consumption, and career opportunities opened imaginations to multiple paths to the future. The shape these aspirations took varied considerably from the perspective of families and the youth. Qutb's mother understood modernity in the usual sense of her generation: as a means of social mobility.[8] In his autobiography, Qutb describes his looming departure to Cairo as a plan devised for him by his mother to restore his family's decreasing land possessions. She perceived success in a professional sense, as defined by the acquisition of a modern education, a job in the state's bureaucracy, and a stable salary. But, besides the understanding of "efendihood" as a means of social mobility—or, in this case, of preventing social descent—Qutb harbored higher aspirations than becoming a bureaucrat. Growing up in his village, Qutb came to picture his efendi future as associated with life in Cairo, the cleanness of his school, and the elegance of the efendi outfit. Soon, however, this naïve vision would evolve into a sense of calling that was to radically transform not only his family's condition, but that of the entire Egyptian nation.[9]

Compared with the previous generation of efendis, or those of a lesser social standing, Qutb was relatively privileged. Unlike many others, who had to spend at least some years in a *kuttāb* (a village school that taught basics of Islam), or those for whom modern schooling was financially inaccessible, Qutb's path to a better future was wide open. In addition to his family's relative financial stability and the status of the oldest son, Qutb's family boasted two Azhar-educated scholars and one efendi—Qutb's uncle, who worked as a teacher and journalist and was ready to host the young Qutb during his studies. Having a relative settled in Cairo was an important asset in sending offspring to the capital, since it saved on rent.[10] In realizing his aspirations, Qutb would follow the path that had already been well trodden by the previous generation of efendis: modern schooling, education in one of Cairo's institutions of higher learning, and

1. Sayyid Qutb in his study years. *Dumu' al-Shu'ara' 'Ala al-Rahil al-Karim Faqid al-Watan wa Za'im al-Sharq Sa'd Zaghlul Basha* by 'Uthman Ibrahim Uways et al. (Cairo: Maktabat al-Amana, 1928), 18. Private collection of Shaaban Yusuf (Cairo); reprinted with permission.

employment in the state bureaucracy. Thus, after completing his primary education and waiting for the winds of 1919 Revolution to subside, Qutb set out for Cairo.

Qutb arrived in Cairo in 1921, at the age of fifteen. After completing his secondary education, he settled for Dar al-'Ulum teachers' training college, founded in 1872. When Qutb enrolled in its preparatory school in 1927 and entered the college two years later, young efendis had already another option for pursuing higher education: Egyptian University. Established in 1908 as a private institution of learning, Egyptian University became a public university in 1925, and, a year later, it shook the intellectual community with the publication of a controversial book on pre-Islamic poetry, *Fi-l-Shi'r al-Jahili*, authored by one of its professors, Taha Husayn. Despite some provocative incidents—or, more likely, because of them—during the following decades the Egyptian University would emerge as the driving force of Egypt's modernity, setting the standards for intellectual research and literature and pushing Dar al-'Ulum down the ladder of modern education.

Qutb's preference for Dar al-'Ulum was most likely determined on practical rather than ideological grounds; it was an institution with a long history and confirmed reputation as the producer of Egypt's teaching staff, whose diplomas guaranteed steady employment and a respectable salary.[11] The Egyptian University, by contrast, was controversial and still very young, although it certainly offered a more fascinating curriculum. It is no surprise that, having arrived in Cairo "like a soldier prepared for the struggle . . . to restore to the family the prestige and money it lost," Qutb could not jeopardize this mission by joining an institution that offered uncertain career prospects. Thus, instead of studying liberal arts and foreign languages, which were part of the Egyptian University's curriculum, Qutb received extensive and practice-oriented training in Arabic, pedagogy, and the sciences of religion necessary for his teaching career.[12] Soon, he would realize that his Arabic-centered instruction formed a hindrance to his professional advancement in the bureaucracy, nourishing his early anticolonial sentiments.

Fortunately, Cairo was larger than the walls of Dar al-'Ulum. The institutional education formed only one part of the entire educational experience of young efendis. A decisive share was acquired through the process of "self-learning" (*takwīn*), based on immersion in the worldly life of literature, individual reading, and participation in Cairo's effervescent political life.[13] The Cairo of the early 1920s offered a rich palette of opportunities for self-learning. Still marked by the revolutionary frenzy of 1919, the capital was absorbed with competitive party politics, as well as a vibrant press, intellectual gatherings in coffeehouses and associations, and a thriving printing industry, which assured the continuous inflow of books, magazines, and periodicals. By choosing a circle to frequent, a type of literature to read, and a party to support, young intellectuals could steer their education in the direction they wished. Sometimes informal education outweighed that acquired through schooling, as in the case of the future historian Ahmad Amin, who, confined to the Azhari track, completed his literary development by attending café gatherings. The poet ʿAbbas al-ʿAqqad, whom Qutb would adopt as his intellectual mentor, did without formal schooling altogether. Having completed only his secondary education, he molded himself entirely through reading and intellectual exchange.

Since the end of World War I, aspiring literati followed ongoing debates on cultural renewal, which, when Qutb arrived in Cairo, reached a heightened pitch. Talk of the need to revive literature had started earlier, when in 1916 young and ambitious poet al-ʿAqqad had argued that genuine literature needed to depart from its ornamental role and to express life by "words of flesh and blood."[14] The criticism of "ornamental poetry" was addressed to the renowned poet Ahmad Shawqi, who had risen to fame a decade earlier as the representative of refined, neoclassical poetry. In 1921, al-ʿAqqad carried the offensive against Shawqi even further, when, together with his friend Ibrahim al-Mazni, he published a pamphlet of literary criticism, *al-Diwan*, in which he called for the "new school" in poetry that would privilege the content instead of the form.

From this point, the confrontation between "the new" and "the old" in culture would become a routine feature of the interwar Arab cultural press. Placing on the frontline between "the new" and "the old" a variety of issues such as language, aesthetics, and Western reception, these debates took a critical turn with the intervention of Azhar.[15] The legal proceedings undertaken by the religious establishment against the prominent sharia judge ʿAli ʿAbd al-Raziq, for his 1925 book that questioned the religious foundations of the caliphate, and, a year later, against his friend Taha Husayn for his opus on pre-Islamic literature shifted the debate on literature to the issue of Islam. The proportions that the controversies of the 1920s took cannot be fully understood without taking into consideration the preceding decades, during which two intellectual groups sniped repeatedly at each other in the press. Rather than being normative categories that expressed a view on modernity, "the new" and "the old" were embodied by concrete individuals. On the side of the self-proclaimed "new", there was a "gang of Taha Husayn," as his detractors loved to call it,[16] composed of a handful of intellectuals loosely connected to the Egyptian University, the Liberal Constitutionalist Party, and its organ *al-Siyasa*.[17] Those assigned to "the old" equally maintained with each other bonds of friendship or discipleship: the poet Mustafa Sadiq al-Rafi'i, the cosmopolitan pan-Arabist Shakib Arslan, and Muhammad al-Ghamrawi were all associated with an important hub of intellectual activism of the Nahda generation, the Salafiyya Bookstore and Publishing House.[18] By assessing texts and positions, intellectuals took into account various pieces of background information on their authors marked by past offenses and gratifications. It is therefore necessary to return to the prehistory of Qutb's arrival to Cairo in order to see how emotions of sympathy or animosity were embedded in the practices of intellectual socialization that shaped the content of modernity.

Salafis of Literature

One of the sources of apprehension Muhammad al-Ghamrawi expressed in his 1938 response to Qutb was the latter's lack of respect to elders. For him, it was unimaginable how Qutb, aged thirty-two, could criticize al-Rafi'i, who was not only more than twenty years his senior, but had also just passed away. Such a lack of respect was not specific to Qutb, in al-Ghamrawi's view, but indicated more largely that the reform movement has taken a wrong path. "Perhaps one of the worst evils of the age of transition is the rebellion that overtook the youth," al-Ghamrawi pondered:

> Before our times were affected by this evil, people would resolve their differences by returning to the basics established by the received religion, custom ['*urf*], or the ancient *adab*, whose rulings had been defined, criteria clarified and foundations given a firm root throughout the ages. A junior was not to encroach on his teacher in [matters] in which he was still a novice or of recent learning. If a junior acted in a way going against the opinion of a senior, he knew he was wrong, and if he wasn't convinced by his teacher's opinion . . . in matters of language, literature or religion in which he might have his own judgment, he never criticized, slandered or laughed off his teacher. He would not even think of exposing him to the mockery of the others.[19]

In the debates on cultural renewal, the invocation of the patriarchal obligation of deference to one's seniors was common. In 1924, Husayn came into the sight of Rashid Rida, the editor of the influential *al-Manar*, as a troublesome student who disrespected his teachers. Rida was shocked by the obituary Husayn wrote on his late teacher of Arabic, Muhammad Mahdi, in which, despite its generally sympathetic tone, Husayn mocked Mahdi's inability "to adapt to new life": "His friends and students who loved and leaned to him would listen to him with amusement. . . . They would smile at him but upon his leaving would explode in laughter, not out of sarcasm, but of affection and love." For Rida, the revered professor Mahdi deserved unconditional respect, not affection.[20] During his own lifetime, Mahdi had complained of Husayn's bad manners as well. He reportedly compared him to "an empty pot on fire" who launched himself into scientific debates unprepared and considered that "all science was in the books."[21] One could only guess the reaction of the poet al-Rafi'i when he read Husayn's review of his *Rasa'il al-Ahzan fi-l Falsafa al-Jamal wa-l-Hubb* (Letters of Sorrow in Philosophy of Aesthetics and Love), in which the latter compared his writing to the torture inflicted by the interminable process of giving birth.[22] Al-Rafi'i emphasized the youth of his interlocutor, arguing that what he called "the new" was, in fact, inexperience disguised as self-confidence.[23]

There is no doubt that Husayn's intentionally provocative attitude as displayed in the press had antagonized fellow intellectuals. But the debate on youth's lack of deference to their seniors reflected a larger intellectual turmoil caused by the transformation of textual—and, by extension, political—authority. As has been noted, the expansion of print during the last decades of the nineteenth century triggered the breakdown of intellectual authority organized around the complex system of mentorship.[24] Since time immemorial, the presence of a teacher was necessary to mediate the texts and to ensure their correct interpretation. The science was not "only in the books," as Mahdi implied in his criticism of Husayn, but also embodied by a teacher, whom a junior could not contradict, as al-Ghamrawi pointed out. Since intellectual and social modes of authority were not considered distinct, the right to author a public text was reserved to senior males who had mastered a wide range of authoritative texts. In this context, becoming an author at a young age was a revolutionary act in itself, directed against senior authorities at home and in the wider network of knowledge production. Fully aware of the new opportunities offered by the increasing access to print, efendi youth threw themselves enthusiastically into this revolution and started writing.[25]

Yet it would be wrong to define their activity as a full-fledged rebellion. While revolting against their seniors, Husayn's generation did not entirely disrupt the system of mentorship. Both Taha Husayn and Rashid Rida were the products of the same print revolution that redefined texts from being the embodiment of an authoritative chain of masters to a mere vehicle of communication from the author's mind.[26] In fact, in his own day, Rida had to mount his own rebellion against his seniors in order to pursue the intellectual renewal known as the movement of balanced reform. For this aim, Rida as well as many others used print to challenge the intellectual authority of Azhar through the appropriation of their practices, such as the interpretation of texts or the right to issue fatwas.[27] Rather, they claimed, what print did was amplify the original tension present in the system of mentorship between the urge to rebel and the obligation of deference to senior authority.[28] By providing new spaces from which the rebellion could be prepared and mounted, print allowed successive generational renewals to take place. In the case of Husayn's generation, these new spaces were made available by the emergence of the new political system based on party politics.

The intellectual divide between "the new" and "the old" largely followed a break within the political order, propelled by the 1919 Revolution and the resulting creation of a parliamentary system in 1923. For Husayn's generation, the events of 1919–23 represented a powerful generational marker that they diligently recorded in their autobiographies and novels.[29] They contributed significantly to the building of the new parliamentary system with which they fused their identity as the architects of a new literary order. As young and skilled writers, these intellectuals worked for competing partisan periodicals as editors, journalists, staff writers, or freelance contributors of poetry and essays. Joining a political party was not only a modern way to seek national liberation and social change, but it also provided better opportunities to rise within the ranks of bureaucracy, which fell under the control of ruling political parties. This new political configuration redefined the lines of distribution of intellectual authority:

political parties took on the task of intellectual consecration while nationalist leaders assumed the place of the mentors. The anticolonial movement conducted through the framework of a political party and its associated legitimist means of political action, such as elections and negotiations, provided a crucial element of their intellectual authority. In many regards, their literary activity was auxiliary to their larger mission of creating a new political community of the territorially conceived Egypt.[30]

Rather than dismantling the system of mentorship, the *udabā'* generation turned to an alternative pool of mentors associated with the parliamentary system. It is not surprising that Ahmad Lutfi Sayyid, the editor of the journal of the Umma Party, *al-Jarida*, is commonly known as the "teacher of the generation" (*ustādh al-jīl*). Indeed, he was a "teacher," not only in the sense of providing an ideological orientation for some of the future literati, but also by facilitating their rise in the emerging intellectual infrastructure. It is under his protection that Husayn placed himself, gaining access to the press, party politics, and the newly founded Egyptian University.[31] Having met Lutfi Sayyid in 1907 with a view to publishing an article in *al-Jarida*, Husayn was fortunate to become part of his select intellectual circle, which largely shaped modern intellectual production during the interwar period. Formed by 'Ali 'Abd al-Raziq's family and held together through the decades by bonds of kinship, friendship, and discipleship,[32] the circle exerted its influence in different sites of intellectual practice: it provided the editorial staff for *al-Jarida*, and, later, for the mouthpiece of the Liberal Constitutionalist Party, *al-Siyasa*; it assumed control of the Egyptian University (from 1922); and it held a glittering salon for elite journalists, politicians, and writers.[33] Instead of following the scholarly authorities of the fields of knowledge that he sought to reform, Husayn styled himself after the teachings of his European professors at the Egyptian University and drew upon his political network to obtain support for his intellectual positions.

Likewise, 'Abbas al-'Aqqad chose his mentors from fields of intellectual practice other than poetry. He drew inspiration from multiple national leaders and newspaper editors, striking a close relationship with Muhammad Farid Wagdy. "A man behind the matter," as al-'Aqqad affectionately called him for his absent-mindedness and interest in spiritual matters, Wagdy edited the journal *al-Dustur*, where al-'Aqqad found his first job in journalism.[34] But it was al-'Aqqad's involvement in the Wafd political party especially that contributed to his intellectual fame. Following the 1919 Revolution, al-'Aqqad became a prominent member, assuming the editorship of the weekly supplement of the party's mouthpiece, *al-Balagh al-Usbu'i*; running for elections; and obtaining the recognition from Saad Zaghlul himself. Upon the latter's death, al-'Aqqad produced his official biography. Within the political-literary establishment, he was known as "the giant writer" after the title bestowed upon him by Zaghlul and was promoted as "the prince of poets" during a celebration organized for his honor by Wafdist youth.[35]

The effects of the symbiosis created between party politics and literature were wide ranging. Notably, it prevented the constitution of an autonomous literary community that would be immune to partisan rivalries. It is telling that, until the creation of the first high-brow literary magazine, *al-Risala*, in 1933, writers published their texts mostly in the weekly supplements of the partisan press, which made it difficult for them to access the writings of their rivals.[36] This feature also discouraged the formation of nonpartisan literary initiatives that risked being swallowed by partisan rivalries. As we will see later, one such victim of the system was the Apollo Poet Society, founded in 1932 as a nonpartisan poetry forum but forced to close down two years later under political pressures. If the parliamentary system allowed for the Husayn's generation to reinvent literature as part of their rebellion against senior Nahda intellectuals, their association with party politics would be the reason for their fall following the postwar collapse of the parliamentary order.

The intellectual trends that came to represent literary modernity should therefore be considered in the light of their effectiveness in disrupting the patriarchal authority of the Nahda generation. The most prominent of them were the Romantic version of literature and the principle of scientific skepticism. Husayn discovered literature while still studying in Azhar, which immediately appeared to him as a tool "to break the chains of Azhar": "As far as I know, nothing in the world can exert so strong the influence for freedom as literature, especially for the young," he wrote.[37] As a young man going to school in the 1900s, Husayn experienced public writing as a means of emancipation. But he certainly carried the transgressive aspect of literature much further by turning his experience of liberation into an ideology of literature. By portraying literature and Azhari scholarship as "two departments of knowledge" that were impossible to reconcile, or "two worlds" that one could only bestride by leading "a double life," Husayn laid the groundwork for the myth of Islam's incompatibility with literature.[38] At the foundation of this representation, young efendis struck out on an initial quest for freedom in regard to their traditional environments. But, to establish themselves as the new intellectual authority, they had to push the rebellion further and create new fields of knowledge.

In the field of imaginative literature, the most efficient instrument for achieving this end was Romanticism. Notions associated with Romantic literature, such as an understanding of poetry as the channel for emotional expression, had reached Arab intellectuals as early as the end of the nineteenth century, but it was the interwar generation who succeeded in establishing Romanticism as the new literary modernity.[39] The notion of literature as a window into one's subjectivity went against the dominant neoclassical canon of that time, which developed in symbiosis with the manuscript movement prompted by the expansion of print from the mid-nineteenth century onward. The excavation of medieval Arab texts incited reformist scholars to experiment with Abbasid literary forms by combining them with commentary on public affairs. If neoclassicists innovated in terms of content, they were keen to preserve classical Arab literary forms regarded as the pinnacle of aesthetic beauty and linguistic mastery. What young Arab Romantics revolted against was not merely neoclassical aesthetics, but also the method of training on which the acquisition of such skills was predicated. If the classical notion of poetry as a craft, mastered as a result of long periods of learning, memorization, and immersion, was gradually abandoned in the nineteenth century, modernist writers pushed this redefinition forward.[40] By shifting literary criteria from the requirement to polish the form to the expression of one's subjectivity, they emphasized their interiority as legitimate subject matter for intellectual expression, allowing them to claim authority at a young age. To be sure, this shift did not mean that their poetry was as spontaneous as they claimed. Complex rules of composition, such as the following of a poetic meter and rhyme, applied to Romantic poetry as well, and immersion in reading and memorization remained essential tools for mastering them. Romanticism transformed not so much the practice of poetry as the discourse surrounding it.

The field of scientific inquiry witnessed a similar transformation. As in literature, the *udabā'* generation reshaped knowledge by redefining norms and practices that authorized it. In the emerging field of the humanities, such a change was enacted through the principle of scientific skepticism (*tajarrud*) that during the 1920s and 1930s became the battle cry of the entire generation. "They closed the door of *ijtihād* in *adab*, as scholars of jurisprudence and theologians closed the doors of jurisprudence and rational theology (*kalām*)," Husayn wrote in the revised version of his *Fi-l-Shi'r al-Jahili*, the book that could rightfully be considered the manifesto of scientific detachment.[41] He thus set out to open these doors and to explore the history of pre-Islamic Arab literature anew. In doing so, he gave to *tajarrud* a double meaning: detachment from all types of emotional bonds, be they religious, historical, or nationalist, susceptible to distort the results of an investigation, and detachment from all the layers of scholarship covering the topic. Husayn claimed to follow the method of Descartes, who had urged scholars to "detach themselves from everything they had known before," to "free oneself from all these multiple heavy chains that impede our free movement of body and reason."[42] It was only by pursuing this method, Husayn claimed, that it would be possible to disburden the Arab heritage of its accumulated interpretations and to engender the right conditions for a civilizational revival.

The principle of *tajarrud* was a scholarly escape from frustrations that many of Husayn's peers had experienced during their studies. Their memoirs are filled with complaints that the tangled commentaries of their teachers only obscured the original texts they were teaching. Ahmad Amin, a future professor at Cairo University who had attended Azhar in his youth, recalled a shaykh's lesson in these terms: "He read the text, then the commentary and I understood them. But then he soared, offering comment on and objections to the wording and answers to the objections, of which I understood nothing."[43] Speaking about himself in the third person, Husayn described his studies in similar terms: "He memorized the tradition and understood it, but showed not the slightest interest in the shaykh's analysis, which reminded him too well of explanations given by the Imam of the mosque in his country village."[44] Al-'Aqqad adopted the same attitude in the realm of poetry: "The generation which appeared after Shawqi were not in the least influenced by him, either in their language or the spirit of their poetry," he wrote. "They read directly the Diwans of the Ancients, studied them and admired in their style whatever they found agreeable."[45] The principle of *tajarrud*, associated with scientific detachment, became a norm of the intellectual authority of this generation, providing the main criterion of identification for their rivals. Scholars of the Salafiyya Bookstore and Publishing House mocked these writers by calling them "*mutajarridūn*" (the detached ones), intentionally misspelling the label of "*mutajaddidūn*" (the renovators) that modernist writers claimed for themselves.[46] They correctly understood that the young writers' call to disregard secondary sources was directed against those scholars who had produced them. In many cases, they were those scholars.

In the humanities, the principle of scientific skepticism functioned as the equivalent of Romanticism in literature. Both served as tools for invalidating the arguments of authority on which the existing intellectual traditions were built. Both were directed against the notion of knowledge as accumulation that not only conveyed certain ideas but also implied certain social relationships. In many ways, Romanticism and *tajarrud* had the same effect in the humanities as the Salafi creed had for balanced reform two decades earlier. To regenerate Islam and to foster a civilizational revival, balanced reformers had embraced Salafi theology as a means of chipping away the late Sunni tradition that was judged too speculative and conducive to divisions.[47] They had similarly emphasized the need to access the knowledge of the ancients in its original and unmediated form, posing a challenge to Azhar's institutional monopoly on the interpretation of scriptures. It was through their efforts that the terms *taqlīd* and *ijtihād*—literally "following" and "critical thinking"—were taken out of their legal context and turned into a mechanism of social change.[48] What the *udabā'* generation did was to shift the discussion from law to literature and to renovate it by the means of the same principle of *ijtihād*.

In order to reinvent literature anew, Husayn's generation advocated for a departure from the embodied intellectual authority to one of abstracted order no longer invested in human relations. Romanticism, scientific skepticism, and freethinking provided them with tools of emancipation, while the new political configuration ensured a privileged position to use them. Yet, following their rise to fame, they reproduced the same type of authority against which they had revolted in their youth. They conceived their literary movements as deeply embedded in their personal genius. Those who positioned themselves as their disciples transmitted their masters' personal genius through the practice of tribute in exchange for the expectation of inserting themselves into the modern intellectual genealogy of *udabā'*. This was crucial not only for one's initiation into literary arts, but also for the advancement of careers, since, by the interwar period, Husayn's generation largely controlled the literary marketplace by supervising periodicals, advising publishing houses, and holding key positions in Egypt's cultural bureaucracy. The centrality of personal genius, the *udabā'* constitutes a structural feature of Egypt's literary order that, in many regards, is valid to this day: the impossibility of reinventing literature without having to carry out an open rebellion against the mentors.[49]

The Demise of the Nahda Generation

The story of the rise of the founders' generation would be incomplete without shedding light on those intellectuals who came to be perceived as representing the side of reaction. A significant portion of these intellectuals were associated with an important hub of reformism, the Salafiyya Bookstore and Publishing House. Founded in 1909 as a joint partnership between two damascene émigrés, Muhibb al-Din al-Khatib and 'Abd al-Fatah Qatlan, the Salafiyya Bookstore and Publishing House emerged as the most vocal opponent of Husayn's intellectual generation. While the venture has been analyzed from the perspective of the religious reform movement, it was less discussed in relation to its significance to literature.[50] Yet a close-up of the Bookstore's intellectual network allows us to observe how intellectuals associated with the diverse Nahda culture came to forge its identity around the defense of Islam. A crucial element in this process was the alliance of the Bookstore with Azhar in the controversies over Husayn's and 'Abd al-Raziq's books. It was the Bookstore that published and distributed for free Azhar's ruling on 'Abd al-Raziq's case, which stripped him of the qualifications of judge.[51] While it was Azhar that framed 'Abd al-Raziq's and Husayn's writings as blasphemy, the Bookstore greatly contributed to the spread of its rhetoric through its numerous publishing activities.[52]

The Salafiyya Bookstore and Publishing House embodied the overlap between multiple historical trends and generations that shaped the cultural revival of the last decades of the nineteenth century: it was overwhelmingly neoclassicist in literature, Arab Ottomanist in politics, and balanced reformist in its vision of reform. The convergence of these intellectual trends within the Bookstore's microcosm is not surprising. Concomitantly emerging in different parts of the declining Ottoman Empire, these trends fed into each other, shaping a distinctive intellectual generation that came to identify itself with a particular understanding of Arab heritage.

First of all, the Bookstore should be located within the expanding print industry and its associated concerns for manuscript printing and trade. It was conceived initially as a commercial venture for printing and selling ancient manuscripts, responding to the manuscript hunt that gripped Ottoman cities at the turn of the century. The "discovery" of ancient Arab texts provided an impulse for the development of the balanced reform movement, coming to shape its main principles: the importance of Arab heritage for political change, the "rediscovery" of the transnational Muslim community, and the erosion of the traditional authority of *'ulamā* based on the oral transmission of knowledge.[53] Those who are remembered today as prominent reformist figures were personally engaged in the manuscript edition. Scholars such as Muhammad 'Abdu and Rashid Rida made use of their personal networks to track down manuscripts that were being kept in private households scattered across the empire. The possession of a press allowed these texts to be printed. Rida relied extensively on his press *al-Manar* to publish manuscripts, on some of which he collaborated with Muhammad 'Abdu.[54]

Muhibb al-Din al-Khatib, the main figure behind the Salafiyya Bookstore and Publishing House venture, was equally attracted to the manuscript business. Born in 1886 in Damascus, he grew up surrounded by Syrian reformers, who advocated the revival of Arab culture through the rediscovery of its heritage. From his youth, al-Khatib combined his passion for the Arab past with vigorous campaigning to expand Arab political influence within the Ottoman Empire.[55] When he settled in Cairo in the late 1910s, he carried his ideas into the Egyptian capital and worked to realize them through his publishing activities in the Bookstore. In Cairo, al-Khatib had access to a voluminous manuscript collection through his friendship with Ahmad Taymur, the encyclopedist, book collector, and cofounder of the association dedicated to manuscript editions *Jama'iyya Nashr al-Kutub al-'Arabiyya*. Hailing from an aristocratic family that boasted connections to the royal court, Taymur was the host of one of the most thriving scholarly houses in Cairo, where Muhammad 'Abdu himself held a salon.[56]

Regardless of the associations that its name might now evoke, the Salafiyya Bookstore and Publishing House did not specialize in the publication of religious books.[57] Nor was the movement of balanced reform exclusively about Islam. It certainly aimed to reshape Islam, in the sense of stripping from its message elements deemed incompatible with Western understanding of rationalism, but the movement was equally concerned with the revival of other sources of knowledge, such as the natural sciences, linguistics, and literature. Islam was not understood as a category separate from other types of knowledge; rather, it was perceived as running underneath multiple ways of understanding the reality to which it provided meaning. Notably, *adab* was the field to which reformist intellectuals accorded significant attention. They recognized the importance of imaginative literature for the Arab cultural revival, which could be harnessed either to political ends, such as the strengthening of Arab national bonds, or used as an efficient tool to communicate useful content and "polish" the mores of the population.[58] The historical proximity of the Salafiyya Bookstore and Publishing House to the manuscript edition movement explains why its associates were so fond of neoclassical literature, especially the poet Ahmad Shawqi. For Arab reformists to come across a "living" poet who was composing verses in Arabic language "of a similar and even higher quality than Turkish poetry" was an exciting discovery that promised an imminent cultural revival.[59]

Another piece of evidence that the Bookstore was not exclusively defined by religious concerns is its intellectual network. The diversity of personalities who became involved in the establishment's activities by writing to its periodicals, printing their books in its press, or simply spending time in its library suggests that the Bookstore had functions that ranged far beyond its religious concerns. During the 1920s, the Bookstore had become a vibrant hub of intellectual exchange and a necessary stop for visiting scholars who flocked to Cairo by the routes of communication set up during the Nahda. Al-Khatib, who lodged just above the Bookstore, spent his days in the shop receiving visitors. His nephew, poet 'Ali al-Tantawi, reportedly encountered in the Bookstore "the crème of the men of *adab* and science" upon his arrival in Cairo in 1928.[60] Among them was the aforementioned Ahmad Taymur, who used to go to the Bookstore on a daily basis to read or to join ongoing conversations. There, al-Tantawi also met the poet al-Rafi'i, who, being unhearing, communicated with the others through writing. Al-Khatib had known al-Rafi'i since his college years in Istanbul, and they maintained their friendship through correspondence.[61] It was therefore natural that after al-Khatib settled in Cairo and acquired the press, al-Rafi'i used it to publish his works.[62]

Muhammad al-Ghamrawi, Qutb's opponent in 1938 battle, was another guest of al-Khatib. Born in 1893 in Zifta, an Egyptian town in the Nile delta, al-Ghamrawi graduated from the Teachers' Training College with a diploma in the sciences. He was fortunate to receive a scholarship for studying in London, becoming after his return a professor of chemistry and medicine at the Egyptian University. Despite his focus in natural sciences, al-Ghamrawi was a profoundly devout Muslim and moved in circles associated with Islamic activism. He was one of the founders of the Young Men's Muslim Association, launched the Salafiyya Bookstore and Publishing House in 1927, contributed articles to the Muslim Brotherhood's periodical *al-Nadhir*, and supervised the scientific section of the Azhar's periodical, *Nur al-Islam*. Hasan al-Banna, the founder of the Muslim Brotherhood, recalls meeting him in the Bookstore, in whose presses al-Ghamrawi published his famous critical response to Husayn's revised version of *Fi-l-Shi'r al-Jahili*.[63]

Perhaps a more unexpected visitor to the Bookstore was the poet Ahmad Zaki Abu Shadi. Born in 1892, Abu Shadi would come to prominence as the founder of the Apollo Poet Society, with which Qutb would associate himself in 1932. In some accounts of Egypt's literary history, Abu Shadi is portrayed as an advocate of unabashed Westernization who experimented with very new forms of poetry, including blank and free verse. Perhaps he was, but in the 1920s he demonstrated loyalty to an intellectual circle whose members would emerge as the most violent opponents of modernist writers. Abu Shadi regularly contributed essays and poems to the Bookstore's periodicals, published his books in its press, and was spotted spending time in its library. His association with the Bookstore illustrates how one could become part of an intellectual circle for reasons that were anything but ideological. His relationship with al-Khatib was, in fact, inherited from his father, the prominent lawyer and journalist Muhammad Abu Shadi, who owned the building in which the Bookstore was located.[64] It is hardly surprising that, upon his return to Cairo after obtaining a medical degree in London, Abu Shadi turned to printing services that were within a hand's reach. Similar factors explain the connection of Muhammad and Mahmud Taymur to the Salafiyya Bookstore and Publishing House, whose presses these two pioneers of the Egyptian novella used to publish their first works. In their case, the Salafiyya Press clearly represented a choice of convenience, since their father, Ahmad Taymur, was linked to its owner by bonds of friendship.

Throughout the second part of the 1920s, intellectual bonds based on friendship, kinship, or neighborhood sociability gradually acquired a more ideological bent. The threat of "atheism" (*ilḥād*) that many of the Bookstore's intellectuals detected in 'Abd al-Raziq's and Husayn's writings directed their activities toward a more narrowly defined version of Islam. It also provided the circle with a sense of mission that solidified the bonds between its members. Scholars, novelists, poets, and other writers now invested at least a part of their talent to defend a notion of culture connected to Islam and Arab nationalism. Abu Shadi contributed to this struggle as well; in his poems and essays he urged liberal intellectuals to stick with time-honored literary forms and to preserve the close association of literature with Islam, the Qur'an, and Arab nationalism.[65] Abu Shadi's activity against *mutajarridūn* illustrates perhaps best of all the importance of group solidarities in shaping one's ideological stands. His example challenges the assumption that it was the type of education, the degree of exposure to Western knowledge, or the generational factor (Abu Shadi was several years younger than Husayn) that determined one's intellectual stances.

To understand the clustering of the Salafiyya circle around the defense of Islam, one should consider the social and political setbacks its intellectuals experienced during the 1920s. 'Abd al-Raziq's and Husayn's books were the last straw in a series of frustrations accumulated over the decades, some of them related to regional developments that invalidated the past political commitments of the circle. Its key members belonged to the last generation of Ottoman Arabs, who, in their youth, had taken part in transnational activism for the establishment of a strong Arab political entity from the ashes of the Ottoman Empire. Al-Khatib was active in the Istanbul scene of clandestine associations promoting Arab cultural and political rights;[66] shaykh Muhammad al-Khidr Husayn zigzagged Ottoman cities fighting the French occupation in Northern Africa and taking part in "German Jihad";[67] Shakib Arslan was personally involved in the military campaigns of the vanishing Ottoman Empire.[68] But, instead of the birth of an Arab unity, throughout the 1920s they witnessed the fall of the Ottoman Empire, the loss of Iraq and Greater Syria to mandatory powers, the triumph of Kemalism in Turkey, and the abolishment of the caliphate. The only silver lining for supporters of Muslim unity was the expanding influence of King al-Sa'ud in the Arabian Peninsula.

Now, young intellectuals threatened to strip the Salafiyya intellectuals from their qualifications on the local scene. They immediately perceived 'Abd al-Raziq's and Husayn's invitation to think of politics and history outside their authoritative grip as a harbinger of a Kemalist-like secular state in Egypt. But these writings alone perhaps would not have sparked such anxieties had their authors not been affiliated with a rising institution calling for an uncompromising break from the past: the Egyptian University. To be sure, in turn-of-the-century Egypt, each founding of a new educational institution precipitated anxieties. But the creation of the Egyptian University in 1908, and especially its transformation into a public institution of learning in 1925, posed a new set of challenges.

These challenges were related to the university's advocacy for an unbending policy of rupture with the established scholarly community. First and foremost, this policy applied to its recruitment strategies: with the exception of one Azhar and a few Dar al-'Ulum graduates, it relied heavily on European teaching staff.[69] Second, this attitude was further amplified by Husayn's personal efforts in reforming education. Many of Husayn's writings on culture could be read as an offensive against the existing institutions of higher education in Egypt. If his autobiography *The Days* is directed against Azhar, a number of his later books, such as *Fi-l-Adab al-Jahili* (1927) and *Mustaqbal al-Thaqafa fi Misr* (1938), advocated for a closure of those institutions from which the Nahda intellectuals had graduated or for which they worked—notably, the future Sayyid Qutb's alma mater Dar al-'Ulum.[70] These suggestions sparked an outcry from those scholars who felt they were their target. "The tyranny of the university over education is a blow against education, and the despotism of an individual on *adab* is a setback for *adab*," Ghamrawi declared in 1929. For him, Husayn's call to shut down educational institutions was outrageous, since the university was too young to claim a monopoly on education. Established as a public institution just recently, he argued, it was still in its "stage of experimentation" and had not produced any outstanding scholars. Concerning literature, "we are aware of only one professor," he added, referring to Husayn.[71]

Others, such as the poet al-Rafi'i, similarly reproached Husayn for his arrogance toward the local community of scholars. Since Husayn's subject matter, the history of *adab*, could not be considered a science given that it was devoid of tradition, it was crucial to submit his findings to the debate of the scholarly community (*ahl al-adab*). Without its approval, Husayn's scholarship consisted of bits of information called "science," audacity defined as "criticism," prejudice labeled "opinion," and imitation of Orientalists (*taqlīd*) called "independent reasoning (*ijtihād*).[72] Overall, the Bookstore's intellectuals contested the scientificity of Husayn's writings, given that he conceived them outside of the procedures of their scholarly approval.

By the 1930s, al-Khatib's impression that the train of reform had derailed had come to be shared by many intellectuals of his generation.[73] It was the end of a certain intellectual culture, marked by an anti-Ottoman Pan-Arabism, the practice of manuscript editing, and the importance of publishing as a means of social reform. A new form of intellectual culture took its place, which inscribed its modernizing mission within the legal setting of party politics, territorial nationalism, and a redefined meaning of literature as detached from political and religious concerns. They correctly understood that the breaking-with-the-past rhetoric, amplified by the irreverent behavior of the youth, their calls for accessing ancient knowledge in its original and unmediated form, and the rising institutional power of the university, foreshadowed their intellectual demise. Published at a time when the intellectual prestige of shaykhs was at its lowest, Husayn's *Fi-l-Shi'r al-Jahili* epitomized the generational change.[74]

It remains difficult, however, to trace substantial differences in the advocated solutions to social, political, or cultural problems that would have justified either camp's position as traditional or modern. Both modernist writers and the Bookstore's circle called for a middle-path reform solution combining, to different degrees, European thought with the Arab heritage; both recognized Western intellectual references as authoritative; and both were mixed in terms of the education their members had received and included efendis and shaykhs. They were divided, though, by their respective intellectual networks, each of which was embedded in a particular intellectual culture, web of personal relationships, and system of political and institutional support. By striking an alliance with conservative elements of Azhar and by increasingly aligning its intellectual orientation with the rising Saudi state, the Bookstore's circle condemned itself as part of the stagnant Azhari culture. Its demise was equally due to the overwhelming victory of the *udabā'* generation in taking control of the discourse of modernity.

A Perfect Disciple

As unabashedly confrontational writers, Husayn's generation would come to represent all that Sayyid Qutb would be fascinated by: boldness, erudition, and an unlimited taste for success. By the time of Qutb's graduation from Dar al-'Ulum in 1933, authors like Husayn, al-'Aqqad, Ibrahim al-Mazni, and Tawfiq al-Hakim had established themselves as figures of authority. For many writers who joined Cairo's intellectual scene in this decade, this generation represented the modernity they wished to emulate. However, since the access to literary life was mediated through the structures of sociability, their cultural orientation was largely dependent on the randomness of social encounters. Qutb's literary beginnings were primarily shaped by two forms of social bonds he created after his arrival to Cairo: his discipleship to 'Abbas al-'Aqqad, and the poetic circle of peers formed in Dar al-'Ulum, which later transited to the Apollo Poet Society. Qutb's literary career and project depended on his skills in navigating between these two forms of sociability and their conflicting demands of loyalty.

Qutb was introduced to the poet al-'Aqqad by his uncle not long after his arrival in Cairo.[75] His uncle, who accommodated young Qutb in Cairo, probably knew al-'Aqqad from his involvement with the Wafd party; similarly to the famous poet, he held a party membership and worked for its newspaper, *al-Balagh*. As was common, Qutb initiated himself into literature through party politics. Like his uncle and al-'Aqqad, he joined the Wafd party and gained access to its press. From 1925, Qutb's poems started appearing in the Wafdist press, *al-Balagh*, and its weekly supplement edited by al-'Aqqad, and in 1928 his elegy "A Prayer at Saad's Grave" was featured in a poetry collection published on the occasion of Saad Zaghlul's passing.[76] At around the same time, Qutb began attending al-'Aqqad's weekly salon, held in the poet's apartment in Heliopolis, encouraged by its proximity from his uncle's house in Zaytun and al-'Aqqad's immense library.[77]

It would not take long for Qutb to identify himself as al-'Aqqad's disciple, or *murīd*, the term that originates from Sufi tradition to describe the symbiotic relationship between a novice and his guide, but was used in literature also to define discipleship. In his first book of criticism, *Mahammat al-Sha'ir fi-l Hayat*, published in 1932, Qutb purposefully located himself within al-'Aqqad's "literary school," adopting his confrontational attitude to Shawqi's poetry and the "old school" in literature.[78] Qutb

2. ‘Abd al-‘Aziz ‘Atiq in the Apollo Poet Society. *Apollo* 1, no. 6 (February 1933): 679. Private collection of Shaaban Yusuf (Cairo); reprinted with permission.

likened his commitment to al-‘Aqqad’s movement to a religious creed, *‘aqīda*, that he promised to defend as a “believer defends his faith.”[79] If, in this equation, poetry stands for *‘aqīda*, then al-‘Aqqad is the prophet and his “school” is the message (*risāla*). “If I can’t be credited for being a messenger of this literary creed,” Qutb declared, “I am committed to be amongst its strongest partisans and protectors, working as much as I can to strengthen its pillars and to expand its edifice.”[80] With the reform of literature having begun, Qutb saw himself as a soldier charged with its further expansion.

At the time of publishing his first book, Qutb had a more intimate circle of poets, comprised of his comrades of Dar al-‘Ulum. Consistent with his early fascination with poetry, it included the poets ‘Abd al-‘Aziz ‘Atiq and Fayid al-‘Amrusi. Born in 1906, the same year as Qutb, all three poets graduated from Dar al-‘Ulum in 1932. At the dawn of their careers, the young men exchanged unpublished manuscripts and faithfully supported each other’s literary beginnings in print.[81] In his preface to ‘Atiq’s first poetry collection in 1932, Qutb expanded on their friendship, attributing to it his capacity to closely follow ‘Atiq’s creative growth.[82] In Qutb’s first book on poetry, published the same year, Qutb cited ‘Atiq’s verse as an example of genuine poetry.[83] ʻAtiq, for his part, was equally appreciative of Qutb's poetry and praised it in an essay published in the Apollo magazine.[84] Both ʻAtiq and Qutb were known as the disciples of ʻAbbas al-ʻAqqad, or "the Aqqadians" (*ʻAqqadiyyūn*)—a title that they wore proudly.[85] Both were committed to the defense of his "new school" in poetry, defined against the neoclassical canon. When in 1935 Qutb published his first poetry collection, *al-Shati' al-Majhul*, it was another member of the *shilla*, Fayid al-ʻAmrusi, who reviewed it in Dar al-ʻUlum's official bulletin. Being a poet and a critic himself, al-ʻAmrusi published on his friend's *diwan* two extended studies, one of them analyzing the collection's treatment of the love theme (*ghazl*), the other focused on aspects that would become signature features of Qutb's poetry: the significance of symbols, shadows, images, and dreams.[86] After graduation, the trio became associated with the Apollo Poet Society.[87] When, in 1933, *al-Risala* magazine was established, the poets rushed to publish their poems there.

Qutb, ʻAtiq, and al-ʻAmrusi shared not only the classrooms of Dar al-ʻUlum, but also a similar vision of poetry. They absorbed the newest literary fashions, associating themselves with the trendiest type of poetry: the poetry of affect (*shiʻr al-wijdān*).[88] Introduced by the Lebanese poet Khalil Mutran and later developed by al-ʻAqqad's circle, the poetry of affect gave primacy to an honest and accurate expression of the poet's interiority. The themes of tombs, ghosts, and rebellion populate the trio's poetry to the extent that some critics found their fascination with darkness a bit excessive. In a review of ʻAtiq's *diwan*, the poet Ibrahim Naji criticized the mood of pessimism, anger, and resentment, asking, "Where is the light, youth, love of life?"[89] Another critic observed a similar exaggeration of melancholy in Qutb's collection. "We would have loved to get something substantial from this despair (*ka'āba*) or to discern some sort of philosophy of life," the critic stated.[90] But the gloomy, pale-faced trio proceeded undisturbed by these criticisms, arguing that their melancholy was an honest reflection of Egypt's political situation, in which "everything pushed to complain, everything stung with pain."[91]

The founding of the Apollo Poet Society in 1932 provided Qutb with new literary friendships. Conceived as a platform for creative exchange that would circumvent the political factionalism that divided the

3. Poet Tahir Abu Fasha. *Apollo* 1, no. 5 (January 1933): 549. Private collection of Shaaban Yusuf (Cairo); reprinted with permission.

community of poets, Apollo brought together different trends and generations, publishing side by side English poetry (both in translation and the original), neoclassical poems, and religious Sufi hymns. The neoclassical poet al-Rafiʿi wrote in the periodical, as did, for a brief period, his rival al-ʿAqqad. Hailing from a wealthy family, Abu Shadi boasted connections with the intellectual elite of the time, which was predominantly neoclassical in taste. Perhaps this explains his appeal to the khedivial poet Ahmad Shawqi to assume patronage of the association.

In contrast to Abu Shadi, Qutb surrounded himself with poets of a social background similar to his. Having arrived from outside of Cairo to study in Azhar or Dar al-ʿUlum, the members of his group, including the poets Mukhtar al-Wakil, Ahmad Mukhaymar, Tahir Abu Fasha, and Mahmud Abu al-Wafa, were of humbler origins.[92] "The bohemian" (*al-būhīmī*) and "the miserable" (*al-bā'is*), respectively, Abu Fasha and Abu al-Wafa took pride in their misery, regarding their vagabond lifestyle as the guarantee of their literary freedom.[93] Accompanied by the Apollo's poets, Qutb was spotted in the most distinguished poetical gatherings in the interwar period: the *nadwa* in the upscale district al-Hilmiyya, the salon held by the poet sheikh Hasan al-Qayati in his house in Sokkariyya in the old Cairo, and coffeehouses scattered around the editorial offices of *al-Ahram* and the National Library in Bab al-Khalq. Significantly, the Salafiyya Bookstore and Publishing House was also located in Bab al-Khalq, contributing to the neighborhood's intellectual reputation. Observing poets in a café in Bab al-Khalq, a correspondent in *al-Risala* wrote in 1939:

> They sit in the company of their brothers and fellows from the University, Dar al-ʿUlum and the Faculty of Arabic Language, holding their cases from which they pull out the newest literature and poetry. . . . A book that has hardly been printed is already in their hands. Not a single essay or poem published in the press escapes their attention and if they don't like it they laugh and parody it.[94]

A chronicler of Cairo's literary life, ʿAbbas Khidr, recounts that Qutb used to come to Hilmiya to join Apollo's poets, who were sitting around Abu Shadi. This is how Khidr met Qutb, initiating a friendship that lasted until Qutb's incarceration in 1954. Residing in Helwan, Qutb used to miss his last train and would have to spend the night in Khidr's tiny apartment, which also hosted the vagabond Abu Fasha. With his young, unruly peers, Qutb took part in pranks organized by the group. Once he was involved in extorting cash from the tenderhearted al-Qayati under the false pretext of his detention by the police. On another occasion, his circle staged a fictitious ceremony of honors (*ḥaflat al-takrīm*) in a mockery of the prominence accorded to this type of ceremony in traditional circles of poetry.[95]

The devastating literary feud that pitted al-ʿAqqad against the Apollo Poet Society between 1933 and 1934 highlights the structural constraints imposed on poets by the system of mentorship based on the embodied type of authority. The controversy functioned as a test of Qutb's loyalty, during which he chose to take the side of al-ʿAqqad against his circle of peers and to attach his literary identity to the personal genius of his mentor. The Apollo controversy took place in the midst of the youth agitation that swept the universities and streets in the 1930s, reaching its peak in the 1935 uprising.[96] Having started with Abu Shadi's review of al-ʿAqqad's freshly published collection, *Wahi al-Arbaʿin* (Revelations at the Age of Forty), it rapidly evolved into a full-fledged war involving growing numbers of writers, periodicals, and increasingly personal attacks. At the start of the battle, in the spring of 1933, Qutb seemed still unaffected by its escalating tone. He continued to publish laudatory comments on the Apollo poets and even compared Abu Shadi's poetry to al-'Aqqad's style without drawing any conclusion about the superiority of either.[97] It took Qutb a year to throw himself fully into the battle and to launch an offensive against the Apollo's group, accusing it of cronyism, self-promotion, and overflowing confidence.[98] Severely damaged by the controversy, the Apollo Poet Society ceased to exist by the end of 1934.

One could speculate on the motivations that pushed Qutb into the battle. But the time gap between its beginning and Qutb's involvement suggests that it was not a spontaneous move motivated by his mere fascination with al-'Aqqad's poetry. Rather, it seems that Qutb's dependency on his mentor had been slowly building up in the background, pointing to the structural factors that underpinned literary solidarities. The political developments of the early 1930s played a crucial, if not a decisive, role. In June 1930, in an authoritarian bid for power, the king appointed Isma'il Sidqi to form a government. A series of events marked the following three years of Sidqi's rule, including the abrogation of the 1923 constitution, the removal of Taha Husayn from the university's deanship, and the nine-month imprisonment of al-'Aqqad under the pretext of lèse-majesté. Naturally, all this made his government particularly unpopular among the intellectual elite, most of whom belonged to the opposing Wafd and Liberal Constitutionalist parties. The decade witnessed another major shift in politics: Husayn's transition from the Liberal Constitutionalists to the Wafd party. After this move, he found himself in the same political camp as al-'Aqqad, and the two literary giants sealed their alliance when Husayn crowned him "the prince of poets."[99] At the political juncture at which two intellectual heavyweights pledged allegiance to the Wafd, Abu Shadi committed an irretrievable error and appealed to Sidqi's government for funds. Abu Shadi had already been suspected of complicity with Sidqi's government; in fact, his detractors had sniffed out three poems authored by him in Sidqi's honor, which he justified by the fact that Sidqi was a close family friend.[100] But his willingness to associate himself further with Sidqi's authoritarian government delivered a fatal blow to his association.

Such a political situation might explain why Qutb saw the need to publicly dissociate himself from Abu Shadi's intellectual project. With the increasing politicization of the Apollo battle following Husayn's association with the Wafd, it was perhaps too risky to stay uninvolved. This could have thrown suspicion on Qutb's political loyalties, cost him the sympathy of influential literati, and deprived him of access to the periodicals they edited. His involvement in the battle, on the contrary, opened the doors to journals that saw the controversy as part of the Wafdist political agenda, such as al-ʿAqqad's *al-Jihad* and Husayn's newly launched *al-Wadi*. Qutb was not the only poet to desert Apollo in favor of al-ʿAqqad; he was preceded by Kamil al-Kilani, the future celebrity of children's literature, and his friend the "miserable poet" Mahmud Abu al-Wafa. The collective nature of defections points to the transformative power that literary conflicts played in a highly politicized intellectual field. Functioning as a test of loyalty, the controversy redefined friendships and redistributed positions by forcing the participants to approach the political frontlines. In a situation in which literary identities, aesthetic positions, party politics, and personal relationships were deeply intertwined, any skirmish had the capacity to evolve into a wide-ranging political conflict.

Throughout the following decade, Qutb's dedication to al-ʿAqqad rose to the level of devotion. In his articles, he never missed an opportunity to demonstrate his loyalty to the famous poet and commitment to his literary school. In the battle waged in *al-Risala* magazine in 1938, Qutb took upon himself the task of defending al-ʿAqqad against al-Rafiʿi disciples. There, he openly declared his "infinite zeal and enthusiasm" (*shadīd al-ghīra wa-l-taʿaṣṣub*) for his mentor, criticized the label of "the prince of poet's" as insufficient to match his gifts, and justified al-ʿAqqad's bad temper by his literary genius.[101] Such a display of devotion needs to be understood as part of the tacit agreement that binds a master and a disciple. By positioning himself as al-ʿAqqad's disciple, Qutb claimed for himself the share of the latter's authority. While doing so, he helped to anchor the modernist movement of poetry in al-ʿAqqad's personal genius.

Literary criticism provided the most appropriate means to translate this relationship into the forms of literature. As we have seen, in his first essay on poetry Qutb had fixed for himself the task of turning al-ʿAqqad's poetry into a literary school. This meant deriving from his poetry a steady form, aesthetic principles, and a certain "philosophy of life"; Qutb named it "the school of the living logic" (*madrasat al-manṭiq al-ḥayawī*), defined by a complex interplay between rationality and feelings.[102] But instead of detaching this school from al-'Aqqad's personality, he contributed to root it in his personal genius. By turning his mentor's poetry into a "school," Qutb put himself forward as its specialist, claiming the authority of the inventor. His public declarations of loyalty stemmed from his burning ambition to establish himself in the field of which the famous poet had been the origin and legitimizing principle.

Qutb not only based his activity of criticism on al-'Aqqad's aesthetics, but also made the relationship part of its theory. Qutb's theory of criticism rested on the conviction that a close familiarity with the author was necessary for understanding his oeuvre. Qutb subscribed to this idea early on, when he wrote the preface to 'Atiq's poetry collection, and developed it further in his criticism of al-'Aqqad's poetry. The conviction that proximity to the author conferred upon the critic the authority to speak about his poetry reflects the Romantic emphasis on authenticity. Since honesty is the supreme criteria of literary evaluation, there is no better way of measuring it than a close friendship. But such a view is also consistent with Qutb's integral outlook on literature. Al-'Aqqad represented for him a "school of life and literature" whose greatness resided precisely in the flawless harmony (*tanāsuq*) between his art, philosophy, politics, and social conduct.[103] Such an organic understanding of literature bears traces of the "ideology of personality" (*shakhsīyya*) that was paramount in al-'Aqqad's philosophy of literature—what al-'Aqqad (and, consequently, Qutb) identified as genius, or an extraordinary human being gifted with privileged access to the source of inspiration. Al-'Aqqad maintained that only personalities produced authentic poetry.[104] The function of criticism was therefore double: to use a piece of literature as the means to understand the author's literary genius, and, inversely, to study the author to understand the art that emerged from him. This is what Qutb meant when he stated that "the personality of the poet is part of the *diwān*": both a poet and his oeuvre needed to be analyzed together to acquire a full image of the divine that spoke through them.[105]

Nevertheless, the relation between al-ʿAqqad and Qutb was not an uncomplicated one. As ʿAli Shalash has noted, al-ʿAqqad was rather erratic in distributing recognition for his disciples, including Sayyid Qutb.[106] Qutb's feeling of the lack of his mentor's support in public would be one of the reasons that precipitated his breaking off from his mentor following World War II, as will be discussed in chapter 3. Yet Qutb's claim of his status of discipleship to al-ʿAqqad was not merely one-sided. Al-ʿAqqad did read Qutb's books, which the latter diligently dedicated to him, and seemingly facilitated his rise in *al-Risala* magazine.[107] Al-ʿAqqad had refused to associate himself with *al-Risala* as long as it employed his rival al-Rafiʿi as the head writer. Following the latter's passing in 1937, al-ʿAqqad took his place, and Qutb's presence increased in the magazine as well. By the 1940s, Qutb was already writing a regular column of literary criticism and would occasionally replace the aging al-ʿAqqad as the lead writer, becoming the magazine's most prominent contributor, after his mentor. Qutb's position in *al-Risala* significantly contributed to his fame and influence, on which he would capitalize in his postwar political activism.

Qutb's status of discipleship to al-ʿAqqad explains his secular position on literature taken in his 1938 battle in *al-Risala*, cited in the beginning of this chapter. In the context in which these positions were associated with people, Qutb allied himself with the camp of his mentor. Commenting on al-ʿAqqad's rivals' inclination to didacticism, Qutb marked a distinction between art and sermon, *adīb* and sheikh, literature and moral mission. He argued against the Bookstore's understanding of literature, which ascribed to it the mission to uphold morality and Muslim unity. To the end of his life, Qutb identified himself as a freethinker and despised the intellectual culture of al-Azhar.

However, the affirmation of literary autonomy vis-à-vis religion did not entail the rejection of alternative forms of spirituality. While playing the role of a diligent disciple, Qutb was able to develop an original project of poetry that resembles his mentor's aesthetics only in form. The difference resided in the place both authors accorded to rationality in apprehending the world. While al-ʿAqqad never ceased to promote rationality as the only reliable tool of social advancement, Qutb considered that reason falsified the perception of the world. Instead, Qutb based his aesthetics on emotional spirituality that poets can access through inspiration. It is precisely the association between the irrationality and truth that would lead Qutb to accord to Islam a central place in the arts and culture. Yet, in doing this, he took the opposite path of balanced reformers: instead of considering the arts as the vehicle of social reform, he saw them as the means to purify the faith. This is the story of the next chapter.

2

Our Own Brand of Modernity

In December 1947, after having completed and handed in for printing his manuscript *Mashahid al-Qiyama fi-l-Qur'an* (Scenes of Resurrection in the Qur'an), Qutb wrote a disclaimer and rushed to add it to the book's conclusion. *Mashahid* was a continuation of Qutb's earlier book, *al-Taswir al-Fanni fi-l-Qur'an* (Artistic Picturing in the Qur'an, 1945), which explored the means of aesthetic expression used in the Qur'an. Both books argued that the scripture employed particular aesthetic devices to strengthen its persuasive effect, which consisted of choosing words and expressions with specific sonic properties for the composition of scenes. A particular mood created by these devices accompanied the content of revealed verses and "opened up" human cognition to the monotheistic creed. But, nearly three years after the publication of *al-Taswir*, Qutb came to realize that he had overlooked a substantial problem, related to his usage of the word "art" (*fann*) in the context of Qur'anic studies.

In his disclaimers, added to the first edition of *Mashahid* and the third edition of *al-Taswir*—published in 1947 and 1952, respectively—Qutb explained that by "artistic" he did not mean "forged, invented or purely imaginative." What he meant instead was "the beauty of demonstration, harmony of rendition and ingenuity of production." He noted, "I am amazed that the word 'artistic' is automatically attached to the realm of fiction, invention, or fabrication that lies outside of the reasonable. . . . Why is it so? Isn't it possible to represent the truths of reality in an artistic and scientific way without denying their factuality? Is it because Homer composed the Iliad and Odyssey from legends? Or is it due to the fact that liberated arts practiced by European novelists, storytellers and playwrights were not intended as a representation of reality? This is art, but not the only form of art."[1]

Pointing to Qutb's unease about associating the arts with the realm of phantasy, these disclaimers read as self-defense in anticipation of a controversy similar to the one that had just shaken Egypt's intellectual community: the Khalafallah affair. In 1947, a doctoral student named Muhammad Ahmad Khalafallah submitted to the university's Faculty of Arts his dissertation on storytelling in the Qur'an.[2] Partly under the pretext of disrespect to Islam, Khalafallah was failed by his examining professors.[3] Similarly to Qutb, who some months later hurried to specify the meaning of "art," from September to October 1947 Khalafallah published a series of elaborative essays in *al-Risala* magazine, explaining his intended usage of the notion of "legend" (*usṭūra*). Like Qutb, he claimed to have used the term not in the sense of falsehood, myth, or illusion, but according to the meaning intended in the Qur'an, as the stories recorded by the ancients. "We should stick to this meaning," Khalafallah suggested, "rather than the one implying imagination."[4]

These methodological anxieties were part and parcel of a broader intellectual movement in interwar Egypt aiming to dissociate modern forms of knowledge from their European origins. From the 1930s onward, Egyptian writers, poets, and playwrights from the *udabā'* generation became increasingly vocal about the colonial underpinnings of European modernity. Collectively, they came to the belief that freedom of thought, scientific skepticism, and the arts as they were understood in Egypt bore traces of Europe's troubled relationship with its religious heritage, which called into question their universal validity. But, they emphasized, they arrived at this conclusion not from a position of faith, as in the case of their religious rivals, but one of doubt, following the realization that modern science was, on some level, unable to contest faith.

Considered together, these anxieties epitomized the dilemma that accompanied the process of knowledge formation in most colonial contexts: how to create a modern intellectual culture that would be equally free from the alleged constraints of tradition and foreign colonial domination.[5] Writers from the *udabā'* generation aimed to solve this dilemma by crafting a local version of modernity that would combine the modern methods of inquiry, such as *tajarrud*, with the Islamic faith. As the most appropriate ground for this monumental task, they chose to focus on Egypt's Islamic heritage in order to revive it and render it accessible to modern readership. As a result, they produced biographies of the Prophet Muhammad and the Companions and reconsidered the sacred texts of Islam in the light of modern means of investigation.

It was in such an intellectual atmosphere that Qutb developed his interests in the fields of poetry, literary criticism, and Qur'anic aesthetics. His projects emerged from the limited space bounded on the one side by the religious establishment, and on the other by a Western modernity marred by cultural biases against Islam. Mirroring the intellectual trends of the 1930s, Qutb fashioned his aesthetic theory in line with the epistemology that accorded a significant attention to the metaempirical realm of existence. If, as we have seen in the previous chapter, Qutb subscribed to the principle of literary, artistic, and scholarly autonomy from religious interference, his intellectual project was far from secular. Rather, it drew upon mystical spirituality, bearing traces of Sufi metaphysics, the arts of Qur'anic recitation, psychoanalysis, and other intellectual traditions that acknowledged the significance of the unseen, or *ghayb*.

This chapter tells the story of how modern literati came to accept the existence of a reality beyond the sphere of the knowable, which humankind has to confront on the basis of faith rather than on the modern sciences. Rather than analyzing this movement in terms of "a shift to Islamic topics," as it came to be known in Western scholarship, this chapter regards it in relation to the rise of the *udabā'* writers to the position of Egypt's cultural elite and their aims to impose themselves as a counterhegemonic force of colonial domination.[6] Having acquired the status of autonomous and influential literati, modernist writers now channeled their energies in advocating for the "national literature" (*al-adab al-qawmī*),[7] revising their ideas to fit pedagogical pursuits, and creating their own version of Islamic history.[8] All these endeavors were part of their aspiration to create an authentic and scientific brand of Egypt's modernity.

"Freedom of Thought" vs. "Freedom to Mock Religion"

"Nine years ago I read Voltaire's play Muhammad and felt ashamed that its author is counted among free-thinkers (*ashāb ḥuriyat al-fikr*)," Tawfiq al-Hakim reminisced in an essay published in 1935. "The extent to which the Prophet was insulted there amazed me." But even more revolting than the play was the fact that Voltaire had dedicated it to the pope, with a letter of praise for Christianity. By kneeling down to the pope, al-Hakim argued, Voltaire betrayed his commitment to protect the rational sciences from religious interference. As if that were not enough, not one of the Western architects of the Enlightenment—including Jean-Jacques Rousseau, who had critiqued Voltaire's works—took the trouble to protest against the play. This convinced al-Hakim that the so-called "freethinkers" in the West applied freedom of thought only selectively. "From that day on," he confided, "I have been feeling as if I had lost a dear thing to me: the faith in the integrity of freedom of thought."[9]

What Voltaire had betrayed with his offensive play was the principle that modernist writers had elevated as the prerequisite for intellectual inquiry: the principle of scientific detachment (*tajarrud*). As discussed in the previous chapter, the principle of detachment and its corollary value of freedom of thought had been a veritable credo of Egyptian modernist writers during the 1920s. Repeated throughout their writings, *tajarrud* expressed the need to unshackle the primary sources of Arab heritage from their secondary interpretation and, by doing so, to emancipate themselves from the scholarly authority of the Nahda generation. This process resulted in making human reason the ultimate means of investigation, considered to be universal and guaranteeing the global applicability of scientific methods and results. In the 1930s, the universality of modern science began to be questioned extensively. In their books and essays, modernist writers expressed their suspicion that freedom of thought as it was understood in Egypt was the product of a specific European history marked by the conflict between scientists and the church. They reached this conclusion, they confessed, while reading Western scholarship on Islam. The way Orientalist scholars dealt with Islam and the Prophet in their works stood in stark contrast to their proclaimed values of objectivity. In fact, Egyptian modernist writers noted, their scholarship uncritically reproduced stereotypes that had seeped into their rational thought from the medieval Christian hostility to Islam.

One of the first to question the integrity of scientific detachment was Muhammad Haykal. In his best-selling book *Hayat Muhammad* (The Life of Muhammad), published in 1935 as a commentary to *The Life of Mahomet* by French Orientalist Emile Dermenghem, Haykal noted that Western scholars fell short of objectivity when it came to Islam. As in the case of al-Hakim, his first reaction was astonishment: "One is amazed (to observe) that Christian hostility to Islam remained so strong in the age called the era of light and science."[10] The argument of freedom of thought had become a disguise for pushing through lies about Islam, Haykal argued, and, by means of imperialism and cultural domination, for depriving Egyptians of the capacity to seek their own truth and freedom.[11] 'Abbas al-'Aqqad was equally concerned with the question of how to avoid reproducing Western biases against Islam while practicing freedom of thought. In the introduction to his version of the prophet's life, *'Abqariyya Muhammad* (The Genius of Muhammad, 1942), he narrated an incident that took place thirty years previously, when a young man, "a stranger to (al-'Aqqad's) group of friends," spoke offensively about the Prophet in the midst of a discussion about Thomas Carlyle's book *Heroes and Hero Worship*. This man, al-'Aqqad explained, was a braggart who thought that insulting the Prophet testified to his erudition in modern sciences.[12] To remedy this false opposition and to prove the contrary, al-'Aqqad set out on an intellectual adventure that unfolded over the next ten years: to write biographies of the Prophet and his Companions.

The challenge those writers faced was indeed monumental. They aimed at reaching a convincing synthesis between the principle of *tajarrud* and the Islamic faith that would serve as the basis for authentic modern culture and science. The principle of free inquiry was necessary to maintain their autonomy from the scholars of religion, while respect for the Islamic faith assured their independence from Western scholarship. The creativity and force of argumentation that writers poured into this task reflected the anxieties of explorers setting out into uncharted territory. After all, they were inventing a new epistemological position based on the premise that religion and modern science sought the same truth. Were the prejudices involved in Orientalist readings of Islam due to the dishonest application of the principle of scientific detachment or to the fact that, forged in opposition to the Christian Church, this principle inherently contained the denial of spiritual truth? Egyptian writers provided various answers to this question.

For al-Hakim, to remedy the false opposition between science and religion was to adopt a position of extreme impartiality in research. This is the method that he defined and attempted in his 1936 play *Muhammad.* According to al-Hakim, the method consisted of simply recording the events "as they really happened" without any intervention on his part; his role as a writer was to merely reduce "the barrier of history between them and the reader" by making history seem as contemporary as possible. "And if, after all this work, this image appeared to people as genuinely majestic," he wrote, "its majesty originates in its own reality, and not because of an enthusiastic writer's apology, or a fanatic author's disapproval."[13]

But the line between apology and disapproval was sometimes too thin to negotiate. In al-'Aqqad's *'Abqariyya*, it took the shape of his argument about the semantic difference between "reverence" (*tawqīr*) toward and "embellishment" (*tajmīl*) of Islamic personalities. The difference between the two, he argued, resided in the level of honesty involved in their historical representation. In contrast to the method of *tajmīl*, which consisted of attributing to Islamic personalities qualities and powers that they did not possess, the method of *tawqīr* adhered faithfully to historical reality, while not renouncing the right to make these humans appear "worthy of praise and reverence." Al-'Aqqad illustrated his argument with the example of the description of a wealthy man: the method of *tawqīr* would consist of listing the properties that he possessed and passing over those he did not, while *tajmīl* would mean inventing new qualities, violating the requirement of honesty inherent in the modern method of history. The same applied to the depiction of the spiritual wealth of Islamic heroes, al-'Aqqad argued. The times were in dire need of reverence, he said, in order to rehabilitate the heroes of Islam who had been unjustly vilified by the destructive infighting between scientists and scholars of religion, and the subsequent rise of leftist ideologies that denied the existence of human greatness altogether. Al-'Aqqad's method of history springs from the tension between two methods of historical investigation: on the one hand, the modern method of history whose requirement of objectivity might result in the negative portrayal of Islamic heroes, and, on the other, the approach of "artificial embellishment" that al-'Aqqad ascribes to scholars of religion.[14] One way to avoid slipping into one of these two extremes was, for him, to taint historical objectivity with a feeling of reverence.

The most elaborate and, in a way, radical solution to the tension between rational investigation and Islam was devised by Haykal. In the final conclusion of several editions of his biography of the Prophet *Hayat Muhammad*, he resorted to the argument that Egyptian intellectuals would use repeatedly to define their relationship to religion as different from the one in the West. He argued that the protracted struggle between scientists and the Church in Europe has led to the establishment of individualism and materialism as the basis of its civilization, which is best illustrated by its primary attention to the economic well-being of populations. In contrast to the Western comprehension of freedom as a secularized and individualistic value unfit to form the basis of community, in Islam freedom stems from religion itself, Haykal argued. The Islamic version of freedom lies precisely in the absence of the religious institution and its power to impose truths, which allows the individual to maintain his personal connection to God.[15] This connection is mediated by individual reason and not social pressure, fear, or an emotional quest for belonging, as in contexts governed by religious institutions. Haykal posited human rationality as the final and the most adequate judge of Islam, reminding his readers that the sacred texts encouraged humans to observe the universe and deduce from its orderly arrangement the fact of the existence of a superior, organizing reason. The teachings of Islam, he concluded, were thus equivalent to the methodology of modern science.[16]

In the manner of al-'Aqqad, who redefined the principle of *tajarrud* by associating it with the reverence of Islam, Haykal preserved the inviolability of the principle of scientific detachment by distinguishing it from its practice. Put differently, if human reason was the same across cultural divides, he emphasized, thinking was not. While based on rational means of investigation, Islamic reasoning (*al-tafkīr al-islāmī*) differs from the Western one. While Western thinking (*al-tafkīr al-gharbī*) was shaped by its conflict with the Church, resulting in its dissociation from emotion, in Muslim countries the synthesis between feeling and reason was preserved.[17] This particularity manifested itself in Islam's refusal to hold human reason as an unlimited means of access to truth that leads thinkers to question the existence of empirically inaccessible reality. According to Haykal, religious faith emerged from precisely the point at which the capacity of reason to understand existence ceased. Such an integral approach to science, which placed within its purview the spiritual and psychological aspects of human nature, was, in Haykal's view, a necessary contribution to humankind. It had a capacity to bring happiness to humankind that the rational sciences lacked, as well as the potential to resolve issues before which "abstract logic" stood confused, unable to either accept or refuse them. For Haykal, the life of the Prophet was the most appropriate topic to study in order to realize these benefits, for it allowed his embodied link between humans and the Creator to be understood.[18]

In redefining the scientific basis of Egyptian modernity, Haykal agreed with other representatives of the *udabā'* generation that Islam was incontestably a rational religion. Not only was it fully consistent with—or, rather, superior to—the European norms of rational investigation, but the Revelation itself had an inherently rational essence. Commenting on Haykal's *Hayat Muhammad*, Tawfiq al-Hakim emphasized his success in revealing the rational essence of the Prophet's message. It was by pursuing the method of "rational demonstration" (*al-tadlīl al-'aqlī*) and appealing to "pure reason" (*al-'aql al-mujarrad*), al-Hakim claimed, that Haykal demonstrated that Muhammad's prophecy resided in his ability to grasp the nature of the bond connecting the universal order and the Creator. "The biggest miracle in this world is the absence of miracles, because everything works according to a precise order," al-Hakim wrote. Setting out from the rationalist perspective, Haykal disproved the existence of miracles in Islam, al-'Aqqad depicted the Prophet as exceptional but still human being, and al-Hakim spoke of God as "the organizing reason." As al-Hakim maintained, "Religion, science and art were the three threads that were given to our limited and blind human race to hold on in its guidance to the infinite Light, which is God."[19] Writers affirmed in unison that the conflict between religion on the one hand and science and the arts on the other was, therefore, a false debate.

The argument of the rationality of Islam was hardly a new discovery; in fact, it had been a widely accepted truth within the movement of balanced reform. The affirmation that scientific skepticism and freedom had been practiced by the pious ancestors of Islam was the cornerstone of Muhammad 'Abdu's entire intellectual enterprise, continued by his heirs.[20] Roughly ten years before the *udabā'* writers reached a conclusion that the conflict between religion and science was a Western invention, Muhammad al-Khidr Husayn, a sheikh and an associate of the Salafiyya Bookstore and Publishing House, maintained that in Islam reason was not distinct from faith, attested to by the fact that all its rational sciences originated from within the realm of religion.[21] In fact, al-Khidr Husayn formulated this argument in his criticism of Husayn's *Fi-l-Shi'r*, which he accused of applying to Islamic history principles and debates that were alien to it. Other members of the Bookstore's circles also pointed out that, contrary of Husayn's invitation to put aside religious considerations in the pursuit of a scientific truth, freethinking needed to be based on the respect of Islam.[22] They insisted on the difference between "freedom of thought" and "freedom to mock religion," echoing the previously cited al-'Aqqad's fury against a braggart who sought to prove his erudition in modern sciences by insulting the Prophet.

To be sure, by claiming the rationality of Islam, the *udabā'* eagerly located themselves within the heritage of Muhammad 'Abdu and some of his heirs.[23] Yet they seemed to ignore scholars who equally claimed his heritage, such as those associated with the Salafiyya Bookstore and Publishing House. Not only had they chosen to ignore their scholarship on Islam, but they also made them carry responsibility for creating the impression of science's opposition to religion and indirectly pushing the Egyptian youth to imitate the West. In his essay "al-Difa' 'n al-Islam," al-Hakim stated that, before Husayn and Haykal took it upon themselves to correct this false opposition in their books, no one in the East stood up to defend Islam.[24] Rather, al-Hakim claimed, the East reacted to the degrading Orientalist image of the Prophet by sinking into a deep slumber. In a similar fashion, Haykal and al-'Aqqad justified their contributions to Islamic history by the absence of modern scholarship on Islam, other than the writings produced by Orientalists and "rigid scholars" (*jāmidūn*).[25] They discarded both types of scholarship as invalid, since both maintained the thesis of Islam's incompatibility with science: the former by reproducing Christian stereotypes of Islam, the latter by conflating any scientific investigation of Islam with disbelief.[26]

By claiming the middle-road position between Orientalists and local scholars of Islam, the *udabā'* sought to impose themselves as the new cultural elite, in charge of creating an authentic Egyptian modernity. While borrowing the argument of Islam from Nahda scholars in order to distinguish themselves from European scholars, they based their scholarship on the particular type of authority they claimed to embody: the authority of a freethinker. In their writings, the *udabā'* generation insistently claimed to have arrived to the Islamic truth by the means of freethinking and not the "blind fanaticism" that characterized the Orientalist and local scholarship on Islam. Although redefined to include the feeling of reverence for Islam, the capacity of freethinking provided the main justification of their position as the founders of an authentic modern culture.

Sounds and Visions

At a time when al-Hakim and Haykal were writing their biographies of the Prophet, Qutb was a freshly graduated poet who had just published his first poetry collection. Heated debates on freedom and Islam, and postulations about the spiritual essence of the East as opposed to Western materialism, thus formed the intellectual mainstream that accompanied Qutb's first steps into literature. When, in 1945, he sat down to write his first book on Qur'anic aesthetics, he had already read Haykal's *Hayat Muhammad* and al-'Aqqad's *'Abqariyyat* series and was certainly familiar with the argument regarding the cultural specificity of Islamic sciences. His dash to the printing house to add a disclaimer to his understanding of arts as something integral to Islam suggests that, as an aspiring member of Egypt's cultural elite, Qutb sought to contribute to these debates. But his studies on the Qur'an did not merely reproduce established patterns of research. In addition to presenting an important contribution to the burgeoning field of Qur'anic aesthetics, Qutb's work shed new light on debates of reason and Islamic faith. As a poet trained in the tradition of Romanticism and characterized by a deep distrust of human reason, Qutb disagreed with the *udabā'* on the rationalist basis of Egypt's cultural modernity. Rather than reason, he argued, it was the affective realm of human cognition that provided the connection between individuals and God. Crucial to this connection was the knowledge communicated by visions under the effect of sounds.

In the introduction to his *al-Taswir al-Fanni fi-l-Quran* (1945), Qutb reminisced about his childhood, when, as a boy, he used to listen to Qur'anic recitation in his village house.[27] Qutb was exposed to the Qur'anic recitation during the seasonal recitations, *khaṭma*, held in his house on religious occasions and during which invited guests would recite the complete text of the Qur'an.[28] Although lacking in understanding of the exact meanings of the verses, Qutb was able to experience the Qur'an through the visions that the recitation stirred in his young imagination. How and through which aesthetic devices the Qur'an achieved such an effect was the question that Qutb set out to explore in his research on Qur'anic aesthetics. The secret of the emotional power of the Qur'an was not a new subject; in fact, it had formed a fundamental principle of the centuries-long Islamic practice and arts of the Qur'anic recitation. Well before Qutb noticed that the Qur'an addressed not only the mental faculties of humans, but also their senses, the arts of reciting the Qur'an had emphasized the importance of melodies in rousing the emotions of the listener. The ideal recitation "is that in which the tongue, the mind, and the heart share."[29] The tongue, mind, heart communicate the sound, the meaning, and the emotional response to the human existence, respectively. What Qutb aimed to do in his *al-Taswir* was to explore specifically the Qur'an's literary means of producing the emotional effect, a sort of inner music created by the text's evocative scenes, arranged sonorities, and musical rhythms. Initially planned as a subject for his academic dissertation, Qutb conceived his research on the aesthetic dimension of the sacred book as a long-term scholarly commitment. He envisioned writing a number of studies on the topic, including a comparative analysis of the storytelling in the Torah and the Qur'an, a deeper exploration of the concept of "affective logic," and a study of the style of Qur'anic aesthetics.

These works were intended to be published in the New Library of the Qur'an collection, which Qutb had established within the prestigious publishing house Dar al-Ma'arif in the 1940s.[30] Yet, interrupted by his political commitment after World War II, his project resulted in the publication of only two books: *Al-Taswir al-Fanni fi-l-Qur'an* (1945) and *Mashahid al-Qiyama fi-l-Qur'an* (1947).

Unlike his work on poetry, in which Qutb emphasized the author's freedom to express his emotional states through language, his research on the Qur'an had scientific purposes. Qutb diligently applied norms that had been established as the hallmark of modern scientific methods decades earlier. They were, essentially, the following: to study the Qur'an for extra-religious purposes, to approach it as a primary source independent from the rich literature of exegesis, and to treat the text as a whole by looking for the underlying patterns. Qutb's commitment to the first principle—to study the Qur'an from a purely aesthetic perspective—formed the point of departure for his research. As he states in the introduction of *al-Taswir*, his aim was "to collect artistic images in the Qur'an . . . to reveal the pattern of their arrangement and the way they construct an image, all this while focusing on a purely aesthetic aspect [of the Qur'an] without consulting linguistic, philosophical, jurisprudential, or any other existing studies."[31] By applying the second principle, to study the Qur'an as a primary source independent from the existing scholarship, Qutb aimed to "liberate" the Qur'an from the dry scholarship of Islamic rational sciences and to render to the sacred text its pristine magic.[32]

Lastly, Qutb's commitment to approach the Qur'an as an integral whole led him to identify a consistent aesthetic language in which the Book was revealed: the method of, as he called it, artistic picturing (*manhaj al-taṣwīr al-fannī*). One of its features, according to Qutb, was a perfect harmony (*al-tanāsuq al-fannī*) between the aesthetics on the one hand and the formal content of the verse on the other. Specifically, this perfection consisted in the way the mood created by the images, scenes, and music corresponded with and strengthened the effect of the verses. As an example of such coordination, Qutb cited the following verse: "Indeed, the worst of living creatures in the sight of God are the deaf and dumb, those who don't use their reason" (8:22). The word for "living creatures" used in the verse was *dawwāb*, the term referring to all crawling creatures, including animals and humans. For Qutb, the choice of this particular word reflected the Qur'anic intention to associate the reference to unbelievers with the image of bestiality. The perfection of the verse consisted in the correlation between the suggestion of unbelief, the image of bestiality, and the vocabulary of dumbness, all of which created a single, harmonious mood.[33]

However, while framing his study according to modern research methods, Qutb reproduced a number of truths associated with the sciences marked as traditional—namely, Sufism and the Qur'anic recitation. Notably, Qutb's aesthetic theory of the Qur'an resonates so well with the concept central to the Qur'anic recitation: *taṣwīr al-ma'na*. In the arts of reciting the Qur'an, *taṣwīr al-ma'na*, or picturing the meaning, refers to the mastery in adapting melodic tone and vocal technique to the meaning of the verse.[34] Accordingly, the voice and melody of the recitation should match the text, to better communicate its meaning, so that "when [the listener] hears about threats and the condition of withholding of the forgiveness he shrinks with fear as if he were dying, and when he hears about the magnanimity and the promise of forgiveness he rejoices as if he were flying with joy."[35] Qutb's notion of *al-taṣwīr al-fannī* is similarly defined by a correlation—not between the sound and meaning, but the image and meaning: "Through palpable imaginative images, it [*al-taṣwīr al-fannī*] expresses intellectual meanings, psychological states, perceptible events, visual scenes, human types, and human nature," he explained.[36] Yet, in his understanding of *taṣwīr*, sounds and images were interrelated. "We need to broaden the meaning of *taṣwīr* in order to appreciate the horizons of the artistic representation in the Qur'an," he stated. "It is a representation by a color, a movement, an imagining, as well as a melody. . . . Description, dialogue, the sound of words, the melody of expressions, the music of the context, all participate in drawing the picture that fills the eye and the ear, senses and imagination, emotions and thought."[37] Put differently, Qutb did not conceive the image as restricted to the realm of the visual; he claimed that the Qur'an's aesthetic language penetrated humans through all their senses. As Charles Hirschkind and Ellen McLarney have noted, Qutb's notion of an image referred to the faculty of imagination that drew the image in the mind's eye rather than to its strictly visual sense.[38]

But Qutb aimed to go beyond the mere postulation of the intricate relationship between sound and vision. While digging into the Qur'anic text, he thought he had solved one of the Book's oldest puzzles: the secret of its inimitability. The fact that so many people had converted upon hearing the Qur'anic recitation in early Islamic history had long preoccupied scholars of Islam, who, Qutb claimed, were simply looking for reasons in the wrong place. All the sciences related to the exegesis, such as grammar, rhetoric, jurisprudence, and philosophy, had mistakenly considered human intelligence as the infallible gateway to knowledge. Even scholars of rhetoric, Qutb noted, had failed to grasp the significance of the emotional effect of the Qur'an, preoccupied as they were with the rational dichotomy between a word and its meaning (*lafẓ wa ma'na*).

There was, however, an exception: the ninth-century grammarian 'Abd al-Qahir al-Jurjani had noted the aesthetic beauty of Qur'anic verses, but he failed to explore its significance.[39] However, it was not these scholars' fault, Qutb conceded, for they lived in a particular time dominated by the scientific prestige of Aristotelian logic and scholastic theology (*kalām*).[40] By making this argument, Qutb joined the balanced reformers in their criticism of the extreme scholasticism that dominated the postclassical Islamic tradition. However, while denouncing its scholasticism, Qutb eagerly embraced another element of the same tradition: a pronounced tendency to esotericism.[41] Rather than reason, Qutb argued, the secret of Qur'anic enchantment resided in the particular correspondence between the language of the Qu'ran and the human affective apparatus. Departing from this observation, Qutb developed a complex theory of perception that explains how affective impressions are sedimented into a solid religious creed.

Qutb's theory of perception rests on a distinction that provided a bedrock for his all intellectual projects: the binary between emotion and reason. In his literary criticism, this binary corresponded to his differentiation between a false and a genuine poet. Poets who relied on reason, Qutb contended, were content with recording and transmitting the aspects of reality that were empirically accessible for nearly everyone. In contrast to this type of poet, which Qutb compared to a photographer (*muṣawwir*), the genuine poet articulated a chain of impressions that conveyed an empirically inaccessible reality.[42] In other words, instead of recognizing a poet from his skills of expression, Qutb defined a poet as characterized by the extraordinary capacity of feeling. Accordingly, he identified the art of poetic creation as *taẓlīl*, or shading, which referred to the poet throwing shades to reveal one side of the reality and leave another imagined.[43]

In his Qur'anic studies, the emotion/reason binary gained a new level of complexity. In his theory of perception, he ascribed affective and rational faculties to two different realms of human cognitive apparatus—affective logic (*al-manṭiq al-wijdānī*) and the logics of reason (*al-manṭiq al-dhihnī*). The affective faculties of perception possessed not only a distinctive form of logic that arranged the received impulses into an orderly pattern, but it had its own "sensory memory" (*al-dhikrat al-shu'ūriyya*), which organized the poetic inspiration into rhymed verses.[44] Qutb claimed that, by transmitting the message of the revelation, the Qur'an activated both of these realms: it addressed to reason the formal content of the verse while simultaneously stimulating the affective realm through aesthetics.[45] The faculties of intuition (*badāha*), spiritual insight (*basīra*), and feeling (*iḥsās*) belonged to the affective realm, and all cooperated in rooting the belief deep within the human psyche. By describing how the affective logic turned a mentally received message into a belief, Qutb did not differentiate between religious and nonreligious beliefs (*'aqīda*). Rather, he considered both to be the products of the same cognitive operation: by being processed through affective logic, the message was imbued with "emotional heat," thus becoming a passionate, intense, and action-driven faith. It was precisely this type of faith—pure, ardent, and sincere—that Qutb attributed to the Islam of the first generation of Muslims.

For his entire intellectual career, Qutb remained fascinated by the effects of sound. In his poetic creation, he conceived of his poems as a sonic experience with the capacity to stir imagination. His poetry is populated with vocabulary referring to an auditory environment: the whispers, murmurs, hidden calls, songs, and clatter of the material world. As in his theory of Qur'anic aesthetics, in his poems Qutb doesn't differentiate between the auditory and the visual worlds, and sounds possess the capacity to generate visions, shadows, sights, and specters. Qutb's appreciation of the sound in poetry stems from his definition of literature as creations that "[address] the emotion" (*'aṭifa*). Departing from this definition, in his first book on literary criticism, *Mahammat al-Sha'ir fi-l-Hayat* (1932), Qutb offers a classification of fine arts according to their efficiency to move emotions: music came first, followed by singing, poetry in the third place, and visual arts in the fourth.[46]

Qutb's appreciation of music might appear surprising, as he was one of the fiercest adversaries of radio broadcasting of Egyptian popular music. Since the 1930s, Qutb had been regularly accusing the prominent singers of the time, such as Muhammad Fawzi, Farid al-Atrash, Layla Murad and, above all, Muhammad 'Abd al-Wahhab, of spreading vice through music.[47] In his articles directed against these musicians, Qutb was concerned not so much about the preservation of social morality as by the numbing effects that music might have on political will. In line with his late conceptualization of emotion as the seat of passionate action, Qutb's criticism of popular music reflected his anxiety over its devastating effects on the population's capacity to fight for its postcolonial future. In the 1950s, Qutb's interest in music took shape in the introduction he wrote to the second edition of poetry collection authored by his friend the poet Mahmud Abu al-Wafa. Intended as religious songs for children and comprising notes of composition, Qutb praised the collection as a laudable effort to communicate religious meanings to the youth.[48]

Yet, in his eyes, all these attempts were feeble when compared to the perfection obtained by the Qur'an in arranging meanings and sounds. As a text that managed to reach and move the hearts of so many people, the Qur'an represented for Qutb the pinnacle of attunement between a text and human affective cognition. None of the literatures that followed the Revelation succeeded in taking the Book as a literary inspiration, Qutb maintained, including the old Arabic *adab*, which reproduced the themes and styles of pre-Islamic literature. Thus, with these conclusions, Qutb opened up for himself and his contemporaries the path to literary innovation based on the Qur'anic example—the path to which he would return several years later, with his effort to devise a specifically Islamic aesthetics.

The Appeal of the Hidden

The discussion of the centrality of the sound/vision nexus in Qutb's aesthetic theory would be incomplete without addressing the question of knowledge. The significance attributed to the affective by Qutb stems from his conviction that observed reality represented only a superficial aspect of the larger whole. This larger whole, Qutb believed, could be accessed through artistic inspiration, which originated from beyond consciousness. Since his childhood, Qutb had been fascinated by the occult. He grew up in a village in which the belief in a parallel reality of the unseen, or *ghayb*, occupied a solid place. As recorded in his *Tifl min al-Qariya*, dervishes, saints, malign spirits, and magic books inhabited Qutb's childhood world. He eagerly took part in the activities organized around the occult, such as chasing spirits (*'afarit*) or helping female villagers to influence their destinies by casting spells derived from books of magic that he owned.[49] As he confessed, his later education dispelled many of these popular beliefs. Yet some of them remained deeply ingrained in his imagination: "But inquire of his dreams and visions today," Qutb wrote in his autobiography. "They will tell you that . . . the spirits [*'afarit*] that inhabited his mind in childhood and youth will inhabit his imagination forever."[50]

These lines were prophetic, since curiosity about the origin of the unseen would remain Qutb's persistent quest. His ambition to identify the manifestations of the unseen in the physical world ran through his different intellectual interests, including his poetry, literary criticism, gothic prose, studies of the Qur'an, and writings on Islam. Certainly, each field of intellectual practice channeled this existential quest into new avenues of expression, contributing its reshaping. Yet there is little doubt that it was this nagging obsession over the nature of the unseen that provided the driving force to Qutb's intellectual life, impelling him to transit through different fields of knowledge in search of answers.

First of all, poetry, as it was redefined during the interwar, provided Qutb's childhood intuition about the unseen with a solid epistemological grounding. Reshaped under the influence of Romanticism, poetry came to be widely considered as a reliable means to access knowledge. The assimilation of poetry into epistemology was not only a result of the primacy that the Romantics attributed to aesthetics in the pursuit of epistemic goals; it can also be related to Yoav Di Capua's observation of the centrality of the question of "knowing" in interwar Egypt, before the focus shifted to the question of "being" following World War II.[51] Curiosity about what could be known, and to what degree of certainty, was shaped by two main epistemological orientations identified by Omnia El Shakry in her research on the modern fields of knowledge in Egypt: Romanticism and positivism.[52] Romanticism considered that "all reality was spiritual, derivative from a living spirit, and thus knowable only by human spirit as well."[53] Since knowing was equated with living, abstract reason was dismissed as inadequate to the task of comprehending existence. In contrast to the Romantic distrust of empirical reason, positivism rejected as illegitimate all that could not be observed empirically. Unsurprisingly, these two orientations presented themselves as intrinsically dichotomous. Romanticism was deductive, while positivism was inductive; the former posited the existence of an "essence" of society, while the latter was based on data; and, importantly, the former postulated the specificity of Arab sciences, while the latter was committed to the universal mode of knowledge production. But, in practice, El Shakry reminds us, "such dichotomies . . . continuously broke down . . . as tensions between the ideas of social reform as a positive scientific project and a culturally specific moral project of social uplift became apparent."[54]

As if epitomizing such a tension, Qutb subscribed to both of these epistemological orientations. As Alain Roussillon's work has shown in great detail, Qutb's reformist ethos was deeply embedded in a positivist mindset. As a social reformer, Qutb volunteered to design social reform projects and advocated the use of statistics and observation-based solutions to cure poverty and disease. His legacy as a positivist-minded social reformer is visible in his essays published in the monthly bulletin of the Ministry of Social Affairs, *Majallat al-Shu'un al-Ijtima'iyya* (The Journal of Social Affairs), to which he contributed between 1939 and 1945.[55] His reformist ethos also runs deeply through his autobiographical novel *Tifl min al-Qariyya* (1945), which, as Roussillon has observed, represents Qutb as an efendi-to-be, who since his early days was driven by the prospect of saving his village from ignorance through science.[56]

4. Sayyid Qutb in the 1930s. *Apollo* 1, no. 3 (February 1932): 234. Private collection of Shaaban Yusuf (Cairo); reprinted with permission.

Such concerns were hardly applicable to poetry, which, in Egypt, developed in tight symbiosis with Romanticism. Qutb's poetry and essays on literature are permeated with Romantic vocabulary, demonstrating that his interest in arts responded to a larger metaphysical anxiety. Qutb understood the universe as an organic, self-forming whole that he interchangeably defined as "the truth" (*ḥaqīqa*), "the ideals" (*al-muthul al-ʿuliyya*), or "the life" (*ḥayat*). Qutb maintained that reason provided a distorting sense of reality, by conveying only a manifestation of it, or a single perspective. His definition of literary creation as "shading" therefore referred to his conception of the empirically accessible reality as consisting of "shades" of the larger whole. Such a combination of two visibly contradictory epistemological orientations was made possible by Qutb's division of his intellectual work into two distinct fields of practice: the politico-social sphere, animated by the struggle for independence and social justice and pursued through party politics, and the sphere of literature, which was considered to communicate knowledge through artistic inspiration. As we will see in chapter 3, this division of the tasks between the political and literary will break down following World War II, when the rise of commitment in literature and the fall of the parliamentary system invalidated the notion of knowledge as detached from political action.

If empirical faculties were powerless to provide access to knowledge, Qutb suggested, a certain degree of insight to the existence can be achieved by the transcending experience of living in the physical world. "A poet is more knowledgeable of the truth than a philosopher," he stated, "because he plunges into life, he senses its sensations and feels its feelings, interacts with it, and then, narrates what he feels or what [the life] wants him to say about itself."[57] Put differently, if the totality is inaccessible, artists can at least approximate it through their art by describing it from a myriad of perspectives. Endowed with extraordinary capacities of feeling, or "the right to connect" to the universe, the poet, according to Qutb, was someone who dwelled on the threshold between the empirical and metaempirical levels of reality and passed "hidden truths" to humankind.[58] The channel of communication between the here and now and the hidden face of the reality was the irrational realm, inhabited by feelings and the imagination. Accordingly, poets accessed these truths through emotions and transmitted them by means of expression, which stirred the emotions of others. The sphere of the irrational thus featured as an invisible thread of communication that connected poets, humankind, and the all-encompassing whole. This is how Qutb ended up associating his early interest in the unseen, or *ghayb*, with the realm of the affective, *wijdān*.

Qutb was not a philosopher setting up innovative trends in epistemological thinking. He was unconcerned about the precise terminology in describing his observed phenomenon, and he did not reference his ideas; he backed up his writings with approximate versions of scientific and philosophical theories. Instead, Qutb was a young and tremendously ambitious poet, who, like many of his contemporaries, probably picked most of his ideas from late evening conversations in coffeehouses and literary associations, or from books passed around in his circles, which offered reworked versions of theories.[59] As a result, the philosophical notions that lurk beneath Qutb's theory of aesthetics provide a valuable insight into the intellectual mishmash of the interwar period, and the ways in which an aspiring poet was able to absorb it and turn it into a wellspring of poetic inspiration. This intellectual setting was primarily characterized by the productive blending of different mystical and spiritual traditions with modern scientific trends. As has been noted, Islamic and modern scientific certainties were not necessarily articulated as mutually exclusive categories of thought and were often taken as tools for intellectual experimentation. The interwar period witnessed numerous attempts to fuse Sufism and existential philosophy, Sufism and psychology, or Islam and philosophical notions inspired by rational sciences and Bergsonian philosophy.[60]

"A particular name struck the poet's mind. Suddenly, he looked around and saw the owner of this name waving at him": the secret of this type of predictive knowledge preoccupied Qutb as a poet.[61] His interest in certain intellectual traditions thus depended on their ability to provide insights for this quest. Qutb drew from a diversity of intellectual traditions delimited on the one side by Sufi metaphysics, and on the other by spiritual tendencies within the rational sciences. The overarching principle of Qutb's aesthetic position is the notion of the "oneness of existence" (*waḥdat al-wujūd*).[62] Central in Sufi metaphysics, where it was attributed to the twelfth-century philosopher Ibn Arabi, the notion of *waḥdat al-wujūd* signified the unity of God, or the universe, beyond the apparent multiplicity of its forms. The highest aim on the Sufi path of learning was *fanā'*, or the extinction of oneself through union with God. But in colonial Egypt, separated from its Sufi context, the principle of oneness traveled freely across the borders of various fields of knowledge, pervading the majority of artistic and scientific inquiries. There, the postulation of unity easily blended with European philosophical traditions of holism and idealism, with Romantic notions of the Absolute, or with the latest European intellectual fashions for theosophy and spiritualism.[63]

The centrality of this notion in Qutb's epistemic position is not surprising, since the principle of *waḥdat al-wujūd* was a popular topic of discussion among poets, who formed his poetic *shilla*.[64] For Qutb, the principle of oneness formed the prime criterion of beauty: "The nature of beauty is such that it does not reside in fragments," he noted, but in the ways "in which these fragments cohere with each other."[65] As a result, the mission of a poet was to pierce the secret of the way different manifestations of reality interact, affect one another, and form oneness. It was the complexity of the task that created the legendary "poet's anxiety."[66] The holistic paradigm of thought would form the bedrock for Qutb's later intellectual ventures, spanning his literary criticism, scrutiny of Islam as a totalizing social system, and late Islamist conceptualization of the relationship between man and the universe. As he progressed in his intellectual work, fragments of the universe would gradually be patched together, coming to form a harmonious whole and thereby reduce his intellectual anxiety to nothing.

Sufism was not the only one to shape Qutb's vision of human connection to the unseen. The other was the positivist sciences themselves, whose capacity to explain existence was widely doubted in 1930s Egypt. Passionate debates over Einstein's theory of relativity, the existence of the ether, the latest findings in psychoanalysis, electricity, and matter opened intellectual imaginations to the possibility of the existence of multiple layers of reality.[67] Many in Egypt saw Einstein's theory of relativity as proof of the existence of a spiritual realm. Qutb was one of them, and he cited Einstein's theory of relativity to support his claim that our spatiotemporal perception of time was illusory, and that the universe pulsated to another dimension of temporality that was absolute, nonlinear, and knowable only by the spirit.[68]

The anxiety over the finitude of human time is one of the major themes of his poetry collection; *al-Shati' al-Majhul* (The Unknown Shore), published in 1935. There, Qutb expresses his longing to reach "the other shore," which stands for the hidden dimension of reality, where neither the time nor distinction between self and others exists.[69] This anxiety is related to another transversal theme of his writings: the quest for eternity. In his early poetry, Qutb envisaged two ways of gaining a temporary access to the eternity: the experience of love, and the return to his native village, whose stillness reminded him of the relativity of time.[70] Later, Qutb added religion as the source of eternity. Qutb's conviction that humans can realize themselves fully only in the metaphysical realm of existence is crucial for understanding his postwar transition to Islamic activism.

Psychology was another science that allowed Qutb to deepen his curiosity about the hidden. Like many of his contemporaries, Qutb shared an overwhelming fascination with psychoanalysis that gripped scientists, professionals, and writers in interwar Egypt. As a teacher, Qutb was naturally interested in pedagogy and its auxiliary sciences, such as psychology. He read the *Majallat 'Ilm al-Nafs* (The Journal of Psychology), the Egyptian journal of psychology that translated and discussed European psychology, and socialized with its contributors. He seems to have been close to the influential Egyptian scientist Yusuf Murad, the founder of the *Majallat 'Ilm al-Nafs* and more largely of the modern science of psychology in Egypt. Drawing from Freudian psychoanalysis, Murad also founded an approach he termed "integrative psychology," which presented the self as the unity of psychic, bodily, and societal aspects.[71] Together with Amina al-Sa'id, a writer and the founder of the famous women's magazine *Hawa*, Qutb collaborated with Yusuf Murad on a series of children's books in 1946, in line with his concern for education.[72] It is probably from Murad that Qutb borrowed the notion of "integrative method" (*al-manhaj al-takamulī*) to define his critical approach, characterized by the consideration of the aesthetic, historical, and psychological factors of a literary piece.[73]

More crucially than providing him with terminology, the Egyptian psychology supplied Qutb with scientific evidence of the existence of *ghayb*. In particular, its notion of the unconscious (*la shu'ūr*) was considered by Qutb as a version of his notion of *wijdān*, or the faculty through which *ghayb* communicated self-knowledge to humans.[74] To put it another way, psychology definitely convinced Qutb that the realm of human perception that played the major role in apprehending existence was the one that laid beyond reason: the sphere of emotions, visions, dreams, and the imagination.

As a result, Qutb developed his aesthetic theory in a tight symbiosis with psychology. In his early career, Qutb even envisioned literature as an auxiliary science of psychology that could help to solve the puzzles of the human soul. In this regard, in the mid-1930s he introduced a column in *al-Usbu'* periodical titled "Psychology and Poetry," in which he published essays analyzing through poetry psychological states induced by love, such as jealousy and doubt.[75] The theme of alternating states of jealousy and doubt that accompany the experience of love also preoccupied Qutb in his sentimental novel *Ashwak* (Thorns), published in 1946. However, in his later literary criticism, Qutb expressed his doubts over the capacity of psychology to grasp the secret of the origin of artistic inspiration. In spite of being the science that stood closest to literary criticism because it shared the same object of study—namely, emotions—psychology, according to Qutb, suffered from the same flaw that characterized the majority of scientific inquiry: its uncritical reliance on rational logic.[76] Furthermore, he was unconvinced by the Freudian theory of the arts as a technique for the sublimation of repressed individual instincts and desires and leaned towards Jung's vision of the arts as the product of an intrinsically positive force—the collective unconscious.[77] Such a vision was more consistent with Qutb's earlier Romantic definition of inspiration as the power of the divine. Inspiration emerged not from instincts, Qutb insisted, but from the "mysterious power of which we know neither its essence nor function but which works towards humankind's sublimation without us detecting it."[78]

How did all of these intellectual references fit into the hierarchies of knowledge in Qutb's epistemological framework? Understanding this will allow us to recognize the significance of the shift that Qutb underwent in his studies of Qur'anic aesthetics. Before he accepted the Qur'an as the ultimate source of true knowledge, Qutb refused to accord such primacy to any other criterion of truth besides his own subjectivity: "The theory of the universal unity might be new in the world of science and some Sufi schools," he stated. "But since a long time ago, humans have possessed this knowledge deep within their nature, and even more the nature and the vision of the life of poets."[79] The poet's knowledge of the universe was part of the truth acquired by intuition (*badāha*), and all the other sciences did, whether they were empirical or religious, was to confirm it. In the end, such a conception of truth was fully in line with the concept of *waḥdat al-wujūd*, which maintained that knowledge was one, and that multiple sciences provided only fragments of it.

If, according to Qutb, all knowledge was intuitive and subjective, was there any possibility of an objective truth that could be shared by others? This epistemological question seems to have preoccupied Qutb throughout his efforts to devise a solid scientific basis for his theory of literary criticism. The difference between the capacity to communicate a subjective experience of life and the transmission of empirically observable reality, accessible to "ordinary humans," was the main principle that distinguished a false poet from a genuine one in Qutb's writings. Likewise, in *Mahammat al-Sha'ir fi-l-Hayat*, he stated that emotional attunement was crucial for the agreement on a common truth.[80] Qutb argued that each poet was incomparable to others in terms of his emotional experiences, philosophies of life, representations of the universe, and more generally, "way of feeling" (*ṭarīqat al-shuʿūr*). Yet, despite these reservations, Qutb agreed to the existence of some type of a shared truth that stemmed from humankind's "emotional reservoir" (*al-raṣīd al-shuʿūrī*), a concept of Qutb's reminiscent of the Jungian notion of the "collective subconscious." The mission of literature thus lay in its contribution to this common fund of emotions: the aesthetic expression of highly individual emotional experiences flowed into this wellspring on which other humans drew in order to expand their faculties of feeling.[81] The common reservoir of emotions featured in Qutb's aesthetic theory as a sort of objective truth.

Islam: Emotional or Rational Religion?

Qutb's studies on Qur'anic aesthetics led him to significantly reconsider his definition of truth as subjective. Like his intellectual forerunners, who were led to rethink their positions on reason and scientific freedom on the basis of their scholarship on Islam, Qutb had to face the inevitable question of the epistemological status of the sacred book. The postulation that scenes and stories recorded in the Qur'an are aesthetic devices intended to pass on the Islamic monotheistic creed implicitly undermined the factuality of the events they narrated. It seems that hesitations regarding the status of these narratives had seeped into Qutb's research on the Qur'an, hindering his progress: "I will not deny that doubts [*shubhat*] presented themselves to me while I was researching the subject of the story and the scenes of Resurrection in the Qur'an. Is this all intended to be something that had happened for real, or is some of it thought of as merely images and allegories?" he confessed in the disclaimer he added to his *Mashahid* in 1947. "I stood long facing these issues. But, among the historical or rational truths, I was unable to find the only truth I could rely on in my judgment of the Qur'an. It was out of the question for me to submit the Qur'an to judgments of assumption or probability [*al-dhann wa-l-tarjīh*]."[82] Eventually, Qutb resolved the tension by resorting to the same argumentative turn that Haykal had used before him: to admit the veracity of the Qur'an based on the absence of any proof to the contrary. Once we deprive the Qur'an of its status as revealed truth, he reasoned, we stand in front of two basic paths to verify its factuality: history or reasoning. But, he continued, neither of the two can yield decisive evidence. First, reason provided deficient access to knowledge, and, secondly, historically trustworthy scriptures that were as chronologically close to the recorded events as the Qur'an simply did not exist.[83]

These observations forced Qutb into an epistemological cul-de-sac, resulting in his reflection on the connection between the revealed and the subjective truths. To begin with, his Qur'anic studies led him to conclude that there was a paternity between arts and religion. Both addressed the same part of the human cognitive apparatus, the "affective logics," and both provided access to the metaempirical reality knowable only by spirit. The idea of a primordial connection between the arts and religion would form the core of Sayyid and Muhammad Qutb's theory of Islamic literary aesthetics (which I will discuss in chapter 4). Moreover, the epistemological dilemmas encountered in the course of his research reduced Qutb's youthful anxieties about the origin of truth. From its internal location, as intuitive knowledge located in the depths of subjectivity, the truth moved to its external site, the scripture and history. As a result, subjective and objective insights into the truth were fused into its unique source—the Qur'an.

In regard to the intellectual mainstream of interwar Egypt, Qutb's stance on the emotional nature of the Islamic faith was rather unorthodox. As we have seen, Egyptian writers who ventured into the history of Islam all seemed to agree that Islam was a rational religion. Unsurprisingly, Qutb's argument for the emotional nature of Islam did not fail to attract criticism. One of the intellectuals who challenged Qutb's understanding of Islam was 'Abd al-Mun'am Khalaf, a teacher and essayist who wrote for *al-Risala* magazine and was deeply committed to the cause of Pan-Arabism. One year Qutb's junior, Khalaf attended Dar al-'Ulum with him, graduating in 1932. But, unlike Qutb, who, after his studies, became associated with Egypt's modernist writers, Khalaf moved in circles connected to balanced reform: he frequented the Bookstore, took part in the establishment of the Young Men's Muslim Association, and wrote in the Muslim Brotherhood press.[84] The paths of Khalaf and Qutb crossed in late 1948, when the latter invited him to join the editorial staff of the periodical he edited, *al-Fikr al-Jadid*, and both men stayed friends. But, back in 1945, Khalaf had some reservations concerning Qutb's research on Qur'anic aesthetics.

The question of the origin of religious belief within the human cognition was Khalaf's long-term interest, resulting in the publication of his book *al-'Aql al-Mu'min* (The Believing Reason) in 1951. As a profoundly pious scholar, equally conversant in Islamic traditions and modern cognitive sciences, Khalaf detected some flaws in Qutb's theory of cognition. First, he pointed out that Qutb's audacious claim to have understood the secret of Qur'anic inimitability bordered on blasphemy. If humans were able to solve the puzzle of the secret power of the Qur'anic text, he said, they could easily reproduce it and the scripture would lose its distinctive quality. More crucially, Khalaf disagreed that the Islamic faith was located somewhere else than in reason. Islam was first and foremost a rational religion, Khalaf insisted, whose power of attraction resided in the soundness of its monotheistic creed, its perfect system of justice, and its respect of human dignity. Rather than the occult (*ghayb*), he continued, the Islamic creed was based on the knowable. The channels of access to the divine message were mental faculties, such as the senses, intuition, and rational judgment, and the means of processing this message were rational methods, such as "induction, reminiscence, meditation, differentiation, verification and judgment."[85]

Further, Khalaf emphasized the fluctuating nature of the affective realm, which received impressions in a transient fashion and was unable to consolidate them into a firm religious belief. If any faith was rooted in the affective logics, he said, it was paganism, which was communicated mostly through symbols, representations, and images. In Islam, faith acquired through affective arousal would be feeble, shaky, and prone to reversals, since it would be grounded in feelings of fear or fascination in the face of the unknown.[86] To support his argument, Khalaf pointed out that Qutb's theory overlooked an important issue: the incapacity of the affective faculties to differentiate between wrong and right beliefs. If, as Qutb maintained, images, scenes, and rhythms instilled faith in the existence of the unknown, how was this faith transformed into a monotheistic creed?

Khalaf's question stressed the difference between the belief in the Creator and the belief that this Creator was one and undivided. In contrast to the process of belief described by Qutb, which attributed to the affective faculties the task of opening up the mental realm for its reception, Khalaf maintained that it was first seeded in the rational realm and then extended to the emotions. To consider otherwise, he observed, was to blindly follow non-Muslims who conceptualized their religions as opposed to logic, assigned each to a separate realm of human cognition, and reduced the role of religion to its mere psychological function.[87] Here, Khalaf inferred that the separation between heart and reason that underpinned Qutb's theory was imported from Christian Europe, defined by the conflict between scientists and the Church.

Qutb firmly maintained his positions. To Khalaf's notion of emotion as a medium of transient impressions that did not sediment into reason, he opposed his own definition, which saw the affective realm as a repository of universal truth. As such, Qutb argued, it was the home of both the arts and religion, which, as "twin trees growing from the same root" (*ṣinwān*), provided the two points of access to the absolute. The only condition was that art be an honest expression of the author's subjectivity and not function as a simple decorative ornament.[88] Setting out from this particular notion of the arts, Qutb concluded that all religious creeds contained within themselves an artistic core. While in Judaism and Christianity the artistic element was incorporated into the core of the doctrines—in the form of legends in the case of the first and the tragedy of Jesus in the case of the second—the Qur'an achieved the same religious aim by means of expression.

Qutb's debate with Khalaf contrasted two diametrically opposed visions of spirituality, one stemming from the tradition of poetry, and the other representing the reformed version of Islam. Although Qutb never abandoned his belief that emotion provided the link to the spiritual, he took note of Khalaf's remarks and made a place for reason in his next intellectual project, the book *al-'Adala al-Ijtima'iyya fi-l-Islam* (Social Justice in Islam). From that point on, Qutb would affirm that Islam was not limited to the sphere of private devotion, but also ordered worldly affairs. Redefining his former vision of spirituality according to his Islamic activism, Qutb depicted Islam as a two-dimensional system whose successful application in society depended on the proper working of each part: the emotional face regulating belief and trust in the necessity of the Islamic social order, and the rational face that ensured the proper management of everyday affairs. With his commitment to Egypt's sociopolitical struggles, Qutb came to accept the significance for human life of the rational, corporeal, and material—the spheres that he despised so intensely during his time as a poet.

Undoubtedly, Qutb's acceptance of Islam as a rational faith was related to his gradual insertion within the intellectual tradition of Muslim reform through his activism in the ranks of the Muslim Brotherhood from 1951. With *al-'Adala*, Qutb's writings took a clear apologetic turn, based on his desire to convince his readers of the superiority of Islamic social solutions over their "imported" competitors, communism and capitalism. Adjusting his intellectual persona to the requirement of *da'wa*, which was by no means exclusive to Islamic activism but formed a general framework for intellectuals in postwar Egypt (as the next chapter will show), he accepted the need to submit Islam to rational debate.

Yet, political activism aside, it is important to acknowledge the often-neglected role that the intellectual legacy of modernist writers played within Qutb's Islamist thought. Both thematically and methodologically, Qutb's writings on Islam followed the pattern established by renowned writers throughout the interwar period. Thematically, with his research on Qur'anic aesthetics, Qutb drew on the precedent set by famous Egyptian literati who ventured into the field of Islamic scholarship to seize from the balanced reformers the last bastion of their intellectual authority: religion. With their novel approach to Islam, writers took up the balanced reformers' mission to reform Islam, albeit with different means and goals. They aimed to make Islam appealing to a young and educated readership through compelling storytelling, accessible language, and innovative readings of Islamic history. With this literature, they aspired to draw young people closer to their local heritage, and further from the blind imitation of Western modernity, as part of their overall ambition to establish Egypt's authentic modernity. In so doing, these writers were careful to distance their intellectual authority from that embodied by scholars of religion. Rather than the established Islamic certainties, their point of departure was reasoning based on the principle of freedom of thought.

Methodologically, too, Qutb's Islamist project bears traces of Egypt's literary modernity. The core requirement of valid scientific research, the principle of *tajarrud*, remained the essential method for uncovering the primordial essence and efficiency of Islam in Qutb's Islamist thought. He would qualify the secondary, exegetical literature on Islam as oppressive "intellectual rubbish," which obscured the pristine Qur'anic connection to emotions. Qutb's obsession with "method" (*manhaj*) in his scientific research also permeated his Islamist writings. But, after he lost his faith in the capability, and the right, of humans to understand existence, his attention shifted from "the method of research" to the "method of life and action."

In a sense, by means of his Islamic activism, Qutb picked up the project where Muhammad Haykal had left it, turning it into a political battle. The parallels that cut across Qutb's and Haykal's intellectual positions are numerous. Initiated in *Hayat Muhammad*, the mission of saving humankind from the looming danger of self-annihilation that stemmed from the Western civilization took a more concrete shape in Qutb's activism for Islamic dominance. In their own way, both writers denounced the alienating effect of sociopolitical systems based on materialism and argued for the need to infuse civilization with a spiritual essence. The primacy of the spiritual was not only Haykal's concern, but that of the whole generation of interwar literati. It was shared by al-'Aqqad, who distinguished himself as a committed antimaterialist, and even the incurable rationalist Taha Husayn, who conceived literature as embedded in the realm of spirituality. From the years following World War II, spiritual orientation in the arts would become increasingly contested, spelling the end of the interwar generation of literati.

3

Bringing the Social Back In

In January 1945, Sayyid Qutb, already an established literary critic and the editor of the prestigious *al-Risala* magazine's literary page, published a review of the young novelist 'Adil Kamil's work *Milim al-Akbar* (translated as *The Magnificent Conman in Cairo*, 2020):[1]

> Reader! You need to read this book. Not because you will agree with everything it says, but because it will spark your emotions—whether those of satisfaction or of anger—and will invite you to think on issues of literature, art, morals and socio-economic systems with a prospect of rejecting and breaking them down, or defending them and sticking to them. And if the book is capable of stirring your emotions in such a way, it breathes life even if at the end it throws you to hell! . . . *Milim al-Akbar* is a novel about the class struggle cast in the artistic mold. As such, it is part of the literature of social consciousness to which crowds of intellectuals, socialists and communists in particular, are calling today all over the Arab world. There is certainly a value of this type of literature, especially in our times. But what is reproachable is the fanaticism of its supporters who seek to impose it on all artists as if it was a tax liability owed to society. Humankind is not limited to this or a couple of future generations; it consists of all generations since the eternity of life. What is more, [humankind's] demands are not limited to the physical needs of drink and food. Even in the most tiring moments, it stretches to the infinite levels of the horizon and turns to the colors of pure and absolute art![2]

Published three years before Qutb became involved in Islamist activism, this passage summarizes the dilemma in which he found himself in the wake of World War II. On the one hand, he expresses enthusiasm about the novel's power to create strong feelings about social injustice that he believed were conducive to concrete action. The novel tells the story of the relationship between Milim (literally, a penny), the son of a hoodlum who decides to lead an honest life but is unjustly imprisoned, and Khaled, the son of an influential and morally corrupt pasha, who idly philosophizes about a just society but is unable to give up his privileges. Qutb perceived in the novel the increasingly widespread criticism of established political, social, and cultural elites, who were seen as responsible for Egypt's failure to achieve Egypt's independence and promote its development.

While criticism against the ruling elites as such was not entirely new—the rebellion against the established parliamentary system had been rising since the mid-1930s—the imperative to use literature as the voice of this criticism was. Before this requirement was conceptualized as "commitment" (*iltizām*) under the influence of Jean-Paul Sartre's writings on literature, it was known to Qutb as "literature of social consciousness" (*adab al-wa'ī al-ijtimā'ī*), of which he seemingly approved for its potential to uncover social injustice and mobilize revolutionary energies for political change. But, while the political value of this type of fiction was beyond dispute, Qutb was unsure about its literary worth. Its preoccupation with the pressing socioeconomic issues that characterized Egypt's postwar intellectual generation clashed with his broader understanding of art as transcendent of the limits of physical time and space. This ambivalence characterized Qutb's more general attitude toward the Left and the associated intellectual trends that provided the postwar rebellion with its main theoretical ground: communism, "committed literature," and social realism. Politically, Qutb felt himself to be in the same camp as the Left, but he was a world apart from its larger epistemological perspective, which he criticized for limiting itself to the satisfaction of material human needs. What becomes apparent from Qutb's vigorous postwar criticism of communism and its materialist epistemology (*māddīyya*) is his former idea that the superior aim of any this-worldly action is spiritual sublimation—the ambition that provided the core idea of his aesthetic project.

Turning to postwar developments in Qutb's intellectual career, this chapter argues that his tension with the Left provides the key to understanding his transition to Islamist activism from 1948 onward. Just before his departure to the United States on an educational mission at the end of 1948, Qutb completed his major work on the Islamic social and political system, *al-'Adala al-Ijtima'iyya fi-l-Islam*, embarking on his career as an Islamist ideologue. But Qutb's evolution in this new intellectual direction cannot be fully understood without taking into account his commitment to revolutionary politics. The surge of new opportunities in culture prompted by the postwar economic boom and the accompanying rebellion against political, social, and cultural elites provided the perfect conditions for Qutb to reinvent himself as a revolutionary intellectual committed to social change.

His first move was to break off from the interwar generation of writers, who had become increasingly targeted for their failure to bring about independence and social justice. Instead of being treated as generation of mentors, as had been the case during the interwar period, Egypt's literary luminaries, such as Taha Husayn, 'Abbas al-'Aqqad, Tawfiq al-Hakim, and Ibrahim al-Mazni, became associated with the corrupt elite who had benefited from decades-long colonial rule. But, while Qutb fell out with his former mentors politically, he still adhered to the old understanding of literature he had developed under their wing: as the product of a spiritual experience situated outside the rational sphere of perception and reality that can be apprehended through reason. This understanding of art, and of the intellectual project more broadly, was one that Qutb's new "materialist" intellectual circles could not accommodate. In this context, Islamism provided him with an alternative way of elaborating a specific ontology, a model for social organization, and a mode of political action.

Instead of viewing Qutb's Islamist commitment as a break from literature, this chapter argues that it served as a conclusion of his aesthetic project—after Qutb had adjusted it to accommodate the urgency of social and political action in line with the postwar requirement of intellectual commitment. To document this transition, the chapter first attends to developments in the intellectual field in postwar Egypt and then follows the steps of Qutb's increasing involvement in the rebellion, both intellectually and from the perspective of his reconfigured networks. It concludes with an analysis of Qutb's model of the Islamic social order, asking how his Islamist commitment affected his former positions on politics, faith, and the arts.

The Fall of the *Udabā'*

In Egypt, as in many other parts of the colonized world, the end of World War II in May 1945 ushered in a new political era. Not everyone welcomed Egypt's participation in the war on the side of the Allies, but many came to believe that the Allied victory would accelerate Egypt's exit from the colonial system. By January 1946, British reluctance to grant the country unconditional independence had become apparent. The creation of Israel in 1948, experienced as a brutal amputation of the Arab world, represented the biggest betrayal of postwar promises. Many came to believe that Egypt's destiny was to be realized not through diplomatic exchange and negotiations but direct street action. What followed was the increasing radicalization of Egypt's political life, marked by demonstrations, repression, and political assassinations. Governments rose and fell, undermined by corruption scandals, party bickering, and growing popular impatience with stalled development and the British occupation.[3] Expanding trade union activism brought attention to the problem of poverty, pushed agrarian reform to the top of political agendas, and channeled intellectual energies into the fight for social justice. For many, Egypt had been standing on the brink of revolution for some time before it was finally brought about by the 1952 Free Officers' military coup.

The seeds of postwar radicalism had been present since the 1935–36 uprising, when thousands of students went out into the streets to protest the political status quo. The uprising favored the emergence of a new type of political actor: a youth frustrated with institutional politics and associated with extraparliamentary radical groups, such as the Muslim Brotherhood, Young Egypt, and communist movements.[4] As we saw in chapter 1, the 1919 revolution and the 1923 constitution had enshrined the party politics as the hegemonic system of national struggle and the Wafd party as its lead actor. With the expansion of radical youth movements, the association between institutional politics and the national cause began to break down. While the uprising in the 1930s failed to dislodge political parties from their positions of power, it did spread a perception that party politics (*hizbīyya*) paralyzed political action and divided the nation.

Following the end of the war, radical extraparliamentary movements increased in influence. Not only were they already fully established organizations supported by institutions, resources, and, in the case of the Muslim Brotherhood, connections at the highest political levels, but their activism was buoyed by the increasing visibility of poverty. To be sure, the so-called social question (*al-qaḍīyyat al-ijtimaʿīyya*) had been a part of political agendas since the interwar period, as illustrated by the creation of the Ministry of Social Affairs in 1939. But, in line with the general institutional outlook on modernization, poverty was primarily understood as a statistical and scientific problem that could be solved by means of targeted reforms.[5] By the end of the war, this understanding began to wane. Under the pressure of growing labor and trade union activism and the spread of socialist ideas, poverty started to be seen as a primarily structural problem, the eradication of which demanded a comprehensive reshuffling of class relationships. The reformulation of the social question occurred in tandem with the shifting status of the working class: instead of being viewed as the object of institutional reform solutions devised in ministerial cabinets, it became the main actor both in its own emancipation and in that of the rest of the world.[6]

The shift in the perception of poverty occurred as the result of the wartime economic boom that redefined Egypt's social class landscape. During the war, the sharp decrease in the import economy and the presence of the Allied armies in Egypt temporarily created a vast internal market with sufficient resources to support local industries. With the establishment of the Middle East Supply Center—an agency created to organize production and procurement of the Allied forces in the Middle Eastern theater—Egypt became the war's major producer, supplying the Allies with a wide range of commodities including sugar, alcohol, textile, soap, shoes, and cement.[7] On the one hand, the expansion of local industries encouraged the migration of the rural poor, who joined the factories and urban centers, filling the ranks of the indigenous working class. On the other, the economic boom fostered the emergence of a new class of businessmen, who had enriched themselves by serving the British war effort and trading scarce commodities. The contrast between the working proletariat, jammed into crowded neighborhoods, and the nouveaux riches, who indulged in luxurious consumption, brought social inequality to light, and sparked indignation.[8] Postwar popular culture attests to the extent of public outcry directed to the class of suddenly rich Egyptians, popularly referred to as the "war profiteers" (*athriyā' al-ḥarb*). Depicted as grotesquely obese, incredibly ignorant, and lacking in taste and refinement, the nouveaux riches were regularly caricatured in magazines. A visual document of the rise of the "profiteer" class can be seen in the 1946 film *Black Market*, where they are portrayed as unprincipled parasites.[9] Postwar cinema, theater, and music singled out these alleged profiteers as the main culprits for the cultural decay, as responsible for having turned theaters and cinema halls into cabarets and actresses into belly dancers.[10]

Yet, beyond the moral outcry, the newly emerging class should be credited for causing the postwar cultural revival. By investing in cinema and publishing industries, the alleged profiteers created new opportunities for budding artists, writers, and film directors, thereby contributing to breaking the cultural monopoly held by the interwar generation of "founders." Cinema, in the first place, appeared as a particularly lucrative business to invest in. The inflow of cash into the hands of both producers and consumers resulted in the dramatic increase of film production outside the monopoly of the Studio Misr, created in 1934 by Egyptian industrialist Tala'at Harb.[11] The postwar period also saw an outburst in publishing in its different sectors. In the commercial sphere, new dailies were launched that catered to the interests and tastes of the nouveau riche—for example, the daily *Akhbar al-Yawm* (The News of the Day), founded in 1944 by journalists 'Ali and Mustafa Amin, which enticed readers with a new type of journalism, mixed news with gossip, entertainment, and full-page pin-ups of American models.

Political groups such as the Left, less concerned with commercial profit, also benefited from the publishing boom. Encouraged by the World War II struggle against fascism, the Left in Egypt emerged as an assertive force whose social influence outweighed its numerical strength. As in many colonized countries, the impact of the Left went beyond its organizational boundaries and seeped into the hegemonic readings of postwar global politics. By attributing the political, social, and cultural maladies of

Egypt to capitalist domination, the Left helped to redirect popular anger from its traditional enemy—the British colonizer—to the local elites accused of growing too comfortable with the colonial system. Partly, the leftist influence was due to its extensive publishing activities, which provided the main means of its activism: various groups launched weeklies, founded publishing houses, and established study groups.[12] Rather than being fostered by the wartime economy, the Egyptian Left supported its publications by subscriptions or the private funds of its well-off members.[13] A case in point is activist Henri Curiel, who used his father's money to open the left-wing library al-Midan, which translated and distributed Marxist literature.[14]

Likewise, following the war, the Muslim Brotherhood could finally stabilize its presence in the publishing market. The Islamist organization had been notoriously unsuccessful in securing press; its outlets were regularly shut down, and members with the license to publish them either departed the organization or were expulsed.[15] Until 1946, the Muslim Brotherhood put out a few irregular weekly magazines, but no dailies. Since 1943, its weekly magazine featured regular complaints of paper shortages, causing price increases and delays in publication, forcing the Brotherhood to reduce its capacity from weekly to bimonthly.[16]

The situation changed when the Brotherhood welcomed in its ranks Muhammad Hilmi al-Minyawi, a successful businessman and, according to his former business partner, a "war profiteer."[17] Having worked for the prestigious ʿIssa and Mustafa Halabi Press, during the war al-Minyawi became one of the major paper suppliers in Cairo. According to Saʿid al-Sahhar, the owner of Misr Publishing House, al-Minyawi had access to the storage of British military troops, which allowed him to establish his own paper business in Cairo.[18] In 1946, al-Minyawi helped the Muslim Brotherhood to purchase two companies, allowing the Brotherhood not only to end its paper shortages, but also to establish its own printing house and launch a daily newspaper for the first time in its history.[19] The same year, he convinced Saʿid al-Sahhar to open a joint publishing venture, Dar al-Kitab al-ʿArabi, for which each of them would provide the paper and the printing equipment. After their falling-out in 1951, Dar al-Kitab al-ʿArabi went to the Muslim Brotherhood, whose top officials would hold unofficial meetings.[20] Al-Minyawi's contacts and resources were instrumental for Sayyid Qutb's postwar intellectual career as well: several months before his arrest in 1948, amid the Brotherhood's crackdown, al-Minyawi founded the weekly periodical *al-Fikr al-Jadid* and invited Qutb to become its editor. As we shall see, this journal was crucial for Qutb's self-reinvention as a revolutionary intellectual and his transition to the Muslim Brotherhood.

Although suffering from paper shortages, Sa'id al-Sahhar from the Misr Publishing House was also able to expand his business, thereby providing opportunities for budding writers. Encouraged by the literary debut by his younger brother, 'Abd al-Hamid al-Sahhar, in 1943 Sa'id al-Sahhar launched a series aimed at promoting the works by beginning authors, the Publishing Committee for University Graduates (*Lajnat al-Nashr li-l Jama'iyyīn*). The narratives associated with the committee emphasize the disadvantaged position of the authors it published: deprived of influential mentors, they could not access a publishing market "monopolized by the big names."[21] One of those marginalized authors was the future Nobel Prize laureate Naguib Mahfuz, who, despite having his novels recognized by local literary prizes, was unable to find a publisher. Printing on cheap paper and with limited circulation, the committee was able to bring to light a number of postwar authors, including Naguib Mahfuz, 'Ali Ahmad Bakathir, and 'Adil Kamil, the author of *Milim al-Akbar*, cited in the beginning of this chapter.[22]

Facilitated by the rise of a new class of businessmen, the creative outburst following the war affected the literary field in two significant ways. Firstly, it generated the feeling of the general decline of cultural taste in Egypt, where it became hostage of the class of "profiteers" who encouraged rapid, cheap literary production. The observed spread of vulgarity in culture sparked different battles, such as the defense of "highbrow art" (*al-fann al-rafi'ī*) or the struggle for "clean culture" in which Qutb assumed a prominent role, as I discuss later.[23]

Secondly, the postwar cultural renewal precipitated the fall of the interwar intellectual generation, who found themselves associated with the corrupt political and economic elites. Different intellectual groups had their specific grievances against the generation of the "founders," but all agreed that the time had come for them to vacate their place. Young authors accused the established writers of nepotism, through which they perpetuated their antiquated literary tastes; leftists denounced them as ivory-tower intellectuals who willingly ignored the oppression and misery of the country's poor; and Islamists emphasized their role in the "Westernization" of Egyptian culture (*taghrīb*), allowing colonial domination to take root in people's hearts. In practice, these different registers of criticism were fused, attributing to the 1919 literary generation various—and sometimes contradictory—iniquities. It was obvious that the postwar developments broke the aura of sanctity that had for so long surrounded these literary giants and opened the path to a full-fledged generational struggle.

The novel *Milim al-Akbar*, published in 1944 by committee member ʻAdil Kamil, captures the budding authors' postwar frustrations. Its introduction opens with a dialogue between the author and the novel's protagonist, Milim, who is devastated after the novel fails to be selected for a literary prize by Egypt's Language Academy. He recounts the humiliating scrutiny to which he was subjected, followed by the decision of the jury to postpone the competition in the absence of deserving candidates. "The goal became a mirage" (*al-hadaf istaḥālu suraban*), Milim sighed, alluding to another novel that had also been rejected by the academy, *al-Sarab* (The Mirage), authored by Kamil's friend Naguib Mahfuz.[24] The sense of a literary breakthrough as a mirage permeates many accounts of the period, attesting to the difficulty young writers faced in getting their works published, read, and approved by the literary establishment. One of the accusations the juniors addressed to the seniors was the latter's literary conservatism.[25] Among the seniors who sat on the committee for the academy's literary competitions was Ahmad Hasan al-Zayyat, editor of *al-Risala* and author of the book that became the object of mockery of the youth, *Difaʻ ʻn al-Balagha* (For the Defense of Rhetoric). As a measure to protect "highbrow literature" from the "profiteers'" harmful influence, al-Zayyat suggested to writers to return to the ancient and largely discredited science of rhetoric.[26] But for ʻAdil Kamil, al-Zayyat's book was a monument of the stagnant literature from which he and his friend Mahfuz unsuccessfully attempted to break out.[27]

The intellectual groups associated with the Left conducted the offensive against the *udabā'* on another front: their lack of commitment to Egypt's sociopolitical struggles. Throughout the 1950s and 1960s, the issue of literary commitment, or *iltizām*, would become a rallying cry of the postwar generation, which would become the orthodoxy of the postcolonial cultural elite.[28] But years before this new criterion of intellectual authority came to be conceptualized as "committed literature" (*al-adab al-multazim*), young intellectuals were already thinking of ways of serving politics with literature. In the postwar discussions, this principle was loosely framed as the requirement of literature to "connect to life," to "serve a goal," or, as in Qutb's formulation, to transmit "social consciousness."[29]

The weekly *al-Fajr al-Jadid*, founded in 1945 by a group of young Marxists, was one of the earliest advocates of this trend. The journal's involvement in the antifascist struggle and its solidarity with writers engaged in the French Resistance provided the channel through which the notion of commitment reached Egyptians. The "purification" of the Egyptian intellectual life from the "reactionary writers and intellectuals, who . . . presented the threat to the national cause" was one of the objectives *al-Fajr al-Jadid* had set for itself.[30] One such "reactionary writer" was Qutb's literary mentor 'Abbas al-'Aqqad, whose visceral anticommunism had turned him into the personal enemy of the Egyptian Left. Called a "spineless old sheikh" who served British imperialism,[31] al-'Aqqad was regularly mocked in the Leftist press, and his "genius," mentioned in reference to his *'Abqariyyat*, became an object of irony.[32] But the journal did not spare its criticism of other old-guard writers, such as Ibrahim al-Mazni, Salama Musa, or Tawfiq al-Hakim. The latter might have never imagined that the title of "ivory tower" intellectual that he had claimed for himself in his *al-Risala* column "From Ivory Tower" (Min al-Burj al-'Aji) would become an accusation aimed at his entire generation.[33]

At this stage, writers were divided on the concrete form the commitment should take in a literary work. The call of the juniors to produce literature of social and political relevance seemed to be more of a credo, or a principle, than a literary school or a movement. Frustrated by seniors' incapacity to bring about social and political change, the juniors clustered around this credo, which they pointed as a weapon against prominent writers. A discussion initiated in 1949 by the literary critic and Qutb's friend Anwar al-Mi'ddawi captures the confusion that reigned on the issue. The debate was launched after al-Mi'ddawi claimed that al-Hakim was "living in his own world, not the one of the people."[34] This statement elicited a perplexed reaction from one of al-Hakim's fans, who had always considered him to represent life-inspired literature, as shown by his *Yawmiyyat Na'ib fi-l-Aryaf* (Diary of a Country Prosecutor, 1937). In his response, al-Mi'ddawi insisted that *Yawmiyyat* represented al-Hakim's youthful writings, from which he had departed with his works on "visions, ghosts and legends."[35]

The discussion of what "life-inspired literature" (*adab al-ḥayāt*) concretely meant continued over several issues, drawing in al-Hakim and Taha Husayn themselves, both of whom objected to al-Mi'ddawi's understanding of the relationship between literature and life, claiming that literature that is not connected to life simply did not exist. According to Husayn, writers are inevitably affected by the same daily experiences as common men. Moreover, he claimed, a writer does not need to be directly involved in an experience in order to be able to depict it artistically; he can grasp it "through reading and listening."[36] For his part, al-Hakim added that "life" had a broader meaning than its mere representations in the external world; in fact, it encompassed the internal impressions of a writer as well. Al-Mi'ddawi responded by laughing off these objections and gave an example of literature that was detached from life: Taha Husayn's recent novel *Shajarat al-Bu's* (The Tree of Misery). The portrayal of provincial life, which provided the setting for the novel's plot, was not convincing, al-Mi'ddawi pointed out, because the author wrote it in his house, situated in the upscale neighborhood Zamalek. "To write about life and people in an Egyptian village while seated in his room in Zamalek is like depicting the life and people at the North Pole while living on the Equator!" al-Mi'ddawi argued.[37]

Calls for reshaping Egypt's culture to fit its upcoming postcolonial future reached the Muslim Brotherhood as well. Following the war, young intellectuals associated with the Brotherhood had become increasingly vocal on the colonial underpinnings of Egypt's national literature. Purging its history and literature from the colonial effects demanded an extensive project of rewriting the humanities of Egypt. One of those responsible for this reorientation was Anwar al-Jundi. Born in 1917, al-Jundi exemplified the trajectory of many young Egyptians of his generation, for whom joining radical political groups was part of the youthful quest for action rather than a lifelong ideological commitment. In 1946, he started writing for the Muslim Brotherhood's journal and rapidly became one of its main cultural commentators. In his essays, he portrayed Western imperialism as operating through Egypt's cultural institutions, media, and established writers, all of whom conspired to normalize the British occupation. In an issue of the Brotherhood's journal published on March 6, 1948, al-Jundi announced his intention to rewrite the modern history of the Muslim regions.[38] Convinced that World War II ushered in a new cultural awakening (*yaqaẓa*), al-Jundi described the interwar period as marked by unchecked Westernization (*taghrīb*) propagated by the established writers.

In some way, al-Jundi's project differed from that of his leftist peers: instead of denouncing the *udabā* for their indifference to the country's pressing needs, he accused them of being the pawns of Western cultural domination. But both projects converged in dismissing the 1919 intellectual generation as historically obsolete, ripe for replacement by the upcoming national culture. In fact, the Islamist vision differed from the leftist only in the form and content that would characterize this new postcolonial culture in the Egypt of the future. The commonalities between the two visions are due to the fact that al-Jundi represented more than the Muslim Brotherhood; his call to reshape culture in the light of Egypt's impending independence matched that of an entire postwar generation—Islamists, leftists, and independents combined.

Al-Jundi epitomized his generation not only in his assessment of the 1919 generation, but also in his shifting organizational sympathies. He did not stay in the Brotherhood for long. After its transition to the underground following its dissolution in 1948, he joined *al-Risala* as a cultural commentator, and easily found a place within the Nasserist cultural establishment after the 1952 coup. Such a trajectory—the beginnings in an extraparliamentary organization followed by the wholehearted adhesion to the Nasserist project—was common to the postwar intellectual generation as a whole.

Disciple Becomes a Master

In many regards, Qutb's postwar career shifts were facilitated by the cultural and political ebullition that followed World War II. As a literary critic and an employee of the Education Ministry, he closely followed the rising challenge to the cultural establishment and took an active role in fomenting it. By the end of the war, Qutb reached a comfortable position in the state bureaucracy. He had entered the Education Ministry just after his graduation in 1933, and during the following years he moved between different departments, settling down in the Auditing Bureau for Research and Projects.[39] According to the documents related to his professional mission to the United States, where he was sent to familiarize himself with the American educational system in 1948, Qutb was by that time supervising an Auditing Bureau subdepartment specializing in teaching syllabi.[40] This was a fourth-ranking position within the eight-rank system of the civil service, with a corresponding salary of thirty-three pounds per month.[41] Although middle-ranking, it was a respected position, as suggested by the luxurious treatment Qutb received during his stay in the United States. Lasting between November 1948 and August 1950, his visit did not go as planned. Suffering from a health condition, Qutb was hospitalized three times, exempted from the obligation to receive a diploma, and accorded a comfortable trip back to Egypt by plane with three-day stops in Rome, Paris, Geneva, and London, all covered by the ministry.[42]

Observing the rising revolutionary tide against the political establishment, Qutb took steps to distance himself from the party political system. His transition to revolutionary politics would be gradual, reaching its end point in October 1952, when, frustrated with the direction the July Revolution was taking under military command, Qutb resigned from the Education Ministry and joined the Muslim Brotherhood. By the mid-1940s, Qutb had initiated a shift in his public intellectual persona: from an organic intellectual associated with party politics and the Wafd to a revolutionary and prophetic ideologue aligned with universal values.[43]

Firstly, against the backdrop of the crumbling prestige of the parliamentary order, Qutb left the Wafd party and began accusing political parties of dividing the nation via the press.[44] Around the same time, he ended his relationship with the official bulletin of the Ministry of Social Affairs, *Majallat al-Shu'un al-Ijtima'iyya* (The Journal of Social Affairs), in which he had once placed so much hope for its potential to solve the problem of poverty. Qutb had been writing in the *Majallat* since its founding in 1939 and praised in his articles welfare initiatives undertaken by the Ministry, such as the creation of Rural Social Centers by the ministry's Fellah Department and the translation of the founding text of the British welfare system, the Beveridge report.[45] From the mid-1940s Qutb stopped speaking in the name of state institutions. Instead of as an expert associated with the system, he positioned himself as its critic, with privileged access to its rampant corruption and inefficiency.[46]

This alteration in rhetoric was certainly due to the lifting of martial law in October 1945, which unleashed the frustrations accumulated during the war.[47] However, Qutb's transition to revolutionary politics expressed a more significant shift in terms of political action. Not only had his rhetoric changed, passing from the expert talk to revolutionary slogans, but he had also redefined his public loyalties in favor of social and political groups associated with radical politics. Qutb closely followed and commented upon the crackdown of anticolonial resistance in the Arab region, which encompassed the French repression in Syria, Lebanon, and Algeria, where it led to the Setif massacre in 1945, to events in Egypt, where an anti-British demonstration resulted in a bloodshed in May 1946. As a result, Qutb lost his faith in a representative political system, coming to view its legalist policies, such as elections or diplomacy, as artifices to maintain the colonial status quo. Instead, he urged his readers to adopt means of action that accorded the significant place to the people (*al-sha'b*): political journalism and activism, such as sit-ins, demonstrations, and popular resistance.[48]

Qutb's transition to revolutionary politics was followed by his dramatic falling-out with the generation of his mentors. In 1947, Qutb published a passionate article in which he accused the *udabā'* of having betrayed the national cause. The list of crimes he addressed to the prominent writers was long: alliance with corrupt political parties, imperialist propaganda, indifference to social justice, elitism, luxurious lifestyles, promotion of a vulgar culture, and, above all, betrayal of "literary consciousness."[49] Published in his edited weekly *al-'Alam al-'Arabi*, this article was the first stone in what would become an avalanche of criticisms of the *udabā'* during the following years. Soon after, in February 1948, Qutb announced his departure from al-'Aqqad's "literary school." Characterized by the excessive rationalism, al-'Aqqad's poetry, Qutb explained, represented a phase in the history of literature that needed to cede place for a new type of poetry.[50]

In his campaign against the *udabā'*, Qutb did not shy away from targeting his former mentors by name. He accused Tawfiq al-Hakim of hypocrisy in regard to his anticolonial politics: this long-term "lover of France," Qutb argued, switched his loyalty to the anticolonial camp as soon as it became trendy, as evidenced by his trip to Syria to support the evacuation of the French colonial troops in April 1946.[51] Likewise, Qutb accused al-'Aqqad of combating social justice out of his paranoid fear of communism and blamed Taha Husayn for going to Europe for his regular summer vacation instead of attending to his work in the Ministry of Education after he became its minister in 1950.[52] After al-'Aqqad, al-Mazni, and al-Hakim joined *Akhbar al-Yawm* as columnists in 1946, Qutb began accusing the *udabā'* of selling themselves out to the tabloid press and, in this way, contributing in the spread of vulgarity in Egypt. Qutb profoundly despised *Akhbar al-Yawm* and considered it the representative of "the press of breasts and thighs."[53] "*Akhbar al-Yawm* was originally founded to combat the people and to protect the exploiters," *al-Fikr al-Jadid* wrote in 1948.

> In doing this, it "rents" Tawfiq al-Hakim to write a few lines in the column Qafs al-Ittiham [The Accusation Cage] since he doesn't mind to serve as a cover for the newspaper's collaboration with the exploiters as long as he gets paid. . . . The journal also employs men like al-'Aqqad and al-Mazni, who, in their old age, do not care about anything except amassing fortune by all possible means.[54]

Qutb's campaign against the *udabā'* was violent and persistent. Without any doubt, it rested on a widespread realization that the colonial education on which this generation had built its notoriety made them unfit to lead Egypt to its cultural emancipation. But the political contestation was equally fueled by the temporary collapse of the system of mentorship predicated on embodied intellectual authority. As discussed in chapter 1, the generation of the *udabā'* founded their authority on the Romantic notion of genius and the ideology of personality (*shakhsīyya*), which relegitimized the preprint institution of mentorship in modern terms. Young authors accessed the literary market by claiming discipleship to prominent authors in their dedications and prefaces, which the latter were willing to contribute to their books in exchange for ensuring their perpetuity through the practice of tribute.

The emergence of new cultural players devoid of mentors in postwar Egypt had shaken this arrangement to the core. The theme of "ungrateful disciples" and "bad masters" who favored certain writers at the expense of others permeated the postwar cultural press. Historian Ahmad Amin urged disciples not to disown their masters, hoping that a personal reconciliation would help to contain the widening rift between writers.[55] In his 1947 article against the *udabā'*, Qutb blamed his former mentors for promoting their sycophants—or, as he called them, "the tails and accompanying chorus"—at the expense of "honorable men."[56] Likewise, writing in 1946 a review of Naguib Mahfuz's novel *al-Qahira al-Jadida* (The New Cairo), Qutb explained the silence with which the novel was received by critics with the fact that Mahfuz lacked protections. "One of the signs that literary criticism reached today the state of neglect . . . is that such a book passes without unleashing a literary and social storm," he wrote. "Is it because of the author's youth?" Recalling that al-Hakim owed his literary success to his early discipleship to Husayn, he added: "Or is it because . . . Naguib Mahfuz and his like among the youth do not throw themselves and their art into anyone's arms except those of their readers?"[57]

During his life, Qutb had been a dutiful disciple who applied himself in reading, reviewing, and commenting on the works of the *udabā'*. He had built his expertise in criticism by diligently studying the texts of his mentors and attempting to derive from their production a literary school. In exchange, he hoped to become their successor when his turn comes. However, by the end of the war, Qutb reached a conclusion that he had been deeply wronged by the system. Despite his absolute loyalty, his mentor al-ʿAqqad refused to write an introduction to Qutb's first book,[58] and instead he promoted writings of dubious quality.[59] Moreover, a similar attitude characterized the entire generation of his mentors, who refused to publicly engage with Qutb's intellectual production. In 1951, Qutb wrote:

> I have been a disciple [*murīd*] in the full meaning of the word of a man from your generation whom you all certainly know. I have been a friend to many others. I wrote about all of them without exception, and explained their opinions, presented their books and analyzed their works as much as I could. Then my turn came. . . . Then my turn came to publish books after having published essays, articles, and poems. I was late to begin publishing books, since I insisted on climbing to the minaret without a ladder. . . . The first book I published was . . . *al-Taswir al-Fanni fi-l Qur'an*. . . . What was the reaction of my teacher [*ustadhī*]? What was the reaction of your entire generation? What was the reaction of the entire generation of seniors in regard not only to this book but all the other ten I published until now?

Apart from two references by al-Hakim and al-Mazni, there had been an overwhelming silence, Qutb noted bitterly.[60] Qutb's public response to Ahmad Amin's call for generational reconciliation published in *al-Thaqafa* magazine demonstrates that the system of mentorship is prone to being denounced as the source of corruption when the expectations related to its promises are not met. If the system stops being functional, it becomes perceived as the fertile ground for practices of nepotism or favoritism—or, to employ a more recent expression, *shillaliyya*. The rising criticism of the *udabā'*, fueled by the emergence of new market-reliant cultural players, provided Qutb with the opportunity to channel his frustration into more structural criticism. With the rising revolutionary storm against the prominent writers, Qutb understood the reason of the literary stagnation in Egypt: the nepotism and cultural colonialism of the *udabā*.

Instead of remaining an eternal disciple of the founders' generation, Qutb channeled his energies into becoming a master himself. The cultural venues that mushroomed in the wake of the war thanks to profiteer investments provided an opportunity. At the end of 1944, Qutb came into contact with the aforementioned Publishing Committee for University Graduates, the series established by the al-Sahhar family in the Misr

Publishing House. Rapidly Qutb became an integral part of its numerous activities. He began regularly attending the committee's weekly meetings, held in the Misr Publishing House in Faggala Street every Tuesday, during which the collective decided on the books to be published.[61] From 1945, Qutb's publications began appearing in the committee's press: in 1945, it published his book cowritten with his siblings, *al-Atyaf al-Arba'a* (The Four Phantoms), in 1946 his autobiography *Tifl min al-Qariyya* (A Child from the Village), and in 1949 and 1951 the two editions of his bestseller *al-'Adala al-Ijtima'iyya fi-l Islam* (Social Justice in Islam). In 1947, using his expertise in children psychology, Qutb cooperated with the novelist and cofounder of the committee 'Abd al-Hamid al-Sahhar, on the first series of religious literature for children, *Qassas al-Anbya'* (Tales of the Prophets).[62] At the same time, Qutb introduced the committee to his younger brother, Muhammad, who throughout the 1970s and 1980s would achieve renown as a Saudi Arabia–based Islamic scholar. It is noteworthy that the committee's press published Muhammad Qutb's first book: a collection of translated European stories entitled *Sukhriyat Saghira* (Little Mockings).

In parallel, Qutb began discussing the books published by the committee in his literary column in *al-Risala*. Qutb's literary criticism provides the most telling illustration of the way friendships created in the Misr Publishing House were reflected in the print. Since 1942, Qutb's criticism in *al-Risala* had mainly revolved around the writings of the *udabā'* authors in line with Qutb's plans to publish these essays as a book.[63] However, from late 1944 onward, Qutb began shifting his literary focus in favor of the committee's young authors, starting with the review of Mahfuz's novel *Kifah Tiba* (The Battle of Thebes).[64] In the following years, Qutb regularly discussed in *al-Risala* novels by authors associated with the committee, such as 'Abd al-Hamid al-Sahhar, 'Adil Kamil, 'Ali Ahmad Bakathir, Naguib Mahfuz. For the committee's circle, Qutb represented an asset; a recognized literary critic with regular access to the reputable *al-Risala* magazine, Qutb was highly instrumental in promoting these authors, who, while having found a publisher, still had hardly anyone to read their work. Years later, Mahfuz would confess that when he met Taha Husayn after the 1952 revolution, the latter had never heard of him, while al-Sahhar recounted how he and Mahfuz desperately attempted to attract the attention of the "giants" by sending them signed copies of their first novels.[65] It was followed by disappointment when the novelists discovered that one of the "giants" had sold these copies to a bookstore in exchange for books he was more interested in reading.[66]

In addition to promoting them through literary criticism, Qutb took his young colleagues under his wing in the journals he supervised, often providing them with their first experience in journalism. In 1947, Qutb was invited to associate himself with the journal *al-'Alam al-'Arabi* (The Arab World), which was created as a regular outlet of the publishing house established by two employees of the Dar al-Ma'arif publishing house, 'Adil al-Ghadban and Yusuf Shehata.[67] A poet with a publisher's talent, 'Adil al-Ghadban had known Qutb since some time. It was thanks to his friendship with al-Ghadban that Qutb established the series Al-Maktabat al-Qur'aniyya (The Qur'anic Library) in Dar al-Ma'arif, where he published his research on Qur'anic aesthetics. When in 1945 al-Ghadban founded the periodical *al-Kitab* (The Book), Qutb became one of its contributors, and when the latter assumed the editorship of *al-Fikr al-Jadid* in 1948, al-Ghadban published his poetry there.[68] Responding to the increasing interest in Arab international politics, *al-'Alam al-'Arabi* published mostly essays by Arab dignitaries or politicians.[69] Such an elitist touch presented a sharp contrast to the publications by the authors in Qutb's personal network that he brought to the journal: committee members 'Abd al-Hamid Guda al-Sahhar, Naguib Mahfuz, and Wadi' Filistin; poets from Qutb's *shilla* of Dar al-'Ulum, Fayid al-'Amrusi and Mahmud Abu al-Wafa; and Qutb's brother Muhammad.

In a slightly different composition, Qutb's circle followed him to another periodical that he was invited to supervise in 1948, the weekly *al-Fikr al-Jadid* (The New Thought). Qutb's involvement in *al-Fikr al-Jadid* provides the central story in his postwar transition to revolutionary politics, Islamism, and the organization of the Muslim Brotherhood. As mentioned above, *al-Fikr al-Jadid* was founded by Muhammad Hilmi al-Minyawi, a businessman and an influential member of the Muslim Brotherhood with a seat in its Consultative Assembly. Most probably Qutb met al-Minyawi through the al-Sahhar brothers, with whom he was acquainted since at least 1945. As a pious family of merchants, al-Sahhars were on good terms with the Muslim Brotherhood. The novelist ʿAbd al-Hamid al-Sahhar extensively consulted Hasan al-Banna for his biographies on Islamic personalities, who agreed to write a preface to his book on the Prophet's companion Abu Dharr al-Ghifari.[70] Al-Sahhar even attempted to introduce the founder of the Muslim Brotherhood to his friend Naguib Mahfuz, but unsuccessfully.[71] ʿAbd al-Hamid's older brother, Saʿid al-Sahhar, cooperated with al-Minyawi in the creation of a shared publishing house, Dar al-Kitab al-ʿArabi, in 1946. The venture represented a genuine meeting point between the committee and the Muslim Brotherhood where the authors associated with both collectives published their works. It was Dar al-Kitab al-ʿArabi that published the second round of Qutb's books on Islam (after the first round was published by the committee's press), plays by committee author ʿAli Ahmad Bakathir, and writings by prominent Muslim Brothers such as the popular shaykh Muhammad al-Ghazzali and the thinker ʿAbd al-Munʿam Khalaf (whom we encountered in chapter 2 debating with Qutb on rationality in Islam).[72] After al-Sahhar and al-Minyawi fell out in 1951, Dar al-Kitab al-ʿArabi became the publishing arm of the Muslim Brotherhood. It was there that the organization printed its official statement supporting the Free Officers coup in summer 1952.[73]

The periodical *al-Fikr al-Jadid* was another venture where writers and Muslim Brothers joined forces to bring down Egypt's cultural establishment. The launch of *al-Fikr al-Jadid* in January 1948 was enthusiastically welcomed by the Muslim Brotherhood, who perceived it as a sister publication that would continue its struggle.[74] Starting with the first issue, Qutb began promoting Islam as the remedy to Egypt's social and moral maladies. While editing *al-Fikr al-Jadid*, Qutb was also writing a more elaborate study on Islam and social justice that would be published in 1949 and become his all-time bestseller, *al-ʿAdalat al-Ijtimaʿiyya fi-l-Islam*. The editorial team of *al-Fikr al-Jadid* almost entirely consisted of Qutb's intellectual circle, which seconded him in his struggle against colonialism, corruption, and cultural vulgarity. This circle included poets, writers, and intellectuals that Qutb had met during different stages of his career: his friends from the study years (Fayid al-ʿAmrusi, ʿAbbas Khidr, and Mahmud Abu al-Wafa), authors encountered through the committee (ʿAbd al-Hamid al-Sahhar, Ibrahim al-Waʿili, and ʿAbd al-Munʿam

Shumayyis); and his three siblings (Muhammad, Amina, and Hamida Qutb). These authors rubbed shoulders with intellectuals associated with the Muslim Brotherhood: Muhammad al-Ghazzali, Azhari poet Sadiq Ibrahim ʿArjun, and renowned Islamic thinker Fathi Osman.[75]

In *al-Fikr al-Jadid*, Qutb made unbridled attacks against Egypt's cultural establishment. Assisted by his editorial team, he adopted a direct tone in accusing wealthy elites of cultural domination, social oppression, and moral decay. The journal pushed for the reform of public service in order to eliminate the "slave mentality" (*ʿaqalīyyat al-ʿabīd*) that Qutb credited with all types of oppression in Egypt, and it denounced moral decay, which consumed people's energies and distracted them from the issues that he viewed as essential in Egypt on the verge of independence: the fight against imperialism and social oppression. The journal called to purge Egypt's educational institutions—such as schools, the university, and the Education Ministry—of the colonial effects so deeply imprinted on mentalities and policies by decades-long British domination.[76] Without any doubt, *al-Fikr al-Jadid* offered to Qutb a much larger space of autonomy than his previously edited *al-ʿAlam al-ʿArabi*, and his intellectual agenda seemed to sit well with the goals of the Muslim Brotherhood.[77] Years later, Qutb would fondly remember his *al-Fikr al-Jadid* circle, comparing it to a "battalion" (*katība*) united in the battle to achieve a "clean culture."[78]

Given Qutb's towering role in the committee and *al-Fikr al-Jadid*, it is not surprising that he was highly esteemed among his younger companions. While reading their book reviews and memoirs or listening to their interviews, one cannot miss the fascination that the postwar generation held for Qutb. Publicist Muhammad Sulayman Fayad discovered Qutb through his fiery writings in *al-Risala* and immediately became a fan. Living in his native Nile delta town of Mansura, Fayad went to explore its public libraries in search of Qutb's books.[79] For him, Qutb represented a committed intellectual who had descended from the ivory tower and joined the masses.[80] Wadiʿ Filistin, a translator and a future literary critic, met Qutb for the first time in 1945 in the Committee. The two men shared a taxi home and started a friendship that would last until Qutb's execution in 1966.[81] It might not be a stretch to say that Filistin initiated himself into literary criticism partly through writing reviews of Qutb's books. Between

1945 and 1947 he had already published four of them.[82] Ibrahim al-Wa'ili, an Iraqi intellectual studying in Cairo who back in 1945 had flirted with the Marxist *al-Fajr al-Jadid* and in the early 1950s would join the equally Leftist Lebanese periodical *al-Adab*, praised Qutb as "a free soul, both in mind and consciousness . . . neither a 'rented' politician, nor a turbaned [*sheikh*] trading in religion."[83] The playwright 'Ali Ahmad Bakathir dedicated to Qutb a poem that he composed for the occasion of the latter's *al-Taswir al-Fanni fi-l-Quran*.[84] Naguib Mahfuz called Qutb "the voice of the new generation."[85]

Such a favorable reception of Qutb's works among the postwar intellectual generation is not surprising, given that Qutb often acted as their mentor. In addition to promoting young writers through his column in *al-Risala*, Qutb wrote prefaces to their books, which he attempted to place with reputable publishers. For example, it was with Qutb's help that writer and critic 'Abd al-Mun'am Shumayyis published his first book. Entitled *Suqut al-Qahira* (The Fall of Cairo) and published in 1951 by Dar al-Kitab al-'Arabi, the book explored the various ways cultural vulgarity corrupted different arts in Egypt—music, the theater, the cinema, and literature—and was prefaced by Qutb himself.[86] In a 1945 letter to Taha Husayn, Qutb solicited Husayn—who at that time supervised the periodical *al-Katib al-Misri* (The Egyptian Scribe) and had privileged access to its publisher—to publish or at least to "write a word" on a manuscript by one of his protégés, 'Imad al-Din 'Abd al-Hamid.[87] Qutb's mentor status did not go unrecognized. Speaking about his presence on the Committee, Wadi' Filistin rejoiced that, despite his advanced career status, Qutb "did not see harm in encouraging them either by publishing his works in the Committee series or by writing reviews of its members' books."[88] Filistin spoke of Qutb's involvement in the Committee as "encouragement" (*tashjī'*), a word commonly used for mentorship. Therefore, it should come as no surprise that some of Qutb's young companions followed him in his Islamist adventure.

An Organic Intellectual

During the years between the publication of *al-Fikr al-Jadid* in 1948 and the joining of the Muslim Brotherhood in 1953, Qutb reached the summit of his intellectual career. Favored by the revolutionary upsurge, he became a highly solicited public speaker who gave public talks, spoke on the radio, and wrote in the most famous antiestablishment newspapers. The publication of *al-Fikr al-Jadid* only lasted for several months. Shortly after its closure, at the end of 1948, Qutb departed for the United States to pursue a professional training mission for the Education Ministry. His return in the 1950s coincided with the release of Muslim Brothers from prison, where thousands of them had been sent during the 1948 crackdown on the organization prompted by the assassination of Prime Minister Mahmud al-Nuqrashi. In order to erase its bloodied reputation, the Brotherhood returned to political life with a new strategy aiming to stress its intellectual face. Enjoying a wide reputation thanks to the commercial success of his *al-'Adala al-Ijtima'iyya fi-l-Islam*, Qutb would become a key figure in this strategy.

Following the restoration of its legal status in 1951, the organization put at Qutb's disposal a wide range of periodicals and publishing opportunities, in which he assumed a central place. Starting with 1951, Qutb became the lead writer in the Brotherhood's periodicals launched the same year, such as the weekly *al-Da'wa* (The Call) and the monthly *al-Muslimun* (Muslims), which addressed the international Muslim audience. In parallel, the Brotherhood took charge of reprinting and distributing Qutb's books: in 1952, it reprinted his *Ma'arakat al-Islam wa-l-Ra'smaliyya* (The Battle between Islam and Capitalism) and *al-'Adala al-Ijtima'iyya fi-l-Islam* and placed them under the insignia of the organization, attesting to its willingness to incorporate Qutb's production in the Brotherhood's official corpus.[89] In addition, Qutb's press articles aroused the interest of young Muslim Brothers, who, following their release from prison, created the small publishing venture the Committee of the Muslim Youth (*Lajnat al-Shabab al-Muslim)* in Cairo. Throughout the 1950s, the committee became the major translator, publisher, and distributor of Pakistani authors, providing the channel through which the writings by the Indo-Pakistani scholar Abu al-'Ala al-Mawdudi reached Egyptian readership.[90]

Fascinated by Qutb's prolific intellectual production, the Committee collected his essays and in 1953 published them as a book soberly titled *Dirasat Islamiyya* (Islamic Studies). The book was prefaced by the sixty-seven-year-old revered Islamic activist, Muhibb al-Din al-Khatib, to whom we were introduced in chapter 1, as the key figure of the Salafiyya Bookstore and Publishing House. In a sense, with his preface Qutb obtained the recognition from the circle with which he had been at odds in his early career, as demonstrated by his feuds against poet Abu Shadi in 1934 and the disciples of poet Mustafa Sadiq al-Rafiʿi in 1939, also discussed in chapter 1. As the Syrian scholar and al-Khatib's nephew, ʿAli al-Tantawi, has noted, "In the beginning, I was in one camp [*ṣaff*] and he was in another. . . . Then, he got closer to us with his book *al-Taswir al-Fanni fi-l-Qur'an* . . . and created what I was unable to create when he wrote "al-Zilal."[91]

Between 1951 and 1953, Qutb had been an active member in the Brotherhood's intellectual circles. Yet he still enjoyed the status of an independent intellectual, which he would mention in his own articles.[92] As much as to the Brotherhood, Qutb was associated with other press outlets published by antiestablishment groups. He wrote in *al-Ishtirakiyya* (Socialism), the mouthpiece of the former Young Egypt, and held a regular column in *al-Lawa al-Jadid* (The New Brigade), which was supervised by the future minister in Nasser's government Fathi Radwan.[93] In the months leading up to the 1952 Free Officers coup, Qutb's articles insisted on the urgency of creating a national front composed of antiestablishment groups, such as the Muslim Brotherhood, Young Egypt, and the National Party, to confront the coalition of "reactionaries" consisting of big landowners, capitalists, and colonizers. Following the Free Officers' coup in the summer of 1952, Qutb's main focus shifted to the necessity of purging the state bureaucracy, radio, and press of the elements of the bygone age. As someone close to the extraparliamentary camp, Qutb was one of the two "Brotherhood personalities" considered for a high position within the ruling organ of the revolution, the Liberation Rally.[94] Unsatisfied with the track the revolution was taking, Qutb refused and in December 1953 presented his resignation to the Ministry of Education.

After spending two years in the Brotherhood's circles, Qutb officially joined the organization in 1953. The shift in his status is visible in the fact that it is only after becoming a member that Qutb was entrusted with official responsibilities—specifically, the supervision of the department in charge of the Brotherhood's intellectual activities, Qism Nashr al-Daʿwa

(Department of Call Propagation).[95] Qutb's appointment as head of the department went against the Brotherhood's regulations, which limited administrative positions to Muslim Brothers with long-term memberships. Decided by the General Guide Hasan al-Hudaybi, Qutb's appointment was probably intended to strengthen al-Hudaybi's camp, facing divisions over its policy regarding Nasser's rule. Notably, Qutb and his intellectual network might have provided the counterweight to the influential Muslim Brother who has been in charge of the Brotherhood's press for decades: Salih 'Ashmawi, al-Banna's comrade-in-arms and the founder of *al-Da'wa* newspaper. Together with Muhammad al-Ghazzali and other two Brothers, in December 1953 Salih 'Ashmawi was expelled from the organization, which took away his *al-Da'wa* newspaper.[96]

As head of the department, Qutb initiated two major intellectual projects. To compensate the loss of *al-Da'wa*, Qutb started working for the revival of the *Majallat al-Ikhwan al-Muslimin* (Journal of the Muslim Brotherhood). The journal's publication faced a number of challenges, and Qutb reportedly outdid himself in overcoming them. The first challenge was to find the place where the editorial team could meet. After working for some time from the offices of his former employer *al-Balagh al-Usbu'i*, Qutb and his editorial team eventually had to leave and had to work in the waiting room of the Bab al-Luq train station. After having finally settled in elsewhere, the project was hit by another calamity: the arrest of Qutb on January 13 amid the clashes between students belonging to the Brotherhood and the Liberation Rally in Cairo University.[97] Interrupted for around four months, the journal's production resumed with Qutb's liberation in April 1954. However, the journal faced yet another challenge: the transport strike that prevented Qutb from reaching downtown Cairo from his residence in Helwan to attend editorial meetings. Qutb circumvented this obstacle by renting a horse carriage, and the journal finally saw the light on May 20, 1954.[98] In the journal's editorial team, Qutb injected some new blood from his *al-Fikr al-Jadid* circle: 'Abd al-Mun'am Shumayyis, 'Abd al-Hamid al-Sahhar, Fathi Osman, and Qutb's siblings Amina, Hamida, and Muhammad.

The second project launched by Qutb as the head of the Department of Call Propagation was one that would lead to his arrest and fifteen-year prison sentence: the publication of secret pamphlets. Outlawed in 1954 and its weekly publication shut down, the Muslim Brotherhood decided to join the secret pamphlet warfare launched by the resumption of the negotiations for the evacuation of British troops on the part of Nasser's regime, in which both anti- and pro-governmental forces took part.[99] Chief among the Brotherhood's pamphlets was a two-paged mimeographed publication entitled *Al-Ikhwan fi-l Ma'araka* (The Brotherhood in Struggle) for which Qutb had ordered the purchase of the Ronéo machine, which permitted the cheap publication of tracts in large numbers.[100] While little is known about this pamphlet, it is clear that its publication provided the basis for Qutb's arrest and imprisonment in November 1954. His interrogation in December 1954 focused on his role in publishing it while the press mocked him as "the minister of tracts" (*wazīr al-manshūrāt*).[101] By joining the Brotherhood and assuming its official responsibilities, Qutb regained the status of an organic intellectual, which he had abandoned with his resignation from the Wafd party. After a short period of glory as an independent intellectual, achieved notably in *al-Fikr a-Jadid*, Qutb fully entrusted his talents and his fate to the Muslim Brotherhood.

Dominant biographical accounts on Qutb tend to see his postwar rebellion against Egypt's cultural establishment and the ensuing transition to Islamism and the Muslim Brotherhood as the effect of his literary failure.[102] Citing Qutb's confessions on his inability to obtain recognition from prominent writers, these accounts draw on the observations of the highly contested literary center while ignoring the margins, where new cultural spaces and actors were emerging—indeed, bursting with new writers, poets, filmmakers, publishers, and intellectuals who mixed their creative production with radical politics and passed from one organization to another in search of opportunities of action. Beyond rivalries in the leadership, young Egyptians easily transited from leftist organizations to the Muslim Brotherhood, without necessarily viewing them as incompatible, since they both catered for the cause that mattered the most at this historical juncture: national independence and social justice.[103] The example of Iraqi intellectual Ibrahim al-Wa'ili, who wrote to the Leftist *al-Fajr al-Jadid*, to Qutb's *al-Fikr al-Jadid*, and to the voice of Arab existentialism, *al-Adab*, is an example of a much larger trend.

Neither did the postwar generation have a problem with Islamism—at least initially. Although a minority of them continued in Islamist activism after the rise of Nasser's regime, in the late 1940s and early 1950s many saw Islamism as a viable solution to Egypt's political, social, and cultural problems. In his 1951 *Suqut al-Qahira*, 'Abd al-Mun'am Shumayyis urged for a larger representation of Islamist activists among Egypt's cultural leaders.[104] Other members of Qutb's intellectual circle wrote rave reviews of his Islamic books and echoed his ideas in their essays.[105] Others espoused Islamic solutions in their novels. The ultimate victory of Islam in the struggle between capitalism and communism, depicted in 'Ali Ahmad Bakathir's 1953 novel *al-Tha'ir al-Ahmar* (The Red Revolutionary), echoed Qutb's vision promoted in his *Ma'arakat al-Islam wa-l-Ra'smaliyya*. Against the backdrop of the Cold War international competition between "imported" solutions to heal Egypt's as well as the entire world's maladies—namely, communism and capitalism—Islamism had the undeniable advantage of its authenticity. It carried the promise of efficiency in reform (because of being in tune with the beliefs of "the masses," or so the argument went) while its local origins guaranteed the emancipation of the mind necessary to ensure full independence. Hardly restricted to the Muslim Brotherhood, the potential of Islam to provide a solid ground for the construction of Egypt's postcolonial state was widely accepted among the postwar generation.

But—Qutb's overwhelming personality aside—for most of the authors associated with his postwar intellectual circle, Islamism was a passing fling, its allure consisting of its anti-imperialistic promise. Additionally, the period from the mid-1940s to the mid-1950s proved to be a mere parenthesis in the longer Egypt's march to the postcolonial future. Prompted by financial investments, creative outburst, and ideological blending, these years represented a revolutionary opening when everything seemed possible. Recalling the postwar years, Marxist intellectual Anouar Abdel-Malek compared Egypt's political scene to "an open stadium in which everyone was invited to play; a stadium whose gates soon were shut."[106] This opening was closed with the rise of the Nasserist state and the banishment of Islamists in 1954. Following the consolidation of Nasser's rule in 1954, the prestige of prominent *udabā'* who had been targeted and accused was restored. The postwar intellectual generation lost its generational unity, dispersed in prisons or integrated into the ranks of Nasser's expanding bureaucracy. While those who remained in the Muslim Brotherhood were sent to prison following the 1954 crackdown, others adapted the rest of their careers to the demands of the Nasserist state. Qutb's former companion ʿAbd al-Munʿam Shumayyis, Muslim Brother Anwar al-Jundi, and cofounder of the Publishing Committee ʿAbd al-Hamid al-Sahhar became part of the Nasser's cultural bureaucracy committed to its goals (which I will discuss in chapter 5).

The productive ideological blending that characterized the period between the end of World War II and the 1952 revolution seems also absent from historical accounts that tend to represent the period from a partisan historiographical perspective.[107] The same applies to literary history; the generation of the committee's authors doesn't have any other identity than that of "the fathers of the sixties generation,"[108] while its most renowned representative, Naguib Mahfuz, preferred to insert himself in the genealogy of the *udabāʾ* instead of claiming the distinctive identity of his postwar intellectual circle.[109] However, to disregard this historical period is to overlook the formative years of many intellectuals who, following the 1952 revolution, would become part of the intellectual elite of the Nasserist postcolonial state. For some, like Qutb, this period was much more than a formative time: it provided him with the conditions to reinvent himself as a revolutionary intellectual committed to the task of creating an Islamic society.

Social Justice in Islam

There is little doubt that Qutb's commitment to Islamist activism represented a sea change in his intellectual career. Not only did he start to advocate for Islam as a political and social solution to Egypt's and the world's maladies, but he also threw himself into oppositional politics and reinvented himself as a revolutionary intellectual. But how did this commitment affect his previous stances on politics, the arts, and religion? What type of conversion did the transition signify? Was it religious conversion or political? To answer these questions, we need to take a closer look at Qutb's first and major work on Islam and social justice: *al-'Adala al-Ijtima'iyya fi-l-Islam.*

Published by the Misr Publishing House in 1949 as part of the Publishing Committee for University Graduates series, *al-'Adala* was the most successful of Qutb's books during his lifetime. Between its publication in 1949 and his death in 1966, it went through six editions, some of which were diligently revised by the author. Examining the book from the perspective of Qutb's earlier writings on social reform, notably published in the official publication of the Ministry of Social Affairs, *Majallat al-Shu'un al-Ijtima'iyya,* Alain Roussillon suggested that the new element in *al-'Adala,* when comparing its arguments to Qutb's former positions on social change, is the means by which Qutb suggests that this change can be achieved. Instead of prioritizing science as the instrument to end entrenched underdevelopment and the British occupation, as he did in his earlier texts, with *al-'Adala* Qutb begins to advocate a spiritual conversion as a prerequisite of any successful reform. According to Roussillon, the core change that *al-'Adala* entails is Qutb's transition from science to spirit as the means of modernizing society.[110]

It is possible, however, to suggest another reading of the type of transformation that Qutb underwent with his commitment to Islamic activism. It emerges when we consider his Islamist writings not solely from the perspective of his expertise on social reform, but also from that of his literary works. As we have seen in chapter 2, a spirit broadly defined as the realm of the irrational and identified with emotion had always been, for Qutb, the means to access knowledge and elevate the human condition. Endowed with extraordinary capacities of feeling, a poet or a writer had a mission to maintain humankind's connection to the realm of the eternal. The sharp distinction between reason and emotion on which Qutb based his understanding of existence allowed a certain compartmentalization of functions assigned to these faculties: reason was charged with the task of managing the affairs of daily life, while the emotional connection to the afterworld guaranteed spiritual well-being. As seen earlier, this compartmentalization allowed Qutb to use distinct epistemologies in different spheres of intellectual activity; he relied on positivism in his reformist writings and referred to Romantic metaphysics in his literary works. But it is precisely this compartmentalization that can prevent us from seeing that the importance of the spiritual did not suddenly appear with Qutb's Islamist commitment, but had been the core element of his aesthetic project all along.

Rather than Qutb's transition from scientific to spiritual tools for achieving a social change, I see it as following from his disenchantment with institutional politics and his subsequent commitment to oppositional activism. Like other efendis, Qutb had always been concerned with social reform and change; otherwise he would not have become involved in party politics on the side of the Wafd. But in the period preceding World War II he had delegated this issue to institutional politics and its associated means of action—elections, negotiations, diplomacy, and top-down administration of reform. His handing over of the business of reform to institutional politics explains why Qutb wrote so little on politics prior to World War II: politics was done through elections, and not the effort to shape public opinion through incendiary public writing. The delegation of reform to legal politics allowed Qutb to develop his artistic project in isolation from the sufferings of the sensate world and in line with a broader Romantic contempt for the material dimension of human existence. Put simply, while the role of institutional politics was to take care of the population's social needs, the mission of poetry was to cater to its spiritual growth.

Postwar developments shook this division of labor to the core. Not only had institutional politics proved itself incapable of solving the multiple crises of the sensate world, but socially detached literature appeared to have been involved in deepening them. This situation created a fertile ground for the circulation of various versions of intellectual commitment, which Qutb passionately seized, reinventing himself in the process. In fact, Qutb himself had been a socially detached (or even an ivory-tower) poet, during the interwar period. It had been a natural position for someone with such a strongly expressed distrust of human reason and disdain for the empirical world. Following the postwar shift from the priority of knowledge to that of action, Qutb surrounded himself with restive youth, took a stand against parliamentary politics, and abandoned his inward-looking poetic creation in favor of revolutionary politics.

This emerging intellectual order, defined by the urgency to act, was also a source of tension for Qutb. He did not feel entirely at ease with the intellectual trends that accompanied his rebellion and provided its main theoretical basis: the Left, committed literature, social realism, and other trends that Qutb considered to have emerged from the epistemological background of materialism (*māddīyya*). This tension is visible in Qutb's hesitant and somewhat contradictory appreciation of leftist trends. In some writings, Qutb seems to appreciate in communist movements their potential to direct popular energies against capitalism, colonial dependence, and social injustice.[111] Yet in others he criticized them for their limited ambitions in relation to the satisfaction of basic human needs such as those for food, shelter, and clothing.[112]

Qutb's review of Kamil's *Milim*, which opened this chapter, offers perhaps the best illustration of Qutb's ambivalent position on the Left. While Qutb praises the novel for its capacity to arouse indignation at injustice, which he believed was conducive to concrete action against the established order, he is also unsure about the novel's artistic value. In appreciating it, Qutb is loyal to his earlier understanding of art, which he had viewed as something that transcends the spatial and temporal limits of the sensate world and its temporary struggles. Qutb's later Islamist works, published before his imprisonment, are replete with similar—but more self-assured—intellectual engagements with the Left, with which he felt himself to be in the same camp politically, but from which he was worlds apart from a broader epistemological perspective. As a result, Qutb faced a dilemma: how could he pursue the literary vocation of humankind's spiritual sublimation at a time when this type of literature had become a synonym for social and political conservatism? And how, at the same time, was he to harness literature to the purpose of national and social advancement without compromising its higher aims of transcendence?

Islamism provided the solution to this dilemma. As a set of symbols open to interpretation, Islam offered elements from which Qutb was able to elaborate a specific ontology, sociopolitical order, and mode of political action. Postwar developments allowed Qutb to realize that it was impossible to sublimate humans spiritually without diminishing the suffering of their physical bodies. "Empty stomachs do not know high meanings," he explained in *al-'Adala*.[113] It draws people into mental slavery and drives them right into the communist fold, he warned in *al-Ma'araka*.[114] Qutb came to the conclusion that a complete system was needed to take care of both levels of existence, spiritual and material, by implementing social justice on earth while at the same time maintaining the spiritual bond to the afterworld. Such a reformulation came at the price of a major revision to his previous theory of human perception, predicated on the distinction between reason and emotion. The revision of the emotion/reason connection that had formed the core doctrine of his aesthetic project is visible in his fiery opposition to the understanding of Islam as located exclusively in the emotional realm (*fī ma'zil wijdānī wa 'ālam al-ḍamīr*) and therefore reduced to ritualized practices of worship (*'ibadāt*).[115] But Qutb also firmly positioned himself against the opposite extreme: the placing of Islam in the exclusive realm of rational thinking and its transformation into a science or a philosophy.[116] What Qutb suggested instead was to fuse these two levels of perception by means of his theory of the Islamic state and to make their reciprocal action the main condition of its success.

How did this system work concretely? In al-*'Adala*, Qutb stated that the material institutions of the Islamic state had to be firmly anchored in the Islamic faith, which acted as "the internal psychological feeling" (*al-shu'ūr al-nafsī al-bāṭin*) of the legitimacy of these institutions. But in order to instill this feeling, human consciousness had to be emptied of all values and beliefs produced socially, such as the fear of social degradation or the quest for power and wealth—a process that Qutb termed "the absolute emotional emancipation" (*al-taḥarrur al-wijdānī al-muṭlaq*). Only when it was supported from the "inside" of human consciousness would the Islamic social system be successful in its "outside" realization, Qutb claimed.[117]

Such an emancipation was a necessary means to convince individuals to voluntarily put the collective interests above the individual needs and desires. But, at the same time, the inner conviction that Islam provided the best model for social organization had to be continuously supported and confirmed by the Islamic state's realization on the material level. Without the observed advantages of the Islamic social system, the inner belief in the justice of this system might eventually fade away.[118] As a result, it was only the existence of Islamic state institutions on the material level that would ensure the realization of spiritual goals. Contrasting his social theory with Christian and communist epistemologies that placed emphasis on the inward and outward aspects of existence, respectively, Qutb presented Islam as taking care of both, which reciprocally validated Islamic faith on its different cognitive levels: an emotional faith in God and a rational belief in the perfection of the sociopolitical system.[119]

Qutb's theory of the Islamic state was the result of the introduction of the issue of politics into his aesthetic project. The connection between the two is especially salient in his theory of Islamic literature (*al-adab al-islāmī*), discussed in detail in the next chapter. In a short essay on Islamic literature published a few months before his arrest in 1954, Qutb continued to define art as an inspired expression of a higher spiritual truth. What changed in relation to his earlier Romantic vision of the arts was the mission that Islamic literature was to fulfill in the sensate world: the command to serve for the improvement of the human condition. In line with the postwar centering of intellectual work on the value of political action, Qutb defined his Islamic literature as "guiding art" (*al-fann al-muwājih*) that would strive to elevate humankind both materially and spiritually.[120] This is how Qutb managed to argue that his Islamic political and aesthetic theory was a more progressive ideology than that of the progressives of the time: the Left.

4

Literature in the Margins

The previous chapter ended with an image of different political and cultural antiestablishment groups working together to bring down the monarchy, as represented by the *udabā'* generation, parliamentary regime, and "moderate" means of political action, such as elections and negotiations with occupying forces. In imagining the shape of Egypt's independent society, revolutionary groups of varying political orientations blended Marxist critique, such as social justice and anticapitalism, with the demands of the Muslim Brotherhood, such as the importance of moral—or "clean"—culture in securing intellectual and territorial autonomy. With the arrival of the Free Officers Revolution in the summer of 1952, the doctrinal fluidity and indetermination of the postwar period started to dissipate. By attempting to tame and co-opt activists, Free Officers contributed to fissuring of the ranks of the antiestablishment camp. Part of the process of the postrevolutionary crystallization of political identities was the drive to better define the terms that in postwar activism were merely used as slogans.

One of these terms was *niẓām*, or the sociopolitical order of the future independent state, which provided the main battlefield for intellectual polemics. The questions of private property and class struggle were identified as the main points of conflict between Marxist and Islamist intellectuals. Another battlefield was literature and the notion of *iltizām*. As we have seen in the previous chapter, while the notion of *iltizām* served as a unifying slogan in postwar criticism of the *udabā'*, years after the 1952 Revolution intellectuals started to question the concrete meaning of literary commitment. Commitment to what exactly? How did it relate to Marxism and its avatar, social realism? What did "realism" mean? Was it the commitment to the improvement of mortal or spiritual life?

By the mid-1950s, Qutb had taken some distance from literary affairs—not because he broke with literature, but in line with the general trend of postwar politics. Qutb understood that producing literature without rethinking its epistemological basis would only lead to reproducing colonial literatures of the interwar years. He came to the conclusion that culture was a reflection of a larger epistemological order, such as materialism, or *māddīyya*, in the case of social realism and idealism, or *mithālīyya*, which provided the basis for Romanticism and for literary production of the interwar generation. Realizing that Islam needed a similar system of thought, Qutb started working on a project that would remain his focus until his death: the creation of an Islamic epistemology, *al-taṣawwur al-islāmī*. As a mere emanation, or a branch, of *al-taṣawwur al-islāmī*, literature was, as a result, pushed to the margins.

However, the renewed war on literature and commitment that pitted Taha Husayn and young Marxists against each other in 1954 provided the occasion for Qutb to publish a short essay on specifically Islamist literature (*al-adab al-islāmī*). Published in *Majallat al-Ikhwan al-Muslimin*, Qutb's essay invited fellow Muslim Brothers to invest in Islamist literary production that would be more attentive to the spiritual dimensions of humankind than Marxist literature. It was Qutb's brother Muhammad and sisters Hamida and Amina who picked up the idea of *al-adab al-islāmī* and channeled their energies to make it a reality.

This chapter examines Qutb's project of *al-adab al-islāmī* from the historical perspective of attempts to differentiate Islamist culture from its rival forms, which were dismissed as vulgar or blasphemous. Examining the debates on the production of fiction and poetry published in the reformist and Islamist press throughout the first five decades of the twentieth century, it traces the conceptual history of *al-adab al-islāmī* in order to identify the debates surrounding the construction of a specifically Islamic cultural heritage. What type of *adab* was deemed acceptable, and under what conditions did it evolve into being labeled as Islamist? How did Qutb's proposed idea of Islamist literature differ from and resemble former Islamist approaches to highbrow and popular culture?

In responding to these questions, this chapter examines Islamist literary production in historical continuity with similar debates that were taking place in the press of balanced reform. The reason for this is the fact that Muslim youth organizations, such as the Young Men's Muslim Association (YMMA) and, to a lesser degree, the Muslim Brotherhood, inherited a significant portion of their literary heritage from the movement of balanced reform. Considering the movement of balanced reform and Islamism together allows us to grasp the direction in which literary sensibilities evolved, revealing the importance of generational and class dynamics in the appreciation of different genres. The chapter is organized around a discussion of three different initiatives of creating a specifically Islamic culture: the project of an Islamic Iliad initiated by the key figure in the Salafiyya Bookstore and Publishing House, Muhibb al-Din al-Khatib in the 1930s; the attempts to create Islamist popular culture, such as fiction, theater, and religious anthems; and the project of Islamist art elaborated by Sayyid and Muhammad Qutb in the first years of the Revolution.

Looking for an Islamic Poet

In August 1933, the leader of the Muslim Brotherhood, Hasan al-Banna, published a short essay praising "two poets of Islam": Muhammad Sadiq 'Arnus and Muhammad Hasan al-Nijmi.[1] What did al-Banna mean by "poets of Islam," and how different were they from poets understood broadly? Judging from the poetry of 'Arnus and al-Nijmi published in the periodicals associated with the Salafiyya Bookstore and Publishing House, "poetry of Islam" was defined by the commitment to multiple causes with which the Bookstore's circle identified itself during the late interwar period. "When he spoke, cried, rejoiced, or wished," al-Banna wrote of 'Arnus, his friend and a long-term companion in the Muslim Brotherhood, "it was always for the sake of Islam's victory." Naturally, when 'Arnus wrote poetry, he did so also for Islam.

Born in Upper Egypt in 1895 and 1875, respectively, 'Arnus and al-Nijmi were not only talented poets but also active members of the emerging Islamic associational scene in Cairo. In addition to being a member of the Muslim Brotherhood, 'Arnus was involved in the pious association Ansar al-Sunna al-Muhammadiyya, founded in Cairo in 1926; worked as an editor of the association's mouthpiece, *Hadi al-Nabawi* (The Prophet's

Guidance); and contributed poetry to Muhibb al-Din al-Khatib's numerous periodicals.[2] Differently from 'Arnus, who wore the garment of a sheikh, al-Nijmi dressed as an efendi. He served as a secretary of a branch of the YMMA, founded in Cairo in 1927 by the al-Khatib's initiative. Both authors wrote poetry that reflected their commitment to the Salafiyya circle and its struggles: rhymed commentary about public affairs, the struggle against "Westernizers" and poetry composed on the occasion of social events in al-Khatib's circle.[3] Rather than by aesthetic principles, their qualification as Islamic poets stemmed from their proximity to the network that identified itself with the defense of Islam.

Al-Banna's talk on Islamic poets reflected rising anxieties of the Bookstore's circle that the arts, and reform more generally, were taking a wrong path. Not only had the reform movement been hijacked, in their view, by secularists such as Taha Husayn, but also the arts were increasingly detached from their service to the Arab political unity and social cohesion. The birth of the interest in specifically Islamic poetry embodies the shift in interest of an important portion of balanced reformers from the reform of literature to the defense of Islam. Traditionally, literature occupied a central role in the balanced reformers' effort to reinvigorate the arts of language and to combat the scholasticism and formalism of the postclassical tradition.[4]

Muhammad 'Abdu held that the decline of literary language and eloquence was one of the reasons for Arab cultural stagnation. He spent great effort in tracing and editing manuscripts in order to revive the rich literary tradition of the classical period and was the driving force behind the introduction of Arab literature in al-Azhar.[5] In the same vein, 'Abdu objected to the use of the colloquial Arabic in Egypt's satirical periodicals, which frequently targeted him.[6] A number of intellectuals involved in the reform movement were poets themselves, and even more of them translated poetry. A cosmopolitan gentleman, Shakib Arslan loved both reading and composing poetry, and it was Rashid Rida who published his collection of poems in 1935.[7] Likewise, Muhibb al-Din al-Khatib was enamored with the Ottoman poetry that he voraciously read and translated during his youth. When he came across Ahmad Shawqi's work while pursuing his studies in Istanbul, he could not measure his excitement that poetry of a similar quality to Ottoman existed in his native Arabic.[8] Soon he became familiar with other contemporary Arab poets, such as Khalil Mutran, al-Kashif, and al-Rusafi, whose verses he quoted in his correspondence. The visit of the Bengali poet Rabindranath Tagore to Cairo in 1926–27, during which he was received by the King Fu'ad and encountered Ahmad Shawqi, sparked a wave of enthusiasm among the Salafiyya circle. Its members cited Tagore's poetry as the example of a reformed *adab* and credited his visit with the literary awakening in Egypt.[9] Al-Khatib expressed his admiration of Tagore by writing his biography.[10]

The literary awakening meant the realization that Arab poetry was in dire need of a reform. First, reformers maintained, it needed to be detached from its customary role of being recited on social occasions and placed at the service of the community.[11] Viewed from the perspective of the debates that flared up in Egypt after World War II, literature advocated by balanced reformers had always been defined by commitment. Al-Khatib placed high expectations on poets for sparking Arab cultural revival and considered them the "owners of the keys to people's hearts" who had the power to forge Arab unity, show the way to the national strength, and purify souls from vice and subservience.[12] Rashid Rida similarly argued for the power of literature to instill pride and love for the Arab nation, as well as its religion and history, and dedicated a section in his journal *al-Manar* to contemporary poetry. As the editor of a highly reputable periodical, Rida regularly received novels authored by journalists, civil servants, and other efendis experimenting with new forms of literary expression. He briefly reviewed their works, praising them for their social benefit or criticizing them if they focused only on love. In one of his earliest comments on the topic, a review of the novel *Al-Yatim* (The Orphan), published in 1898, Rida gave advice concerning the topics on which writers should focus: "The best topics for novels [*riwāyyāt*] are those that guide the youth in general, and students in particular, towards the love of their country and the service of their community according to its present needs. It needs to show them that this cannot be achieved in isolation of actions and virtues of religion."[13]

In their view, one of the beneficial effects contained in modern forms of fiction was the communication of knowledge and norms to the uneducated parts of society in order to reduce the gap between social classes. The entertaining aspect of this type of literature, they argued, was useful for the instruction of the masses, who were unable to access scholarly texts of religion. As such, fiction could be used as the basis for a reformed society, which, by narrowing the divide between the elite (*khāssa*) and the public (*'āmma*), would create "the nation as a chain," as Rida explained in 1908. In his introduction to the novel on the Prophet Muhammad's first wife Khadija, serialized in *al-Manar* the same year, he went as far as to draw a parallel between Muhammad 'Abdu's scholarly texts, which only learned men could digest, and novels intended for the less educated.[14] By suggesting the use of fiction as the medium of instruction, reformers worried about the harm that the spread of literacy could inflict on the so-called "vulnerable" parts of society, such as women and the youth.[15] Expanding literacy to populations that had traditionally been excluded from the circuit of formal education precipitated anxieties about upsetting social hierarchies. Reformers attempted to offset the risks by putting all the responsibility on the shoulders of the authors, who were expected to handle their newly given right to a public voice with care, by following tacit rules of form and content.[16]

The rise of Romantic notions of literature as the unhindered expression of an author's subjectivity significantly reinforced these anxieties. The Salafiyya circle frowned upon al-'Aqqad's open attacks against the poetry of Ahmad Shawqi,[17] and they warned against the dangers of blindly imitating the West in literary expression.[18] Taha Husayn's discussion on Abu Nuwas, the Abbasid poet famous for his "bawdy" poetry that invoked drinking and sexual desire,[19] and Salama Musa's promotion of *al-adab al-makshūf* (erotic literature) as a means to relieve psychological tensions in Egyptian society, sent a shock wave through reformist circles.[20] Taking a position against the severing of the link between *adab* and morality, reformers argued that Musa's *al-adab al-makshūf* was the exact opposite of *adab*—namely, *qillat al-adab* (vulgarity).[21] In 1927, al-Khatib took a firm stand against the notion of "arts for the art's sake" in his editorial in *al-Zahra*. Denying that it was freedom that defined the arts, he pondered, "Does a poet or artist live for himself or the community? If he lives for the community, does he want [his art] to be like cocaine that pleases and harms, or like a flower that pleases and is beneficial?"[22] In his view, the degree of freedom allowed in the arts should reflect the level of progress achieved in a given society, and if Western nations were immune to the potential harms inflicted by noncontrolled literary production, the fragile nations of the East could not afford such a luxury. As long as the Arabs were in decline, al-Khatib maintained, artists were defined by their task to provide strong spiritual foundations to a united, industrious, and morally upright Arab nation.[23]

The shift of reformers from the task of revitalizing language through the edition of classical manuscripts in light of concerns of morality created a tension between aesthetics and morality in their appreciation of the arts. On the one hand, the intellectuals of the Salafiyya Bookstore and Publishing House argued for the preservation of the literary style of the period stretching from pre-Islamic to early Abbasid literature,[24] and they considered classical poets (such as Bashshar bin Burd, al-Buhturi, or the compiler of *Nahj al-Balagha* Sharif Radi) and prose writers (such as al-Jahiz and Ibn al-Muqafa') as the paragons of eloquence.[25] The preservation of classical eloquence was, in their view, necessary to confront the calls to simplify written Arabic and to prevent more significant reforms from taking place, such as those in Turkey, where Mustafa Ataturk's decision to replace the Arabic alphabet with the Latin script condemned to oblivion the rich Ottoman book culture.[26] On the other hand, the threat of the corrupting influence of classical authors on untrained readers led them to revise their previous stances on some poets. The appreciation of the eight-century poet Bashshar bin Burd—who reportedly spread atheist views, composed erotic poetry, and was executed on the orders of the Abbasid caliph—epitomized this tension. Despite his scandalous reputation, Bashshar bin Burd was one of the most appreciated classical poets among the Bookstore's intellectuals.[27] This contradiction illustrates the situation in which reformers found themselves when reframing their cause around the defense of Islam: they remained loyal to their earlier commitment to uncovering classical Arab tradition, and they devoted themselves to their new role as the guardians of morality and religion.

The anxieties sparked by the rise of Taha Husayn's generation, who claimed that literature (*adab*) should be committed to nothing but freedom, provided the backdrop for the need to create a specifically Islamic literature. The urge to establish an "Islamic poet" appeared with the passing of Ahmad Shawqi in 1932. For many, his death signaled the end of an epoch. Writing his obituary, al-Khatib lamented the "intellectual chaos" (*fawḍa fikrīyya*) that characterized the decade in which poetry had become the property of "propagators of atheism," "tavern dwellers," and those who composed poetry to please their passions.[28] For him, Shawqi's work represented the highest living example of what modern literature should look like. From the perspective of the form, he followed the classical styles of Arab eloquence, while writing on issues relevant to the cause of Islam and Arabs, as evidenced by his collection *Duwwal al-'Arab wa 'Uzama al-Islam* (The States of Arabs and the Great Men of Islam) published in 1923.

Just before Shawqi's death, al-Khatib had tasked him with "a very big mission": to compose a *diwān* that would stand as a monument to the past glories of Islam of equivalent importance as "the Greek Iliad by Homer, and the Persian Shahnameh by Fardusi."[29] Shawqi agreed, but he passed away before al-Khatib could pay him a visit to discuss the details. The mission was then passed on to another neoclassicist poet, Ahmad Muharram. Another poet, Ahmad Zaki Abu Shadi—who was associated with the Salafiyya Bookstore and Publishing House and whom we encountered in chapter 1 as the founder of the Apollo Poet Society—enthusiastically supported the decision to confer the mission on Muharram, a truly "Islamic poet" capable of sparking "Islam's awakening in literature and arts."[30] Departing from Muharram's example, the poet that he personally admired, Abu Shadi insisted that Islam could not necessarily be served by didactic literature or the celebration of the Arab past, but rather by the capacity of poetry to convey its spiritual meanings. The epic, entitled *Diwan Majd al-Islam*, or the "Islamic Iliad," was completed before Muharram passed away in the mid-1940s.

In the coming decades, the Bookstore's circle would witness sporadic attempts to spark the movement of "Islamic poetry," without tangible success. In 1944, a young Azhari student named Mustafa Ahmad al-Rifa'i al-Labban returned to the topic of Islamic poetry and attempted to define it as poetry composed by Shawqi, Muharram, and al-Nijmi. A loyal reader of *al-Manar*, an associate of al-Khatib's circle, and a member of both the

YMMA and the Muslim Brotherhood, al-Labban was a vocal proponent of the need to reform the arts along the lines of Islamist commitment. He was one of the earliest voices to draw attention to the benefits that popular forms of culture, such as fiction and cinema, could have on society if placed at the service of Islam. But, in describing specific features Islamic poets were expected to embody, al-Labban did not depart from the established identification of Islamic poets with the historical themes of Arab greatness.[31]

In many regards, poetry defined as Islamic corresponded to the neoclassical canon that balanced reformers personally admired. Yet the emerging need of poets to label their poetry as Islamic indicated a desire to snatch literature from the hands of "tavern dwellers and propagators of atheism" and to place it at the service of Islam. These attempts laid the foundations for the specific literary heritage to which Islamist movements would refer as their own. The effort to create a specifically Islamic culture were continued by those who considered themselves legitimate successors of the Salafiyya circle: the efendi youth of the YMMA and the Muslim Brotherhood.

The Rise of the Youth: Short Stories, Theater, and Religious Anthems

Dominated by poetry, the Salafiyya Bookstore and Publishing House showed little interest in fiction. The limited concern for storytelling did not stem from ideological opposition to this particular genre. As we have seen, reformers recognized the potential of novels and short stories to communicate beneficial content through entertainment. The circle's limited concern for prose was more likely related to the lack of individuals interested in writing stories for them to publish. It could also be attributed to the factors of social class and the traditional modes of distribution of authority, which privileged seniors over the youth. Traditionally, the movement of balanced reform was driven by men of nobility. Muhammad 'Abdu's family belonged to the rural elite of the Nile Delta that claimed Prophetic descent and held the position of village mayors (*'umda*). Rashid Rida came from a similar background in Tripoli and held the distinctive title of *sayyid*, indicating noble descent.[32] As seen earlier, the Salafiyya circle counted among its allies prominent Arab dignitaries such as the Druze prince Shakib Arslan or Ahmad Taymur, whose family boasted a friendship with Muhammad ʿAli. Even the younger members of the circle, such as the poet Abu Shadi or the future editor Mahmud Shakir, hailed from prominent intellectual families who had the interest in the print-initiated reform and sufficient means to undertake it.[33]

As a quintessential efendi genre, fiction came to the fore as the result of the gradual handover of the Islamic mission to the emerging middle-class youth. Starting with the late 1920s, Egypt's associational scene saw the proliferation of youth organizations: the founding of the YMMA in 1927, and a year later of the Muslim Brotherhood. These organizations attest to the gradual shift of Islamic activism from the hands of intellectual nobility to middle-class youth, who relied on new modes of action, distrusted conventional politics, and formed alternative grassroots political movements. Such a development was consistent with the rise of youth activism in the 1930s, a decade marked by the prominence of scout culture, the emergence of radical youth organizations, frequent street demonstrations and university strikes, and the formation of paramilitary wings of established political parties.[34]

Within the reform movement, the handing over of the leadership from seniors to juniors took place gradually as well. Modeled after the Egyptian branch of the Young Men's Christian Association, the YMMA represented this transition, being an organization in which the importance of the youth had been recognized but the command was still kept in the hands of the seniors. Instead of an organization run by the youth, the YMMA was founded *for* the youth, which was placed under the attentive eye of sheikhs. Created by the core members of the Salafiyya Bookstore and Publishing House—namely, al-Khatib, Ahmad Taymour, and sheikh al-Khidr Husayn—the YMMA accorded limited visibility to the youth.[35] All its administrative and editorial positions were occupied by local dignitaries. Instead, young members of the organization filled the ranks of Rover troops (*jawwāla*) or acted as lay preachers.[36] Despite its portrayal as a youth organization, the YMMA was governed by the vestigial rules of the distribution of authority: young people were associated with action, and elders with knowledge. Illustrative in this regard is the title "sheikh of the Muslim youth," by which the president of the YMMA, 'Abd al-Hamid Sa'id, was sometimes called.[37]

With the expansion of the Muslim Brotherhood, middle-class youth rose to the forefront of Islamic activism. It was precisely the frustration with the elitist bent of the reform movement that prompted Hassan al-Banna—a regular visitor to the Bookstore and a member of YMMA—to create his own organization.[38] Founded in 1928 in Ismailia, the city situated on the bank of the Suez Canal, the Brotherhood first recruited its members from artisans, traders, and drivers working for the Suez Canal Company, but, with its move to Cairo in 1932, its demographics changed to include urban-educated youth.[39] At its onset, the Brotherhood devised a number of policies intended to ensure the organization's financial and ideological autonomy from wealthy notables—autonomy that would later earn them the accusation of being a "state within the state." One of these policies consisted of launching internal campaigns to generate funds in which members themselves bought shares and became owners of the Brotherhood's institutions.[40] It was by means of such campaigns that the organization acquired its own printing press in the mid-1930s and emancipated itself from the influence of reformist figures on whom it had relied during its formative phase.[41] While the first periodical of the Brotherhood, published between 1933 and 1938, still partly relied on the authority of senior scholars such as the retired Dar al-'Ulum teacher, the "sheikh-philosopher" Tantawi al-Jawhari, who acted as its editor, and Muhibb al-Din al-Khatib, who, in exchange for two pounds, gave the Brotherhood access to its printing services, the production of its later journal *al-Nadhir* (The Warner), launched in 1939, was fully produced by the members of the organization.[42] In fact, by the mid-1930s al-Banna had become a figure of authority himself, as indicated by his assumption of the editorship of *al-Manar*, which had stopped publishing in 1935 following Rida's passing. Although he still had to be introduced by the sheikh al-Azhar Mustafa al-Maraghi, al-Banna's takeover of *al-Manar* suggests that at this point he had acquired sufficient legitimacy to position himself as Rida's intellectual heir.[43]

The shift of intellectual authority from intellectual nobility to the efendi class went hand in hand with the promotion of forms of cultural expression that were associated with youth culture such as novellas, theater plays, and religious anthems (*anāshīd*). In 1928, young writer Muhammad ʿAli Gharib attempted to introduce fiction into the Salafiyya circle's periodicals. Entitled "Session with the Satan," the story depicted Kemalist reforms as the Satan's ploy, who seduced the army to abandon religion, abrogate the caliphate, liberate women, and adopt Western dress. But, instead of the promised power and glory, the reforms brought famine and a wave of suicides.[44] Muhammad ʿAli Gharib was one of those authors who rarely make it into literary histories; he was less of a writer than an active member of the vibrant Cairo's literary scene, who started his literary career in al-Khatib's journal, *al-Fath*, moved on to other venues (such as the *Apollo* magazine or *al-Risala*), and reached the peak of his publishing activity under Nasser.[45]

Two years later, the idea of using fiction to transmit didactic content was picked up by the young intellectual Mustafa al-Labban. As a committed member of the circle, he aimed to introduce fiction in a systematic way, creating a section in *al-Fath* entitled "al-Qassas al-Diniyya" (Religious Stories). In his description of the section, he explained that his purpose was to popularize Islamic themes among the youth. "The youth rush upon illustrated magazines, which publish novels and stories to which they lean and get passionate about," he lamented. "At the same time, they push religious magazines away for their assumed dryness that inspires boredom to their bursting souls which long for fun and the taking-off."[46] Thus, al-Labban concluded, the most efficient way to spark the youth's interest in religion was to provide them with Islamic stories. In the following months he regularly published stories that portrayed young men on the path of *al-daʿwa*, denounced the indiscriminate pursuit of Western ways of life, or aimed to show the correct way to approach women for marriage.

In 1935, *al-Fath* welcomed another novella writer, this time from faraway Indonesia. Pursuing his studies in Azhar, ʿAbdallah bin Nouh al-Indunusi was also a poet and one of the future influential scholars of Islam in Indonesia. Under the headline of "al-Qissat al-Khayaliyya" (Fictional Story), he published three utopian stories.[47] This was followed by the emergence of yet another section dedicated to short stories, entitled "Islamic Short Stories Not for Children."[48] Different qualifications of novella—religious, fictional, or "not for children"—indicated a certain confusion around the genre.

The attempts to spark the movement of Islamist fiction continued in the Muslim Brotherhood's press. In the August 1933 issue of the *Jaridat al-Ikhwan al-Muslimin*, Hasan al-Banna introduced a section for short stories under the headline of "al-qassas al-waqaʿīyya" (Realistic Stories). Al-Banna inaugurated the section by authoring a novella himself, which provided the main template for what Islamic stories should look like. Entitled "Uncle Sayyid," the story is built on al-Banna's memories as a schoolboy, when he, together with his classmates, would gather around the school's aged janitor Sayyid to listen to him speak about Andalusia. The old man's stories, al-Banna noted, contained two critical elements that guaranteed the utility of storytelling: entertainment and a lesson from history. While the captivating storytelling attracted al-Banna's interest as a child, he understood the historical meaning of the tragedy of Andalusia only in adulthood.[49]

Short stories became a regular feature of the Brotherhood's other periodical, *al-Nadhir*. Mostly written by ʿAli Yusuf ʿAllam, the stories reflected efendi anxieties and concerns in the midst of the uprising against the British. One story published in *al-Nadhir* is of particular interest in the context of our discussion on Islamism and fiction, since it hints at the young Muslim Brothers' vision of the arts; it describes an artist from Upper Egypt, who, convinced that art belongs to the realm of the soul, abandons himself to spirituality, excessive piety, and asceticism. But all of this changes upon his arrival in Cairo, where he gets involved with women, gambling, and dubious associates. From a kind-hearted and shy young man, he develops into a witty, cunning, and life-loving bohemian. From his former idea of art as a matter of soul, he comes to believe that art consists of elegance and finery and is not related to any obligation to live a virtuous life. The story reaches its climax when the artist falls in love with his friend's fiancée while drawing her portrait and attempts to seduce her. Yet, as bad deeds bring retribution, the girl turns out to be the lover of a wealthy man. Deeply disappointed, the artist listens to the advice of his friend and joins the Muslim Brotherhood.[50] In the succession of events that bind together the dangers of the artistic milieu in Cairo, male friendship, the corruption of women, and local notables, the story aims to present the Muslim Brotherhood as the way to salvation.

If, in the circles of Islamist activists, storytelling became the privileged form of expression, poetry still retained its appeal. Yet its function had changed: it was set to melody (*talḥīn*) and turned into galvanizing religious anthems (*anāshīd*) intended to maintain the high spirits of the youth. Since the YMMA was the Bookstore's offspring, it was the circle's poets that took up the mission of creating songs for the organization. In 1928, Ahmad Muttalib, Ahmad Muharram, Hafiz Ibrahim, and Ahmad Shawqi took part in the poetry competition organized by the Bookstore. But the winner was the poet Mustafa Sadiq al-Rafiʿi, whose poem "Rabbuna Iyaka Nadʿu" (O Lord, To You We Pray) was selected as the YMMA's anthem.[51]

The Salafiyya Bookstore and Publishing House had yet another challenge to face: to find an appropriate composer to pick a melody for setting al-Rafiʿi's poem to music. In 1934, al-Khatib published a desperate editorial in which he admitted that all the efforts to turn this poem into a *nashīd* had been in vain. Among the reasons that made finding a composer difficult, al-Khatib cited the decline of musical culture in Egypt, which favored songs on love and passion instead of those reminding the Egyptians of the values of nation, sacrifice, and courage. But today, al-Khatib continued, with the visit of Iraqi and Palestinian scouts to Cairo, the time had come to take concrete steps toward the creation of a morally responsible melody.

To this effect, the YMMA set up a Committee for Uplifting Anthems and Nationalist songs in Egypt and Arab Countries (Lajna li-Tarqiya al-Aghani al-Qawmiyya fi Misr wa Bilad al-ʿArabiyya), and announced a competition for "patriotic, moral and social" poems, which would be based on enthusiasm and advocacy of the association's principles. Over three hundred poets, writers, and musicians were brought together to discuss the practical ways to use music to stir up enthusiasm among the Egyptian youth.[52] One of those invited was the composer and songwriter Muhammad ʿAbd al-Wahab, who had just hit the Egyptian cinematic scene with his 1933 debut film *al-Warda al-Bayda* (The White Rose). In the course of a decade, ʿAbd al-Wahab would turn from a gifted musician sympathetic to the patriotic concerns of the Islamic organization into a symbol of imperialism and cultural decay widely decried by the guardians of high culture.[53] At approximately the same time, in 1934, the Muslim Brotherhood acquired their first *nashid*. The poem was composed by sheikh Ahmad Hasan al-Baquri, a senior figure in the Brotherhood who would join the government of the Free Officers following the Revolution in 1952. Entitled "Ya Rasul Allah" (O Prophet of the God), the poem was melodized and turned into the anthem of its Rover Scout Unit.[54] Later, this highly popular anthem was replaced by another one, entitled "Huwa al-Haqq Yahshud Ajnadahu" (Justice Mobilizes Its Soldiers), created by the Brotherhood's long-term member and secretary ʿAbd al-Hakim ʿAbdin.[55]

To fully grasp the significance of these initiatives, it is crucial to consider them in relation to the increasing anxieties concerning popular culture during the interwar period. By the 1930s, the feeling that popular culture had been lost to the entertainment industry was shared by many exponents of high culture, including Sayyid Qutb. Concerns about popular culture rose in parallel to the increasing role the means of its transmission—radio, cinema, and illustrated magazines—came to play in the lives of Egyptians during this period.[56] The YMMA's initiative to bring together poets, musicians, and "other representatives of popular art" (*fann*) under its roof represented precisely an attempt to reverse this situation by snatching popular culture from morally dubious and irresponsible artists and redirecting it toward the Islamic vision of reform. This aim echoes al-Labban's motivations for writing fictional Islamic stories, which, he hoped, would help to redirect the attention of the youth from illustrated magazines to religious publications.

These initiatives met with a certain degree of success in the area of theater. As has been noted, theater is definitely the genre in which the Brotherhood, as well as other Islamist groups, managed to leave its footprint.[57] In the ranks of the Muslim Brothers, the high level of attention paid to theater was certainly due to the personal interest of one of the founding members of the organization: the brother of Hasan al-Banna, ʿAbd al-Rahman al-Banna (al-Saʿati). Two years al-Banna's junior, ʿAbd al-Rahman facilitated the Brotherhood's expansion in Cairo when he turned his own association into the Brotherhood's Cairo office.[58] ʿAbd al-Rahman was a young man of many talents; he excelled in poetry and history, supplied the Brotherhood's press with a number of enthusiastic poems, and wrote a series of essays on Islamic personalities published under his supervised historical section in the Brotherhood's first periodical. He merged these two interests by producing historical theater plays. For his first play, published in 1933, he chose a classical Arab poet, Jamil Buthayna, as the subject of the play, which put forward the virtues of chaste love. Advertised as an example of "chastity, loyalty and emotion" and of the Islamic teachings applied to family life, the play was an immediate success.[59] Its performance was financially supported by the Ministry of Education and involved many famous actors of the time, such as Georges Abyad, Mahmud al-Maliji, and Fatima Rushdi.

Encouraged by the success, al-Banna produced a number of edifying plays set in the Islamic past. Some of the plays were staged in the restricted framework of the Muslim Brotherhood, but many others reached out to a general theater audience. In fact, rather than being an activity exclusively reserved for the members of the Muslim Brotherhood, its organized theater activities often relied on cooperation with famous actors, producers, and musicians. The Brotherhood's theater notably collaborated with a rising folk singer, Malak, who performed al-Banna's rhymed theater play Su'di, as well as with the famous composer Ahmad 'Abd al-Qadir. As a result, al-Banna's plays were performed in popular cultural venues such as the opera or the theater of Ezbekiyya.[60] The expansion of theatrical activities associated with the Brotherhood to general audiences testifies to its considerable success in gaining leverage in popular culture.

Al-Banna's personal influence aside, the appeal of theater within the Brotherhood can also be explained by its changing target audience, which shifted from essentially intellectual and educated social strata (as was the case in the Bookstore) to the masses. Theater provided both the most efficient means of reaching a wider audience and the most convenient framework for involving the Brotherhood's members in the activities of the organization. According to the historian 'Asim Talima, almost every branch (*shu'ba*) of the Muslim Brotherhood had its own theater troupe, which was founded within its student section and in which members were trained to act.[61] An amateur playwright and a member of the Brotherhood, Mahmud 'Abd al-Halim narrated his experience of founding a theater troupe within the Brotherhood's branch in Fuwwa village, located in the governorate of Kafr El Sheikh. According to ʿAbd al-Halim, upon his arrival in the village there was no entertainment offered to the population, which provided a golden opportunity for the Brotherhood to establish its own theater and thereby transfer "Islamic ideas into the minds of peasants and youth." ʿAbd al-Halim wrote two plays portraying historical events in Islam, both in classical Arabic. But in order to better reach the peasantry, he decided to compose another play in colloquial Arabic on a well-worn anti-Semitic canard: a warning against usurious practices by Jewish loan-bankers. ʿAbd al-Halim concluded, perhaps not without exaggeration, that the initiative was a roaring success: it was attended by "thousands" and changed the lives of many people in the village, including a wealthy notable who, blown away by the Brotherhood's performances, made the pilgrimage.[62]

In the period following World War II, culture labeled "Islamic" or "religious" had acquired a stable presence in Egypt. The YMMA had founded its own theater troupe, which performed in general theater venues from the mid-1940s. Even Azhari students succeeded in forming their own theater troupe in 1949 after years of efforts to persuade the Azhari authorities of the benefits of this art.[63] The ranks of the Muslim Brotherhood witnessed an increase in authors interested in writing religious plays. Sabir ʿAbdo Ibrahim produced a series of plays on the Prophet's Companions, and the famous playwright ʿAli Ahmad Bakathir contributed some of his plays to the Brotherhood's press.[64] The Azhari sheikh Ahmad al-Sharbasi, who in Nasser's time would become one of the first preachers on television, wrote religious scripts for the stage and cinema. The majority of theater plays produced by the Brotherhood, YMMA, and Azharis fall within the most common definition of Islamic art, which had as its setting the history of Islam and intended to act as a lesson or as a guide for behavior. In order to differentiate their religious-oriented art from rival forms of theater, Islamic theater had to respect certain limitations, such as the historical accuracy of the events portrayed, the absence of women performers, and the interdiction against performing the roles of Prophets.[65]

However, the line of division between forms of culture cultivated in the circles of Islamic activism and the other forms of arts remained vague. Like modernist writers of the *udabā'* generation, who by the 1930s set out to produce entertaining and easily accessible stories about Islam, Islamists also attempted to use entertainment as means of disseminating Islamic norms and ideals. Despite the crisis of confidence that shook the Egyptian literary community following World War II, described in chapter 3, cultural production by modernist writers was cited by the Muslim Brothers as being consistent with the aims of the *da'wa*. Anwar al-Jundi compared the plays produced by fellow member of the Muslim Brotherhood Anas al-Hijaji to Tawfiq al-Hakim's theater plays; another writer cited writings by Husayn, al-Hakim, al-Mazni, and Zaki Mubarak as examples of excellent literature, and the Muslim Brotherhood included Haykal's *Hayat Muhammad* in the reading list of its training program for preachers.[66] Sayyid and Muhammad Qutb's theories on Islamist aesthetics would dramatically reverse this situation, drawing a sharp line of division between Islamist and other forms of art.

The Qutb Brothers and the Theory of Islamist Aesthetics

Sayyid Qutb published his short essay on Islamist literature in May 1954, in reaction to the heated debates on commitment and the arts that opposed the dean of Arab letters, Taha Husayn, and young Marxist intellectuals. Started by Husayn with a routine piece on literature, the confrontation was part of the longer struggle that the emerging postwar generation was waging against the *udabā'* under the pretext of the latter's lack of political commitment, as seen in the previous chapter.[67] Qutb followed the debate from prison, where he was sent after the January 1954 clashes between the Muslim Brotherhood with the regime's Liberation Rally, and after his release in April wrote his own contribution to the debate. In an essay published in the first issue of his edited *Majallat al-Ikhwan al-Muslimin* under the title "Manhaj al-Adab" (The Method of Literature), Qutb distanced himself from both Husayn's and Marxist understandings of literature. Islam, he argued, had its own vision of the arts, which rested on its particular epistemology, *al-taṣawwur al-islāmī*, with respect to humankind, universe, and life.[68]

Responding to the broad issue of commitment that preoccupied Egypt's intellectuals since the late 1940s, but published in a marginal periodical of the Muslim Brotherhood, Qutb's essay aimed to open the discussion on the form the arts should take to fit with the Islamist anticolonial commitment. Indeed, Qutb's article prompted an avalanche of contributions by fellow Muslim Brothers who grappled with the notion of *al-adab al-islāmī* and its connection to the traditional arts produced in Muslim lands. One of the contributors to the debate was Qutb's younger brother, Muhammad. A poet, translator, and rising author in his own right, Muhammad Qutb expanded on his criticism on Husayn's and Marxist visions on arts and suggested a third solution to their respective notions of literature "the art for the art's sake" and "the art for the society": arts had to serve the society, while resting on stable foundations of religion.[69] Almost a decade later, when Qutb was languishing in Nasser's prison, Muhammad Qutb returned to the topic with a more elaborate study. In his book *Manhaj al-Fann al-Islami* (The Method of Islamist Art), published in 1963, he suggested a sweeping theory of Islamist aesthetics, providing guidelines for artistic production for those who followed the Islamic way of life. Muhammad Qutb described the superiority of his approach relative to dominant Western intellectual and artistic trends, demonstrated the primordial link between religion and the arts, and specified the way in which the Islamic worldview influenced the process of artistic creation. In his selection of literary pieces that qualified as Islamic, Muhammad Qutb included short stories produced by his two sisters, Amina and Hamida. Since its inception, the project of Islamist literature was a genuine family affair.

It is unusual to consider the two Qutb's brothers' intellectual work jointly. An age gap of thirteen years separated Sayyid and his brother Muhammad, born in 1906 and 1919, respectively. Sayyid seems to have been more of a father to Muhammad than an equal partner in an intellectual exchange, just as he was to his other younger siblings, sisters Amina and Hamida, born in 1927 and 1937. The towering role played by Sayyid in Muhammad's intellectual formation is attested by his influence on his brother's educational career, as well as on the channeling of his interests toward literature. It was Sayyid who advised Muhammad to enroll at the Faculty of English Language and Literature in Cairo University to acquire expertise in Western literatures and intellectual trends.[70] It was also Sayyid who initiated his siblings' literary beginnings in the family's common project dedicated to the memory of their late mother, the 1945 book *al-Atyaf al-Arbaʿa* (The Four Phantoms). It was also Qutb who prefaced and facilitated the publication of Muhammad's first translated anthology in 1947.[71] That Muhammad had been the locus of Sayyid's particular aspirations is suggested by the fact that it was to him that Sayyid dedicated his first poetry collection in 1935.

However, from the early 1950s, it becomes increasingly difficult to distinguish the Qutb brothers' intellectual contributions from each one another. Sayyid and Muhammad Qutb seem to have been in constant conversation while developing the comprehensive paradigm of the Islamic worldview on humankind, universe, and life in which their respective fields of expertise complemented each other perfectly. Sayyid's contribution consisted of his two-decades-long experience as a literary critic, while Muhammad, as a graduate in English studies, provided his extensive knowledge of Western intellectual and artistic trends. His fluency in English, a language that Sayyid did not read, and his familiarity with psychoanalysis (Muhammad Qutb was a Freudian in his youth),[72] allowed him to bolster his brother's insights with criticism of the Western ideological trends of materialism, realism, and idealism. The symbiosis between the two men was such that Muhammad Qutb did not even bother to cite his brother's name when referencing his early writings on the art of representation in the Qur'an.[73] Starting with the publication of Muhammad Qutb's book *al-Insan bayn al-Maddiyya wa-l-Islam* (Human Being between Materialism and Islam, 1951), which marked his departure from Freudian thought, the two brothers completed each other's intellectual worlds. Their cooperation fulfilled Sayyid's aspiration expressed in the dedication of his first book in 1935 that his sixteen-year old brother become his "extension and his heir."[74]

The project of *al-adab al-islāmī* was born from the attempts to create a cultural identity for postcolonial Islamist commitment that differed from literatures promoted by both the Muslim Brotherhood and Marxists.

This project sits entirely on Sayyid Qutb's vision of aesthetics developed throughout his career as a literary critic. Central to this vision is the understanding of arts as the expression of the inspired soul, or *wijdān*. As we saw in chapter 2, Qutb—together with other writers of his generation—conceived his aesthetic project in line with the modernist opposition to literary tradition of balanced reformers criticized for addressing the mind and not the heart. In the 1938 battle in *al-Risala*, discussed in chapter 1, Qutb had accused Muhammad al-Ghamrawi, a member of the Bookstore's circle, of using literature for social goals and, as a result, confusing it with preaching. In Qutb's project of Islamist literature, this initial hostility to the cultural endeavors of balanced reformers was preserved, taking the shape of criticism of the literatures produced by the Muslim Brotherhood, who, as we have seen, inherited a substantial part of the balanced reformers' literary goals. The Islamist literature was not about morality, Sayyid Qutb explained—nor did it portray heroes of Islam who were supposed to act as models for behavior, Muhammad Qutb added. "Islamist literature does not necessarily speak about Islam!" he wrote. "Certainly, it is not the preaching [*wa'ẓ*] nor the incitement to follow virtues. It is neither the abstract truths of faith put in a philosophical form. None of this even qualifies as art!"[75]

From the mid-1950s, the Qutb brothers slightly revised Sayyid Qutb's former aesthetic project in line with their newly developed theory of Islamic worldview, or *al-taṣawwur al-islāmī*, the notion that would consume Sayyid Qutb's intellectual energies for the years to come. Interest in the Islamic worldview came as a result of the multiple postwar paradigmatic shifts in politics and culture discussed in the previous chapter: the shift from the problem of knowledge to the urgency of action, the increased attention to sociopolitical matters, the demise of the *udabā'* generation, and the widening rift between Islamist and Marxist intellectuals. The urgency to develop the Islamic worldview that would provide an overarching explanation of human existence stems from Qutb's observation that similar systems of thought existed for the Left and the Romantic tradition of the fallen *udabā'*: materialism (*māddīyya*) and idealism (*mithālīyya*). This perspective is visible in the fact that both brothers interpreted the 1954 controversy between Husayn and young Marxists as not concerning literature per se, but as an expression of a much larger confrontation between idealism and materialism.[76]

In his book *Manhaj al-Fann al-Islami*, Muhammad Qutb pursued his criticism of both paradigms, which, in his opinion, were marred by numerous shortcomings. Since art is the reflection of a particular prevalent paradigm, he explained, Hegelian idealism gave rise to Romanticism, which distinguished itself by its concern with the supernatural, geniuses, and heroism. But such a refuge in the world of dreams and the supernatural provoked a reaction in the opposite direction, ushering in an era of materialism. Started by Darwin, continued by Freud, and more recently applied to the social realm by Marx and Engels, materialism, Muhammad Qutb continued, found its expression in the school of realism. The change from Romanticism to realism entailed a shift from portrayals of the supernatural to those of material reality; from an interest in heroes to attention to the "common man"; from the themes of subjectivity to the pressing needs of society; and from excessive spirituality to a focus on humanity's animalistic drives and desires. This transformation was necessary, Muhammad Qutb argued, because the function of the arts was to serve society. However, pushing the representation of humans to the extreme of their animalistic nature severed the link between humankind and the surrounding universe and denied man's spiritual element, thus presenting a distorted view of human nature. Worse, it led to the popularization of "carnal literature" (*al-adab al-jinsī*) and the lowering of man under the pretext that his weaknesses, instincts, and drives were part of human reality.[77]

Convinced that the current wave of materialism would eventually recede, Sayyid Qutb took upon himself the task to devise a similar system of thought for Islamism. He named it *al-taṣawwur al-islāmī* and defined it as the foundation for various Islamic engagements with reality, such as the sociopolitical order or artistic creation. Qutb described *al-taṣawwur al-islāmī* as vertically connecting all levels of human existence: human nature (*fiṭra*), the sociopolitical order (*niẓām*), and the cosmic order (*nāmūs*). The incorporation of the notion of the Islamic worldview in Qutb's intellectual makeup led him to redefine the human faculties that he had earlier credited with the role of receiving artistic inspiration. Instead of the affect, or *wijdān*, Qutb began speaking of human nature, or *fiṭra*. The difference between *fiṭra* and *wijdān* is that the former is not just any type of soul, but its primordial and unsoiled version, which has been created by God to be in harmony with all other aspects of existence. In other words, *fiṭra* was *wijdān* that had been transformed by the Islamic worldview. Accordingly, once an artist opened himself to Islam and his soul was purified of distorted visions of reality, all his actions, including his artistic creation, would be automatically in tune with *al-taṣawwur al-islāmī*. As the Qutb brothers explained, no particular effort was required to produce an Islamist literature, assuming that its author was a genuine artist.[78] In fact, even non-Muslim writers, such as the Hindu poet Tagore or the Christian writer John Millington Synge, wrote excellent pieces of Islamist literature.[79]

Such a refashioning of the human soul was consistent with Qutb's changed vision of truth. In his early aesthetic theory, Qutb defined the truth as something an artist could partially access by the means of their extraordinary capacities of feeling. After his Islamic awakening, Qutb arrived at the conclusion that all these efforts were meaningless, since the truth had already been revealed and given to humanity. It was fully realized in the Qur'an, which by the same token was a perfect piece of art, and a book of "artistic inimitability" (*al-'ijāz al-fannī*).[80] Echoing the neoplatonic understanding of beauty, both Qutb brothers associated it with order and harmony, rather than with chaos and randomness.[81] The perfect harmony according to which the universe worked was, in their opinion, a proof of the existence of a superior mind. Beauty resided precisely in these bonds that made out of existence a unified whole.[82] What an Islamist artist could hope to achieve was to get closer to the supreme piece of art of the Qur'an by demonstrating through their art some of the connections binding the universe together. As Muhammad Qutb emphasized it, "[Islamist art] emerges from the encounter between beauty and truth."[83] Since beauty and truth were interconnected, the assumption that arts and religion stood in opposition to each other was based on a false understanding of both aesthetics and religion, which, Muhammad Qutb explained, worked hand in hand to draw humankind closer to God. By sharpening human senses to the surrounding beauty, which was nothing else than the signs of God (*ayāt al-ulūhīyya*), the arts deepened religious faith.[84]

At the time Sayyid Qutb was writing his essay on Islamist literature, in May 1954, the cultural identity of Egypt's postcolonial state was not yet set. When Muhammad Qutb undertook the writing of his book in 1963, the context had changed. Not only had the crackdown of the Muslim Brotherhood stamped out the dreams of the Islamic identity of the Egyptian independent state that in the mid-1950s still seemed within reach, but also leftist notions of realism and committed literature imposed themselves as the new orthodoxy. Although the texts by Sayyid and Muhammad Qutb aimed at the same goal of setting the direction for the creation of an authentic postcolonial culture, their target against which this culture was defined shifted: it was no longer limited to the old guard Egyptian literati as Taha Husayn, but encompassed their former comrades-in-arms, Marxist intellectuals, who by the 1960s came to dominate the Arab intellectual scene.

The theory of Islamist aesthetics developed by the Qutb brothers bears traces of these struggles for influence among Egyptian intellectuals and mirrors the changing alliance between Islamists and Marxists. Like Qutb's social order of Islam, which was presented as the alternative to capitalism and communism, the method of Islamist literature was conceived as a third way between the paradigms of idealism (*mithālīyya*) and materialism (*māddīyya*) and their avatars in the arts, Romanticism and realism. It was not only the third but also a middle way that, in a manner reminiscent of Hegelian dialectics, presented a synthesis of the best elements of these ideological paradigms and claimed to surpass them. Firstly, the Qutb brothers redefined the Marxist version of committed literature, *al-adab al-multazim*, by including in its scope spiritual goals. Similarly to the Marxist understanding of literature, Sayyid Qutb explained, Islam aimed to end social oppression and to improve the material conditions of humankind. However, it did not stop there, but ensured spiritual and psychological well-being as well.[85] "[Islamist art] is a committed art [*al-fann al-multazim*]," Muhammad Qutb wrote.

> But not in the narrow sense of commitment. It is not committed to a certain school [*madhhab*], nor is it a didactic art that promotes an idea by the means of a sermon or direct propaganda. It is necessarily and

> only committed to the cosmic order [*nāmūs*] in its aesthetics, harmony, balance, and smoothness. It aims to create a virtuous human-being [who lives] in accordance with the cosmic order and does not deviate from it. [Islamist art] seeks this aim by showing the beauty and ugliness understood widely and encompassing feelings, thoughts, behavior, and conduct, to make the soul long for beauty and flee from ugliness without being pressured to.[86]

As they redefined the notion of *iltizām*, the Qutb brothers similarly reshaped the understanding of realism (*waqaʿīyya*). Both authors insisted that Islamist art was more realistic than Marxist art. First of all, it was realistic because it objected to the mythical and idealistic representation of humans. But, contrary to materialist objections to idealism, the Islamist arts did not deny the reality of the metaphysical dimension of human nature, which is known to be created both the material and spiritual elements, clay and God's breath. Thus, a genuine realism needed to take into account the spiritual dimension of the human in its artistic portrayals, which is exactly what Islamist literature aspired to do.[87]

One of the main points of difference between Islamist realism from its rival Marxism was its attitude to the representation of human weakness. Sayyid and Muhammad Qutb emphasized that the materialist tendency to focus on weaknesses turned a blind eye to the human capacity for surmounting them,[88] while, in her short story collection focusing on prison experience, Hamida Qutb argued that both moments of weakness and strengths were part of human experience.[89] As an example of the Islamist realism, Muhammad Qutb cited a 1946 short story by his friend and the cofounder of the Publishing Committee for University Graduates, ʿAbd al-Hamid al-Sahhar, entitled "Hamazat al-Shayatin" (The Temptation of Demons), which depicted a young man who falls under the influence of vice, loses his spiritual purity, and eventually commits a sin. But al-Sahhar doesn't stop here, Muhammad Qutb stressed; he ends his story with the scene of repentance. "The scene of repentance is a spot of light in the dark continent of sin," Muhammad Qutb wrote. "Then he opens the door to the light . . . and leaves you with an image of a sparking light!"[90] Religious awakening following a personal crisis or an intense physical pain, the inner battle between good and evil, or the depiction of the human bewilderment in front of the unknown would be established as the major themes of Islamist literature.

The conversation and rivalry with Marxist intellectual trends reflected themselves not only in the realm of ideas, but also in social relationships. The story of Qutb's involvement with *al-Adab* magazine provides the most vivid example of the alliance and the subsequent falling-out between Islamist and Marxist intellectuals. Founded by the Lebanese intellectual Suhayl Idris in Beirut in 1953 and modeled on the Sartrean notion of literary commitment, *al-Adab* aimed at creating a new type of literature that would correspond to the postcolonial future of Arab societies. Rapidly, the magazine imposed itself as the key literary venue and a laboratory for Arab existentialism.[91] At the moment of the founding of *al-Adab*, Qutb together with his sister Amina followed the whole generation of postwar intellectuals to the promising magazine, still convinced that his project of emancipation fit within its postcolonial agenda. Through the intermediary of literary critic Anwar al-Mi'ddawi, Suhayl Idris invited Qutb to join the magazine's editorial board as an Arab literary critic of the first rank."[92] Qutb did not join the board, but he did remain associated with the magazine. In April 1953, he gave an interview to the journal on the state of Arab poetry,[93] while in July and November his sister Amina published two short stories there.[94] After making her literary debut in a collaborative book, *al-Atyaf al-Arba'a*, in 1945, Amina was a rising poet and storyteller in her own right. As a periodical that embodied the intellectual revolt of the postwar generation and carried the promise of the postcolonial cultural grandeur, *al-Adab* was a fitting place for her stories.

However, the cooperation between the Qutb family and *al-Adab* lasted for less than a year. Coinciding with the increasing hostility between the Muslim Brotherhood and Egypt's revolutionary regime, the Qutb family realized that they understood literary commitment differently than *al-Adab*. In its December 1953 issue, one of the regular writers and the member of the editorial board, Lebanese translator Munir al-Ba'albaki, dismissed Amina Qutb's short story "Awham" (Illusions) as inconsistent with the goals of committed literature. Depicting a man (curiously resembling her brother Sayyid Qutb), who experiences an existential crisis after the death of his dog and becomes aware of the absurdity of material life, Amina Qutb's story qualifies as *al-adab al-multazim* as it was defined by the Qutb brothers.[95] Yet al-Ba'albaki disagreed with the story's disdain for the mortal affairs of humans and qualified it as "the dangerous absurd, which aroused the distaste for human life and portrayed it as an illusion and the biggest irony."[96]

Muhammad Qutb reacted to this assessment with hurt feelings. In his article published in the *Majallat al-Ikhwan al-Muslimin* in 1954, he fustigated *al-Adab* for criticizing a piece by his sister (whom he identified simply as an "Egyptian storyteller") and accused it of promoting a reactionary stance to religion. While agreeing that Marxism embodied the anticolonial stance in literature, Muhammad Qutb accused its adepts of a major setback: the blind following of Marx's false ideas on religion. He pointed out that if Islam had been the source of oppression in the past, today it was acting as a powerful catalyst of uprisings throughout the Muslim world.[97] Qutb family's involvement with *al-Adab* would not be its last encounter with the proponents of Marxist literary commitment. At the end of the 1970s, prominent Marxist intellectual Mahmud Amin al-'Alam ran into Hamida Qutb in Paris, where he now lived, hoping to escape the campaign of denasserization launched by Nasser's successor Anwar al-Sadat. Hamida fled to Paris after her liberation from prison in 1972.[98] However, at the time of their meeting, the short cooperation of Qutb's family with *al-Adab* was a memory of the past. Convinced that the proponents of committed literature were definitely taking a secular road, Qutb embarked on his own project of formulating an Islamist version of politically conscious art.

This project would be interrupted by the sweeping crackdown on the Muslim Brotherhood in autumn 1954 that sent thousands of its members, including Sayyid Qutb, to prison. Yet Qutb's 1954 article on *al-adab al-islāmī* left a deep imprint on the Muslim Brothers, who continued their attempts to create an Islamist literature in prison. Imprisoned after the second wave of arrests of the organization in 1965, Ahmad Ra'if, a playwright and future publisher, took part in the cultural activities organized in the cell, which inspired him to write an Islamic utopian play called *al-Bu'd al-Khamis* (The Fifth Dimension).[99] Similarly, Amina Qutb continued writing stories and published them as a collection, *Fi-l-Tariq* (On the Road), in the 1960s. After being consigned to prisons for nearly two decades, Islamist literature accomplished an impressive return after the Arab defeat in the 1967 war, the liberation of Islamists from prison by Nasser's successor Anwar al-Sadat, and the rise of the Gulf States, where many Egyptian intellectuals found refuge. The Islamist cultural scene shifted eastward from Cairo, and the genre flourished during the 1980s, 1990s, and early 2000s. These decades witnessed the fame of the prolific Egyptian storyteller Naguib al-Kilani, considered to be the most famous representative of *al-adab al-islāmī*,[100] the speedy popularization of the genre in Turkey, and the founding of the International League for Islamic Literature in Lucknow, later transferred to Riyadh.[101] It was only in 1998 that Hamida Qutb, who had been writing all along, resolved to publish her first short story collection, *Rihla fi Ahrash al-Layl* (A Journey into the Darkness of the Night). Encouraged by this debut, she published two other collections just before passing away in 2012 in her residence in Paris.[102]

The late production of *al-adab al-islāmī* bear traces of Qutb's initial idea developed amid the Islamist competition and conversation with their former Marxist comrades-in-arms. Qutb's formative influence on the later production of Islamist literature is visible in the fact that most of its proponents continue to define it as the reflection of *al-taṣawwur al-islāmī*.[103] However, one could wonder whether in these writings the difference of Qutb's literary project is maintained from the didactic art. The genre's tendency to tip the balance between aesthetics and didacticism in favor of the latter seems to undermine Qutb's original project conceived in opposition to literary goals of morality promoted by balanced reformers and the Muslim Brotherhood.[104] In the decades that followed Qutb's execution, the criteria qualifying a particular text as Islamist was gradually reduced to a minimum condition of "clean literature," referring to the absence of sexual content.[105] The debate on whether or not Islamist literature ever existed that opposed Muslim Brothers following the publication of Qutb's piece in 1954 never stopped dividing the Islamist literary scene, and the partisans of the inclusive definition of the genre seemed to gain the upper hand.[106] Such a fraught development of Islamist literature is due to the ambivalence of Qutb's notion of *al-taṣawwur al-islāmī*: it remained unclear what degree of self-transformation was required to be able to compose Islamist literature. What is clear, however, that writing in the mid-1950s Qutb envisaged a much more profound transformation of the Arab self than later authors ever imagined, since the creation of a new, transcendental Arab identity was part and parcel of the postcolonial project of state-building. How the posited relationship between the faith, *ʿaqīda*, and the state informed Qutb's prison writings is the topic of the next chapter.

5

State and Faith

In the spring of 2008, Egyptian publisher Ahmad Ra'if handed me a copy of Sayyid Qutb's renowned book *Ma'alim fi-l-Tariq* (Milestones). As a Muslim Brotherhood sympathizer, Ra'if was one of the thousands of young Islamist activists arrested following the exposure of the "1965 Organization" in the summer of 1965, to which Qutb was attributed the leading role. Inquired about this controversial opus, which was used in Qutb's trial as evidence of his violent intentions against Nasser's regime, Ra'if smiled and said, "It's a piece of *adab*, and it was never intended to be understood literally."[1] This statement clearly contradicts Qutb's own vision as described in *Ma'alim*, which he conceived as a guidebook for political action. However, the Muslim Brotherhood had become comfortable with the characterization of Qutb's late writings as literature. By pointing to Qutb's literary reputation, the Islamist organization aims to save its intellectual legacy on two levels. First, assigning the title of *adīb* to Qutb allows the relativization of *Ma'alim's* subversive character by claiming the author's right to the freedom to think and to create. Secondly, by suggesting that *Ma'alim* was a piece of *adab*, and that, as such, it was not intended to be taken literally, the Muslim Brotherhood sought to absolve Qutb of the bloodied legacy of the radical jihadist movements that ravaged the Arab region in the decades following his death. And yet efforts to assimilate Qutb's late thought into literature have been met by the utmost resistance among the Brotherhood's opponents, who continue to insist on Qutb's association with violence as a way to keep Islamists far from both politics and literature.

The roots of the controversy around Qutb's reputation—was he a man of letters, or a leader of a violent armed organization?—hearken back to the most dramatic years of his life, which coincided with the rise, consolidation, and collapse of the Nasserist state. During the years that spanned the 1952 Revolution and Qutb's execution in 1966, the Egyptian state had significantly transformed. Within the cultural sector, the mission of an *adīb*, as well as his place in society, shifted considerably. With literature subjected to the goals of the Nasserist "cultural revolution," and authors placed under strict state surveillance, writers lost much of the symbolic privilege they had enjoyed under the monarchy. To be sure, writers still formed a substantial part of the cultural elite, as evidenced by the enduring prestige of the 1960s generation in contemporary Egypt, but their talents were only applauded so long as they fit in with the aims of Nasserism, which they themselves had little power to shape.[2] In fact, in the field of cultural production, the limelight shifted from *udabā'* to *mufakkirūn*, or intellectuals, who were expected to provide the Arab state with an ideology. Rather than *udabā'*, in Nasser's Egypt the main driver of change and progress had become the Arab state, supported by those groups of intellectuals that proved themselves indispensable for its survival—namely, journalists and technocrats.[3] In contrast to the universalist knowledge of the Nahdawi intellectual centered upon the elitist "highbrow art" (*al-fann al-rafi'ī*), the 1960s intellectual felt at home in the reconfigured media landscape, knew how to navigate between the capricious power demands and the preservation of minimal space of autonomy, and leaned toward realism and entertaining writing styles.

This chapter focuses on the so-called radical phase of Qutb's life, stretching from his imprisonment in 1954 and the writing of Qutb's major prison work, *Ma'alim fi-l-Tariq*. Starting with the transformation of Egypt's cultural scenery following the 1952 Revolution, which included its subjection to the state's control, the reconfiguration of its media landscape, and from the 1960s onward the promotion of Islam as part of the official ideology of Arab socialism, the chapter turns to the confined world of prison, where Qutb worked on *Ma'alim*. Published in Cairo in 1964, *Ma'alim* is the text on which Qutb's intellectual legacy has been built, providing the grounds for his influence within Islamist movements and the basis on which his reputation as a terrorist ideologue has been created. Qutb's biographers—sympathizers and detractors alike—tend to explain the production of *Ma'alim* as a result of the torture inflicted on the Muslim Brotherhood following the crackdown in 1954, Qutb's isolation in prison, and the authoritarian nature of the Nasserist state.[4] Without dismissing these factors, this chapter takes a different approach and locates the text within the intellectual themes that dominated Egypt in the 1960s: notably, the ideologization of culture and the increased significance of the Arab state as the key agent in forging a new postcolonial Arab subject.

As Yoav Di Capua has noted, the 1960s witnessed the rise of the powerful pan-Arab state, which imposed itself as the central producer of postcolonial Arab subjectivity. "The difference between the decolonization struggles of the 1950s," Di Capua writes, "and those of the 1960s was that, as opposed to the 1950s, which emphasized the physical liberation of national territory, the 1960s ushered in the understanding that anticolonial struggles were about not simply reclaiming national space, but much more profoundly, the inner liberation of the human subject."[5] This shift, observed mostly in relation to secular postcolonial projects, affected Islamists as well. The switch from the decolonization of society to the decolonization of the self was epitomized in Qutb's transition from his interest in socio-political order (*niẓām*) to the desire to conceptualize a comprehensive system that would provide the basis for Islamic action and thought: Islamic concept and method (*al-taṣawwur w-al-manhaj al-islāmī*).

This chapter argues that his book *Ma'alim fi-l-Tariq* should be equally read in the context of the 1960s postcolonial projects, specifically as a particular rendering of the widespread faith in the state's capacity to forge a postcolonial Arab subjectivity. Across Arab nationalism and Islamism, ideology, or *al-'aqīda*, was posited as the emancipatory force of human consciousness capable of forging a new Arab or Muslim man who would create a postcolonial society. But, rather than its Islamist dimension, the particularity of Qutb's postcolonial project was to conceive the human liberation outside the purview of the powerful pan-Arab state. When Qutb published *Ma'alim*, in the mid-1960s, Islam was not an anathema in Nasser's political field. Quite the contrary: encouraged by the post-1962 Nasserist search for ideology, Islam was posited as a major resource for marking Arab socialism as different from Marxism. The second half of the decade, and before the devastating Arab defeat in the 1967 war against Israel, witnessed an upsurge of books that vehemently argued for Islam's compatibility with Islam. Rather than Islam, Qutb's "crime," for which he would be accused of conspiracy and executed in 1966, was to portray the Arab state as an obstacle for human liberation, not as its main agent. In his *Ma'alim*, the dialectic relationship between the state and subjectivity took the shape of his theory of Jahiliyya and its effect in shaping one's faith, or *'aqīda*. Contrary to the dominant view that entrusted the mission to shape the Arab subject to the all-powerful pan-Arab state, Qutb defined human freedom as opposed to the state's power.

By drawing attention to the significance of the state, Qutb's *Ma'alim* marked a major historical turn in Islamic activism. It redirected Islam's revolutionary potential from the Cold War competition with communism and capitalism to the confrontation of the Arab state, setting the direction that radical trends of Islamism would follow after Qutb's execution. The development of competing visions of Egypt's postcolonial futures, which, either on the Arab nationalist or Islamist side, were centered upon the state, paved the way to the ultimate confrontation between Nasser's regime and the Muslim Brotherhood.

The Rise of the State in Culture

The July Revolution carried great expectations of change that was to take place in the cultural realm. As has been discussed earlier, the years preceding the fall of the monarchy in 1952 were marked by a widespread feeling that cultural production in Egypt was taking the wrong path. From across the ideological spectrum of postwar Egyptian politics, writers pointed to different maladies that, according to them, plagued the Egyptian cultural scene. Some were concerned about the increasing commodification of culture that spread vulgarity and sapped people's ability to contribute to the building of a postcolonial society. Others expressed their frustration over the suffocating rules of writing that kept culture enclosed within the stagnant image of the medieval *adab*. Many intellectuals, including Sayyid Qutb, explained the corruption of culture by borrowing from the all-pervasive Marxist lexicon that pointed to the responsibility of the old-guard men of letters. Such pundits claimed that the *udabā'* unconsciously sustained Egypt's colonial situation through their reliance on Western cultural references and their dependency on local power structures that made them incapable of reforming themselves, let alone lead Egypt to freedom. As a solution to these cultural ills, many called for the increased state regulation of cultural production. Rebellious authors exhorted the state to prohibit immoral content in popular culture, regulate the publishing market, and provide writers with the means of subsistence, preventing their turning to the entertainment industry.[6] In fact, the demands for more state intervention in culture were paralleled by similar requests in many other fields of ideological production, foreshadowing the rise of statist ideologies.[7] The cultural policies brought about by the revolution would largely exceed these demands.

Upon assuming power, the Free Officers took upon themselves the task of reorganizing culture. Their first steps in this direction were rather modest, being largely dictated by their needs for unmediated access to the population. Wary of alienating the media in these early days of the upheaval, the military men set out to create parallel means of communication without dismantling the existing media infrastructure. One of the first institutions to be established under the revolutionary regime was the Ministry of National Guidance, created in 1953 and placed under the supervision of Fathi Radwan, a political activist and the founder of the National Party and its mouthpiece *al-Lawa' al-Jadid*. Under his energetic but short-lived direction, the ministry took control of the radio and set up plans to establish television broadcasting that would materialize in 1960 with the construction of the Maspero tower.[8] In the print media, officers followed a similar policy of establishing their own press outlets and set up the publishing house Dar al-Tahrir, which published the periodical *al-Tahrir* (The Liberation), and, from 1954, the daily *al-Jumhuriyya* (The Republic) and the cultural magazine *al-Risala al-Jadida* (The New Message). Throughout the following years, the military regime communicated with writers through two trusted officers and attentive observers of Egypt's cultural scene: Anwar al-Sadat and Yusuf al-Siba'i.

Responding to the demands for increased state presence in culture, officers began setting up an institutional framework for cultural activities. Under the initiative of the novelist in uniform Yusuf al-Siba'i —"the pioneer of cultural security," as he was sarcastically called by Tawfiq al-Hakim—the 1950s saw the emergence of a host of institutions, such as the Club of Storytelling (*Nadi al-Qissa*, 1953), the Writers' Association (*Jama'iyyat al-Udaba'*, 1955), and the Supreme Council for the Protection of Arts, Literatures and Social Sciences, and, lastly, the Ministry of Culture (1958).[9] Though tailored to provide for different cultural needs, including the production of inexpensive pocketbooks, the organization of debates and encounters, and the distribution of literary prizes, these institutions took up the task of regulating literary life that had previously been carried out informally by private publishing houses. Their mission also consisted in culturally representing the Nasserist state within transregional postcolonial cultural institutions, such as the Congress of Arab Writers and the Afro-Asian Writers' Association.[10]

In parallel, the cultural infrastructure inherited from the past began slowly to die out. The two cultural giants of monarchical Egypt dedicated to highbrow literature the magazines *al-Risala* and *al-Thaqafa*, closed in 1953 for financial reasons.[11] Other cultural remnants of the past age fell victim to the campaigns of repression launched by the regime to silence its opponents. The purges targeting the Wafdist press and university professors of Marxist leanings that followed the March crisis in 1954 resulted in the dismantling of the networks of the liberal intelligentsia.[12] By the late 1950s, there were hardly any magazines where Egyptian writers could publish their work. Left with few options, many of them turned to cultural outlets published overseas, such as the Lebanese *al-Adib* (A Man of Letters) and *al-Adab*.[13]

Such a prudent coexistence of intellectuals and the military regime reached its end by the late 1950s. The new decade dawned with a feeling that spectacular political victories, such as the Non-Aligned Movement and the nationalization of the Suez Canal, were not being matched on the economic front. By the early 1960s, the seemingly all-powerful pan-Arab state, supported by an extensive bureaucracy and intelligence apparatus, started showing signs of ideological fatigue that Sharif Yunis calls "the failure of the ideology of 'the sacred march'" (*al-zahhaf al-muqaddas*).[14] The failure of the union with Syria in 1961, economic difficulties, and the all-consuming war in Yemen added to the overwhelming feeling of despair. The Nasserist state thus proceeded to critique itself and examine past mistakes, raising an accusing finger to intellectuals. The famous controversy over "the crisis of intellectuals," initiated by Nasser's confidant Muhammad Hasanayn Haykal in the newspaper *al-Ahram*, signaled a change in the regime's policies toward the intellectual community. The tacit agreement about nonintervention in each other's affairs that had provided the basis for communication between writers and the state during the 1950s came to an end. Now, intellectuals and producers of culture were required to grant to the regime "their hearts and, as a result, their ideas."[15]

Throughout 1961, a handful of Egyptian thinkers debated in the press and at conferences the reasons for the apparent passivity of intellectuals regarding Nasser's revolution.[16] They concluded that the 1952 revolution had failed to "liberate" them from the ivory towers in which they sat in isolation from the social realities of the country.[17] It was consequently decided that Egypt was in dire need of a full-fledged cultural revolution that would harness its intellectual energies for the construction of the Nasserist state. As part of the campaign of nationalization that accompanied the launch of the policy-changing National Charter (1962), the state proceeded to take control of the Egyptian press. Private press groups, such as *Akhbar al-Yawm*, *Ahram-Hilal*, and *Ruz al-Yusuf*, were placed under the authority of the nation's single political party, the Arab Socialist Union. The nationalization of the press was, according to Yunis, the officers' response to its alleged failure to produce "serious" content. The spread of tabloid journalism, sensational news, and crime stories during the postwar emergence of the nouveaux riches created a rather unflattering image for the revolutionary regime, which expected the press to communicate its "message."[18]

Following the nationalization of the press, *Akhbar al-Yawm* and *al-Ahram* introduced sections for opinion, the arts, and literature under the expectation of reorienting Egyptian culture in a more responsible direction.[19] Likewise, the state proceeded to nationalize publishing houses. One of them, al-Dar al-Qawmiyya, became the key producer of patriotic, state-sanctioned literature, flooding the market with inexpensive pocketbook collections that thematically organized topics according to different categories of readers, such as workers, peasants, students, or soldiers.[20] A number of periodicals dedicated to different literary genres were also launched.

Some of these magazines, such as *al-Risala* and *al-Thaqafa*, strongly resembled their namesakes published under the monarchy and were explicitly intended to mark Egypt's reconciliation with its cultural past; others, such as *al-Masrah* (The Theater), *al-Shi'r* (The Poetry), *al-Qissa* (The Story), and *al-Nathr* (The Prose), were new. Entrusted to the supervision of famous representatives of various literary arts, these periodicals aimed at pursuing the cultural goals set by the National Charter, as the minister of culture and orientation, Muhammad 'Abd al-Qadir Hatim, made it clear in his introduction to *al-Thaqafa*.[21] Here again, his warning against "intellectual immaturity" and "superficiality" reflected the regime's intention to infuse cultural production with responsibility and gravity. Nasser and his intellectual elite subscribed to the cultural vision of the postwar generation. As seen in chapter 3, this vision called for culture that would raise consciousness, rather than simply entertain. Another element that Nasser "inherited" from the postwar activism was his Islam.

The Revolution Embraces Islam

It would be inadequate, however, to attribute the rise of the state's monopoly in culture only to its top-down policies. This would underestimate the ideological appeal that the transregional Egyptian state and its cultural policies held for Arab intellectuals. For a significant part of the formerly rebellious youth, Nasserism represented a fulfillment of the generational aspirations that had motivated them since the 1930s. Articulated around the urgent need to end British colonial rule and entrenched poverty, these aspirations more generally consisted in the quest for the dignity and authenticity that this generation of Egyptians felt deprived of. The powerful state embodied by Nasser offered a promise of dignity to which many Arab writers and intellectuals enthusiastically surrendered themselves.

Many of Qutb's former comrades-in-arms of pre-1952 activism found a comfortable place in Nasser's expansive media landscape: the radio, the press, cinema, and, from 1961, television. The majority of the nation's interwar poets would be unknown today without that massive audiovisual industry. Such is the case with the poet Tahir Abu Fasha, Qutb's acquaintance from interwar poetry circles, who became famous as a songwriter for

Umm Kulthum, the unparalleled celebrity of the Nasserist era. The same goes for Ibrahim Naji, the renowned poet of the Apollo Poet Society who rose to prominence when his poem "al-Atlal" (The Ruins) was performed by Umm Kulthum. The trajectory of 'Abd al-Mun'am Shumayyis, whom we encountered in chapter 3 as the author of *Suqut al-Qahira* (1951), offers a vivid illustration of the postwar generation's accommodation within Nasser's regime. A former companion of Qutb and a contributor to his edited *Majallat al-Ikhwan al-Muslimin*, in 1951 Shumayyis had conceived of his intellectual mission as that of upholding morality within the Islamic vision of culture. Several years into the revolution, he modeled the rest of his career on the demands of the Nasserist state. He enthusiastically pursued the objectives of Nasser's cultural reshuffling, launched in the mid-1960s, becoming a prolific author of plays for radio and television. Focusing on themes that closely reflected the political line of the state, such as the Arab new man, the construction of the High Dam, the Zionist threat, and the achievements of the revolution, his patriotic books filled the collections of the state-owned al-Dar al-Qawmiyya press. For his untiring efforts, he was honored twice—by President Nasser and President Sadat.[22]

Intellectuals of an Islamic bent did not have to renounce their postwar activism for the establishment of Islamic society to find a welcome in Nasser's booming cultural bureaucracy. The novelist 'Abd al-Hamid al-Sahhar, the cofounder of the Publishing Committee for University Graduates (also seen in chapter 3), is a case in point. Throughout his career, al-Sahhar had never abandoned his dream of witnessing the establishment of an Islam-inspired social system, as first expressed in his 1943 novel on the "Muslim socialist" Abu Dharr al-Ghifari. In 1960s Egypt, al-Sahhar became one of the most prolific scriptwriters of Islamic drama for cinema, radio, and television. He cooperated with the filmmaker Salah Abu Sayf in writing the script for the well-known Egyptian film on the beginnings of Islam, *Fajr al-Islam* (The Dawn of Islam), and his serial biography of the Prophet, *Muhammad Rasul Allah wa Aladhina Ma'hu* (Muhammad, Peace Be Upon Him, and Those Who Are with Him), would be adapted for television following his death. In the 1960s, he reached the highest levels of bureaucracy in the film industry, when he was appointed as the head of the Egyptian General Organization of Cinema.

In many regards, the themes of postwar cultural activism fit well with the audiovisual representation of Nasser's national project. Fiction works produced by the authors of the Publishing Committee, such as 'Ali Ahmad Bakathir, 'Adil Kamil, or Naguib Mahfuz, were easily installed in Nasser's revolutionary tale. Anticolonial struggle and socialist revolution provided transversal themes that could be stitched to both Pharaonic and Islamic history. Although fond of Pharaonic history, Naguib Mahfouz cooperated in writing the screenplay of Youssef Chahine's renowned biography movie *Saladin the Victorious* (Nasir Salah al-Din, 1963) depicting the triumphs of the Arab warrior.[23] Another member of the Publishing Committee, 'Ali Ahmad Bakathir adapted his postwar play *Ma'sat Udib* (The Tragedy of Oedipus), which originally reflected Bakathir's Islamist commitment, to meet Nasserist revolutionary objectives. As noted by Raphael Cormack, Bakathir's 1949 play followed the story of the Athenian tragedy Oedipus Tyrannus to depict the dissolution of the Muslim Brotherhood, with which he maintained friendly relations. In his lectures published in 1958, however, Bakathir offered a new reading of the play that tied it to the achievements of the Nasserist regime. In his reinterpretation of the play, he succeeded even to demonize the group that he was once close to—that is, the Muslim Brotherhood. In fact, Bakathir made the play express the exact opposite of its original approval of the Islamist organization: the accusation that the Muslim Brotherhood traded in religion and sought to destroy the country.[24]

But these twists of the mind were not necessary, since Islam was to become a pillar the pan-Arab state. In many Arab states, the 1960s ushered in the quest of cultural authenticity that would set postcolonial politics apart from Marxism. In their efforts to curb the influence of local communists, many Arab states adopted Islam as the spiritual component of Arab socialism. In Iraq, the general 'Abd al-Salam 'Arif, brought to power by the Ba'ath party in 1963, affirmed his belief in God against the "atheism of communists."[25] With the Egyptian communists being rounded up in Egypt in 1959, Islam became a key reference in Nasser's turn to Arab socialism, as inaugurated by his National Charter of 1962. As Sharif Yunis notes, the whole set of debates that surrounded the notion of "Arab socialism" was infused with the search for authenticity that would maintain its autonomy from Marxism and the socialist camp.[26] The Report of the Charter, issued in 1962 as an explanatory document for the National Charter, firmly established the Islamic roots of Arab socialism, defined by its faith "in God, his message, and religious and moral values"[27] and the "balance between its material and spiritual aspects."[28]

The turn to Arab socialism went hand in hand with the increased visibility of religion in the public representation of Nasser's regime. With the appointment of the officer Husayn al-Shafi'i as the vice president, the influence of the newly nationalized Azhar and Islamic associations such as the Young Men's Muslim Association (YMMA) significantly expanded. As a "believing officer," al-Shafi'i patronized celebrations and religious events, supervised the affairs of Azhar, and personally reassured the people of the regime's commitment to Islam.[29] The year 1964 witnessed the founding of a national radio station that specialized in Islamic programs, Idha'at al-Qur'an al-Karim. It was under Nasser that the first full recitation of the Qur'an was produced and broadcast on the radio. In 1965, Nasser performed the pilgrimage to Mecca for the second time, earning himself the audacious title of "the hero of the revolution and the prophet of Islam." Children in school learned religion from new textbooks produced between 1958 and 1959, which depicted Egyptian society as both religious and socialist.[30] Religious scholars, intellectuals, and writers competed with each other to find the most innovative parallels between Islamic law and Nasser's regime,[31] while Arab readers observed the increase of anti-Marxist literature that argued for Islam's superiority over communism.[32] Unsettled by the upsurge of religious sentiment, Syrian philosopher Sadiq Jalal al-Azm spoke of a "religious hysteria" that was orchestrated and "adopted by state apparatuses—its journalism, media and ministries."[33]

In this ideological quest, books and references of the postwar period on Islamic social justice came back in full force. In 1959, Syrian Muslim Brother Mustafa al-Siba'i published *Ishtirakiyyat al-Islam* (The Socialism of Islam), which drew heavily on Qutb's 1949 book on social justice.[34] In Nasser's Egypt, al-Siba'i's book—endorsed by Nasser himself—became an immediate bestseller. In another context, in 1956 Iranian student 'Ali Shariati came across al-Sahhar's 1946 biography on Abu Dharr Ghifari, the first "Muslim socialist." Highly impressed, Shariati produced its

Persian translation, marking the beginning of his intellectual career as a theorist of Islamic socialism who would inspire the 1979 Iranian Revolution. The undisturbed transmission of the postwar Islamic vision to Nasser's regime of the 1960s is epitomized by al-Sahhar himself. Following the announcement of nationalization laws in 1961, al-Sahhar wrote a public letter to Nasser pleading for the adoption of the "spiritual explanation of history" (*tafsīr al-rūhī li-l-ta'arīkh*) as the foundation of his rule. Echoing Qutb's idea on social justice in Islam, al-Sahhar's letter argued for the benefits of an Islamic economic system over a socialist one, presented Islam as the best alternative to both communism and capitalism, and stressed the importance of spiritual values for the stability and strength of civilizations.[35]

To be sure, the calls for Islamic socialism under Nasser did not make it the only and prevailing trend. Rather, the intentional ambivalence of Nasser's socialism allowed for the coexistence and competition between Marxist intellectuals and those who aimed to set the Arab postcolonial project on the Islamic path. However, Nasser's embrace of Islam during the 1960s allowed for the gradual expansion of the anti-Marxist intellectual class, who focused the postcolonial debates on the themes of intellectual purity, Islam, and Western cultural imperialism (*al-ghazu al-fikrī*). Favored by the devastating Arab defeat against Israel in 1967 and the denasserization campaign launched by Nasser's successor Anwar al-Sadat, these themes would dominate the next decade. It was in the mid-1960s, after a short parenthesis of patriotic writing, that Anwar al-Jundi returned to the topic of Western cultural imperialism (*taghrīb*) that had preoccupied him in the postwar period.[36] Around the same time, Muhammad Qutb completed his manuscript on Islamic arts, discussed in the previous chapter, concluding with a plea for cultural authenticity (*aṣāla*).

Such an intellectual climate favored the circulation of Qutb's intellectual reputation both locally and internationally, despite his imprisonment. In the context of the increasing calls for Islamic socialism, starting in the early 1960s Qutb began publishing a series of paperbacks that contained his vision of Islam developed in prison. His six books produced between 1961 and 1964 were published by legally operating publishing houses, some of which were identified with the Islamist movement (such as Maktaba Wahba), and some others associated with the editorial universe of Azhar (such as 'Issa al-Bab al-Halabi). Even though they were consistent with the general atmosphere of the 1960s, Qutb's writings posited a diametrically opposed relationship between the state and the creation of a new, postcolonial Arab with a whole and unharmed subjectivity.

Sayyid Qutb in Prison: Writing *Ma'alim fi-l-Tariq*

The assassination attempt on Nasser in October 1954 opened a new chapter in the relations between the Muslim Brotherhood and the military regime. The shots fired at Nasser as he addressed the crowd in the Manshiyya Square in Alexandria, and the sweeping crackdown on the Brotherhood that followed, was a culmination of the rising tensions between the regime and the Islamist organization. After some attempts of cooperation following the July Revolution in the summer of 1952, the regime and the Brotherhood started to clash. In January 1954, the Brotherhood was officially dissolved, and some of its prominent members, including Sayyid Qutb, were sent to prison for several months. The military's resumption of negotiations with the British in August provided an occasion for another round of confrontation. In response to the Brotherhood's clandestine activities against the regime, to which Qutb contributed by publishing unauthorized tracts, the regime launched a campaign in the media. Nearly a month before the Manshiyya incident, the Brotherhood had already been accused of national treason, compared to the Kharijites,[37] and labeled as "the party of Satan" and "the enemies of God, of the fatherland and of Arabism."[38]

Qutb's arrest was announced in the state-published daily *al-Jumhuriyya* on November 19. In a series of articles on the efforts to suppress the Brotherhood, Qutb was alternatively identified as a member of its Guidance Bureau, as a journalist, and even as "the Brotherhood's contact within the communist movement."[39] Together with thousands of Muslim Brothers, Qutb was sent to the military prison in an episode that would enter the Brotherhood's memory as one of extreme torture and humiliation. After several months of back and forth between the military prison and the Manyal Hospital, where he was treated for multiple diseases, Qutb was sentenced to fifteen years of hard labor in the Tora prison. He was placed in the prison's clinic instead and granted reasonably good conditions for writing and publishing.[40] Qutb was allowed to receive books from his visiting family and had access to the modest prison library. His collection would include works by Pakistani authors, such as Abu A'la Mawdudi, that were being translated into Arabic in great volume, reflecting the growing prestige of Pakistan within the transnational networks of Islamic activism.

It is commonly accepted that by the end of the 1950s Qutb reached a new understanding of Islam.[41] It was based on Qutb's particular interpretation of the first section of the Muslim profession of faith "there is no deity but God" (*lā ilaha ilā Allah*). Instead of following its usual understanding as an injunction to believe in the oneness of God, Qutb saw it as applying to the sociopolitical realm as well. Accordingly, the Islamic faith was authentic only if practiced in a society organized according to God's revealed law. Departing from this interpretation, Qutb concluded that a genuinely Muslim society no longer existed and needed to be restored if humankind was ever to experience happiness and universal peace. Qutb reached this conclusion while working on his commentary of the Qur'an, *Fi Zilal al-Qur'an* (In the Shadow of the Qur'an), which had been published in installments since the end of 1952. By the early 1960s, others of Qutb's prison books appeared on shelves. With titles such as *Hadha al-Din* (This Religion, 1961), *Khasa'is al-Tasawwur al-Islami* (The Properties of Islamic Conception, 1962), *Mustaqbal Li-Hadha al-Din* (The Future Belongs to This Religion, 1962), *Nahwa Mujtam' Islami* (Toward an Islamic Society, 1960–62), and *al-Islam wa Mushkilat al-Hadara* (Islam and the Problems of Civilization, 1962), these books were released by Cairo publishers affiliated with the Islamist movement, such as Maktaba Wahba or Dar al-Qalam.[42] Although these publications reflected Qutb's prison thought, which perceived Islam as a transformative force of human consciousness and political life, it did not cause an outrage. On the contrary, these books enjoyed a wide readership and went through numerous reprints: *Hadha al-Din* was published in four consecutive editions while *Khasa'is al-Tasawwur al-Islami* and *Mustaqbal li-Hadha al-Din* were each reprinted twice. The enthusiasm with which these books were received suggests that, despite his imprisonment, Qutb enjoyed a wide popularity in Egypt and abroad.

The publication of *Ma'alim fi-l Tariq* in 1964 marked a shift in regard to his earlier prison writings. This shift concerned not so much the content of the book, which restated the urgency to restore Islamic society, but its rhetoric. While, in his former texts, Qutb had used a cautious tone when speaking about the damages caused by man-made political systems—in his *Nahwa Mujtam' Islami* he even presents his ideas as an "opinion" and invites readers to debate and prove him wrong—in *Ma'alim* this humble tone would be gone.[43] Instead, a vocabulary of struggle, confrontation, urgency, and martyrdom saturates the book. While, earlier, Qutb had settled for defining Islam as a radical change in one's entire way of life, conceptual, moral, and social, in *Ma'alim* Islam becomes a revolution (*thawra*): "A revolution against the earthly authority that had usurped the authority of God, a revolution against the conditions established upon this usurpation, a defiance against that authority which issues laws not permitted by God."[44]

The emphasis on the struggle is probably related to the fact that *Ma'alim* was addressed to a particular group: a network of young Islamic activists who, by the end of the 1950s, started to organize themselves with a view of restoring the Brotherhood. The network, which in the mid-1960s would make headlines as the 1965 Organization, emerged out of the encounter between two separate groups of Muslim activists who joined forces and established a study group with contacts all over Egypt and abroad.[45] Familiar with Qutb's commentary of the Qur'an, one of the leading members of the circle, Islamic female activist Zaynab al-Ghazzali, contacted Qutb's sisters, Hamida and Amina, with the intention of obtaining intellectual guidance from their brother. Together with other women of imprisoned Muslim Brothers, Hamida was part of the prisoners' support group, acting as a mediator between prisoners, their families, and other Brothers in hiding, which involved fundraising and distributing finances for the families in need.[46]

Through these underground lines of communication between the prison and the outside world, Qutb's writings began reaching restless activists. The first round of readings delivered by Hamida to Zaynab al-Ghazzali was a stack of manuscript pages of the future *Maʿalim*. "After you have finished reading them, I will send you more," Qutb reportedly instructed the group.[47] The existence of the new readership might explain why the idea of the "vanguard" (*ṭalīʾa*), which was conspicuously absent in his previous prison texts, appeared in *Maʿalim*. As Qutb himself acknowledged, he wrote *Maʿalim* for this vanguard, a group of select individuals with purified faith and a mandate to turn his project of Islamic society into a reality.[48] The rhetorical shift between *Maʿalim* and Qutb's earlier prison works suggests that it was not the mere experience of prison that infused his writing with revolutionary zeal. Rather, it was his contact with a group of dedicated individuals that inspired him to write a guidebook for an Islamic revolution.

Such an impact of the organization on Qutb's intellectual production is also related to his particular theory of action, as developed in prison. At the basis of this theory was Qutb's conceptualization of Islam as a method, *manhaj*. As Henri Lauzière has noted in his work on the Salafi movement, by the 1960s the notion of *manhaj* had become "something of a buzzword" in Egyptian academia. It was Qutb who transferred the concept from literary criticism and psychology to Islamic thought, where it traveled into Salafism, leading to its reframing as an all-encompassing religious ideology, a Salafi *manhaj*.[49] As a result, Islamism in the 1960s as compared to the 1950s shifted from being understood as a sociopolitical system, *al-niẓām*, to its conceptualization as a method.[50] As seen in previous chapter, in prison Qutb reached an understanding that the Islamic system of governance, on which he had spilled so much ink during the 1950s, was in fact just an emanation from a larger, all-embracing Islamic epistemology, *al-taṣawwur al-islāmī*. Qutb reshaped his understanding of communism and capitalism accordingly, viewing them as products of the materialist epistemology, *al-taṣawwur al-māddī*.[51]

The particularity of Islamic epistemology, Qutb argued, lay in its method of reception of the Qur'an, which fused theory and praxis. In *Maʿalim*, Qutb dwells at length on the relationship of the original community of Muslims with the Qur'an. Unlike "theoretical Muslims" (*al-muslimūn naẓarīyyan*) of his time, who take the Qur'an as a closed set of divine truths and injunctions, the first Muslim generation embraced it in fragments in light of their particular needs.[52] Entangled with the prospect of its immediate execution, Qur'anic verses reached them in their original form, free from intellectual speculation. Qutb claimed that the original method of Qur'anic reception had been largely lost as a result of the century-long attempts to reshape it according to man-made epistemologies that encouraged an approach to the Qur'an as a matter of intellectual speculation, entertainment, or culture.[53] Thus, the rebirth of Islam ought to begin with the restoration of its original method of reception, which denied the division between idea and action. "It was the reception of the Qur'an with an intention to put it in practice that produced the first Muslim generation. And it was its reception for the study and entertainment that made all the following generations leave Islam," Qutb argued.[54] Put differently, "*Manhaj* in Islam equals 'the truth.'"[55] It is as important as the faith (*'aqīda*) itself.

Why insist on the corrupting effects of the Qur'an's intellectual reception? The answer to this question lies in the particular connection Qutb established between action and emotion. He maintained that a thought detached from praxis remained confined to the rational realm of human cognition, which paralyzed the capacity to act. In *Hadha al-Din*, Qutb mocked the philosophers who had spent centuries attempting to understand human existence: "They have been using their talents for the wrong reasons" he declared.[56] The mission of humans was not to understand existence and to invent their mode of living accordingly, but to implement a system that had already been given by God. In the process of its implementation, it was precisely the irrational realm of human cognition that played a critical role. If received correctly—that is, by the means of all the existing channels of human perception, such as thought, sensation, intuition, and emotion—Qutb argued that the Qur'anic message takes control of all human faculties, including the power to act.[57] As early as the 1950s, Qutb made clear that it was the passionate drive to action that marked the difference between "idea" (*fikra*) and "faith/ideology" (*'aqīda*): "Indeed, an idea doesn't thrive nor lives in the hearts of individuals and generations except when it becomes a faith," he wrote in 1951. "It [only lives] when adopted by a human as his belief, and when it becomes embodied by a living creature. It is the heat of belief that infuses ideas with life and opens them to the spirit and feelings. This is why the words of the prophets and saints had lived whereas those of philosophers and thinkers had vanished."[58]

The drive to action arising from the Islamic creed is the most original element of Qutb's revised theory of Islam. The association of passionate action with the realm of emotions bears traces of Qutb's Romantic literary education. With his Islamist commitment Qutb departed from his former understanding of reason and emotion as opposing binaries. Instead, he presented a new concept, *fiṭra*, which fused reason and emotion as part of an instinctive and primordial human nature. Nonetheless, the former division between rational and irrational realms of cognition was preserved through a new line of division between the conscious and unconscious aspects of human agency, or *al-jānib al-irādī* and *al-jānib al-fiṭrī*. In restoring the harmony between the social life of humans and the universal order, Qutb argued, humans willfully chose Islam, which, in turn, activated the instinctive part of their agency, *al-jānib al-fiṭrī*, responsible for facilitating the following of Islam in their daily lives.[59] Although Qutb borrowed this distinction from the South Asian scholar Abu al-A'la al-Mawdudi, it sat well with his Romantic notion of *wijdān* as the seat of divine intervention, which operated beyond human willpower.[60] As John Calvert has noted, there is a clear continuity between Qutb's method of the Qur'anic aesthetics developed in the late 1940s and his mature prison thought; both held the Qur'an to be a depository of powerful images that stirred religious imagination.[61] Yet, whereas in his musings over the aesthetic power of the Qur'an, these images communicated the secrets of existence, in his late writings, it is the action that takes precedence over knowledge. As a result, a theory and praxis—or "the word" (*bayān*) and "the movement" (*ḥaraka*)—were perceived to act in tandem for the Islamic restoration.[62] The 1965 Organization represented the movement, while Qutb was the word.

With the change in rhetoric of Qutb's *Ma'alim*, the target of revolutionary action became the oppressive Arab state. This shift is visible in Qutb's reformulation of the term of Jahiliyya, borrowed from South Asian scholars Abu al-Hasan Nadvi and Abu A'la al-Mawdudi. Qutb extensively relied on al-Mawdudi's conceptual apparatus to give his prison writings theoretical consistency. Apart from Jahiliyya, he borrowed the concepts of *ḥākimīyya* (God's sovereignty), *'ubūdīyya* (human obedience to God), and *ṭāghūt* (someone who sets himself as God), as well as redefined the usual concepts of religion (*dīn*) and Islamic law (*sharī'a*).[63]

Qutb had been aware of the modern uses of Jahiliyya at least from 1951, when he encountered Nadvi and agreed to write a preface to his *Madha Khasara al-'Alam bi-Inhitat al-Muslimin* (Islam and the World).[64] Following Mawdudi, there Nadvi redefined the Jahiliyya from its usual meaning as a pre-Islamic historical time to the condition resulting from the abandonment of God's law. Since then, Qutb started to integrate the concept into his own ideological apparatus.[65] In most of Qutb's prison texts, the usage of Jahiliyya still reflected that of Mawdudi: as a condition where God is not held sovereign, referring mostly to Western modernity and its avatars in the Muslim world.[66] But while in these early works Jahiliyya could still allow for ideational interpretation as man-made systems of life applied in the abstractly defined world, in *Ma'alim* it assumes a very material existence. There Jahiliyya is portrayed as a living and all-pervasive physical force, which consciously blocks humankind from Islam and needs to be dismantled by an equally physical struggle. According to Qutb, the material aspect of the present-day Jahiliyya is precisely what marks its difference with its pre-Islamic version: unlike the latter, today Jahiliyya had become an "organized political power" that forbid individuals to receive and propagate the Islamic message.[67] Since these "material obstacles formed by the socio-political orders" stood in between humans and the faith,[68] they needed to be removed to clear the path for the free circulation of the Islamic call.[69] Although Qutb doesn't refer directly to Nasser's regime when defining Jahiliyya, its definition as the "organized political force" clearly mirrors the Brotherhood's experience with the Nasserist state.

The association between Jahiliyya with the state stems from the importance Qutb assigned to the latter in sustaining the faith, *'aqīda*. In his writings, the idea of Islam as a liberating force of human consciousness was not new. As we saw in chapter 3, in *al-'Adala al-Ijtima'iya fi-l-Islam* Qutb posited "absolute emotional emancipation" (*al-taḥarrur al-wijdānī al-muṭlaq*) as the prerequisite for the successful application of Islam to social realities. He argued that, for the Islamic state to function properly, the conviction that Islam provided the best model for social organization had to be sustained by a "deep psychological feeling." Only when it is supported from the "inside" of human consciousness would the Islamic system work in its "outside" realization. It was precisely *'aqīda*, the Islamic faith, that ensured the connection between the inside and outside levels of existence, or between the individual and the collective, by making individuals put the interests of society above their own. In accordance with his distinction between the inward and outward functions of *'aqīda*, Qutb defined Jahiliyya as acting in two directions: from its material manifestation in the state power and from within human consciousness, where it manifested itself as a "false consciousness" populated by factitious beliefs. But, in this equation, it is the material aspect of Jahiliyya that takes the precedence in shaping the faith. This emphasis on the state is visible in Qutb's controversial idea that the Muslim creed was not valid if it was not supported by the corresponding social order, which led him to deny the existence of any truly Muslim society. But if, according to his theory, the Islamic creed cannot be fully practiced in isolation from society, the opposite, however, was possible: the Islamic state could function without being supported from the "inside" by the belief of its subjects.[70] It is not a semantic coincidence that, during the 1960s, *'aqīda* came to signify not only a subjective faith, but also the official ideology of the state.

By assigning to the state the role of upholding the faith, *Ma'alim* signaled a turn in Islamism. It closed the chapter of Islamism as it was defined by the Cold War logic that presented Islam as a pacifier of the polarized post–World War II international scene. Now, Islam was brought home and redirected against the omnipresent Arab state, setting the direction Islamism would take after Qutb's execution in 1966. The shift from Cold War politics of Islamism to the contestation of local Arab regimes appears clearly when comparing Qutb's *Ma'alim* with 'Abbas al-'Aqqad's Islamic writings.

In fact, Qutb's former mentor in poetry, al-'Aqqad, could also be considered as having "turned" to Islam following the war. In this period, he shifted his former interest in Islamic genius, as explored in his prolific series of *'Abqariyyat*, to the study of the historical and philosophical aspects of Islamic *'aqīda*.[71] Produced during the 1950s, al-'Aqqad's prolific work on Islam bears striking similarities to Qutb's *Ma'alim*, suggesting that the latter relied on his former mentor's texts while crafting his own vision of Islam. For example, similarly to Qutb's *Ma'alim*, al-'Aqqad attributed the resurgent power of Islam to its *'aqīda*, defined by its comprehensive and invisible nature, or *shumūl* and *ṣumūd*—the vocabulary that Qutb amply used in his own works.[72] Qutb also borrowed from al-'Aqqad the reading of Islamic history in terms of stages of weakness and of strength.[73]

But al-'Aqqad's vision of Islam still reflected the intellectual climate of the 1950s. In the context of intense Cold War competition for the "hearts and minds" of the colonized nations, belief appeared as a powerful tool in directing the course of global politics. For many Arab intellectuals, the Cold War was primarily a war of beliefs—*ḥarb al-'aqā'id*—from which Islam emerged as a precious resource to ensure spiritual and political autonomy from the competing trends of communism and capitalism. This explains why the question of *'aqīda* and the emphasis on the spiritual foundations of society assumed such importance in early Arab postwar politics. The upsurge of Islamic politics in the 1950s, epitomized by the creation of Pakistan and Indonesia, suggested to al-'Aqqad that Islam was going through the stage of strength.[74] Writing from prison a decade later, Qutb could no longer share this optimism. The crackdown on the Brotherhood and the rise of oppressive Pan-Arab states across the region marked the end of the Islamist moment. In Qutb's view, Islam had entered a stage of weakness, and urgent action was needed to reawaken its potential.

Therefore, Qutb's Islamist project developed in prison should be considered in line with other attempts to create a new postcolonial man that strongly reflected the widespread fascination with the state. Coinciding with Qutb's stay in prison, the Arab nationalist press was animated by a similar curiosity about the connection between *'aqīda* and the state. But for the difference that, in these writings, *'aqīda* was defined as Arab nationalism and not Islam, Marxist intellectuals saw it as the means to emancipate the self from a colonial heritage. "Arabism is the raw material while the state is the matrix into which this material is poured," argued the Iraqi poetess Nazik Mala'ika in the debate that took place in the Lebanese periodical *al-Adab* in the summer of 1960. "Arabism is an emotion [*'aṭifa*], while state is a method [*manhaj*]."[75] While Marxist intellectuals saw the Arab state as the key agent in purging from the Arab self the traces of colonialism with the ideology of Arabism, in his alternative project, Qutb described the Arab state, on the contrary, as the obstacle to human freedom. Both projects revolved around the dialectical relationship between the state and faith/ideology (*'aqīda*), and both therefore exhibited a paradoxical desire for both freedom and state power.

While denouncing the Jahiliyya as an oppressive power that forced upon humans its own *'aqīda*, Qutb demanded no less from the creed-supported Islamic State. In both cases, the state was assigned the paramount role in preserving the corresponding beliefs and, if necessary, correcting them by way of coercive politics. By stating the necessity for harmony between one's beliefs and the ideology of the state, both Islamist and Pan-Arabist projects saw it as their right to check people's innermost convictions. Both mirrored each other in demanding that their respective creeds be fully embraced in order to foster the birth of a postcolonial society. The violence that accompanied their clash during the 1960s echoed the dramatic scope of these totalizing ambitions.

6

The People against Sayyid Qutb

With Arab intellectuals joined to the cause of Nasserism, little space was left for alternative projects of postcolonial emancipation. Even less was available when these visions were understood as deliberately threatening the state. The accusation made against Qutb of conspiring to violently overthrow Nasser's regime in 1965 and his execution in 1966 epitomized the clash between two diametrically opposed postcolonial visions that revolved around the state. The focus of this chapter is the last one and half years of Qutb's life, covering his release from prison in the summer of 1964 and his rearrest eight months later following the exposure of the 1965 Organization.

The clandestine group of Islamist activists formed around 1957 has received sustained and significant academic attention.[1] However, in spite of the wealth of material on the topic, a cloud of mystery still shrouds the precise nature of the group. Was it a paramilitary branch of the Muslim Brotherhood aimed at toppling Nasser's rule as it was depicted by the authorities? Or was it a loosely connected network of peaceful Islamist activists who gathered to read books, as the Muslim Brotherhood's historiography suggests? A wealth of contradictory material exists on the topic, making it difficult to disentangle historical fact from fiction. In this material, memoirs occupy a central place, including one attributed to Sayyid Qutb. Entitled *Limadha 'Adamuni?* (Why Did They Execute Me?) and published for the first time in the 1980s after the assassination of Anwar al-Sadat, Qutb's memoir says more about the context in which it was released than it does about the 1965 Organization. Originally a report of Qutb's police interrogation, signed on October 22, 1965, the document was reportedly acquired by Egyptian journalist and Nasser's éminence grise

Muhammad Hasanayn Haykal and sold to Saudi publishers Hisham and Muhammad ʿAli Hafiz, who included it as the appendix to their periodical *al-Hayat*.[2] Despite the fact that the publishers confirmed the authenticity of the document on the basis that they recognized Qutb's handwriting, the conditions under which it was released make it questionable as a source. In addition to Haykal's implication and the gap of nearly twenty years between its production and release, another issue that raises doubt is the similarity of claims attributed to Qutb to those made by ʿAli ʿAshmawi, a key member of the organization who had been forced to collaborate with Egyptian intelligence. The political sensitivity surrounding the story of the 1965 Organization invalidates its eligibility for historical research.

Instead of attempting to determine the nature of the 1965 Organization, this chapter focuses on the group's influence on Qutb in the process of knowledge production, as well as on the Muslim Brotherhood more broadly. It argues that the public uproar that followed the organization's exposure paved the way for the establishment of schismogenetic discourse against the Muslim Brotherhood. Originally suggested by Georges Bateson and reworked by Walter Armbrust in his analysis of the 2011 Egyptian Revolution, the concept of schismogenesis refers to the routinization of violence as a result of extreme levels of social and political polarization.[3] Schismogenesis occurs when the preexisting order of normality marked by specific ethics and social life is canceled and replaced by a new condition defined by the systematization of violence. As Armbrust has pointed out, the critical moment in creating and maintaining schismogenesis is the national excommunication of an adversary. This excommunication is needed to deprive the adversary of the fundamental attribute of national belonging: grievability. It is by denying the right to be grieved that the enemy can be cast outside the national community and denied the status of a martyr.[4]

This chapter argues that the schismogenesis generated by the 1965 crackdown on the Muslim Brotherhood explains Qutb's absence from Egypt's national historiography. The media campaign unleashed against Qutb in 1965 contributed to the erasure of the previous order of things defined by Qutb's participation in Egypt's vibrant interwar and postwar intellectual scene. By publishing cartoons, editorials, and fiction that ridiculed Qutb, Egyptian intellectuals helped to establish a new, schismogenetic reality in which Qutb was expulsed from history and cast as an icon of absolute evil. Instead of taking his place in history, Qutb exists today as a ghost systematically conjured as a reminder of the Brotherhood's violent intentions. The power of schismogenesis can be measured by its effect on public memory and the pressure placed on his former comrades to renounce him. Importantly, the 1965 anti-Brotherhood campaign laid the groundwork for the decades of knowledge production about Qutb, allowing his violent image to be reactivated on a regular basis.

The Trial and Excommunication

After having spent nine years in prison following his arrest in 1954, Qutb was released in the summer of 1964 for health reasons. Upon his release, Qutb rapidly resumed his weekly salon, held in his house in the Cairo suburb Helwan. Qutb had been holding the salon at least since he returned from the United States in 1951, when it became a necessary stop for transnational Muslim activists who visited Cairo during these critical times. South Asian scholar Abu al-Hasan al-Nadwi, who came to Cairo at that time, remembers driving to Qutb's salon with al-Minyawi, seen in chapter 3, the publisher of one of Nadwi's books.[5] ʿAbdallah ʿAqil, an Iraqi intellectual and a member of the Muslim Brotherhood who studied in Cairo in the 1950s, would fondly remember the international audience of Qutb's salon, which brought together students from across the Arab world.[6] After Qutb's release from prison in 1964, his salon acquired a slightly different shape. After hosting the members of the 1965 Organization at his house several times, Qutb agreed to provide more comprehensive guidance for their intellectual development and political action.[7]

During the months that followed the exposure of the network, Qutb was accused of having led a "semisecret organization" (*tanẓīm shibh sirrī*) that planned to assassinate Nasser, dynamite bridges and power stations, stir up chaos nationwide, and take control of television and radio—all this while arguably being on the way to receiving a shipment of weapons. The campaign against the Brotherhood began with the arrest of Qutb's brother, Muhammad, in late July 1965. As usual for this time of the year, Sayyid

Qutb was spending his summer at his beach house in the Mediterranean seaside resort of Ra's al-Barr, where members affiliated with the organization occasionally visited him. In Ra's al-Barr, Qutb also encountered his old acquaintance from the heyday of pre-1952 literary activism, the critic and translator Wadi' Filistin, whom he enthusiastically embraced without suspecting that it would be the last time.[8] Sayyid Qutb was arrested shortly afterward, on August 9.

In parallel, the police followed the leads to the other ends of the network. According to the memoir of one of the group's core members, Ahmad 'Abd al-Majid, the network's existence was accidentally revealed when an unrelated investigation guided the police to a rank-and-file member who possessed a weapon. Subjected to torture, he revealed names, allowing the police to direct its attention to another gathering spot, an apartment located in the working-class neighborhood of Imbaba. More arrests followed, and more information was divulged by the end of August 1965.[9] The confessions extracted from one of the masterminds of the network, 'Ali 'Ashmawi, opened the way for a full-scale crackdown on anyone suspected of having sympathies for the Islamist movement. Not only had the police acquired the names of thousands of suspects all over the country whom they were now able to locate, but they also had the ultimate proof of the organization's violent intentions: a story of its attempt to purchase a truck filled with weapons. Except for Qutb and 'Ashmawi, there were no other witnesses to this incident, making it easy to use 'Ashmawi's testimony as the evidence against Qutb. As for 'Ashmawi, ostracized by his former comrades, he was used extensively in the regime's propaganda war with the Muslim Brotherhood throughout the following decades.[10]

The motivation behind the 1965 crackdown on the Brotherhood was probably not the mere fact of its attempts to revive its activities. Similar types of activism had existed since the Brotherhood's dissolution in 1954, and yet they were silently dismantled by the authorities without creating a scandal comparable to the one unleashed in 1965.[11] Rather, the renewed confrontation with the Brotherhood responded to the needs of Nasser's regime, which, by the mid-1960s, started showing signs of fatigue. Gone were the days of the building of the revolution that marked the 1950s: the rise of new institutions, the emergence of international alliances, the ambitious projects of development, all accompanied by the spectacular victories at home and abroad, such the nationalization of the Suez canal, the union of Syria, and the launch of the construction work for the Aswan High Dam. The 1960s opened with a series of failures. The secession of Syria was the first blow to the regime, followed by the mediocre results of its first five-year economic plan, and, above all, its open-ended war in Yemen, which by the mid-1960s had turned into an all-consuming quagmire.[12]

Qutb's arrest and trial revealed for the first time the scope of influence of the intelligence services that had been silently growing under Nasser's political shadow. In the summer of 1965, the Nasserist state reached the peak of paranoia over its survival. The Brotherhood's plot was not the only conspiracy revealed that summer. A case was made against the influential journalist and cofounder of *Akhbar al-Yawm* Mustafa Amin, who was accused of spying for the United States. There was also a new case for the legendary Egyptian assassin Husayn Tawfiq, who back in 1946 had murdered a minister and was immortalized as a hero in the famous novel by Ihsan 'Abd al-Quddus, *Fi Baytina Rajul* (A Man in Our House). In 1965, Tawfiq became the center of attention again, but this time as a terrorist who had allegedly planned to assassinate Nasser in the manner of John F. Kennedy and had attempted to purchase weapons from the Brotherhood. There was also an obscure instance of a "secret organization" within the Arab communist party that was said to have been plotting against Nasser.[13] The multiplication of plots probably resulted from the rivalries between intelligence branches that grew particularly heated that summer. The conspiracy provided the pretext for the Military Intelligence Department (MID) to accuse its rival civil security, General Intelligence Directorate, (GID) of inefficiency and to curb its influence.[14] The Muslim Brotherhood's prison narratives support this view, detailing how they were sent back and forth between the military prison and Abu Za'bal (prison facilities respectively supervised by MIDs and GID), where the rival intelligence agencies competed with each other in their use of torture to extract information that could be used against each other.[15]

In crafting the public case against the Muslim Brotherhood, this sophisticated intelligence apparatus relied on the media. Journalists, poets, writers, and intellectuals were expected to put their expertise, humor, and creative skills at the service of the anti-Brotherhood campaign. For this, they were granted unrestricted access to information and to prisons. In December 1954, in the midst of the sweeping arrests of Muslim Brothers, the journal *al-Musawwar* ran a photo report from inside the military prison, where the detained Muslim Brothers were subjected to torture. The story included an interview with Qutb, in which the latter provided sarcastic responses. Referring to the healthy lifestyle of the detainees, Qutb demonstrated several gymnastic moves he managed to perfect while in prison.[16]

During the 1965 crackdown, the media also had direct access to prisons. From early October 1965, the Ministry of National Guidance and Culture began live-broadcasting interrogations of the suspects from the military prison. The following day, transcripts of the interrogations would appear in the state-run *al-Jumhuriyya* with an announcement of whose confessions would be published next. The interviews were carried out by the promising pioneer anchor Hamdi Qandil, who had joined the state television network after its inauguration in 1961. The way Qandil led the interrogations exemplified the voluntary confusion of roles between the media and police investigations. Qandil would start the interview in a manner of an interrogator: "Name? Age? Profession?" Placed in front of the cameras, the culprits confessed their crimes.[17] Suspects were also expected to publicly repent. One of them admitted, for example, that "the Brotherhood's conspiracy was against the homeland and Islam,"[18] while another declared that "terrorist conspiracies do not benefit anyone, and are not in the interest of any human being."[19] These public confessions continued until November 1965, so the audience was thus unable to see the testimony of Qutb, scheduled for December. The staging of these public trials demonstrated the theatricality of Nasser's politics, based on the need to give justice a public face.

In producing anti-Brotherhood rhetoric, the media provided a daily show that mixed reportage with entertainment. While the dailies fed the public with sensation, running lengthy stories on the conspiracy amply illustrated with hand-drawn maps, assassination lists, photos of explosives, and pictures of the suspects, satirical illustrated magazines used

5. Representation of the Muslim Brotherhood in press cartoons. "The Brother. It is not about politics, but human beings." *Sabah al-Khayr*, September 23, 1964, 25. Courtesy of the Egyptian National Library.

parody (fig. 5).[20] While diverse, these articles shared two general themes: the association of the Brotherhood with violence and antirevolutionary forces. These two themes were merged in the genre of dystopian satire that also flourished during the anti-Brotherhood campaign. Dystopian literature had already been popular in the 1954 suppression of the Brotherhood.

In 1954, essays authored by prominent intellectuals and journalists—such as Taha Husayn, the editor in chief of the state-owned al-*Jumhuriyya*, and Mustafa al-Taba'i and 'Ali Amin, renowned *Akhbar al-Yawm* journalists—were collected and published as a book entitled *Ha'ula'u Humma al-Ikhwan* (These Are the Muslim Brothers). One essay, authored by 'Ali Amin, offered a dystopian account of what could have happened had the Brotherhood imposed its rule on Egypt.[21] The pioneer of modern colloquial poetry Bayram al-Tunsi composed a poem prophesying Egypt's return to backwardness under a hypothetical Brotherhood rule.[22] The anti-Brotherhood campaign of 1965 repeated this pattern. One of the first examples of the genre to appear in 1965 was produced by a satirical writer, Mahmud Sa'adni, who serialized in *Sabah al-Khayr* a dystopian story on Qutb entitled "Jama'a Hadha al-Rajul" (This Man's Group). In the Brotherhood's Egypt, so the story began, the son of the exiled king Faruq, Ahmad Fu'ad, reclaimed the kingdom, Qutb and other Muslim Brothers became his pashas, and all other Egyptians were reduced to slavery. Foreigners returned to retrieve their nationalized businesses, chariots replaced cars, and the supply of electricity to villages was cut off to prevent late evening gatherings. As a result of the return of feudalism, crowds of the unemployed filled the streets. "Believe me, these are brothers of darkness, not Islam!" exclaimed Sa'adni. "Sterling is the greatest, glory to the dollar!" he concluded, replacing God in the common religious invocation with the symbols of Western imperialism.[23]

A highlight of the campaign was a volume published by the Supreme Council of Religious Affairs, an institution created in 1961 as a result of Azhar's nationalization. Entitled *Ra'i al-Din fi-l-Ikhwan al-Shaytan* (The Opinion of Religion on the Satanic Muslim Brothers), the book opened with an official discourse by the Grand Imam of al-Azhar, followed by essays by approximately twenty religious scholars, writers, and poets. The

6. Book cover of *The Opinion of Religion on the Satanic Muslim Brothers*. Courtesy of Dominican Institute for Oriental Studies.

book sought to create a long-lasting association between the Brotherhood and violence. Its cover image depicted a wicked creature with wide-set eyes and oversized ears, holding a grenade in one hand and a blood-smeared knife in the other (fig. 6). Drawings of skulls, knives, and blood stains were dispersed throughout the book. Essays verbally reinforced the impressions of violence the illustrations created. Contributors repeated ad nauseum the charges leveled against the Brotherhood by the press, notably the conspiracy to carry out assassinations of state officials and to destroy various symbols of progress realized by Nasser, such as factories, power stations, bridges, and even the High Dam.[24]

Mixing horror with sarcasm provided the basis for schismogenesis, paving the path to Qutb's national excommunication. While the imagery of violence served to deny Qutb the right to be grieved, sarcasm, for its part, sought to deprive him of dignity. Both the imagery of violence and the tone of sarcasm served to dehumanize Qutb in preparation for his execution as part of the new order of normality. How these rhetorical strategies were fused is well represented by a cartoon published in the September 16 issue of *Sabah al-Khayr* (fig. 7). Signed by Ihab, the cartoon depicts the Brotherhood as a disease, called "Brothers Shurum Burum." The symptoms of the disease are demonstrated through eight illustrations representing Qutb. Accompanying captions refer to Qutb's ideological concepts, which the image subverts. For example, the first illustration mocks Qutb's concept of "natural disposition" (*al-isti'dad al-fiṭrī*), which he had used to describe the human predisposition to embrace Islam. The corresponding illustration portrays a toddler with Qutb's face, holding a rattle, wearing a saucepan on his head, and urinating on himself. Other illustrations ridicule Qutb's status as the spiritual guide of the 1965 Organization, such as one representing him as a surgeon removing a patient's heart and brain and throwing them into the garbage bin. Another depicts Qutb prostrating himself in front of an image of a devil in western-style cowboy gear, most probably to suggest his subservience to imperialism. A last illustration suggests a remedy against the Brotherhood's disease: it represents Qutb stabbing himself with a knife.

Why, one might ask, Qutb was identified as the main culprit in the 1965 Organization case, which was a collective project driven by activists outside the prison? In the view of the dominant narrative, Qutb had committed a twofold crime: not only had he openly called for the destruction of the state in *Ma'alim*, but, more crucially, he intentionally misled the youth by framing his vision as Islam. In doing so, it was argued, Qutb failed to fulfill his social responsibility as an elder, which consisted of containing the youthful rebellion instead of instigating it. It was the latter crime that

7. Representation of Sayyid Qutb in press cartoons. "The Brotherhood Shurum Burum," *Sabah al-Khayr*, September 16, 1964, n.p. Courtesy of the Egyptian National Library.

was deemed the most devastating. The age gap between Qutb, who was in his sixties, and his young accomplices, the majority of whom were in their twenties, made it easy to convince popular opinion of his culpability for the conspiracy. The editor in chief of *al-Jumhuriyya*, poet and officer Mustafa Bahjat Badawi, warned against society losing its grip on young people. "It was not the Qur'an that was their constitution," Badawi wrote, referring to the Brotherhood's well-known slogan "the Qur'an is our constitution." Rather, it was "the one written by their leader [*kabīruhum*], entitled *Ma'alim fi-l-Tariq*, which aimed to mislead them and change the meaning of Qur'an. . . . How the youth were permitted to learn Islam from such erroneous sources?"[25]

Famed writer Fathi Ghanim, editor in chief of the weekly *Sabah al-Khayr*, squarely attributed the conspiracy to Qutb's personal hunger for power.

> Why did they seek destruction, burning down and bloodshed? Their senior impostor responds: domination. But he did not provide any explanation or *tafsīr* of the meaning of domination to us, the slaves of the 'Ubudiyya. Clearly, the right to dominate belongs only to the "chosen elite" [*al-ṣafwa al-mukhtāra*], Sayyid Qutb, and their masters who are financing the whole matter,

Ghanim ironized, visibly well-attuned to the vocabulary of *Ma'alim*.[26]

The content of *Ma'alim fi-l-Tariq* provided evidence against Qutb. Passages from the book were widely published in the press, commented upon, and eventually ridiculed. "After reading the first pages from *Ma'alim fi-l-Tariq* by the terrorist Sayyid Qutb, it dawned on me that I was not in front of a book!" the novelist and screenwriter 'Ala' al-Dib began his column. "A black monster leapt from between its pages calling to destroy everything. The sly black monster which grins hastily when you try to catch him, and all smeared in blood repeats the words from the book of God. Then, he quickly walks away passing above ruins and wrecks."[27] In what followed, al-Dib presented a similarly vivid commentary on the book, refuting Qutb's ideas one by one. The observation that Qutb's book was a direct call for violence was made by other commentators as well. A columnist in *Akhir Sa'a* described *Ma'alim* as the founding text of the 1965 Organization that opens with the injunction "Kill immediately!" instead of the conventional *basmala* that should characterize religious publications.[28]

The greatest pressure to refute Qutb's *Ma'alim* fell on the shoulders of Egypt's religious establishment. For the first time since its reorganization in 1961, al-Azhar saw itself given an historical opportunity: to prove its relevance to the Nasserist state by securing Islam against Qutb's subversive ideology. In its mission to counter Qutb's ideas, al-Azhar was supported by another religious institution, the Young Men's Muslim Association (YMMA). Benefiting greatly from Nasser's turn to Arab socialism and the related increase in references to Islam in the representation of his regime, by the mid-1960s the YMMA had significantly expanded. The association had begun to organize conferences of public interest, which were patronized by members of the political leadership. The YMMA reacted to Qutb's conspiracy by convening two conferences, one of which was entitled Laysa min al-Din Fi Shay (It Has Nothing to Do with Religion) and was specifically dedicated to the discussion of *Ma'alim*. A consensus that the book represented "the Satan's call" (*al-da'wa al-shayṭānīyya*) dominated the discussions. Shaykh 'Abd al-Latif al-Subki, the head of the Azhar's fatwa committee, suggested changing the title of Qutb's book from *Ma'alim fi-l-Tariq* (Milestones) to *Mazaliq fi-l-Tariq* (Pitfalls on the Road). Another speaker, poet and supervisor of the YMMA's cultural activities 'Ali al-Jumblati, focused his talk on the most evocative language that could be picked up from Qutb's text to evidence its violent nature, such as "We will have to make great sacrifices," "the revolt against this-worldly authority," or "smashing the systems." Al-Jumblati juxtaposed these citations with information provided by the press of discoveries of weapons, explosives, assassination lists, and maps, in an attempt to demonstrate that Qutb's words matched his intended actions.[29]

While it is true that a vocabulary of confrontation permeates *Ma'alim*, the conditions in which the text was received reinforced its subversive character. Radical rhetoric had been a constant feature of Qutb's political writings since the end of World War II—a time when Egypt called for revolution and when radical language was considered the hallmark of a progressive intellectual. In the mid-1960s, however, the same rhetoric appeared subversive. In a similar manner to Husayn Tawfiq, who went from being considered a glorified assassin of British collaborators to a terrorist, Qutb was portrayed as a bloodthirsty murderer. The decline in esteem mirrored the evolution of Egypt from a colonial society on the brink of revolution to an authoritarian state that dealt with dissidents with an iron fist. This change is perhaps best illustrated by the contrasting associations evoked by Qutb's frequently used expression "smashing the idols" (*taḥṭīm al-ṭawāghīt*). In 1954, Qutb's essay "Tahtim al-tawaghit," which opened his collection of essays published in the same year, *Dirasat Islamiyya*, did not arouse the suspicions of the Azhar magazine editors who reviewed the book. On the contrary, the journal praised Qutb as "a talented author," well known for "his fiery writings against the tyrannical regime of the bygone era."[30] In 1965, however, it was precisely Qutb's unrestrained use of the word *taḥṭīm* (*taḥṭīm al-ṭawāghīt*, *taḥṭīm al-anẓima*) that was held up as semantic evidence of his invitation to violence.

Schismogenesis of Knowledge

Qutb was excommunicated not only from Egypt's present national community, but from its history as well. Following his execution in August 1966, the traces of his literary past began to fade from Egypt's intellectual history. Arabic readers that featured Qutb's poems were removed from educational programs.[31] Some writers, literary historians, and critics withdrew sections on Qutb from post-1966 editions of previously published books.[32] Likewise, poets removed from their collections texts that were related to Qutb,[33] while his name was dropped from subsequent editions of books originally produced with his collaboration.[34] Writers and intellectuals who had been close to Qutb were exhorted to testify in their work against their former colleague. Wadi' Filistin, the former acquaintance of Qutb, refused to disown Sayyid Qutb, attesting that pressures to disown him were indeed real.[35]

Yet a number of authors who had befriended Qutb surrendered to these pressures. One of them was Ahmad Hasan al-Zayyat, a founder and former editor in chief of *al-Risala* magazine, who had facilitated his rise in the magazine back in the 1950s. In 1965, the eighty-year-old al-Zayyat was editing al-Azhar's official magazine. While refraining from public commentary in the initial explosion of the controversy, he broke his silence when Qutb's case briefly resurfaced following his execution in the summer of 1966. In a lengthy and passionate editorial, al-Zayyat listed Qutb's crimes: substitution of Islam by Jahiliyya, monotheism by idolatry, justice by injustice, guidance by chaos, and fraternity by aggression.[36] Another example is Naguib Mahfuz, who adjusted his memoirs to reflect the established schismogenetic discourse. In his 1972 book *Maraya* (Mirrors), Mahfuz included a biographical sketch popularly known to represent Sayyid Qutb. One would expect Mahfuz to share his personal recollections of Qutb from the time they rubbed shoulders in the Publishing Committee for University Graduates. However, Mahfuz's sketch is a reproduction of Qutb's schismogenetic image, representing him as a violent yet failed opportunist.[37]

Writing about the Raba'a massacre in Egypt in 2013, when nearly a thousand Muslim Brothers perished during the dispersal of protests against the deposition of President Muhammad Morsi, Walter Armbrust notes that the preexisting discourse on the Brotherhood facilitated the massacre.[38] The circulation of popular culture infused with anti-Brotherhood sentiment, such as the TV series *Al-Gama'a* broadcast in August–September 2010, helped to crystallize a coherent and frightening image of the organization.[39] Yet this image was also based on older "evidence"—namely, that which had been produced in the 1954 and, especially, 1965 crackdowns on the Brotherhood. Scores of essays, poems, and cartoons published under Nasser's rule were republished in the Egyptian media during 2012 and 2013.[40]

Partly, the efficiency of anti-Brotherhood discourse is due to the fact that the intellectual culture responsible for its production, the "golden sixties," remains unchallenged to this day. There is no doubt that intellectuals who took an active part in the construction of the postcolonial Nasserist state, such as journalists (e.g., Hamid Qandil, Ahmad Rajab, and Fathi Ghanim), writers (Naguib Mahfuz), or poets (Bayram al Tunsi), are figures of intellectual authority in contemporary Egypt. Their opinions and creative contributions to the anti-Qutb campaign of 1965 are therefore posited as uncontestable truths, supported by their intellectual prestige. At the same time, the climate of fear in which they were produced is largely forgotten. A similar pattern can be observed in the academic scholarship on Qutb, and the Muslim Brotherhood more broadly. Memoirs produced in suspicious circumstances, such as Qutb's *Limadha* or 'Ashmawi's *Tanzim*, serve as primary sources in scholarly studies on Islamism. The endless confrontation between the Egyptian state and the Muslim Brotherhood prevents these cultural artefacts from taking their place in history. On the contrary, they are constantly brought back to life to reinforce schismogenetic knowledge of Qutb and to create the impression that history repeats itself.

On the other side of the front line—the Islamist camp—the knowledge produced of Qutb equally serves to maintain the schismogenetic condition. Qutb's execution in August 1966 gave a powerful boost to the publication and dissemination of his books across Muslim-majority countries. Pirated versions of his writings, including of those of no relevance for the Islamist movement such as his autobiography, gothic novel, and literary criticism, flooded the Arab capitals of Amman, Jeddah, Beirut, and Kuwait City between 1966 and the 1970s. As if his existing books were not enough, his essays published in Egyptian periodicals were collected and released as books, giving birth to his *Fi-l-Ta'arikh: Fikra wa Minhaj* (On History: Idea and Method), published in 1967 in Saudi Arabia, and *Ma'araka did al-Yahud* (Struggle against the Jews), published in Beirut in 1970. There were also numerous translations of Qutb's works into Urdu, Malay, Persian, and Turkish.

This short period of uncontrolled circulation of Qutb's intellectual production did not last long. Very soon, efforts were multiplied to put a stop to the unauthorized publishing of Qutb's texts. They were followed by rigorous attempts to interpret, adjust, and manipulate Qutb's intellectual legacy, which resulted in purging from his writings traces of literature, Sufism, and anticolonial and postcolonial Arab thought such as references to Marxism and revolutionary activism. Following Qutb's execution, the authority over his writings passed to his closest intellectual partner and confidante, his brother Muhammad. Upon his release from prison in 1971, Muhammad signed a contractual agreement with Muhammad al-Mu'allim, the owner of the Dar al-Shuruq Publishing House, which acquired the rights to all his and his brothers' writings. After leaving prison, Muhammad Qutb departed for the country where Islamist movements still enjoyed some relevance after the rise of Arab postcolonial regimes: Saudi Arabia. A significant challenge awaited him there, to render Qutb's ideas compatible with the political and religious environment of his adopted country.

First, Qutb's works on art and literature, as well as his collections of poetry, were discarded on the basis that Sayyid Qutb himself had opposed their publication. The publication of Qutb's complete poetry works in 2011 by the Ahram publishing house, favored by the easing of intellectual control in the context of the Egyptian Revolution, sparked a controversy over publishing rights. With granting the rights to publish Qutb's works to al-Shuruq, Muhammad Qutb ordered that his literary texts not be published.[41] These restrictions exert control over Qutb's intellectual legacy.

Second, Qutb's works were purged of allusions to social justice and violence—references that sat uncomfortably with the conservative Saudi state. Thirdly, Muhammad Qutb set out to achieve the challenging task of bridging his brother's conceptual apparatus with the precepts of the Wahhabi tradition.[42] In so doing, he produced lengthy explanations aiming to defend Qutb against the accusations of radicalism, Marxism, and contempt for the Prophet's companions. One of the thorniest issues in this respect was the notion of "unity of existence" (*waḥda al-wujūd*) that—as we have seen in chapter 2—had become a staple of Qutb's entire intellectual production. This notion, which Qutb inherited from his poetic past and incorporated into his Islamic thought, stirred controversy among the Saudi religious establishment. For many religious scholars of the Wahhabi tradition, the claim that God and his creatures formed a unity amounted to sheer blasphemy that challenged the concept of *tawḥīd* and bore traces of Sufi idolatry.[43] In his introduction to his brother's unfinished work *Khasa'is al-Tasawwur al-Islami wa Muqawimatuhu*, published posthumously in 1986, Muhammad Qutb urged readers to disregard his sibling's "puzzling expressions" on the unity of existence in favor of his "more decisive" statements about the distance between God and his creation.[44] Not all of Qutb's ideological adversaries were convinced, and doubts about his religious credentials continue to tarnish his Islamist legacy.

Up to this day, on the both sides of the so-called Islamist/secular divide, the image of Qutb remains schismogenetic. Both sides struggle to perpetuate this image either by constantly reinforcing his excommunicated status through the recirculation of popular culture produced in 1954 and 1965, or by adjusting Qutb's intellectual legacy according to various Islamist orthodoxies. These manipulations have resulted in excluding Qutb from Egypt's rich intellectual and social history. His intellectual collaborations, his references to Sufism, Marxism, and anticolonial activism, have been swept under the rug at the expense of Qutb's representation as an insulated intellectual trapped in the struggle between secularism and Islamism. Significantly, it is by purifying these ideological trends from any traces of historical complexity that their confrontation acquires a moral value as the struggle between the absolute good and evil. Depicted as either a quintessential martyr or as an icon of absolute evil, Qutb is too relevant to contemporary struggles to be left out to history.

The reactivation of the schismogenesis between the Egyptian state and the Muslim Brotherhood, which takes place regularly, albeit with varying degrees of intensity—for instance, in the Tanwir discourse during the 1990s, following the 2005 Muslim Brotherhood's electoral victory, and the 2013 the Raba'a massacre—creates an illusion that Egyptian (and, more largely, Arab) history revolves around the perennial clash between secularism and Islamism.[45] The confrontation that produced the schismogenesis was real, yet it is situated in a particular historical moment that is being continually replayed. This moment is the waning of international focus from the Cold War and the refocusing on local Arab states, either with the intention to protect or destroy them. It was this moment that produced competing claims on the state based on the shared conviction that it was a necessary means to liberate Arab consciousness from the traps of colonialism and to create the new postcolonial Arab self. Qutb's long-standing accusation of *takfīr*—the excommunication of Arab societies from Islam—should be therefore considered in the light of the parallel excommunication of the Brotherhood from Egypt's national community. The mutual excommunication and the bloodshed that followed appeared as the sole exit from the impasse created by the totalizing ambitions of competing postcolonial visions provided by Islamism and Nasserism.

Conclusion

Arts and Religion to Reenchant the World

In 1964, writing his famous opus *Ma'alim* in prison, Qutb reflected on his past:

> The person who is writing these lines has spent forty years of his life in reading and studying almost all aspects of human knowledge. He specialized in some of its branches and studied the others as his leisure pursuit. Then he turned to the wellspring of his faith. He came to feel that whatever he had read so far was as nothing in comparison to what he found here. But he does not regret spending forty years of his life in the pursuit of this knowledge, because he came to know the nature of *Jahiliyya*, its deviations, its pettiness, as well as its noisy and boastful claims![1]

In this rare moment of introspection, Qutb explicitly breaks with his literary past, attributing it to one of the many traps set by Jahiliyya. But, while conceptualizing his life in terms of a rupture, Qutb implies a crucial biographical continuity by suggesting that the forty years spent in the grip of Jahiliyya made him what he had become. Without his past experience, Qutb would not have been capable of identifying the gravity of the threat that the Jahili system presented to humankind, let alone come up with the solution of Islam. Qutb's view of his past reflects the broader worldview he developed toward the end of his life, which was defined by the Manichean struggle between Islam and Jahiliyya. Interestingly, this vision replicates that espoused by Qutb's detractors, who similarly tended to conceptualize Egypt's intellectual history in terms of a struggle—if not between Islam and Jahiliyya, then at least between Islamism and different versions of secular nationalism. Within this hall of mirrors, the idea of struggle provides the organizing principle that structures Egypt's intellectual history.

This book has argued that the perception of Egypt's history as defined by the struggle between Islamism and secularism is produced by schismogenesis. Established during the 1954 crackdown against the Muslim Brotherhood, this schismogenesis has been reactivated with each confrontation between the Islamist organization and the state, including the repression campaigns of 1965 and 2013. It emerges from extreme levels of social polarization and involves attempts to excommunicate the Muslim Brotherhood from Egypt's past and present national community. It not only dictates the historical status reserved to the Islamist organization; it also affects the rest of Egyptian society. The ritual republishing of popular culture produced during past anti-Muslim Brotherhood campaigns allows the national community to tighten its ranks around a shared reckoning of the Brotherhood's crimes. As its most prominent member, accused of having attempted to violently overthrow the state, Qutb is a reference point through which the schismogenetic condition is reproduced. The existing archive on Qutb has been deeply shaped by this condition, which expelled him from history and turned him into a ghost that haunts Egypt in the present.

In order to circumvent the biases inherent in schismogenetic discourse, this book has sought to construct an alternative archive of Qutb's intellectual career. Using all types of text that document the worldly dimension of Egypt's literary life—such as autobiographies, memoirs, tributes, lampoons, rumors, dedications, prefaces, and collections of literary feuds and book reviews—it has followed Qutb's traces in the vibrant interwar and postwar intellectual scenes. The snapshots of his literary life thus collected make him appear to have been an active and opinionated thinker, who traveled easily across different fields of knowledge, befriended famous intellectuals, and spilled out his frustrations in the press. The worldly archive of Qutb's life also suggests the value of reading his biography not from its end point in Islamism, as is usually done, but starting with his life as a poet. This perspective reveals the salience of Qutb's persistent metaphysical drive, which ran through his different intellectual interests, including his poetry, literary criticism, gothic prose, studies of the Qur'an, psychology, and writings on Islam. Setting out from this observation, this book suggested that it was his early experiences of poetry that indirectly steered him in the direction of Islamism.

The origins of Qutb's metaphysical anxiety can be traced back to the modern condition and its redefined understanding of knowledge. The early decades of the twentieth century witnessed the emergence of new notions of truth, which relied on novel ways to access and verify knowledge. A crucial part of this process has been the narrowing down of reality to its sole dimension accessible to human reason, which resulted in the banning of the unseen, *ghayb*, from the scope of the apprehensible world. Instead of being recognized as part of lived human experience, as was the case before the advent of the modern age, the unseen was condemned as superstition and expelled from modern hierarchies of knowledge. First of all, Islam, which in the past authorized a wide range of mystical and esoteric traditions and experiences, was redefined as a rational religion transparent to human reason. After the movement of balanced reform, scholars posited rationalism as the final and the most adequate judge of religion, holding that the sacred texts encouraged humans to contemplate the universe and deduce from their perfect arrangement the fact of the existence of a superior, organizing reason. Modernist writers followed the drive for rationalism initiated by balanced reformers, adding to it their own claim of scientificity—the principle of scientific detachment (*tajarrud*)—which during the interwar period became the battle cry of their entire generation. The postulate that the genuine scientific pursuit consisted of the ability to detach oneself from all types of emotional bonds, be they religious, historical, or nationalist, contributed to aligning reality to its rational perception. As a result of these redefined notions of truth, the world emerged as a deeply disenchanted place with no designated space for *ghayb*.

Poetry, and, more largely literature, was an exception to this drive toward rationalism. If the world of religion and science was disenchanted, that of literature was, on the contrary, enchanted. In reforming literature, modernist writers followed the opposite road to that taken in their reform of religion. Subjected to the influences of Romanticism, poetry was no longer understood in accordance with the neoclassical notion that it should be the ornament of social occasions and the basis for cultural Arab solidarity; instead, it was redefined as the seat of emotion, imagination, and feeling. "The poetry of affect" (*shi'r al-wijdān*), as it was defined by 'Abbas al-'Aqqad, exalted emotion over reason, the senses over the intellect, and the invisible over the visible. As a result, poetry emerged as a space where the connection to the unseen could be experienced and maintained. The potential of poetry to accommodate *ghayb* explains Qutb's passion for this art in his early life.

Qutb's existential anxiety emerged from the gradual shrinkage of the zones where the unseen could be experienced in the world around him. Indeed, his entire intellectual project was driven by the persistent attempt to carve out spaces for *ghayb* in different rational sciences. In literary criticism, this attempt led him to suggest the concept of "affective logic" (*al-manṭiq al-wijdānī*), or the realm of emotion and imagination, through which *ghayb* spoke directly to the human soul. In psychology, Qutb became passionate about the potential of the notion of the unconscious (*lā shu'ūr*) to offer the connection to the unseen. His studies on Qur'anic aesthetics provided the first occasion for the encounter between religion and the arts. From that point onward, Qutb considered them jointly as two different channels to the same metaphysical reality, or a "twin branch" (*ṣinwān*), as he defined it. However, all his attempts to make room for the *al-ghayb* in the realm of rational sciences left him frustrated with the limited capacity of human reason to apprehend experience outside of its control. The decline of Romantic poetry after World War II—condemned as a luxurious activity that only reactionary classes could enjoy—signaled the disappearance of the last bastion of enchantment. While examining the project of Islamist literature, developed by the Qutb brothers in the decades following the 1952 Revolution, one cannot miss their sense of frustration with the path taken by postcolonial politics. Their disappointment was related not only to the brutal suppression of the Islamist movement, but also to the failure of the postcolonial era to reenchant the world. Instead of offering an exit from the reason-dominated world, postcolonial politics only deepened the disenchantment by blessing the Left with final victory. The dominance of materialism (*māddīyya*) in directing postcolonial politics severed the link between humankind and the universe, the Qutb brothers claimed.[2] Combining religion with the arts, their projects of Islamist literature represented the last attempt to reenchant the postcolonial world. Yet this attempt was bound to fail, and during the 1970s and 1980s the ambitious goals of Islamist literature were narrowed down to the enforcement of morality and "clean culture."

The ideological shifts produced by the advent of the modern age took place in a social world inhabited by people and institutions. This book invited the study of Egypt's cultural production as embedded in social practices of intellectual exchange and transmission. Social institutions of literature—associations, coffeehouses, salons, and publishing houses, as well as political parties—played an important role in mediating the production and reception of ideas. The social relationships formed in these institutions exerted power by setting the limits of literature. Informal groupings of *shilla*, which provided the most immediate environment for initiation into the literary milieu, acted as filters through which literary norms were received and practiced on the ground level of intellectual activity. It filtered the reception of norms in two significant ways. First, in the context of interwar intellectual life, in which most knowledge was acquired through the process of self-formation, ideas traveled through social institutions of literature, reaching young intellectuals in their translated, reworked, and adapted versions. Picked up during late evening conversations in literary clubs and coffeehouses or from books passed around in circles, ideas were not necessarily received as fixed certainties but as tools for intellectual experimentation and synthesis.

Social institutions of literature also filtered ideas in another way: by infusing them with the emotional warmth of social relations on which they depended. One of the main suggestions of this book is that modern intellectuals were not only producers of texts, but also social beings embedded in a web of social relations, which provided conditions for their production and naturally directed their application to the realization of sometimes very personal agendas. Kinship, peer friendship, mentorship, discipleship, disputes, and a number of other configurations that tied writers together affected the direction in which the boundaries of literature were pushed. Al-'Aqqad's decades-long conflict with the poet al-Rafi'i, Husayn's reputation as an agent provocateur, and the intellectual mobilization against Qutb in the 1965 conspiracy helped to define the limits of literature, pointing to motifs that were not necessarily related to the content of literary production. Once ideas were out in the social world of literature, it was not only their soundness that counted but also their relationship, whether desired or real, to their producer or transmitter. In a context in which ideas were mediated by people, what also counted was the degree to which these people embodied values that are usually appreciated in the context of pleasurable interaction, such as wit, light-heartedness, or good conversation.

For Qutb, romantic notions of poetry were filtered through the gatherings of his poetic *shilla* of "the Aqqadians," the Apollo association, and, crucially, his discipleship to al-ʿAqqad. The latter played a formative role in shaping not only Qutb's literary taste and ideological worldview, but also the intellectual community with which he identified himself. Involved in multiple strings of social relationships and sites of intellectual practice, he translated romanticism by mixing it with other sources of inspiration, such as philosophy, science, and Sufi religious symbolism. He did not experience it as contradictory to adhere to positivist thinking in his projects of social reform while simultaneously emphasizing the limits of reason in his literary project. Likewise, Qutb's turn to revolutionary politics in the wake of World War II was facilitated not only by the increased value of activism in the intellectual field, but also by a certain configuration of social relations in which Qutb found himself at this time. The feeling of having been betrayed and left behind by the generation of his mentors and the encounter with young and talented novelists willing to transform literature and politics provided him with a new sense of mission and the opportunity to realize it. The principle of *iltizām*, or "commitment," was again filtered through shared experiences in the Publishing Committee for Academics and *al-Fikr al-Jadid* and translated into the struggle for "clean culture." Qutb's Islamist commitment would have been unimaginable without the warm welcome he received from the Muslim Brotherhood. The Islamist organization not only provided him with the opportunity to pursue his spiritual goals but also gave him unlimited access to its intellectual infrastructure, including its intellectual networks, periodicals, publishing initiatives, and the supervision of its cultural department.

Qutb composed his most radical Islamist texts in a context in which the relationship between Islam and national politics once again changed course. During the 1960s, the Nasserist state accepted Islam as the guarantee of the authenticity of Arab socialism and incorporated it into the national project of salvation. While conceiving his Islamist project as the alternative to Nasserism, Qutb shared with it the emphasis on the material structures of the state as the means to preserve the inviolability of the soul, or *'aqīda*. This time, visions produced on the national level of intellectual thought were filtered through thick prison walls, the shared experience of bloodshed inflicted upon the Muslim Brotherhood, and the psychological need to keep alive the hope that it was still possible to change the course of postcolonial politics. On the opposite side of the barricade, Qutb's intellectual heritage was equally mediated. His affiliation with the Muslim Brotherhood—an organization accused of conspiracy against the state—largely determined the way his writings were, and still are, read and understood.

The fluidity of usage to which normative concepts of literature were subjected in intellectual practice explains why the principle of secularism, instituted as the norm in the 1920s, did not confine cultural production to one type of attitude toward Islam. While religion was denied the right to direct change in the formative stage of modern intellectual life, it continued to shape literary sensibilities in multiple other ways. Romantic poets drew inspiration from Sufi metaphysics, writers delved into the Islamic heritage, looking for exemplary personalities and models of political life, and young activists envisioned Islam as a viable political solution. Consider the example of the poet Ahmad Zaki Abu Shadi, who experimented with the most radical forms of poetry while simultaneously adhering to neoclassical aesthetic standards in his work, which was intended for social occasions of the Salafiyya Bookstore circle. Take the poet and novelist Ahmad 'Ali Bakathir, who was part of the Muslim Brotherhood's intellectual networks and published many of his plays in their journal, or the al-Sahhar brothers, who, positioning themselves between literature and the publishing industry, maintained friendly relations with prominent Muslim Brothers while befriending Naguib Mahfuz. The multiplicity of sites of intellectual practice in which intellectuals were engaged allowed a space for creativity, combination, and innovation. There was no clear-cut boundary between Islamists and writers, since, depending on historical circumstances, the lines of division followed more closely the boundaries of class, generation, or spatial limits of neighborhoods than those of strictly ideological origin.

The story of Qutb's life, from his arrival in Cairo at the beginning of the 1920s to his execution in 1966, allows us to trace the constraints imposed on literature by the postcolonial moment. It illustrates the shift from the belief in literature's potential to transform societies to its eventual loss of centrality in the postcolonial project. Literature never fully recovered from the blow it received during the surge of commitment after the war, and writers in Egypt never assumed a status comparable to that enjoyed by *udaba'* under the monarchy. With the rise of postcolonial Pan-Arabist states, the figure of *adib*-politician gave way to technocrats and journalists who became the new intellectual elite. This change took place within a larger shift of priorities from the centrality of thought to that of action.

The growing place of Islam in Qutb's intellectual project reflected these shifts as well. While, in his early works on literature, he conceived of the human mission as geared toward the understanding of existence, in the late 1940s he shifted his focus from understanding to action. Such a change went hand-in-hand with his reconfigured vision of humankind. Qutb had always viewed humans as limited in their capacity to grasp the secrets of the universe and blamed them for excessively trusting their reason. But he had strongly believed in the existence of exceptional human beings who, gifted with extraordinary faculties of feeling, or the "right to connect," could collectively reconstitute the truth and advance humankind's position in the universal order. In his late writings, Qutb no longer shared this optimistic vision. He came to the conclusion that humans were limited, ignorant, and pretentious creatures who blindly followed their passions, desires, and self-interest. He no longer distinguished poets from ordinary men; instead, he stressed their equality in deficiency and weakness. To be sure, Qutb still believed in the existence of geniuses, but their location shifted from the community of poets to the first generation of Muslims—the only ones who, according to Qutb, had succeeded in bringing Islam to life. With Qutb's fading belief in the exceptional nature of poets, literature lost its central position in his project of change. From the overarching scheme of human sublimation, *adab* shrank to a fraction of the experience through which humans uncovered and realized their Islamic worldview.

But, while literature lost its prominence, Qutb's literary education continued to shape Islamist thought and activism in unexpected ways. Moving Islam from the realm of reason to that of emotion was an important innovation that had dramatic consequences. With the denial of reason's capacity to apprehend Islam in its genuine form, Islam was shifted from the grounds of rational debate to the domain of affect-driven action. This was in tune with Qutb's conviction that it was not reason but affect that, being of divine origin, formed the bond between humans and could therefore provide the common ground for creating a community. Yet his understanding of Islam as an emotional experience posited subjectivity as the ultimate criterion of truth, sowing dissension among the faithful and leading to a rash of excommunications of the faithful. Indeed, the resulting proliferation of self-serving interpretations fed violent Islamist movements for at least three decades following his death.

One might wonder, however, to what extent the extraordinary popularity that Qutb's writings enjoyed following his death was due to the sociopolitical climate of their reception, and to what extent this was due to the specificity of Qutb's writing style. After all, Qutb was the author of a theory of aesthetics that held that a certain choice of images, words, sonorities, and musical rhythms had a hidden power of persuasion that operated from beyond the rational realm of perception. Qutb's late texts are permeated with imagery accompanying his descriptions of Islam that conveys a sense of lightness, oceanic vastness, and unobstructed breathing as opposed to the images of narrowness, clutter, and pressure chosen to describe the Jahiliyya. Perhaps this vocabulary reflects the experience of the narrow world of prison confinement in which he was writing. But it certainly resonated with the world in which his works were read: overcrowded, repressive, and unfree societies, gasping under the suffocating weight of Arab postcolonial regimes.

Notes

Bibliography

Index

Notes

Introduction

1. Whether the notion of *al-adab al-islāmī* could be rendered as Islamic or Islamist literature is a matter of debate, depending on whether literatures historically produced in Muslim regions are considered to be part of it. Since Qutb maintained that properly Islamic literature had never existed in history, I chose to adopt the translation that best corresponded to his intended meaning—that is "Islamist literature."

2. Sayyid Qutb, "Manhaj al-Adab," *Majallat al-Ikhwan al-Muslimin*, no. 1, May 20, 1954, 14.

3. Sayyid Qutb, *al-Taswir al-Fanni fi-l-Qur'an* (Cairo: Dar al-Shuruq, 2002), 143–44.

4. *Majallat al-Ikhwan al-Muslimin*, May 20, 1954, and July 29, 1954.

5. Sayyid Qutb, *al-Naqd al-Adabi: Usuluhu wa Manahijuhu* (Cairo: Dar al-Fikri al-'Arabi, n.d.), 103–6; Qutb, *al-'Adalat al-Ijtima'iyya fi-l-Islam* (Cairo: Dar Ihya' al-Kutub al-'Arabiyya, 1958), 249–53.

6. Muhammad Qutb, *Manhaj al-Fann al-Islami* (Cairo: Dar al-Shuruq, n.d.).

7. Sayyid Qutb, *Ma'alim fi-l-Tariq* (Cairo: Dar al-Shuruq, 1992), 137.

8. "Al-Ta'arif bi-l-Rabita," Rabitat al-Adab al-Islami al-'Alamiyya, accessed July 29, 2020, http://www.adabislami.org.

9. See Sabry Hafez's article in response to the protests that took place in Egypt against the reprint of Haydar Haydar's novel *Walima li-'Ashab al-Bahr* by the Egyptian Ministry of Culture: Sabry Hafez, "The Novel, Politics, and Islam," *New Left Review* 5, September–October 2000, accessed July 29, 2020, https://newleftreview.org/issues/II5/articles/sabry-hafez-the-novel-politics-and-islam. For a critical discussion of Hafez's article, see Michael Allan, *In the Shadow of World Literature. Sites of Reading in Colonial Egypt* (Princeton, NJ: Princeton Univ. Press, 2016), 19–25.

10. Allan, *In the Shadow of World Literature*; Lucie Ryzova, *The Age of the Efendiyya: Passages to Modernity in National-Colonial Egypt* (Oxford: Oxford Univ. Press, 2014); Michael Gasper, *The Power of Representation: Publics, Peasants, and Islam in Egypt* (Stanford, CA: Stanford Univ. Press, 2008); Hoda Youssef, *Composing Egypt: Reading, Writing, and the Emergence of Modern Nation* (Stanford, CA: Stanford Univ. Press, 2016).

11. This argument saw an uptick during the 2013 protests organized by renowned Egyptian intellectuals against the nomination to the Ministry of Culture of ʻAlaʼ ʻAbd al-ʻAziz, a professor in cinema studies considered to be close to the Brotherhood. See, for example, ʻAbd al-Muʻti Hijazi, "Sayyid Qutb Badaʼ Shaʻiran wa Intaha Muftiyyan bi-l-Qatl," *al-ʻArab*, September 23, 2013, https://alarab.co.uk/.

12. During the 2013 crackdown of the Muslim Brotherhood, the Egyptian press republished the anti-Brotherhood propaganda produced on the occasion of its 1954 and 1965 crackdowns, see Giedrė Šabasevičiūtė, "Diriger L'Egypte depuis sa tombe: le retour de Sayyid Qutb, 1954, 1965, 2013," *Vacarme* 74 (Winter 2016): 44–49.

13. Samuli Schielke, "There Will Be Blood: Expectation and Ethics of Violence during Egypt's Stormy Season," *Middle East Critique* 26, no. 3 (2017): 205–20.

14. Walter Armbrust defined the discourse on the Brotherhood as schismogenetic, created as a result of extreme political polarization between the state and the Islamist organization, see Walter Armbrust, *Martyrs and Tricksters: An Ethnography of the Egyptian Revolution* (Princeton, NJ: Princeton Univ. Press, 2019), 17, 168–69.

15. This thesis has been suggested by ʻAli Shalash, *al-Tamarrud ʻAla al-Adab: Dirasa fi Tajriba Sayyid Qutb* (Beirut: Dar al-Shuruq, 1994).

16. The Egyptian TV series *al-Gamaʻa* broadcast at the end of 2010 provides an illustration. For the discussion on *al-Gamaʻa*'s contribution to the Brotherhood's phantasmagoric image, see Armbrust, *Martyrs and Tricksters*, 157–80; and Marie Vannetzel, *Les Frères musulmans égyptiens: Enquête sur un secret public* (Paris: Ed. Karthala, 2016), 43–47.

17. For the illustration, see Hilmi al-Namnam, *Baʻthat Sayyid Qutb. Al-Wathaʼiq al-Rasmiyya* (Cairo: Dar al-Kutub wa-l-Wathaʼiq al-Qawmiyya, 2017), 41–67. On Qutb's eccentric sexual behavior, see al-Namnam's interview in Ibrahim ʻIssa's TV show "Mukhtalif ʻAlayhi Maʻ Ibrahim ʻIssa . . . Sayyid Qutb," YouTube, 31:16–33:02, May 20, 2018, https://www.youtube.com/watch?v=iNSDk81SxhY&fbclid=IwAR0Nup_lK8_cOYu3qe9FmbCES37Xlx7E_A5Ux93IDYriqFK6UXzqB786JpQ.

18. The biographic literature on Qutb is vast. The most significant contributions are Shalash, *al-Tamarrud ʻAla al-Adab*; Sharif Yunis, *Sayyid Qutb wa-l-Usuliya al-Islamiyya* (Cairo: Dar Tayba li-l-Dirasa wa-l-Nashr, 1995); ʻAbd al-Fatah al-Khalidi, *Sayyid Qutb: Min al-Milad ila al-Istishhad* (Damascus: Dar al-Qalam, 2007); John Calvert, *Sayyid Qutb and the Origins of Radical Islamism* (London: Hurst, 2010); James Toth, *Sayyid Qutb: The Life and Legacy of a Radical Islamic Intellectual* (New York: Oxford Univ. Press, 2013); Adnan Musallam, *From Secularism to Jihad: Sayyid Qutb and the Foundations of Radical Islamism* (Westport, CT: Praeger, 2005), Alain Roussillon, "Trajectoires réformistes. Sayyid Qutb et Sayyid ʻUways: figures modernes de l'intellectuel en Égypte," *Égypte/Monde Arabe* 6 (1991): 91–139; and Hilmi al-Namnam, *Sayyid Qutb: Sirat al-Tahawwulat* (Cairo: al-Karma li-l-Nashr wa-l-Tawziʻ, 2014).

19. While differing on the orientation from which Qutb had departed—identified, alternately, as "secularism" (Toth, *Life*, 36–55), "Muslim secularism" (Musallam, *Sayyid*

Qutb, 50), "secular nationalism" (Calvert, *Sayyid Qutb*, 126–27), and "literature" (Shalash, *al-Tamarrud 'Ala al-Adab*)—scholars seem to agree that these ideological orientations are opposed to Islamism.

20. Calvert, Sayyid Qutb, 8–10; John Calvert, "Sayyid Qutb and the Power of Political Myth: Insight from Sorel," in "Islam and Modernity," special issue, *Historical Reflections* 30, no. 3 (Fall 2004): 509–28.

21. Yunis, *Sayyid Qutb*. This thesis echoes Angela Giordani's observation that Qutb's Islamism and the national project of literary modernity shared the same mode of thinking in totalities. See Angela Giordani, "To Be an Adib: Sayyid Qutb's Intellectual Biography Reconsidered" (master's thesis, Columbia Univ., 2014).

22. Shalash, *al-Tamarrud 'Ala al-Adab*, 83–87.

23. Cyrus Schayegh and Yoav Di Capua, "Why Decolonization?," *International Journal for Middle East Studies* 52 (2020): 142–43.

24. Yoav Di-Capua, *No Exit: Arab Existentialism, Jean-Paul Sartre, and Decolonization* (Chicago: Univ. of Chicago Press, 2018), chap. 3.

25. Bernard Lahire, *Frantz Kafka: Éléments pour une théorie de la création littéraire* (Paris: Découverte, 2018).

26. Lahire, *Frantz Kafka*, 111–19.

27. Pierre Bourdieu introduced the notion of habitus in his study of the philosophy of Martin Heidegger; see his "L'ontologie politique de Martin Heidegger," *Actes de la recherche en sciences sociales*, no. 5 (1975): 109–56.

28. Lahire, *Frantz Kafka*, 87–146.

29. For example, Calvert, *Sayyid Qutb*, 8; and Toth, *Sayyid Qutb*, 7.

30. Put differently, not all events deemed transformative on the national level are such for an individual life. The methodological flaws inherent in some uses of the context to account for particular situations were pointed out by the defenders of *microhistoria*. See Jacques Revel, *Jeux d'Échelles: La micro-analyse à l'expérience* (Paris: Gallimard & Le Seuil, 1996).

31. See, for example, Hilmi al-Namnam's interview: al-Hurra-al-Qanat-Hurra, "Mukhtalif 'Alayhi Ma' Ibrahim 'Issa . . . Sayyid Qutb," 10:18–12:35.

32. Classic examples are J. Brugman, *An Introduction to the History of Modern Arab Literature* (Leiden: A. J. Brill, 1984); and Albert Hourani, *Arabic Thought in the Liberal Age, 1798–1939* (Cambridge: Cambridge Univ. Press, 1983).

33. For example, M. M. Badawi, *A Critical Introduction to Modern Arab Poetry* (Cambridge: Cambridge Univ. Press, 1975); and Paul Starkey, *Modern Arab Literature* (Edinburgh: Edinburgh Univ. Press, 2006).

34. The most famous example of this approach is Timothy Mitchel, *Colonizing Egypt* (Berkeley: Univ. of California Press, 1991).

35. Khaled Furani, *Silencing the Sea: Secular Rhythms in Palestinian Poetry* (Stanford, CA: Stanford Univ. Press, 2012), 4.

36. Concerning literature, the most significant contributions to this tradition are Furani, *Silencing the Sea*; and Allan, *In the Shadow.*

37. The academic literature produced in this perspective is vast. For the formation of the middle class, see Ryzova, *Age of Efendiyya*; for popular literature, Samah Selim, *Popular Fiction, Translation, and the Nahda* (Cham: Palgrave Macmillan, 2019); for Islamic reform, Leor Halevi, *Modern Things on Trial: Islam's Global and Material Reformation in the Age of Rida, 1865–1935* (New York: Columbia Univ. Press, 2019); for literacy, Hoda A. Youssef, *Composing Egypt: Reading, Writing, and the Emergence of Modern Nation* (Stanford, CA: Stanford Univ. Press, 2016); for politics, Hussein Omar, "Arabic Thought in the Liberal Cage," in *Islam after Liberalism*, ed. Faisal Devji and Zaheer Kazmi (London: Hurst/Oxford Univ. Press, 2017), 17–46; and, for literature, Elisabeth Holt: *Fictitious Capital: Silk, Capital, and the Rise of the Arabic Novel* (New York: Fordham Univ. Press, 2017).

38. In *Politics of Piety: The Islamic Revival and the Feminist Subject* (Princeton, NJ: Princeton Univ. Press, 2005), Saba Mahmood suggests that political Islamist movements are secular since they rely on secular forms of social and political action (40–78).

39. Gregory Starrett, "The Varieties of Secular Experience," *Comparative Studies in Society and History* 52, no. 3 (2010): 631–34.

40. As Gregory Starrett has remarked, "A secular age is a secular age because there is "secularism" somewhere in it, not because secularism is a majority philosophy or even a popular one" ("Varieties of Secular Experience," 634).

41. The notion of secularism suggests that before its advent human life was defined by purity and oneness. As Samuli Schielke has noted, rather, to a sociohistorical reality, purity and oneness belong to the order of imaginaries, aspirations, and strivings. See Schielke, "Is Prose Poetry a Conspiracy Against the Noble Qur'an? Poetics, Humans, and Gods in Contemporary Egypt," *Historical Social Research* 44, no. 3 (2019): 122.

42. For the detailed study of the manifestations of the secular in Palestinian poetry, see Furani, *Silencing the Sea*. On the connections between sound and secularity, see Charles Hirschkind, *The Ethical Soundscape: Cassette Sermons and Islamic Counterpublics* (New York: Columbia Univ. Press, 2006).

43. Schielke, "Prose Poetry."

44. Muhammad Sa'id al-'Aryan, *Hayat al-Rafi'i* (Cairo: Maktabat al-Tijara, 1955), 217.

45. On *shilla*, see Aymon Kreil, "Territories of Desire: A Geography of Competing Intimacies in Cairo," *Journal of Middle East Women's Studies* 12, no. 2 (July 2016): 166–80; on the function of *shilla* in politics, see Robert Springborg, *Family, Power, and Politics in Egypt: Sayed Bey Marei—His Clan, Clients, and Cohorts* (Philadelphia: Univ. of Pennsylvania Press, 1982).

46. Studies on the conditions surrounding the emergence of the sixties and nineties generations in Egypt have shown how aesthetic coherence intersects with other types of

social bonds created between the members of a generation. See Richard Jacquemond, *Entre scribes et écrivains: le champ littéraire dans l'Egypte contemporaine* (Paris: Actes Sud 2003), 202–11; Nancy Linthicum, "The Cultural Newspaper Akhbar al-Adab and the Making of Egypt's "Nineties Generation", *Alif* 37 (2007): 249–50; and Yasmine Ramadan, "The Emergence of the Sixties Generation in Egypt and the Anxiety over Categorization," *Journal of Arabic Literature* 43 (2012): 423–24. See also Giedrė Šabasevičiūtė, "When a Coterie Becomes a Generation: Intellectual Sociability and the Narrative of Generational Change in Sayyid Qutb's Egypt," in *Snapshots of Change: Methodological Approaches to Societies in Transformation*, ed. Yasmine Berriane, Aymon Kreil, Annuska Derks, and Dorothea Lüddeckens (London: Palgrave Macmillan, 2021).

47. Michael Gasper, *The Power of Representation: Publics, Peasants, and Islam in Egypt* (Stanford, CA: Stanford Univ. Press, 2008).

48. Dale F. Eickelman and Armando Salvatore, "The Public Sphere and Muslim Identities," in "Priorities of Social Justice," special issue, *Archives Européennes de Sociologie* 43, no. 1 (2002), 92–115; Teresa Pepe, "Critics, Moralists, and Intellectuals—The Transformation of the Udabā of the Arab Naḥda: A Historical-Conceptual Approach," *Modern Oriente* 99 (2019): 179–202.

49. On these different practices, see Jocelyn Sharlet, *Patronage and Poetry in the Islamic World: Social Mobility and Status in the Medieval Middle East and Central Asia* (London: I. B. Tauris, 2011); Jonathan Berkey, *The Transmission of Knowledge in Medieval Cairo: a Social History of Islamic Education* (Princeton, NJ: Princeton Univ. Press, 1992); and Brinkley Messick, *The Calligraphic State: Textual Domination and History in a Muslim Society* (Berkeley: Univ. of California Press, 1992).

50. On the significance of private salons (*majālis*) in premodern culture, see Nelly Hanna, *In Praise of Books: A Cultural History of Cairo's Middle Class, Sixteenth to the Eighteenth Century* (Syracuse, NY: Syracuse Univ. Press, 2003); and Peter Gran, *Islamic Roots of Capitalism: Egypt, 1740–1840* (Syracuse, NY: Syracuse Univ. Press, 1998), 57–75.

51. On the significance of the salon held by the Lebanese-Palestinian poetess Mayy Ziyada for the intellectual and political development of the early interwar period, see Boutheina Khaldi, *Egypt Awakening in the Early Twentieth Century* (New York: Palgrave Macmillan, 2012).

52. "If my kids were hungry I would grill Taha Husayn and feed them his meat, were it permissible (*halāl*) to serve my kids dog's meat," wrote the poet and critic Zaki Mubarak in his poetry collection *Alhan al-Khulud*. See the quote in Wadi Filistin, *Wadi' Filistin Yatahaddath 'n A'lam 'Asrihi*, vol. 1 (Damascus: Dar al-Qalam, 2003), 246. Credit to Raph Cormack for having brought this quotation to my attention.

53. On this tension in other contexts, see Brinkley Messick, *Calligraphic State*, 203–55; Mitchel, *Colonizing Egypt*, 128–60; and Abdellah Hammoudi, *Master and Disciple: The Cultural Foundations of Moroccan Authoritarianism* (Chicago: Univ. of Chicago Press, 1997), 81–97.

54. Walter Armbrust, *Mass Culture and Modernism in Egypt* (Cambridge: Cambridge Univ. Press, 1996).

55. ʿAbbas al-ʿAqqad, *Rijal ʿAraftuhum* (Cairo: Mu'assasa Hindawi li-l-Taʿalim wa-l-Thaqafa, 2013), 84.

56. ʿAbbas Khidr, *Ha'ula'u ʿAraftuhum* (Cairo: Dar al-Maʿarif, 1998), 120.

57. Taha Husayn, *Hadith al-Arbiʿa*, vol. 3 (Cairo: Dar al-Maʿarif, n. d.), 163.

58. ʿAbd al-Hamid Juda al-Sahhar, *Suwwar wa Dhikrayyat* (Cairo: Maktaba Misr, n. d.), 192.

59. Ryzova, *Age*, 139–73.

60. Ryzova, 197, 211–14.

61. On strolling in *mawlids*, see ʿAbbas al-ʿAqqad, *ʿAbqariyya Muhammad* (Beirut: al-Maktaba al-ʿAsriyya, n.d.), 5; on the habit of Apollo members to meet in a coffee shop in Hilmiyya, see Khidr, *Ha'ula'u ʿAraftuhum*, 46–47.

62. Scholars focusing on the circulation of sciences from Western Europe stressed the degree to which Western notions were modified by the process of reception allowing synthesis to take place. On the reception of Darwinism, see Marwa Elshakry, *Reading Darwin in Arabic, 1860–1950* (Chicago: Univ. of Chicago Press, 2013); on Freudian psychoanalysis, Omnia El Shakry, *The Arabic Freud: Psychoanalysis and Islam in Modern Egypt* (Princeton, NJ: Princeton Univ. Press, 2017); and, on existentialism, Yoav Di-Capua, *No Exit: Arab Existentialism, Jean-Paul Sartre, and Decolonization* (Chicago: Univ. of Chicago Press, 2018).

63. Natalie Zemon Davis, cited in Elshakry, *Reading Darwin in Arabic*, 22.

1. Becoming an *Adib*

1. Sayyid Qutb, "Bayn al-ʿAqqad wa-l-Rafiʿi," *al-Risala*, no. 263, July 18, 1938, 1179.

2. Muhammad Ahmad al-Ghamrawi, "al-Qadim wa-l-Jadid. Naqd wa Tahlil," *al-Risala*, July 4, 1938, 1103–5.

3. Sayyid Qutb, *A Child from the Village*, trans. John Calvert (Syracuse, NY: Syracuse Univ. Press, 2004), 92. Decades later, the Muslim Brotherhood's famed Islamic scholar Yusuf al-Qaradawi also wrote his autobiography under a similar title, *Ibn al-Qariyya wa-l-Kuttab* (A Son of a Village and Islamic Elementary School). See Yusuf al-Qaradawi, *Ibn al-Qariyya wa-l-Kuttab: Malamih Sirah wa-Masirah* (Cairo: Dar al-Shuruq, 2002).

4. On this type of literature, see Samah Selim, *Popular Fiction, Translation, and the Nahda* (Cham: Palgrave Macmillan, 2019).

5. Lucie Ryzova, "My Notepad Is My Friend: Efendis and the Act of Writing in Modern Egypt," *Maghreb Review* 32, no. 4 (2007): 329.

6. Qutb, *Child*, 95.

7. Qutb, 92–94.

8. It was usually mothers, who had better insight into social mobility opportunities and struggled to ensure modern education of their male offsprings; see Ryzova, *Age*, 122–36.

9. Lucie Ryzova defines this sense of mission as part of "efendi subjectivity" (*Age*, 131). Departing from Pierre Bourdieu's tradition, Alain Roussillon calls the same type of worldview "reformist habitus"; see his "Republican Egypt Interpreted: Revolution and Beyond", in *The Cambridge History of Egypt*, ed. M. W. Daly (Cambridge: Cambridge Univ. Press, 1998), 342.

10. Ryzova, *Age*, 186. Qutb as well saw his Cairo-based uncle as a privilege: *Child*, 130–31.

11. Iman Farag, "Les manuels d'histoire égyptienne : genèse et imposition d'une norme, *Genèses*, no. 44 (March 2001): 4–29.

12. The list of the subjects Qutb studied in Dar al-'Ulum is reproduced in the official documents of his 1948 professional mission to the United States; see Hilmi al-Namnam, *Ba'tha Sayyid Qutb . . . al-Watha'iq al-Rasmiyya* (Cairo: Dar al-Kutub wa-l-Watha'iq al-Qawmiyya, 2017), 81. On the instruction of pedagogy in Dar al-'Ulum, see Hilary Kalmbach, "Teaching Teachers How to Teach: Transnational Exchange and the Introduction to Social-Scientific Pedagogy in 1890s Egypt," in *The Long 1890s in Egypt: Colonial Quiescence, Subterranean Resistance*, ed. Marilyn Booth and Anthony Gorman (Edinburg: Edinburgh Univ. Press, 2014), 87–116.

13. Ryzova, *Age*, 161–77.

14. 'Abbas al-'Aqqad, *Diwan al-'Aqqad Arba't Ajza' fi al-Mujallad al-Wahid* (Cairo: Matba'at al-Muqtataf wa-l-Muqattam, 1928), 8.

15. See Salama Musa's essay series, "Suwwar Mujaza' li-Udaba Misr," published in *al-Hilal* from January 1 to July 1, 1924. See also Taha Husayn, "al-Qadim wa-l-Hadith," in *Hadith al-Arbi'a*, vol. 3 (Cairo: Mu'assasa Hindawi li-l-Ta'alim wa-l-Nashr, 2014), 579–82.

16. Al-Sayyid Hasan al-Shakra, "Ibtikar Jadid fi-l-'Ilan 'n al-Nafs. Sa'a Ma' Duktur Taha Husayn," *al-Fath*, no. 75, December 15, 1927, 12-14; Abu Rashiq, "Taha Husayn fi Ghururihi wa Khida'ihi. Kalima 'n Hadithihi al-Akhir fi Nadi Niqabat al-Muwazzafin," *al-Fath*, no. 52, July 7, 1927, 1–3. See also the fictional satire describing the meeting of Husayn's *shilla* in a coffeehouse: "Jama'at al-Ilhad al-Za'ifun fi-l-Manam," *al-Fath*, no. 187, February 20, 1930, 10–11.

17. Taha Husayn, 'Ali 'Abd al-Raziq, and Muhammad Husayn Haykal were members of the Liberal Constitutionalist Party, regularly contributed articles to its organ *al-Siyasa*, and taught at the Egyptian University. Khalil al-Sakakini lectured at the university in 1921 and wrote for *al-Siyasa* as well.

18. For the example of their classification as "the old," see Salama Musa's series in *al-Hilal*, "Suwwar Mujaza' li-Udaba Misr."

19. Muhammad al-Ghamrawi, “al-Qadim wa-l-Jadid. Naqd wa Tahlil,” *al-Risala*, no. 261, July 4, 1938, 1103.

20. Rashid Rida, “Shaykh Muhammad al-Mahdi,” *al-Manar* 25, no. 3 (1924): 219–21.

21. Reported by Muhibb al-Din al-Khatib in “Madha ‘Arafu ‘n Taha Husayn?” *al-Zahra* 3, no. 4 (1926): 271.

22. Husayn, *Hadith al-Arbi‘a*, 694.

23. Mustafa Sadiq al-Rafi‘i, *Tahta Rayat al-Qur’an. Al-Ma‘araka Bayn al-Qadim wa-l-Jadid* (Beirut: al-Maktabat al-‘Asriyya), 14.

24. Mitchel, *Colonizing Egypt* (Berkeley: Univ. of California Press, 1988), 128–58.

25. Lucie Ryzova, “My Notepad Is My Friend: Efendis and the Act of Writing in Modern Egypt,” *Maghreb Review* 32, no. 4 (2007): 323–48.

26. Mitchel, *Colonizing Egypt*, 158.

27. On Rashid Rida’s use of the print as the means of preaching, see Dyala Hamzah, “From ‘Ilm to Ṣiḥāfa or the Politics of Public Interest (Maṣlaḥa): Muhammad Rashīd Riḍa and his Journal al-Manār (1898–1935),” in *The Making of the Arab Intellectual, 1880–1960: Empire, Public Sphere, and the Colonial Coordinates of Selfhood*, ed. Dyala Hamzah (London: Routledge, 2012), 90–127; on issuing fatwas, see Leor Halevi, *Modern Things on Trial: Islam’s Global and Material Reformation in the Age of Rida, 1865–1935* (New York: Columbia Univ. Press, 2019).

28. On this tension, see Abdellah Hammoudi, *Master and Disciple: The Cultural Foundations of Moroccan Authoritarianism* (Chicago: Univ. of Chicago Press, 1997), 81–97.

29. Ryzova, *Age*, 151–54.

30. Israel Gershoni and James P. Jankowski, *Egypt, Islam, and the Arabs: The Search for Egyptian Nationhood, 1900–1930* (Oxford: Oxford Univ. Press, 1986), 77–191.

31. Abdelrashid Mahmoudi, *Tāhā Husayn’s Education: From Azhar to the Sorbonne* (Richmond: Curzon, 1998), 43–52. Ahmad Lutfi al-Sayyid’s influence was wide. At different moments in Egyptian history, he headed the newspaper *al-Jarida*, Egyptian National Library Dar al-Kutub al-Misriyya, Egyptian University, and Language Academy. See his autobiography, *Qissat Hayati* (Cairo: al-Hay’at al-Misriyyat al-‘Amma li-l-Kitab, 1998).

32. According to Walid Kazziha, founded to represent Egypt’s big landowning families, the party emphasized the significance of the kinship bond. See Kazziha, “The Jarida-Umma Group and Egyptian Politics,” *Middle Eastern Studies* 13, no. 3 (October 1977): 373–85.

33. On the salon held in the ‘Abd al-Raziq’s residence, see James Broucek, “The Controversy of Sheikh ‘Ali ‘Abd al-Raziq” (PhD diss., Florida State Univ., 2012), 117, 128–29.

34. ‘Abbas al-‘Aqqad, *Rijal ‘Araftuhum* (Cairo: Dar al-Hilal, 1963), 116–17.

35. Ahmad Zaki Abu Shadi, “Kalima Muharrir,” *Apollo* 2, no. 9 (May 1934): 744.

36. Taha Husayn confessed that he was able to read al-‘Aqqad’s essays previously published in the rival *al-Balagh* only after they were issued in a book format; see Taha

Husayn, *Hadith al-Arbi'a*, vol. 3 (Cairo: Dar al-Ma'arif, 1989), 96. Husayn also feared that the nonpartisan magazine *al-Risala* might not survive political pressures; see Ahmad Hasan al-Zayyat, *Wahi al-Risala* (Cairo: Nahda Misr, 1956), 72.

37. Cited in Mahmoudi, *Tāhā Husayn's Education*, 32.

38. Taha Husayn, *The Days: His Autobiography in Three Parts*, trans. E. H. Paxton, Hilary Wayment, and Kenneth Cragg (Cairo: American Univ. in Cairo Press, 1997), 232.

39. Muhammad Abdel-Hai, "Shelley and the Arabs: An Essay in Comparative Literature," *Journal of Arabic Literature* 3 (1972): 74; M. M. Badawi, *A Critical Introduction to Modern Arab Poetry* (Cambridge: Cambridge Univ. Press, 1975), 68. On Taha Husayn's association to Romanticism, see Pierre Cachia, *Taha Husayn: His Place in the Egyptian Literary Renaissance* (London: Luzac, 1956), 132.

40. Terri Deyoung, *Mahmud Sami al-Barudi: Reconfiguring Society and the Self* (Syracuse, NY: Syracuse Univ. Press, 2015), 124–25; Roger Allen, *The Arabic Literary Heritage: The Development of Its Genres and Criticisms* (Cambridge: Cambridge Univ. Press, 1998), 106.

41. Taha Husayn, *Fi-l-Adab al-Jahili* (Cairo: Lajnat al-Ta'alif wa-l-Tarjama wa-l-Nashr, 1933), 61.

42. Taha Husayn, *Fi-l-Shi'r al-Jahili* (Cairo: Ru'a li-l-Nashr wa-l-Tawzi', 2007), 74–77.

43. Ahmad Amin, *My Life: The Autobiography of an Egyptian Scholar, Writer, and Cultural Leader*, trans. Issa J. Boullata (Leiden: Brill, 1978), 45, 52, cited in Donald Malcolm Reid, *Cairo University and the Making of Modern Egypt* (Cambridge: Cambridge Univ. Press, 1990), 58–59.

44. Husayn, *Days*, 118.

45. 'Abbas al-'Aqqad, *Shu'ara' Misr wa Bi'atuhum fi-l-Jil al-Madi* (Cairo: Maktabat al-Nahdat al-Misriyya, 1953), cited in Badawi, *Critical Introduction*, 87.

46. Al-Khatib, "Ma 'Arafu 'n Taha Husayn," 271.

47. Henri Lauzière, *The Making of Salafism: Islamic Reform in the Twentieth Century* (New York: Columbia Univ. Press, 2016), 44–49.

48. Indira Falk Gesink, *Islamic Reform and Conservatism: Al-Azhar and the Evolution of Modern Sunni Islam* (London: I. B. Tauris, 2010), 66–71.

49. Giedrė Šabasevičiūtė, "When a Coterie Becomes a Generation: Intellectual Sociability and the Narrative of Generational Change in Sayyid Qutb's Egypt," in *Snapshots of Change: Methodological Approaches to Societies in Transformation*, ed. Yasmine Berriane, Aymon Kreil, Annuska Derks, and Dorothea Lüddeckens (London: Palgrave Macmillan, 2021).

50. Henry Lauzière, "The Construction of Salafiyya: Reconsidering Salafism from the Perspective of Conceptual History," *International Journal of Middle East Studies* 42, no. 3 (2010): 377; Catherine Mayeur-Jaouen, "Les débuts d'une revue néo-salafiste: Muhibb al-dîn al-Khatîb et al-Fath de 1926 à 1928," *Revue des Mondes Musulmans et de la Méditerranée*, nos. 95–98 (April 2002): doi.org/10.4000/remmm.234 (accessed July 29, 2020).

51. *Hukm Hay'at Kibar al-'Ulama fi Kitab al-Islam wa Usul al-Hukm wa Hukm Majlis Ta'adib al-Quda' al-Shara'iyyin fi Wizarat al-Huqqaniyya bi-Fasl Mu'allifihi Min al-Qada' al-Shara'i* (Cairo: al-Matba'at al-Salafiyya, 1925). The ruling was distributed for free in the Bookstore; see the announcement in *al-Zahra* 2, no. 2, (1925), 145.

52. The establishment provided its printing and advertising services to Husayn's and 'Abd al-Raziq's critics. As such, it acted as a powerful magnet of more conservative elements of the reformist scene. See the publications by Muhammad al-Khidr Husayn *Naqd al-Kitab al-Islam wa Usul al-Hukm* and *Naqd Kitab fi-l-Shi'r al-Jahili*, published by the Salafiyya Bookstore and Publishing House in 1925 and 1926, respectively; Muhammad al-Ghamrawi, *al-Naqd al-Tahlili li-l-Kitab al-Adab al-Jahili*, published in 1929; and the articles by al-Rafi'i and Shakib Arslan published in the Bookstore's periodicals *al-Hadiqa*, *al-Zahra*, and *al-Fath*.

53. Nadine Picaudou, *l'Islam entre religion et l'idéologie: Essai sur la modernité musulmane* (Paris: Gallimard, 2010), 21–105; Francis Robinson, "Technology and Religious Change: Islam and the Impact of Print," in "How Social, Political, and Cultural Information Is Collected, Defined, Used, and Analyzed," special issue, *Modern Asian Studies* 27, no. 1 (February 1993): 229–51.

54. The duo collaborated on the publication of *Asrar al-Balagha* by the eleventh-century Persian grammarian 'Abd al-Qahir al-Jurjani and *Dala'il al-'Ijaz* by the same author, as well as on the compilation of sayings attributed to the Prophet Muhammad's son-in-law and caliph Ali b. Abi Talib *Nahj al-Balagha*. See Rashid Rida's introduction to the third edition of al-Jurjani's *Dala'il al-'Ijaz fi 'Ilm al-Ma'ani* (Cairo: Dar al-Manar, 1913), h–s; and Rashid Rida, "Kitab Nahj al-Balagha," *al-Manar* 6, no. 16 (November 1903): 787–90.

55. Sayyid Muhammad Rizvi, "Muhibb al-Din al-Khatib. A Portrait of Salafist-Arabist (1886–1969)" (PhD diss., Simon Fraser Univ., 1991), 22–46.

56. Muhibb al-Din al-Khatib, "Sabab Wujud al-Fath," *al-Fath*, vol. 551, Rabi' al-Awwal 2, 1356, 10–12. For the biographical sketch of Ahmad Taymur and his role in the collection and edition of Arab manuscripts, see Ahmed El Shamsy, *Rediscovering the Islamic Classics: How Editors and Print Culture Transformed an Intellectual Tradition* (Princeton, NJ: Princeton Univ. Press, 2020), 102–11.

57. On the discussion on the usages of the *salafīyya* notion during the interwar period see Lauzière, "Construction," 377–78.

58. For example, Muhammad 'Abdu was responsible for the publication of a fictional text, a version of the ninth-century text *Maqamat* by Hamadhani. See El Shamsy, *Rediscovering the Islamic Classics*, 150–51.

59. Muhibb al-Din al-Khatib, "Shi'runa wa Sha'iruna," *al-Zahra* 3, no. 10 (1927): 608–16. For the discussion of literary forms appreciated within the Bookstore's circle, see chap. 4.

60. 'Ali al-Tantawi, *Dhikrayyat*, vol. 1 (Jedda: Dar al-Manara li-l-Nashr, 1985), 262–63.

61. Muhibb al-Din al-Khatib, "Shi'runa wa Sha'iruna," *al-Zahra* 3, no. 10 (1927): 616.

62. The poet Mustafa Sadiq al-Rafi'i was one of the main contributors to al-Khatib's periodicals, especially to *al-Hadiqa*, founded in 1924. One of the earliest publications by the Salafiyya Press was his *Nashid Sa'd Zaghlul* (1922), which was popularized as the first Egypt's national anthem *Aslami Ya Misr.*

63. Hasan al-Banna, *Mudhakkarat al-Da'wa wa-l-Da'iyya* (Kuwait: Maktaba Ufaq, 2012), 56.

64. Ahmad Zaki Abu Shadi, "Naqlat al-Zahra," in *al-Hadiqa: Majmu'at Adab Bari' wa Hikma Baligha*, ed. Sulayman Bin Salih al-Kharasi (Riyad: Dar al-'Asima, 2011), 729–30.

65. See his poem addressing *al-mutajarridūn*, the label the Salafiyya Bookstore and Publishing House reserved for Husayn's group, in "Ila al-Mutajarridin," *al-Zahra* 3, no. 1 (1926), 7. See also Abu Shadi's essay, published in his poetry collection, where he takes a stance against *al-mutajarridūn*: "Al-Sha'ir wa-l-Shi'r. Bahth Falsafi," in *al-Shafaq al-Baqi* (Cairo: al-Matba'at al-Salafiyya, 1926), 45–50.

66. He cofounded Jama'iyyat al-Nahda al-'Arabiyya during his studies in Istanbul: Leyla Dakhli, *Une génération d'intellectuels arabes: Syrie et Liban (1908–1940)* (Paris: Ed. Karthala, 2009), 61–62.

67. The popular name for the Ottoman-German scheme to encourage revolutionary sentiment among Muslim populations in the colonized territories during World War I.

68. In 1911–12, he took to the battlefield in Libya to fight Italian occupation, in 1914 took part in capturing the Suez Canal, and in 1917–18 served as the special emissary to Berlin on behalf of the Ottoman state. See William Cleveland, *Islam against the West: Shakib Arslan and the Campaign for Islamic Nationalism* (Austin: Univ. of Texas Press, 1985), 20–21, 30–31, 39.

69. Reid, *Cairo University*, 87–102.

70. Husayn suggested closing down Dar al-'Ulum and transferring its prerogative of teachers' training to the Egyptian University. This move was interpreted by some as aiming to increase the employment chances for the university's graduates; see Husayn, *Fi-l-Adab*, 11–12; and Husayn, *Mustaqbal al-Thaqafa fi Misr* (Cairo: Dar al-Ma'arif, 1944), 56, 211–23.

71. Al-Ghamrawi, *al-Naqd*, 6–8.

72. Al-Rafi'i, *Tahta Rayat al-Qur'an*, 105.

73. Muhibb al-Din al-Khatib, "Hal Yumkin Taghyr Ittijah Wizarat al-Ma'arif Ba'd Taghyr Wakiliha?" *al-Fath*, no. 668, Rajab 9, 1358, 1–4.

74. Husayn's victory in the controversy catapulted him to stardom. He was frequently solicited for interviews in the Egyptian press, invited to give talks, and dispatched as the Egyptian University's delegate to the International Congress of Orientalists in 1928. For illustration, see a highly flattering interview with Husayn conducted by *al-Hilal* magazine, "Sa'a Ma' Duktur Taha Husayn," *al-Hilal*, January 1, 1927, 34–38.

75. ʻAbd al-Fatah al-Khalidi, *Sayyid Qutb: Min al-Milad ila al-Istishhad* (Damascus: Dar al-Qalam, 2007), 93–94, 136.

76. ʻUways ʻUthman Ibrahim *et al*, *Dumuʻ al-Shuʻaraʼ ʻAla al-Rahil al-Karim Faqid al-Watan wa Zaʻim al-Sharq Saʻd Zaghlul Basha* (Cairo: Maktabat al-Amana, 1928), 18–19.

77. Al-Khalidi, *Sayyid Qutb*, 136.

78. Sayyid Qutb, *Mahammat al-Shaʻir fi-l Hayat wa Shiʻr al-Jil al-Hadir* (Koln: Manshurat al-Jamal), 18–19.

79. Qutb, *Mahammat*, 6. He used *ʻaqīda* as the synonym of *ṭabʻ*, literally an inborn talent opposed to the practice of poetry as craft: Sayyid Qutb, "Bayn al-ʻAqqad wa-l-Rafiʻi," *al-Risala*, April 25, 1938, 693.

80. Qutb, *Mahammat*, 5.

81. Qutb cited ʻAtiq's unpublished poems in his *Mahammat*, 30.

82. Sayyid Qutb, "Khawatir Mutasawiqa fi al-Naqd wa-l-Adab wa-l-Akhlaq," *al-Risala*, December 11, 1944, 1086–88.

83. Qutb, *Mahammat*, 45–46.

84. ʻAbd al-ʻAziz ʻAtiq, "Bayn al-Qadim wa-l-Jadid," *Apollo* 2, no. 10 (June 1934): 919.

85. See the unsigned review of *Diwan ʻAtiq* by ʻAtiq, *Apollo* 1, no. 6 (February 1933): 690.

86. Fayid al-ʻAmrusi, review of *al-Shatiʼ al-Majhul* by Sayyid Qutb, *Sahifat Dar al-ʻUlum*, no. 4 (April 1935): 220–25.

87. Qutb mentions that he used to spend time in Apollo in the company of ʻAtiq and al-ʻAmrusi: Sayyid Qutb, "Apollo wa Shuʻaraʼ," *Apollo* 3, no. 2 (October 1934): 213–14.

88. There is no exact equivalent for *al-wijdān* in English. Taken broadly, the notion refers to the seat of the affective and psychic as opposed to the material experience of the body. In Sufi metaphysics, *al-wijdān* signifies the altered emotional states inferred by the mystical union with God. In this book, I chose to translate it as an affect. For a detailed discussion of various meanings of the term, see Ellen Anne McLarney, *Soft Force: Women in Egypt's Islamic Awakening* (Princeton, NJ: Princeton Univ. Press, 2015), 121–24. For the place of *al-wijdān* in Qutb's aesthetic theory, see chap. 2.

89. Ibrahim Naji, "Diwan ʻAtiq," *Apollo* 1, no. 6 (February 1933): 690.

90. Mahmud al-Khafif, "al-Shatiʼ al-Majhul: Nuzum al-Shaʻir Sayyid Qutb," *al-Risala*, June 10, 1935, 959.

91. Qutb, *Mahammat*, 73–75; ʻAtiq, "Bayn al-Qadim wa-l Jadid," 914–19.

92. Al-Khalidi, *Sayyid Qutb*, 119–22.

93. Although hailing from a wealthy family of merchants in Nile Delta city Damietta, Tahir Abu Fasha liked to pretend he was poor, while Abu Wafa was famous for his failed attempts to earn a living. Reportedly, Ahmad Shawqi was repulsed by Abu Wafa's poverty and refused to meet him. On Abu Fasha, see the memoirs of his occasional host ʻAbbas Khidr, *Haʼulaʼu ʻAraftuhum* (Cairo: Dar al-Maʻarif, 1998), 53; on Abu Wafa, see

"Mahmud Abu al-Wafa," in *Dhil al-'Alam. Qamus al-Tarajim min al-Ashhar Rijal wa al-Nisa' min al-'Arab wa al-Musta'aribin wa-l-Mustashriqin*, ed. Ahmad al-'Alawina (Jedda: Dar al-Manara li-l-Nashr wa-l-Tawzi', n.d.), 208.

94. M. F., "Istitla' Sahafi: al-Andiyya al-Adabiyya fi Misr," *al-Risala*, May 1, 1939, 867.

95. Khidr, *Ha'u'la'u 'Araftuhum*, 40–53.

96. On the 1935 revolution, see Ahmad Abdalla, *The Student Movement and National Politics in Egypt, 1923–1973* (London: Saqi, 1985); and Erlich Haggai, *Students and University in Twentieth-Century Egyptian Politics* (London: Frank Cass, 1989).

97. See Qutb's essays in *al-Ahram*, April 11 and May 28, 1934, cited in Ahmad al-Badawi, *Sayyid Qutb* (Cairo: al-Ha'iat al-Misriyya al-'Amma li-l-Kitab, 1992), 55–57, 56–61.

98. Qutb, "Apollo wa Shu'ara'," 212–15. Qutb's battle against Apollo was mainly conducted in *al-Usbu'*, *al-Wadi*, and *al-Jihad*. See his essay series "Ma'arakat al-Naqd al-Adabi wa-l-Dawafi'ha al-Asliyya," published in *al-Usbu'*, June–August 1934.

99. Ahmad Zaki Abu Shadi, "Kalima Muharrir," *Apollo* 2, no. 9 (May 1934): 744.

100. Ahmad Zaki Abu Shadi, "Abulu wa Juhuduha," *Apollo* 3, no. 3 (November 1934): 284.

101. Sayyid Qutb, "Bayn al-'Aqqad wa-l-Rafi'i," *al-Risala*, no. 251, April 25, 1938, 694.

102. Sayyid Qutb, "al-Sadiqa Bint al-Sadiq . . . li-l-'Aqqad," *al-Risala*, January 24, 1944, 91–93.

103. Qutb, "al-Sadiqa."

104. Al-'Aqqad, *Shu'ara' Misr wa Bi'atuhum fi-l-Jil al-Madi*, cited in Badawi, *Sayyid Qutb*, 15. Qutb echoed the idea of personality in his *Mahammat*, 70–79.

105. Qutb, "Khawatir Mutasawiqa," 10. See chap. 2 on Qutb's attempt to connect literary criticism with psychoanalysis.

106. Shalash, *al-Tamarrud 'Ala al-Adab*, 115–26.

107. The copy of Qutb's *al-Atyaf al-Arba'a* dedicated to al-'Aqqad is available in the latter's personal library, held by the Egyptian National Library Dar al-Kutub. The book is amply annotated, suggesting that al-'Aqqad did read Qutb's books.

2. Our Own Brand of Modernity

1. Sayyid Qutb, *Mashahid al-Qiyyama fi-l-Qur'an* (Cairo: Dar al-Shuruq, 1993), 266–67.

2. Published as *al-Fann al-Qassasi fi-l-Qur'an al-Karim* in 1951 (Cairo: Maktabat al-Nahda al-Misriyya).

3. His two examining professors failed Khalafallah for different reasons. The literary critic Ahmad Shayyib reports that the dissertation contained assertions contradicting Islam—namely, that Qur'anic stories are not to be taken as historical facts. The other examiner, the historian Ahmad Amin, rejected the work for its weak methodology. See

Nasr Hamid Abu Zayd, "The Dilemma of the Literary Approach to the Qur'an," *Alif: Journal of Comparative Poetics*, no. 23 (2003): 28.

4. Muhammad Khalafallah, "Hawla al-Fann al-Qassasi fi-l-Qur'an al-Karim," *al-Risala*, October 13, 1947, 1121.

5. Omnia El Shakry, *The Great Social Laboratory: Subjects of Knowledge in Colonial and Postcolonial Egypt* (Stanford, CA: Stanford Univ. Press: 2007), 4–5.

6. The attempts to create an authentic modernity in Egypt took a similar road as in India; see Giya Prakash, *Another Reason: Science and the Imagination in Modern India* (Princeton, NJ: Princeton Univ. Press, 1999).

7. Selim Samah, *Popular Fiction, Translation, and the Nahda* (Cham: Palgrave Macmillan, 2019), 36–41.

8. See Joseph Massad's discussion on Husayn's ambivalent positions in regard to the public access to Abu Nuwas's poetry in Joseph Massad, *Desiring Arabs* (Chicago: Univ. of Chicago Press, 2007), 62–66.

9. Here, al-Hakim is discussing Voltaire's play *Le Fanatisme ou Muhammad le Prophète* (1742), which was part of the anticlerical literature typical of the French Enlightenment. Tawfiq al-Hakim, "al-Difa' 'n al-Islam," *al-Risala*, April 15, 1935, 579. For a discussion of al-Hakim's play, see Antonie Wessels, *A Modern Biography of Muhammad: A Critical Study of Muhammad Hussayn Haykal's* Hayat Muhammad (Leiden: E. J. Brill, 1972), 10–14.

10. Muhammad Husayn Haykal, *Hayat Muhammad* (Cairo: Mu'assasa Hindawi li-l-Ta'alim wa-l-Thaqafa, 2012), 25.

11. Haykal, *Hayat*, 38.

12. 'Abbas al-'Aqqad, *'Abqariyya Muhammad* (Beirut: al-Maktaba al-'Asriyya, n.d.), 5–6.

13. Tawfiq al-Hakim, *Muhammad* (Cairo: Maktaba Misr, n.d.), 11.

14. 'Abbas al-'Aqqad, *'Abqariyat al-Siddiq* (Cairo: al-Hay'at al-Misriyya al-'Amma li-l-Kitab, 2002), 8–10.

15. Haykal, *Hayat*, 481–85.

16. Haykal, 158–60.

17. Haykal, 481–82.

18. Haykal, 43.

19. Tawfiq al-Hakim, "al-Difa' 'n al-Islam," *al-Risala*, April 15, 1935, 578–80.

20. Nadine Picaudou, *L'Islam entre religion et idéologie* (Paris: Gallimard, 2010), 74–85; Ibrahim Abu Rabi', "Al-Azhar and Islamic Rationalism in Modern Egypt: The Philosophical Contributions of Mustafa 'Abd al-Raziq and 'Abd al-Halim Mahmud," *Islamic Studies* 27, no. 2 (1988): 129–50, 130.

21. Muhammad al-Khidr Husayn, *Naqd Kitab "Fi-l-Shi'r al-Jahili* (Cairo: Mu'assasa Hindawi li-l-Ta'alim wa-l-Thaqafa, 2014), 37.

22. For example, Muhammad al-Sayyid al-Tawil, "Da'iyyat al-Ilhad," *al-Fath*, September 1, 1927, 13–15; and Muhammad al-Ghamrawi, *Al-Naqd al-Tahlili li-l-Kitab al-Adab al-Jahili* (Cairo: al-Matba'at al-Salafiyya, 1929), 52.

23. Haykal, *Hayat*, 70; al-Hakim, "al-Difa' 'n al-Islam," 577–78; 'Abbas al-'Aqqad, *'Abqari al-Islah wa-l-Ta'alim: al-Imam Muhammad 'Abdu* (Cairo: Dar Nahda Misr, 1962).

24. Al-Hakim, "al-Difa' 'n al-Islam," 576.

25. Haykal, *Hayat*, 38.

26. Haykal, *Hayat*, 36–37; al-'Aqqad, *'Abqariyyat al-Siddiq*, 10.

27. Qutb, *al-Taswir*, 7–8.

28. Sayyid Qutb, *A Child from the Village*, trans. John Calvert (Syracuse, NY: Syracuse Univ. Press, 2004), 43–46.

29. Kristina Nelson, *The Art of Reciting the Qur'an* (Cairo: American Univ. in Cairo Press, 2001), 73.

30. Sayyid Qutb, *Mashahid al-Qiyama fi-l-Qur'an* (Cairo: Dar al-Shuruq, 1993), 8. Most probably, this was done with the assistance of his long-standing friend the poet 'Adil al-Ghadhban, who supervised publication projects in Dar al-Ma'arif. See "'Adil al-Ghadhban," in Wadi' Filistin, *Wadi' Filistin Yatahadath 'n 'Alam 'Asrihi*, vol. 1 (Damascus: Dar al-Qalam, 2003), 329.

31. Qutb, *al-Taswir*, 9.

32. Qutb, 9–10.

33. Qutb, 90.

34. Nelson, *Art of Reciting the Qur'an*, 63.

35. These lines are attributed to the Imam al-Ghazzali; cited in Nelson, *Reciting the Qur'an*, 63.

36. Qutb, *al-Taswir*, 36.

37. Qutb, 37.

38. Charles Hirschkind, *The Ethical Soundscape: Cassette Sermons and Islamic Counter Publics* (New York: Columbia Univ. Press, 2006), 154–56; Ellen Anne McLarney, *Soft Force: Women in Egypt's Islamic Awakening* (Princeton, NJ: Princeton Univ. Press, 2015), 121–24.

39. Influenced by the tenth-century controversy on the Aristotelian logic and grammar, the opposition between *lafẓ* and *ma'na*—or wording and meaning—had been the central dichotomy in Arab sciences of rhetoric, with a certain consensus that *lafẓ* was poetically more important than meaning. The contribution by the ninth-century grammarian and the author of *Dala'il al-'Ijaz* 'Abd al-Qahir al-Jurjani was to complicate the dichotomy with his theory of "multiple meanings" that coexist and intertwine in one and the same text. His idea that the surface structure of the text offers just a glimpse of many hidden layers of meaning provided direct inspiration for Qutb's theory that words communicated a series of enchained fragments of meaning. See "Lafz and ma'na," in

Encyclopedia of Arabic Literature, vol. 2., ed. Julie Scott Meisami and Paul Starkey (London: Routledge, 1999), 461–62.

40. Qutb, *al-Taswir*, 30–34.

41. On the postclassical tradition and its critics among the Nahda generation, see Ahmed El Shamsy, *Rediscovering the Islamic Classics: How Editors and Print Culture Transformed an Intellectual Tradition* (Princeton. NJ: Princeton Univ. Press, 2020), chap. 2.

42. Sayyid Qutb, *Mahammat al-Sha'ir fi al-Hayat wa Shi'r al-Jil al-Hadir* (Koln: Manshurat al-Jamal, 1996), 20.

43. Sayyid Qutb, "'Ala Hamish al-Naqd: Baqiyya fi-l-Ma'ani wa-l-Zilal," *al-Risala*, September 4, 1944, 11–16.

44. Sayyid Qutb, *al-Naqd al-Adabi: Usuluhu wa Manahijuhu* (Cairo: Dar al-Shuruq, 2003), 42.

45. Qutb, *al-Taswir*, 226–38.

46. Qutb, *Mahammat*, 12.

47. For example, Sayyid Qutb, "al-Ghina' al-Marid Yankharu al-Khalq al-Misri wa-l-Mujtam'," *al-Risala*, September 2, 1940, 1382–84; "Al-Mutribun wa-l Mutribat Humma al-Tabur al-Khamis fi Misr," *Sahifa Dar al-'Ulum*, July 1940, 52–56; and "Ikhrasu Hadhihi al-Aswat al-Danisa," *al-Risala*, September 22, 1952, 1049–50.

48. Sayyid Qutb, introduction to *Anashid Diniyya ma' Alhaniha al-Musiqiyya* by Mahmud Abu al-Wafa (Cairo: Maktaba Wahba, 1954), 1–2.

49. Qutb, *Child*, 59–96.

50. Qutb, 77.

51. Yoav Di-Capua, *No Exit: Arab Existentialism, Jean-Paul Sartre, and Decolonization* (Chicago: Univ. of Chicago Press, 2018), 51.

52. Omnia El Shakry, *The Great Social Laboratory: Subjects of Knowledge in Colonial and Postcolonial Egypt* (Stanford, CA: Stanford Univ. Press, 2007), 10–14.

53. "Romanticism," *Dictionary of Philosophy*, 272, cited in El Shakry, *Social Laboratory*, 227n57. On the role of Romanticism in shaping social scientific fields in the interwar Egypt, see El Shakry, *Social Laboratory*, 10–14.

54. El Shakry, 11.

55. The majority of Qutb's essays published in the bulletin were collected by Alain Roussillon in his *al-Mujtam' al-Misri: Judhuruhu wa Ufaquhu* (Casablanca: Sina li-l-Nashr, 1993).

56. Alain Roussillon, "Trajectoires réformistes: Sayyid Qutb et Sayyid 'Uways: figures modernes de l'intellectuel en Égypte," *Égypte/Monde Arabe*, no. 6 (1991): 91–139.

57. Qutb, *Mahammat*, 13.

58. Sayyid Qutb, *Al-Naqd al-Adabi: Usuluhu wa Manahijuhu* (Cairo: Dar al-Shuruq, 2006), 31–32.

59. For an illustration of how scientific theories were transformed during the process of their popularization, see Marwa Elshakry's book on the reception of Darwin's theory of evolution, *Reading Darwin in Arabic, 1860–1950* (Chicago: Univ. of Chicago Press, 2013).

60. See Di Capua's discussion on the Egyptian philosopher Abd al-Rahman al-Badawi's efforts to fuse existentialism and Sufism, in *No Exit*, 47–56; El Shakry's analysis on the influence of Sufism on Egyptian psychology, in *The Arabic Freud: Psychoanalysis and Islam in Modern Egypt* (Princeton, NJ: Princeton Univ. Press, 2017); and Charles D. Smith's discussion of Haykal's intellectual formation in *Islam and the Search for Social Order in Modern Egypt: A Biography of Muhammad Husayn Haykal* (Albany: State Univ. of New York Press, 1984), 133.

61. ʿAli ʿAbd al-Rahman ʿAtiyya, ed., *Sayyid Qutb, al-ʿAmal al-Shiʿriyya al-Kamila* 1 (Cairo: Markaz al-Ahram li-l-Nashr, 2012), 12.

62. ʿAbd al-Baqi Muhammad Husayn, ed., *Diwan Sayyid Qutb* (al-Mansurah: Dar al-Wafa' li-l-Tibaʿa wa-l-Nashr wa-l-Tawziʿ, 1989), 31–32; Qutb, *Mahammat*, 37–42.

63. The predominant influence of holism within scientific inquiries in colonial Egypt has been noted by many scholars; in psychology, El Shakry, *Arabic Freud*, 28–29; in Taha Husayn's project of modernity, Angela Giordani, "To Be an *Adib*: Sayyid Qutb's Intellectual Biography Reconsidered" (master's thesis, Columbia Univ., 2014); in the field of Qur'anic commentary, Issa J. Boullata, "Modern Qur'an Exegesis: A Study of Bint al-Shāti's Method," *Muslim World* 64, no. 2 (April 1973): 103–13; and in poetry, where it took the form of the aesthetic requirement of unity of the whole poem, instead of its traditional fragmentation into two-verse fragments.

64. See for example, Ramzi Muftah, "Wahdat al-Wujud," *Apollo* 2, no. 10 (June 1934): 1004–7; and Tahir Abu Fasha, "Wahdat al-Wujud," *al-Risala*, December 18, 1933, 18–19.

65. Qutb, *Mahammat*, 33.

66. Qutb, 41.

67. Charles D. Smith, *Islam and the Search for Social Order in Modern Egypt: A Biography of Muhammad Husayn Haykal* (Albany: State Univ. of New York Press, 1984), 100.

68. Husayn, *Diwan*, 31.

69. ʿAtiyya, *Sayyid Qutb*, 38–39. See his poem "Ila al-Shati' al-Majhul," 47–48.

70. ʿAtiyya, 38–39.

71. El Shakry, *Arabic Freud*, 24.

72. Amina Saʿid, Dr. Yusuf Murad, and Sayyid Qutb, *Rawdat al-Tifl* (Cairo: Dar al-Maʿarif, 1946). Unfortunately, I was unable to locate the copies of the series in Egyptian or European public libraries, and the only reference to these books was the announcement of its publication in *al-Risala* magazine in 1946.

73. Qutb, *al-Naqd al-Adabi*, 253–56.

74. Qutb, 209. In his 1935 poetry collection, Qutb used another translation of "the unconscious" previously suggested by the Egyptian polymath Salama Musa: *al-ʿaql*

al-bāṭin (inner mind). See ʻAtiyya, *Sayyid Qutb*, 41. On Salama Musa's translation of "the unconscious," see El Shakry, *Arabic Freud*, 2.

75. Reproduced in ʻAtiyya, *Sayyid Qutb*, 123–30.

76. Qutb, *al-Naqd al-Adabi*, 208–18.

77. Qutb, 211–12.

78. Husayn, *Diwan*, 30.

79. Qutb, *Mahammat*, 37; Husayn, *Diwan*, 31–32.

80. Qutb, *Mahammat*, 19–20.

81. Qutb, *al-Naqd al-Adabi*, 17–23.

82. Qutb, *Mashahid*, 272.

83. Qutb, 272.

84. ʻAbd al-Munʻam Khalaf was one of the YMMA's youths from 1926. Mahmud Muhammad Shakir, "Jamaʻiyyat al-Shubban al-Muslimin," in *Jamharat Maqalat al-Ustaz Mahmud Muhammad Shakir*, ed. ʻAdil Sulayman Jamal (Cairo: Maktabat al-Khanji, n.d.), 774; al-Tantawi, *Dhikrayyat*, vol. 1 (Jedda: Dar al-Manara li-l-Nashr, 1985), 261.

85. Significantly, Qutb and Khalaf disagreed over the location of *al-badāha*, a term from Sufi metaphysics that could be translated as "intuition" but also as "matter-of-factness." Qutb and Khalaf grouped *al-badāha* with the affective and mental faculties, respectively. ʻAbd al-Munʻam Khalaf, "al-ʻAql al-Mu'min wa-l-Din min Tariq al-Fikr," *al-Risala*, December 17, 1945, 1367–70.

86. ʻAbd al-Munʻam Khalaf, "Munaqashat fi-l-Sayf . . . ," *al-Risala*, June 4, 1945, 584.

87. ʻAbd al-Munʻam Khalaf, review of *al-Taswir al-Fanni fi-l-Qur'an* by Sayyid Qutb," *al-Risala*, April 30, 1945, 453.

88. Sayyid Qutb, "al-Mantiq al-Wijdani wa-l-ʻAqida," *Risala*, July 23, 1945, 780.

3. Bringing the Social Back in

1. Adel Kamel, *The Magnificent Conman in Cairo: A Novel*, trans. Waleed Almusharaf (Cairo: American Univ. Press, 2020).

2. Sayyid Qutb, "Milim al-Akbar: Bahth wa Qissa. ʻAdil Kamil," *al-Risala*, January 1, 1945, 10.

3. Joel Gordon, *Nasser's Blessed Movement: Free Officers and the July Revolution* (Oxford: Oxford Univ. Press, 1992); Tariq al-Bishri, *al-Harakat al-Siyasiyya fi Misr 1945–1953* (Cairo: Dar al-Shuruq, 2002).

4. Lucie Ryzova, *The Age of the Efendiya: Passages to Modernity in National-Colonial Egypt* (Oxford: Oxford Univ. Press, 2014), 153–54; 182, 224. On the rise of the youth as a political actor, see Omnia El Shakry, "Youth as Peril and Promise: The Emergence of Adolescent Psychology in Postwar Egypt," *International Journal of Middle Eastern Studies* 43 (2011): 591–610.

5. Alain Roussillon, "Réforme sociale et politique en Égypte au tournant des années 1940," *Egypte/Monde Arabe*, nos. 18–19 (1994): 197–236; Omnia El Shakry, *The Great Social Laboratory: Subjects of Knowledge in Colonial and Postcolonial Egypt* (Stanford, CA: Stanford Univ. Press, 2007), 145–64.

6. Mélanie Henry, "Le "trésor" révolutionnaire: insurrections et militantisme à Alexandrie en 1946 et 1977" (PhD diss., Aix-Marseille Univ., 2018), 181–89.

7. Joel Beinin and Zachary Lockman, *Workers on the Nile: Nationalism, Communism, Islam, and the Egyptian Working Class* (London: I. B. Tauris, 1988), 257–59; Mona Russel, *Middle East in Focus (Egypt)* (Oxford: ABC-CLIO, 2013), 68.

8. The Alexandrian beaches were the most common display of the social gap. See the observations made by the Iraqi sociologist ʿAli Wardi, who visited the Egyptian port city Alexandria in 1950, cited in Raoul Makarius, *La jeunesse intellectuelle d'Égypte au lendemain de la Seconde Guerre mondiale* (La Haye: Mouton, 1960), 33–34. See also Qutb's impressions recorded during his visit to Alexandria in the summer of 1946 in "Ila Iskandariyya," *al-Risala*, July 22, 1946, 796–98.

9. On the film *Black Market* and the cinematic representation of "profiteers," see Walter Armbrust, "Egyptian Cinema on Stage and Off," in *Off Stage/On Display. Intimacy and Ethnography in the Age of Public Culture*, ed. Andrew Shryock (Stanford, CA: Stanford Univ. Press), 80–82; for their representation in the press, see Walter Armbrust, "Bourgeois Leisure and Media Fantasies," in *New Media in the Muslim World. The Emerging Public Sphere*, ed. Dale F. Eickelman and John W. Anderson (Bloomington: Indiana Univ. Press, 2003), 114–17.

10. See the accounts cited in Saʿid al-Shahhat, *Umm Kulthum wa Hukkam Misr* (Cairo: Maktaba Jazirat al-Ward, 2016), 18–19.

11. Armbrust, "Egyptian Cinema," 82.

12. Rifaʿat al-Saʿid, *al-Sahafat al-Yasariyya fi Misr, 1925–1948* (Cairo: Maktaba Madbuli, 1977); Selma Botman, *The Rise of Egyptian Communism, 1939–1970* (Syracuse, NY: Syracuse Univ. Press, 1988), 33–58; Yoav Di Capua, *Gatekeepers of the Arab Past: Historians and History Writing in Twentieth-Century Egypt* (Berkeley: Univ. of California Press, 2009), 237–46.

13. Makarius, *Jeunesse Égyptienne*, 34–36.

14. Botman, *Rise of Egyptian Communism*, 38.

15. It was the case of *Jaridat al-Ikhwan al-Muslimin* (1933–38), *al-Nadhir* (1939), and *al-Daʿwa* (1951–53).

16. See the advertisement of al-Banna's *Rasa'il*, *al-Ikhwan al-Muslimun*, July 19, 1943, 3; and an apology for the journal's publication delay, *al-Ikhwan al-Muslimun*, October 23, 1943, 9.

17. Saʿid al-Sahhar, *Mawaqif fi Hayati* (Cairo: Maktaba Misr, 1991), 138–45.

18. Al-Sahhar, *Mawaqif*, 133.

19. ʻAdil Ahmad Kamal, *al-Nuqat Fawqa al-Huruf: al-Ikhwan al-Muslimun wa-l-Nizam al-Khas* (Cairo: al-Zahra li-l-ʻAlam al-ʻArabi, 1987), 123. See the description of the Brotherhood's efforts to purchase the land for the establishment of the printing house in Hasan al-Banna, "al-Jarida wa-l-Matbaʻa," *al-Ikhwan al-Muslimun*, January 5, 1946, 4; and ʻAbdo Ahmad Qasim, "al-Matbaʻat al-Islamiyya wa-l-Jaridat al-Yawmiyya," *al-Ikhwan al-Muslimun*, January 12, 1946, 22.

20. The Brotherhood's use of the publishing house to hold unofficial meetings was mentioned by the organization's fourth guide, ʻUmar al-Tilmisani; see Ibrahim Qaʻud, *ʻUmar al-Tilmisani, Shahidan ʻAla al-ʻAsr: al-Ikhwan al-Muslimun fi Da'irat al-Haqiqat al-Gha'iba* (Cairo: Dar al-Mukhtar al-Islami, 1985), 33.

21. Al-Sahhar, *Mawaqif*, 134; ʻAbd al-Hamid al-Sahhar, *Suwwar wa Dhikrayyat* (Cairo: Maktaba Misr, n.d.), 217.

22. The memoirs by Saʻid and ʻAbd al-Hamid al-Sahhar provide a vivid picture of the strategies they used to purchase paper for publishing. In addition to their contact with al-Minyyawi, the publishers printed the committee's novels on wrapping paper purchased from the Alexandria-based company Rakta, or on wet paper after they had dried it with the help of an iron. Al-Sahhar, *Mawaqif*, 133–39; al-Sahhar, *Suwwar wa Dhikrayyat*, 190–91.

23. See, for the illustration, Taha Husayn, *Khusam wa Naqd* (Beirut: Dar al-ʻIlm li-l Malayyin, 1979), 5–13; al-Jahiz, "al-Adab wa-l-Fann fi-l Usbuʻ," *al-Risala*, April 14, 1947, 430; and Mansur Jab Allah, "Mihnat al-Adab fi Misr," *al-Risala*, November 17, 1952, 1288–89.

24. Kamil and Mahfuz submitted their respective novels in manuscript form. Mahfuz's *al-Sarab* was published in 1948, four years later than Kamil's *Milim al-Akbar.*

25. Reportedly, Kamil's *Milim al-Akbar* and Mahfuz's *al-Sarab* were rejected under the pretext that the former was "too political" and the latter "too carnal"; see Raja' al-Naqqash, *Safahat min Mudhakkarat Najib Mahfuz* (Cairo: Dar al-Shuruq, 2011), 160–61.

26. Ahmad Hasan al-Zayyat, *Difaʻ ʻn al-Balagha* (Cairo: ʻAlam al-Kutub, 1967), 22. The key science of the postclassical Islamic tradition in deciphering sacred texts, rhetoric was criticized since the early Nahda period for its tendency to obscure the meaning of texts; see Ahmed El Shamsy, *Rediscovering the Islamic Classics: How Editors and Print Culture Transformed an Intellectual Tradition* (Princeton, NJ: Princeton Univ. Press, 2020), 36–38.

27. ʻAdil Kamil, "Muqadimma fi Ta'adib Milim fi Funun al-Lugha wa-l-Adab," *Milim al-Akbar* (Cairo: Al-Karma li-l Nashr wa-l Tawziʻ, 2014), 49–50.

28. Verena Klemm, "Different Notions of Commitment (iltizam) and Committed Literature (al-adab al-multazim) in the Literary Circles in the Mashriq," *Middle Eastern Literatures* 3 (2000): 51–62; Yoav Di Capua, *No Exit: Arab Existentialism, Jean-Paul Sartre, and Decolonization* (Chicago: Univ. of Chicago Press, 2018), 77–107.

29. In 1947, a columnist in *al-Risala* explained that the crisis of literature in Egypt was caused by its "detachment from the depths of the Egyptian life," and its refusal to

serve any goal, "even if the goal was the fame and glory of an author." Al-Jahiz "al-Adab wa-l-Fann fi-l-Usbu'," *al-Risala*, April 14, 1947, 430.

30. Ahmad Rushdi Salih, "Marhala Jadida fi-l-Fikr al-Misri", *al-Fajr al-Jadid 1*, no. 2 (June 1, 1945): 3. See also Salih's manifesto-like editorial in which he urged writers to adopt the suffering and hopes of the people: Ahmad Rushdi Salih, "Mahammat al-Katib," *al-Fajr al-Jadid 1*, no. 1 (May 16, 1945): 3.

31. "Barid al-Fajr al-Jadid," *al-Fajr al-Jadid 2*, no. 36 (May 29, 1946): 24.

32. See the responses to al-'Aqqad's anticommunist stances expressed in his 1946 book *Fi Bayti*: "Radd 'ala al-'Aqqad" and "al-'Aqqad Lam Yantahi!!! Wa al-'Aqqad la Yazal Yukhaddir al-Sha'b," *al-Fajr al-Jadid* 1, no. 10 (October 1, 1945): 7, 21; *al-Fajr al-Jadid* 2, no. 39 (June 19, 1946): 19; and Isma'il Muhammad, "Fi Bayti: Naqd 'Abbas Mahmud al-'Aqqad," *al-Fajr al-Jadid 1*, no. 8 (September 1, 1945): 16–17, 22.

33. "Radd 'ala al-Mazni," *al-Fajr al-Jadid 1*, no. 8 (September 1, 1945): 5, 19; on al-Hakim, Nu'man 'Ashur, "Al-Quwwat al-Namiyya wa-l-Quwwat al-Munhara fi-l-Adab al-Misri al-Mu'assir," *al-Fajr al-Jadid 1*, no. 7 (August 16, 1945): 2, 22; on Taha Husayn, 'Ali al-Katib, "Mulahazat 'Ala Bahth al-Duktur Taha Husayn: Al-Adab al-'Arabi Bayn Amsihi wa Ghadihi," *al-Fajr al-Jadid 1*, no. 11 (October 15, 1945): 10–11. Although criticized by the journal, Husyan was considered as the most progressive writer of his generation. See "al-Kutub al-Jadida", *al-Fajr al-Jadid 2*, no. 22 (20 February 1946): 15.

34. Anwar al-Mi'ddawi, "Ta'qibat: Tawfiq al-Hakim fi Mizan al-Fann wa-l-Naqd," *al-Risala*, April 18, 1949, 753.

35. Anwar al-Mi'ddawi, "Ta'qibat: al-Fann Bayna Waqi' al-Fikr wa Waqi' al-Hayat, "*al-Risala*, April 30, 1949, 813–14.

36. Anwar al-Mi'ddawi, "Ta'qibat: al-Fann wa-l-Hayat Bayni wa Bayn al-Duktur Taha Husayn," *al-Risala*, June 6, 1949, 953.

37. Al-Mi'ddawi, "Ta'qibat," 954.

38. Anwar al-Jundi, "Kayfa Naktub al-Ta'arikh al-Islami?," *al-Ikhwan al-Muslimin*, March 13, 1948, 10.

39. Sharif Yunis, *Sayyid Qutb wa-l-Usuliya al-Islamiyya* (Cairo: Dar Tayba li-l-Dirasa wa-l-Nashr, 1995), 26.

40. See the mission's official documents in Hilmi al-Namnam, *Ba'tha Sayyid Qutb: Al-Watha'iq al-Rasmiyya* (Cairo: Dar al-Kutub wa al-Watha'iq al-Qawmiyya, 2017).

41. Prior to his resignation in 1952, Qutb would reach the third-ranking position. Al-Namnam, *Ba'that*, 244.

42. Al-Namnam, 198–220.

43. While organic intellectuals intervene in public debates in the name of their professional expertise, prophetic intellectuals are defined by their charismatic commitment to universal issues; on this distinction, see Gisèle Sapiro, "Modèles d'intervention politique des intellectuels: Le cas français," *Actes de la recherche en science sociales*, nos. 176–77, vol. 1 (2009): 8–30.

44. Sayyid Qutb, "'Adilu Baramijaku aw Insahabu Qabla Fawat al-Awan," *al-Risala*, July 6, 1945, 723–24.

45. Sayyid Qutb, "Al-Sakht Dalil al-Hayawiyya wa-l-Hafiz ila al-Mustaqbal al-Jadid," *Majallat al-Shu'un al-Ijtima'iyya*, no. 6 (1941): 44–49; "Mashru' Bifiridj: Ittijah 'Alami la Mashru' Mahali," *Majallat al-Shu'un al-Ijtima'iyya*, no. 4 (May 1943): 21–29. For the Rural Social Centers and the Fellah Department presided over by Ahmad Husayn, see Amy J. Johnson, *Reconstructing Rural Egypt: Ahmed Hussein and the History of Egyptian Development* (Syracuse, NY: Syracuse Univ. Press, 2003), 47–119.

46. Sayyid Qutb, "Dar al-Tarjama wa Nahda Misr al-Thaqafiyya," *al-Risala*, May 7, 1945, 465–66; "La . . . ya Ma'ali al-Wazir: Laqad Akhta'ak al-Tawfiq," *al-Risala*, August 6, 1945, 839–40.

47. John Calvert, *Sayyid Qutb and the Origins of Radical Islamism* (London: Hurst, 2010), 116.

48. Qutb supported the popular resistance against the British troops in the Suez Canal zone prompted in autumn 1951 by the abrogation of the 1939 treaty by the Wafd government: Sayyid Qutb, "Al-An Waqt Kata'ib al-Fida'," *al-Da'wa*, October 16, 1951, 1, 16.

49. Sayyid Qutb, "Bud' al-Ma'araka: Al-Damir al-Adabi fi Misr: Shubban wa Shuyukh," *al-'Alam al-'Arabi*, no. 4 (April 1947): 52.

50. Sayyid Qutb, "Ra'i fi-l-Shi'r bi-l Munasaba Luzumiyyat Mukhaymar," *al-Kitab*, February 1948, 248–57, cited in Shalash, *al-Tamarrud 'Ala al-Adab*, 119.

51. Sayyid Qutb, "Sihr al-Jala'," *al-Risala*, May 6, 1946, 493–94.

52. Sayyid Qutb, "Hal Adab Qad Mat—3?," *al-Risala*, July 30, 1951, 855.

53. Qutb, "Hal Adab Qad Mat—3?," 854.

54. *Al-Fikr al-Jadid 1*, March 3, 1948, 8. See also Sayyid Qutb, *Ma'arakat al-Islam wa-l-Ra'smaliyya* (Cairo: Dar al-Shuruq, 1993), 100–101. Concerning Tawfiq al-Hakim's association with the journal, see Sayyid Qutb, *Kutub wa Shakhsiyyat* (Cairo: Dar al-Shuruq, 1983), 121n1.

55. Ahmad Amin, "Day'at al-Adab," *al-Thaqafa*, August 20, 1951, 6–7.

56. Qutb, "Bud' al-Ma'araka," 52.

57. Sayyid Qutb, "al-Qahira al-Jadida," *al-Risala*, December 30, 1946, 1440–43.

58. Sulayman Fayad, *Kitab al-Namima* (Cairo: Dar Misr al-Mahrusa, 2006), 75.

59. Al-Shalash attributes Qutb's rebellion against al-'Aqqad to the latter's flattering review of *Hadhihi Hiya al-Aghlal* by the Saudi intellectual 'Abdallah al-Qasimi, in *al-Tamarrud 'Ala al-Adab*, 116–19.

60. Sayyid Qutb, "Ila Ustadhina al-Duktur Ahmad Amin," *al-Thaqafa*, September 10, 1951, 7–8.

61. The committee published one book per month. Wadi' Filistin, in discussion with the author, January 2014, Cairo.

62. The series consisted of four parts that Al-Sahhar published until 1951.

63. Qutb announced his forthcoming book *al-Madhahib al-Fanniyya al-Mu'assira* in *Kutub wa Shakhisyyat*, 104, 113.

64. Sayyid Qutb, "'Ala Hamish al-Naqd. Fi 'Alam al-Qissa: Kifah Tiba . . . li-Najib Mahfuz," *al-Risala*, October 2, 1944, 15–21.

65. Naguib Mahfuz, introduction to *Rasa'il Taha Husayn* by Ibrahim 'Abd al-'Aziz (Cairo: Mirit, 2000), 10.

66. Al-Sahhar, *Suwwar wa Dhikrayyat*, 192–95.

67. An exhibition held in April 2013 in Bayt al-Sinari in Cairo contained two documents related to the launch of the journal *al-'Alam al-'Arabi*: Qutb's demand of authorization from his employer the Ministry of Education to assume the editorship of the review, and a request of authorization to launch *al-'Alam al-'Arabi* signed by Yusuf Shehata and addressed to the Ministry of Interior's Office of the Publications Management. On the creation of *al-'Alam al-'Arabi*, see Wadi' Filistin, *Wadi' Filistin Yatahaddath'n A'lam 'Asrihi*, vol. 1(Damascus: Dar al-Qalam, 2003), 329.

68. 'Adil al-Ghadban, "Suwwar al-Mustaghillin," *al-Fikr al-Jadid*, January 15, 1948, 21.

69. It published, for example, the essays by the secretary-general of the Arab League 'Abdallah 'Azzam, the Syrian politician Sabri al-'Asali, and the Lebanese journalist and politician 'Abdallah Mashnuq.

70. Al-Sahhar, *Suwwar wa Dhikrayyat*, 207.

71. Muhammad Shu'ayr, "Najib Mahfuz. Satumdi al-Hayat fi-l Hadiqa wa-l-Nadi wa-l-Ghina'," *al-Safir*, February 8, 2013, https://www.assafir.com/Article/300966/Archive.

72. *Al-Salam al-'Alami wa-l-Islam* (International Peace and Islam, 1951); *Ma'arakat al-Islam wa-l-Ra'smaliyya* (The Battle between Islam and Capitalism, 1952); *al-'Adalat al-Ijtima'iyya fi-l-Islam (Social Justice in Islam)*, 3rd ed., 1952.

73. *Al-Bayan Aladhi Aqarathu al-Hay'at al-Ta'assusiyya li-l Ikhwan al-Muslimin fi Ijtima'iha Ghayr al-'Adi al-Mu'ataqid bi-l-Markaz al-'Amm fi-l-Yawm al-Jum'a 10 min Dhi al-Qa'ada 1371/1 Ughustus 1952* (Cairo: Matabi' Dar al-Kitab al-'Arabi, 1952).

74. *Majallat al-Ikhwan al-Muslimin* published the following announcement in its issue of January 25, 1948, under the heading *al-Fikr al-Jadid*: "Coinciding with the disappearance of *Majallat al-Ikhwan al-Muslimin*, the journal *al-Fikr al-Jadid* is finally launched. [It] carries the Islamic banner, defends the oppressed classed, and reveals the truths of Islamic socialism. We welcome our colleague" (*Jaridat al-Ikhwan al-Muslimin*, January 25, 1948, 12).

75. For an extensive biography of Fathi Osman, see Ghada Osman, *A Journey in Islamic Thought: The Life of Fathi Osman* (London: I. B. Tauris, 2011).

76. Giedrė Šabasevičiūtė, "Sayyid Qutb and the Crisis of Culture in Late 1940s Egypt," *International Journal for Middle East Studies* 50 (2018): 85–101.

77. As the reason for his resignation from *al-'Alam al-'Arabi*, Qutb cites his disagreement over the journal's editorial policy; see Yunis, *Sayyid Qutb*, 26n11.

78. Sayyid Qutb, "Nahwa al-Mujtam' al-Nadhif," in *Suqut al-Qahira* by 'Abd al-Mun'am Shumayyis (Cairo: Dar al-Kitab al-'Arabi, 1951).

79. Fayad, *Kitab al-Namima*, 67–70.

80. See Muhammad Fayad, review *of al-Salam al-'Alami wa-l-Islam* by Sayyid Qutb, *al-Risala*, November 19, 1951, 1319–21.

81. Filistin, *Wadi' Filistin Yatahaddath*, vol. 1, 283–84. Wadi' Filistin, in discussion with the author, January 2014, Cairo.

82. Wadi' Filistin, review of *al-Atyaf al-Arba'a* by Amina, Hamida, Muhammad, and Sayyid Qutb, *al-Risala*, May 7, 1945, 490; review of *al-Madina al-Mashura* by Sayyid Qutb, *al-Risala*, February 25, 1946, 228–29; review of *Tifl min al-Qariyya* by Sayyid Qutb, *al-Risala*, May 6, 1946, 510; review of *Ashwak* by Sayyid Qutb, *al-Muqtataf*, May 10, 1947, 381–82.

83. Ibrahim al-Wa'ili, review of *Ma'arakat al-Islam wa-l-Ra'smaliyya* by Sayyid Qutb, *al-Risala*, February 26, 1951, 261.

84. 'Ali Ahmad Bakathir, "Ila Mu'allif Kitab *al-Taswir al-Fanni fi-l-Qur'an*," *al-Risala*, April 30, 1945, 460.

85. Naguib Mahfuz, review of *al-Taswir al-Fanni fi-l-Qur'an* by Sayyid Qutb, *al-Risala*, April 23, 1945, 432.

86. 'Abd al-Mun'am Shumayyis, *Suqut al-Qahira* (Cairo: Dar al-Kitab al-'Arabi, 1951).

87. The letter was published in *Akhbar al-Adab*, no. 970 (February 2012): 17.

88. Filistin, *Wadi' Filistin Yatahaddath*, vol. 1, 283.

89. Both books were printed in al-Minyawi's Dar al-Kitab al-'Arabi.

90. On *Lajnat al-Shabab al-Muslim*, see Fathi Osman, "Mawdūdi's Contribution to the Development of Modern Islamic Thinking in the Arabic-speaking World," *Muslim World* 93, nos. 3–4 (2003): 446.

91. He refers to Qutb's several volume commentary of the Qur'an *Fi Zilal al-Qur'an*; 'Ali al-Tantawi, *Dhikhrayyat*, vol. 5 (Jedda: Dar al-Manara li-l-Nashr, 1985), 142.

92. Yunis, *Sayyid Qutb*, 177.

93. Entitled "Li-Hisab Man Hadha" (For the Benefit of Whom), the column was introduced in the May 22, 1951, issue of *al-Lawa al-Jadid*.

94. Alongside al-Bahi al-Khuli, the author of the influential book *Tadhkirat al-Du'a* (1953); see Mahmud 'Abd al-Halim, *al-Ikhwan al-Muslimun: Ahdath Sana'at al-Ta'arikh: Ru'ya min al-Dakhil*. Vol 3 (Alexandria: Dar al-Da'wa, 1979), 174.

95. Qism Nashr al-Da'wa was established in 1945 as the supervision organ of the press, internal communication, celebrations, trips, cinema, and radio. See the regulation of the department, "La'ihat Qism Nashr al-Da'wa 1945," IkhwanWiki, accessed July 14, 2020, https://www.ikhwanwiki.com. According to Richard Mitchell, the department verified the compatibility of the publications by Muslim Brothers with the official line of the

organization; see Richard Mitchell, *The Society of the Muslim Brothers* (Oxford: Oxford Univ. Press, 1969), 187–88.

96. Yunis, *Sayyid Qutb*, 177–79; for the expulsion-related reports, see ʿAbd al-Halim, *al-Ikhwan al-Muslimun*, vol. 3, 229–50.

97. For the description of clashes, see Richard Mitchell, *The Society of the Muslim Brothers* (Oxford: Oxford Univ. Press, 1993), 126–27; and Martin Frampton, *The Muslim Brotherhood and the West: A History of Enmity and Engagement* (Cambridge, MA: Harvard Univ. Press, 2018), 231.

98. "Qadiyyat al-ʿAdad al-Awwal," *Majallat al-Ikhwan al-Muslimin*, May 20, 1945, 8.

99. ʿAbd al-Halim, *al-Ikhwan al-Muslimun*, vol. 3, 313–15; Mitchell, *Society of the Muslim Brothers*, 136.

100. Yunis, *Sayyid Qutb*, 184. See Qutb's testimony in the trial of Hasan al-Hudaybi, in *Mahkamat al-Shaʿb: Al-Madhbata al-Rasmiyya li-Mahadir Jalasat Mahkamat al-Shaʿb*, vol. 4 (Cairo: Wizarat al-Irshad al-Qawmi, 1954), 1256–58.

101. "Majlis al-Wizara' . . . Fi-l Sijn!" *al-Musawwar*, December 3, 1954, 16.

102. This thesis is prominent in Shalash, *al-Tamarrud ʿAla al-Adab.*

103. Ryzova, *Age*, 255.

104. Shumayyis, *Suqut al-Qahira*, 74.

105. ʿAbbas Khidr, review of *al-Islam wa-l-Nizam al-ʿAlami*, by Sayyid Qutb, *al-Risala*, January 1, 1951, 19–21; see also the reviews of Qutb's books by Ibrahim al-Wa'ili, Sulayman Fayad, and Sadiq Rustum, published, respectively, in *al-Risala*, February 26, 1951; November 19, 1951, and September 24, 1951.

106. Anouar Abdel-Malek, in discussion with the author, April 2011, Cairo.

107. Di Capua, *Gatekeepers of the Arab Past*, 219–47.

108. The title of a popular biography of the Committee by Muhammad Jibril, *Aba' al-Sittiniyyat: Jil Lajnat Nashr li-l-Jamaʿiyyin* (Cairo: Maktaba Misr, n.d.).

109. See Giedrė Šabasevičiūtė, "When a Coterie Becomes a Generation: Intellectual Sociability and the Narrative of Generational Change in Sayyid Qutb's Egypt," in *Snapshots of Change: Methodological Approaches to Societies in Transformation*, ed. Yasmine Berriane, Aymon Kreil, Annuska Derks, and Dorothea Lüddeckens (London: Palgrave Macmillan, 2021).

110. Alain Roussillon, "Trajectoires réformistes: Sayyid Qutb et Sayyid ʿUways: figures modernes de l'intellectuel en Égypte." *Égypte/Monde Arabe*, no. 6 (1991): 91–139.

111. Qutb, *Maʿaraka*, 19–22.

112. Sayyid Qutb, *al-ʿAdala al-Ijtimaʿiyya fi-l-Islam* (Cairo: Maktaba Misr, 1951), 263–64.

113. Qutb, 48.

114. Qutb, *al-Maʿaraka*, 19–22.

115. Qutb, *al-ʿAdala*, 14.

116. Sayyid Qutb, *Khasa'is al-Tasawwur al-Islami wa Muqawimatuhu* (Cairo: Dar al-Shuruq, 2002), 12–19.

117. Qutb, *al-'Adala*, 35–49.

118. At the same time, the divine origin of the Islamic sociopolitical order allowed Qutb to argue that, since it was not subject to our human perception of temporality, retribution might arrive at an unexpected time and take an unexpected form.

119. Qutb, *al-'Adala*, 48–49.

120. Sayyid Qutb, "Manhaj al-Adab," *Majallat al-Ikhwan al-Muslimin*, no. 1, May 20, 1954, 14.

4. Literature in the Margins

1. Hasan al-Banna, "Sha'ira al-Islam: 'Arnus wa-l-Nijmi," *al-Fath*, no. 357, Rabi' al-Thani 18, 1352, 17.

2. 'Umar al-'Abasu, "al-Sha'ir al-Shaykh al-Adib Muhammad Sadiq 'Arnus," *Rabitat Udaba' al-Sham*, April 31, 2017, http://www.odabasham.net.

3. For example, al-Nijmi composed elegies for the occasion of Ahmad Taymur's and Rashid Rida's passing; see Muhammad al-Nijmi, "Dum'at al-Muslim," *al-Hadiqa*, January 1, 1931, 81–85; and "Usrat Sahib al-Manar," *al-Fath*, January 19, 1936, 13. 'Arnus wrote a poem on the occasion of al-Khatib's arrest in 1914 and a panegyrics addressed to Shakib Arslan; see "Mashi al-Huwayna La Yufid," *al-Fath*, January 31, 1929, 8; and "Ila Sayyid al-Mujahidin wa Mafkharat al-Sharq wa-l-Sharqiyyin al-Amir Shakib Arslan," *al-Fath*, May 9, 1929, 782.

4. El Shamsy, *Rediscovering the Islamic Classics*, 147–58.

5. El Shamsy, *Rediscovering the Islamic Classics*, 107.

6. Ziad Fahmy, *Ordinary Egyptians: Creating the Modern Nation through Popular Culture* (Stanford, CA: Stanford Univ. Press, 2011), 85–87.

7. Shakib Arslan, *Diwan al-Amir Shakib Arslan* (Cairo: Matba'at al-Manar, 1935).

8. Muhibb al-Din al-Khatib, "Shi'runa wa Sha'iruna," *al-Zahra* 3 (1927): 608–16; see also his editorial on Turkish literature, "al-Adab al-Turki fi Thalatha Adwar," *al-Zahra* 3, no. 4 (1926): 209–21.

9. Al-Khatib, "Shi'runa wa Sha'iruna," 608; Mustafa Sadiq al-Rafi'i, "Faylasuf wa Falasifa," *al-Zahra* 3, no. 10 (1927): 355.

10. Muhibb al-Din al-Khatib, *Taghur: Bi'atuhu, Tufulatuhu, Shababuhu* (Cairo: al-Matba'at al-Salafiyya, 1926).

11. Rashid Rida, "Shi'r wa Shu'ara," *al-Manar* 1, no. 9 (1898): 150–53; al-Khatib, "Sh'iruna wa Sha'iruna," 608–9.

12. Al-Khatib, "Shi'runa wa Sha'iruna," 605–21; Muhibb al-Din al-Khatib, "Matmah al-Adab al-'Arabi," *al-Fath*, no. 366, Jumadi al-Akhar 22 1352, 1–3.

13. Rashid Rida, "Riwayyat al-Yatim," *al-Manar* 1, no. 7 (1896): 129–33.

14. Rashid Rida, "Ta'arikh al-Adab wa-l-Islam fi Silk al-Qissas wa al-Riwayyat," *al-Manar* 11, no. 1 (1907): 64–66. For a detailed discussion on Rida's views on social classes, see Dyala Hamzah, "Production des classes moyennes et l'émergence du 'social' pendant la Nahda: Et le confessionnel (al-tā'ifiyya) dans tout cela?," *Egypte-Monde Arabe*, no. 20 (February 2019): 57–78.

15. On women, see Hoda A. Yousef, *Composing Egypt: Reading, Writing, and the Emergence of Modern Nation* (Stanford, CA: Stanford Univ. Press, 2016), 49–75; on peasants, see Michael Gasper, *The Power of Representation: Publics, Peasants, and Islam in Egypt* (Stanford, CA: Stanford Univ. Press, 2008), 72–107.

16. Rashid Rida, "al-Adab al-Sahih," *al-Manar* 1, no. 8 (1898): 133–40. See also al-Rida's discussion on the theater, arguing that the illegality of the means through which a message is transmitted, such as the acting of women, invalidated the message: Rashid Rida, "Tamthil al-Qassas aw Tiyatru," *al-Manar* 10, no. 1 (1907): 38–42.

17. Hasanayn Hasan Makhluf, "Shawqi wa Khusumuhu," *al-Zahra* 4, no. 1, (1928): 638–42.

18. Muhammad Ahmad al-Ghamrawi, "Taqlid al-Adab al-Ifranji," *al-Zahra* 4, no. 1 (1928): 584–88.

19. Joseph Massad, *Desiring Arabs* (Chicago: Univ. of Chicago Press, 2007), 64–66.

20. Muhammad 'Ali Gharib, "al-Khawaja Salama Musa wa Adabuhu al-Mafduh," *al-Fath*, December 22, 1927, 7; "Al-Adab al-Makshuf fi Nadi al-Shubban al-Masihiyyin" *al-Fath*, December 22, 1927, 13.

21. "Hukm al-Quda al-Misry 'Ala al-Adab al-Makshuf," *al-Fath*, no. 336, Dhu al-Qa'da 20, 1351, 2.

22. Al-Khatib, "Shi'runa wa Sha'iruna," 617–18.

23. In support of this argument, al-Khatib cited the example of nineteenth-century German literature which spread a national consciousness among the population, preparing the ground for the political unification of Germany by Otto von Bismark; see his "Matmah al-Adab al-'Arabi," 1–2.

24. Indicative of this trend were multiple reprints of al-Rafi'i's 1926 book *'Ijaz al-Qur'an wa-l-Balaghat al-Nabawiyya*. See Rashid Rida's introduction to its 1926 edition locating the book in the context of the battle against "innovators" in literature: *'Ijaz al-Qur'an wa-l-Balaghat al-Nabawiyya* by Mustafa Sadiq al-Rafi'i (Cairo: al-Maktabat al-Ahliyya, 1926), 15–22.

25. Al-Khatib, "Shi'runa wa Sha'iruna," 619; Shakib Arslan, "al-Shi'r al-Jahili: A Manhul Am Sahih al-Nisba," *al-Zahra* 3, no. 2 (1928): 137.

26. The accessibility of a text was posited as the modern criterion of literary excellence; see Ryzova, *Age*, 199. For illustration, see Haykal's criticism of al-Rafi'i's textbook of literature: Muhammad Hasan Haykal, *Fi Awqat al-Faragh* (Cairo: Maktabat al-Nahdat al-Misriyya, 1968), 198–213.

27. "Bashar bin Burd: Shi'ruhu wa Akhbaruhu," *al-Zahra* 2, no. 1 (1925): 64–65.

28. Muhibb al-Din al-Khatib, "Mat Shawqi," *al-Fath*, no. 315, Jumadi al-Akhira 20, 1351, 1–3.

29. Al-Khatib, "Mat Shawqi," 2.

30. Ahmad Zaki Abu Shadi, "al-Yaqazat al-Islamiyya fi-l-Adab aw al-Fann," *al-Fath*, no. 431, Shawwal 26, 1353, 2–3. See also his "Sha'ir Misr Yahmul Lawa' Majd al-Islam," *al-Fath*, no. 421, Sha'aban 7, 1353.

31. Mustafa Ahmad al-Rifa'i al-Labban, "al-Sha'ir al-Islami," *al-Fath*, no. 814, Sha'aban 1363, 9.

32. Dyala Hamzah, "From 'Ilm to Saḥāfa and the Politics of Public Interest (maṣlaḥa): Muhammad Rashīd Riḍa and His Journal al-Manār," in *The Making of the Arab Intellectual. Empire, Public Sphere and the Colonial Coordinates of Self-Hood*, ed. Diyala Hamzah (London: Routledge, 2013), 94.

33. On Ahmad Zaki Abu Shadi's family, see Joe Garnett's multimedia project, parts of which are published on the Bee Kingdom website, accessed July 2020, https://newsgrist.typepad.com/thebeekingdom/abush%C3%A2dy-family/. On Mahmud Muhammad Shakir, see El Shamsy, *Rediscovering the Islamic Classics*, 200–208.

34. See chap. 3.

35. 'Ali al-Tantawi, *Dhikrayyat*, vol. 1 (Jedda: Dar al-Manara li-l-Nashr, 1985), 261.

36. Mahmud Muhammad Shakir provides an account of the founding of the association from the perspective of a *da'iyya*: 'Adil Sulayman Jamal, ed., *Jamharat Maqalat al-Ustadh Mahmud Muhammad Shakir*, vol. 2 (Cairo: Maktaba al-Khanji, n.d.), 772–77. For the history and activities of its rover section, created in 1929 and commanded by "the father of Egyptian Olympics" Ahmad Damardash al-Tuni, see "Haflat Jawwala al-Shubban al-Muslimin," *Majallat Jama'iyyat al-Shubban al-Muslimin*, March 1940, 366–73.

37. Al-Khatib, "Mat Shawqi," 1–3.

38. Brynjar Lia, *The Society of the Muslim Brothers in Egypt: The Rise of an Islamic Mass Movement, 1928–1942* (New York: Ithaca, 1998), 54–60.

39. Lia, *Society of the Muslim Brothers*, 39.

40. Richard Mitchell, *The Society of the Muslim Brothers* (Oxford: Oxford Univ. Press, 1993), 274–77.

41. Lia, *Society of the Muslim Brothers*, 97–98.

42. "Sahafat al-Ikhwan, Laha Qissa," *al-Ikhwan al-Muslimun*, May 27, 1954, 2.

43. Muhammad Mustafa al-Maraghi, "Tasdir," *al-Manar* 35, no. 5 (1939): 1–2.

44. Muhammad 'Ali Gharib, "Jalsa ma' al-Shaytan: Riwayya Dakhalat fi Bidaya Nihayatiha," *al-Fath*, October 4, 1928, 5.

45. Muhammad 'Ali Gharib's first novel, *Rajulan wa Imra'a* (Cairo: Dar al-Ma'arif, 1945), focused on poverty in the Egyptian countryside. See his short stories in *al-Risala*: "al-Shaykh 'Abd al-Basit Yatazawij," *al-Risala*, July 13, 1936, 1151–53; "Suhrat al-Miliyyunir," *al-Risala*, September 1, 1941, 1106–8; and his article in the *Apollo* magazine

criticizing al-ʿAqqad, "al-Adab Shay'un wa-l-Hizbiyya Shay'un Akhar," *Apollo* 1, no. 9 (1933): 1074–77.

46. Mustafa al-Rifaʿi al-Labban, "Al-Qassas al-Diniyya", *al-Fath*, January 2, 1930, 12.

47. See his short stories "ʿAbd al-Majid bin Khalid," "Ila al-Bayt al-ʿAtiq," and "al-Qariya al-Saliha," *al-Fath*, no. 451, Rabiʿ al-Awwal 26, 1354, 18–19; no. 526, Shaʿaban 20, 1355, 14–16; and no. 565, Jumadi al-Akhira 26, 1356, 6–7.

48. ʿAbd al-Latif, "al-Qissas al-Islamiyya li-Ghayr al-Atfal: al-Mawlid al-Mubtakir," *al-Fath*, no. 585, Dhu al-Qaʿada 18, 1356.

49. Hasan al-Banna, "ʿAm Sayyid," *Jaridat al-Ikhwan al-Muslimin*, no. 9, Rabiʿ al-Thani 18, 1352, 23–24.

50. "Wa Innaha li-Kabira Ila ʿAla al-Khashiʿyyin," *al-Nadhir*, no. 8, Jumadi Awwal 20, 1357, 24–25.

51. *Al-Fath*, no. 106, July 26, 1928, 1.

52. "Al-Anashid al-Qawmiyya: Ijtimaʿ Hafil Bayn al-Shuʿara wa-l-Musiqiyyin," *Majallat al-Shubban al-Muslimin* 5, (1933–34): 588–98.

53. Giedrė Šabasevičiūtė, "Sayyid Qutb and the Crisis of Culture in Late 1940s Egypt." *International Journal for Middle East Studies* 50 (2018): 85–101," 93–94; Walter Armbrust, *Mass Culture and Modernism in Egypt* (Cambridge: Cambridge Univ. Press, 1996), 184–90.

54. "Diwan al-Huriyya. Min Anashid al-Ikhwan al-Muslimin," *Jaridat al-Ikhwan al-Muslimin*, no. 1, Muharram 19, 1353, 25–26.

55. ʿAbd ʿAllah al-ʿAqil, *Min ʿAlam al-Daʿwa al-Islamiyya wa-l-Harakat al-Islamiyyat al-Muʿassira* (Jedda: Dar al-Bashir, 2008), 389–99.

56. Armbrust, *Mass Culture and Modernism*; Frédéric Lagrange, "Musiciens et poètes en Egypte au temps de la Nahda" (PhD diss., Paris VIII-Sorbonne, 1994), 300–302.

57. ʿIssam Talima, *Hasan al-Bana wa Tajribat al-Fann* (Cairo: Maktaba Wahba, 2008), 10–42.

58. Mitchell, *Society of the Muslim Brothers*, 10–11.

59. *Jaridat al-Ikhwan al-Muslimin*, no. 23, Ramadan 4, 1352, 10.

60. Talima, *Hasan al-Banna*, 15–17.

61. Talima, 11.

62. Mahmud ʿAbd al-Halim, *al-Ikhwan al-Muslimun. Ahdath Sanaʿat al-Taʾarikh. Ru'ya min al-Dakhil*, vol. 1 (Alexandria: Dar al-Daʿwa, 1979), 288.

63. Kamil Muhammad ʿAjlan, *Sultan al-ʿUlama* (Cairo: al-Matbaʿa al-Faruqiyya al-Haditha, 1950), 4–5.

64. Published as a book, *Masrah al-Siyyasa* (Cairo: Maktaba Misr, 1952).

65. See, for example, Ahmad al-Sharbasi's response to the *fatwa* published by a Moroccan scholar Ahmad al-Ghumari in response to a play performed by the Muslim Brotherhood, reproduced in Talima, *Hasan al-Bana*, 21–29; see also the conditions listed by the Azhari playwright Kamil Muhammad ʿAjlan, in ʿAjlan, *Sultan*, 6–7.

66. Anwar al-Jundi, "Muhakama," *al-Ikhwan al-Muslimun*, July 13, 1947, 20; "Bayn al-Fikr wa-l-Adab," *al-Ikhwan al-Muslimun*, September 22, 1947, 8; "al-La'ihat al-'Amma li-l-Minhaj al-Thaqafi li-l-Ikhwan," *al-Ta'aruf*, March 23, 1940, 9.

67. This debate will give birth to the famous manifesto on committed literature *Fi al-Thaqafa al-Misriyya* coauthored by Marxist intellectuals Mahmud Amin al-'Alam and 'Abd al-Azim Anis; see Yoav Di Capua, "The Intellectual Revolt of the 1950s and 'The Fall of Udabā,'" in *Commitment and Beyond: Reflections on/of the Political in Arabic Literature Since the 1940s*, ed. Friederike Pannewick and George Khalil (Wiesbaden: Ludwing Reichert, 2015), 89–104.

68. Sayyid Qutb, "Manhaj al-Adab," *Majallat al-Ikhwan al-Muslimin*, May 20, 1954, 14.

69. Muhammad Qutb, "al-Fann wa-l-Mujtam'," *Majallat al-Ikhwan al-Muslimin*, May 27, 1954, 14.

70. Sayyid Qutb, "Introduction," in *Sukhriyyat Saghira*, by Muhammad Qutb (Beirut: Dar al-Rafidayn, 2017), 8.

71. Muhammad Qutb, *Sukhriyyat Saghira* (Cairo: Lajnat al-Nashr li-l-Jama'iyyin, 1947).

72. Muhammad Qutb, *al-Insan Bayn al-Maddiyya wa-l-Islam* (Beirut: Dar al-Shuruq, 1989), 9–10.

73. Muhammad Qutb, *Manhaj al-Fann al-Islami* (Beirut: Dar al-Shuruq, 1981), 141n1, 156n1, 179n1.

74. 'Atiyya, *Sayyid Qutb*, 33.

75. Qutb, "Manhaj al-Adab," 14; Qutb, *Manhaj al-Fann al-Islami*, 6.

76. Qutb, "Manhaj al-Adab," 14; Qutb, "al-Fann wa-l-Mujtam'," 14.

77. Qutb, *Manhaj al-Fann al-Islami*, 45–64.

78. Qutb, "Manhaj al-Adab," 14; Qutb, *Manhaj al-Fann al-Islami*, 182-83.

79. Muhammad Qutb included these authors as the exemplars of Islamist literature; see Qutb, *Manhaj al-Fann al-Islami*, 199–202, 212–21.

80. Qutb, *Al-Taswir*, 25–35.

81. Doris Behrens-Abouseif, *Beauty in Arabic Culture* (Princeton, NJ: Marcus Wiener, 1999), 37–43.

82. Qutb, *Manhaj al-Fann al-Islami*, 92, 141; Sayyid Qutb, *Mahammat al-Sha'ir fi-l-Hayat wa Shi'r al-Jil al-Hadir* (Koln: Manshurat al-Jamal, 1996), 38–45. According to this vision, art based on materialist or idealist worldviews was devoid of beauty, since both overemphasized one type of bond connecting humankind to the world.

83. Qutb, *Manhaj al-Fann al-Islami*, 6.

84. Qutb, 5–6.

85. Qutb, "Manhaj al-Adab," 14.

86. Qutb, *Manhaj al-Fann al-Islami*, 157.

87. Qutb, 11–13, 45–63.

88. Qutb, "Manhaj al-Adab"; Qutb, *Manhaj al-Fann al-Islami*, 46–58.

89. Hamida Qutb, *Rihla fi Ahrash al-Layl* (Cairo: Dar al-Shuruq, 1998), 8–9.

90. Qutb, *Manhaj al-Fann al-Islami*, 58.

91. On the magazine *al-Adab*, see Di Capua, *No Exit: Arab Existentialism, Jean-Paul Sartre, and Decolonization* (Chicago: Univ. of Chicago Press, 2018), 64–69.

92. Di Capua, *No Exit*, 68.

93. "Hal Usib al-Shi'r al-'Arabi bi-Naksa? Jawab al-Ustadh Sayyid Qutb," *al-Adab* 1, no. 4 (April 1953): 25.

94. Amina Qutb, "Awham," *al-Adab* 1, no. 11 (November 1953): 37–39; "'Id al-Su'ada," *al-Adab* 1, no. 7, (July 1953): 58–60.

95. Qutb indeed had a dog named Tut, who was taken for a stray dog and shot down. Qutb described the dog in "Min al-'Amaq," *al-Risala*, January 20, 1947, 80–82. He also had a cat named Susu, also described by Amina Qutb in her story. Qutb marked the death of Susu in his poem "Mawt Susu," *al-Muqtataf*, no. 4 (November 1937): 460.

96. Munir al-Ba'albaki, "Qara'tu fi-l-'Adad al-Madi fi-l-Adab," *al-Adab* 1, no. 12 (December 1953): 55.

97. Qutb, "Al-Fann wa-l-Mujtam'," 14.

98. According to al-'Alam, Hamida was his student in Paris VIII and Ecole Normale, where he was teaching. However, I haven't found any evidence that Hamida Qutb pursued her education in Paris. Mahmud Amin al-'Alam, in discussion with the author, April 2008, Cairo.

99. The play was published in the 1980s; see Christian Szyska, "On Utopian Writing in Nasserist Prison and Laicist Turkey," *Die Welt des Islams* 35, no. 1 (April 1995): 95–125.

100. On Najib al-Kilani and *al-adab al-islāmī*, see Christian Szyska, "Najib al-Kilani on His Career, or How to Become an Ideal Muslim Author," in *Conscious Voices*, ed. S. Guth, P. Furrer, J. C. Bürgel (Beirut: Orient-Institut, 1999), 221–35.

101. Kenan Çayir, *Islamic Literature in Turkey: From Epic to Novel* (New York: Palgrave Macmillan, 2017); Stephan Guth, "Islamist Belles Lettres—Bourgeois and Secular: Interesting Parallels between Ali Nar's Arilar Ülkesi (The Bees' Island, 1994) and Texts from German Enlightenment," in *Uluslararasi Karsilastirmali Edebiyatbilim Kongresi, Sakarya Üniversitesi, Adapazari, 07–08 Eylül 2006: Kongre Bildirileri*, ed. B. Baytekin and T. F. Uluc (Serdivan: Sakarya Üniversitesi Basimevi, 2006), 312–26.

102. *Nida' ila al-Diffat al-Ukhra* (Cairo: Dar al-Shuruq, 2000); and *Awba ila al-Maladh* (Damascus: Dar al-Qalam, 2011).

103. "Al-Ta'arif bi-l-Rabita," Rabitat al-Adab al-Islami al-'Alamiyya, accessed July 29, 2020, http://www.adabislami.org. On al-Kilani's definition of *al-adab al-islami*, see Szyska, "Najib al-Kilani on His Career."

104. Magdalena Kubalek, "Paraenetic Character of Modern Islamic Prose," *CLEaR* 3, no. 1 (May 2016): 19.

105. Magdalena Kubalek, "Should the Culture Be Engaged? Modern Islamic Literature and Its Religious and Political Engagement," *International Journal of Culture and History* 2, no. 1 (March 2016): 55–56; Husam Tammam and Patrick Haenni, "De retour dans le rythme du monde: Une petite histoire du chant (ex) Islamiste en Egypte," in "Islam et politique en méditerranée au 20e siècle," special issue, *Vingtième Siècle: Revue d'histoire*, no. 82, (April–June 2004): 91–102.

106. See, for example, an article by ʻAbd al-Quddus Abu Salih, a poet and a member of the International League of Islamic Literature, "Qadiyyat al-Adab al-Islami," *Aluka*, May 5, 2011, 2020, https://www.alukah.net/literature_language/0/31650/.

5. State and Faith

1. Ahmad Ra'if, in discussion with the author, April 2008, Cairo.

2. Richard Jacquemond, *Entre scribes et écrivains: le champ littéraire dans l'Egypte contemporaine* (Paris: Actes Sud 2003), 53; Marina Stagh, *The Limits of Freedom of Speech: Prose Literature and Prose Writers under Nasser and Sadat* (Stockholm: Almqvist & Wiksel International, 1993).

3. For the changing role of journalists in monarchic and republican Egypt, see Sonia Temimi, "D'un journalisme à l'autre: contours d'une identité professionnelle et évolution de son rapport au pouvoir politique, 1923–1970," *Égypte/Monde Arabe*, nos. 4–5 (2001), accessed July 29, 2020, https://doi.org/10.4000/ema.864. For the significance of the technocratic class in Nasser's Egypt, see Roel Meijer, *The Quest for Modernity: Secular-Liberal and Left-Wing Political Thought in Egypt, 1945–1958* (London: Routledge Curzon, 2002); and Anouar Abdel-Malek, *Egypte, Société Militaire* (Paris: Ed. du Seuil, 1962).

4. For example, Haddad Yvonne, "Sayyid Qutb: Ideologue of Islamic Revival," in *Voices of Resurgent Islam*, ed. John L. Esposito (Oxford: Oxford Univ. Press, 1983), 67–98; Gilles Kepel, *Muslim Extremism in Egypt: The Prophet and the Pharaoh* (London: al-Saqi, 1985), 26–29; Hasan Hanafi, *al-Din wa-l-Thawra fi Misr, 1952–81* (Cairo: Maktaba Madbuli, 1989), 167–300; and John Calvert, *Sayyid Qutb and the Origins of Radical Islamism* (London: Hurst, 2010), 204.

5. Di Capua, *No Exit*, 174.

6. See, for example, Shumayyis, *Suqut al-Qahira*, 22–23.

7. Roel Meijer, "L'élaboration d'un modernisme autoritaire: les intellectuels de gauche et la réforme de la société égyptienne dans les années 1950, *Cahiers d'histoire*, no. 105–6 (2008): 203–34; Di Capua, *No Exit*, 108–30.

8. Fathi Radwan, *72 Shahran maʻ ʻAbd al-Nasir* (Cairo: Dar al-Huriyya, 1985), 127.

9. Lama'i al-Muti'i, *Mawsu'a Nisa' wa Rijal fi Misr* (Cairo: Dar al-Shuruq, 2003), 826. See also Yusuf al-Sharuni, *Rihlat al-'Umr ma' Najib Mahfuz* (Cairo: al-Majlis al-A'ala li-l-Thaqafa, 2010), 5.

10. Jacquemond, *Entre scribes*, 34–37.

11. 'Ali Shalash, *Dalil al-Majalat al-Adabiyya fi Misr, 1939–1952. Bibliughrafiyya 'Amma* (Cairo: al-Majlis al-A'la li-l-Kitab, 1985), 38.

12. The "March crisis" refers to a series of events during which a broad coalition of opposition forces challenged the Free Officers' rule in March 1954. See Joel Gordon, *Nasser's Blessed Movement: Free Officers and the July Revolution* (Oxford: Oxford Univ. Press, 1992), 139–41; and Anouar Abdel-Malek, *Egypte, Société Militaire (*Paris: Ed. du Seuil), 1962, 210–11.

13. Yusuf al-Sharuni, in discussion with the author, June 2014, Cairo.

14. Sharif Yunis, *Nida' al-Sh'ab: Ta'arikh Naqdi li-l-Idiyulujiyyat al-Nasiriyya* (Cairo: Dar al-Shuruq, 2012), 347–400.

15. Anouar Abdel-Malek, *Egypt: Military Society; The Army Regime, The Left, and Social Change under Nasser* (New York: Random House, 1968), 190, cited in Di Capua, *No Exit*, 129.

16. See the overview of the debate in Abdel-Malek, *Egypte*, 191–98.

17. Rami Ginat, *Egypt's Incomplete Revolution: Lutfi al-Khuli and Nasser's Socialism in the 1960s* (London: Frank Cass, 1997), 103–4.

18. Yunis, *Nida'*, 420; Fathi Ghanim, *Ma'araka Bayn al-Dawla wa-l-Muthaqqafin* (Cairo: Dar Akhbar al-Yawm,1995), 51.

19. Yunis, 421–24.

20. Yves Gonzalez-Quijano, *Les gens du livre: Edition et champ intellectuel dans l'Égypte républicaine* (Paris: CNRS Éditions, 1998), 54–55.

21. Muhammad 'Abd al-Qadir Hatim, "Hadhihi al-Majalla," *al-Thaqafa*, July 22, 1963, 1–2.

22. "'Abd al-Mun'am Shumayyis," in *Tatima al-A'lam li-Zarakli*, by Muhammad Khayr Ramadan Yusuf (Beirut: Dar Ibn Hazm, 2002), 36.

23. On how Youssef Chahine's cinematography fit with Nasser's national project, see Malek Khouri, *The Arab National Project in Youssef Chahine's Cinema* (Cairo: American Univ. in Cairo Press).

24. See Raphael Cormack, "Oedipus on the Nile: Translations and Adaptations of Sophocles' Oedipus Tyrannos in Egypt, 1900–1970" (PhD diss., Univ. of Edinburgh, 2017), 169–89.

25. Olivier Carré, "Utopies socialisantes en terre arabe d'Orient," *Tiers-Monde* 19, no. 75 (1978): 539.

26. Yunis, *Nida'*, 370–82.

27. Yunis, 370.

28. Yunis, 382.

29. For example, see his discourse on the occasion of the second conference of the Academy of Islamic Research in 1965, “Nasrat al-Haqq,” *Majallat al-Shubban al-Muslimin*, June 1965, 5. During the crackdown on the Muslim Brotherhood in 1954, al-Shafi‘i was in charge of reassuring the population that the repression of the Islamist organization did not signify the officers’ hostility to Islam. See Gordon, *Nasser’s Blessed Movement*, 105.

30. Gregory Starett, *Putting Islam to Work: Education, Politics, and Religious Transformation in Egypt* (Berkeley: Univ. of California Press, 1998), 78; Olivier Carré, “L’idéologie politico-religieuse nassérienne à la lumière des manuels scholaires,” *Politique étrangère*, no. 4 (1972) 535–53.

31. Yunis, *Nida’*, 558–59; Gonzalez-Quijano, *Les gens*, 107. On how Nasser’s turn to Islamic socialism affected literature, see Yusuf ‘Izz al-Din, *al-Ishtirakiyya wa-l-Qawmiyya wa Ithruha fi-l-Adab al-Hadith* (Cairo: n.p., 1976), 82–83.

32. A host of intellectuals who rose to prominence under Anwar al-Sadat, such as Muhammad Jalal Kishk, wrote their first anti-Marxist books under Nasser.

33. Sadiq Jalal al-Azm, *Naqd al-Fikr al-Dini* (Beirut: Dar al-Tali‘a li-l-Tiba‘a wa-l-Nashr, 1970), 154.

34. Calvert, *Origins of Radical Islamism*, 165.

35. Included in his *Suwwar wa al-Dhikrayyat* (Cairo: Maktaba Misr, 1981), 220–37.

36. Anwar al-Jundi, “al-Taghrib wa al-Thaqafa al-‘Arabiyya,” *al-Aqlam*, April 1, 1965, 27–33.

37. Gordon, *Nasser’s Blessed Movement*, 178.

38. Sayyid ‘Abd al-Hafiz, “Hukm Shara‘i fi Jama‘at al-Ikhwan al-Muslimin,” *al-Jumhuriyya*, October 2, 1954, 3.

39. “Mahkamat al-Sha‘b Tuwasil Nazr Qadiyyat ‘Isabat al-Irhab,” *al-Jumhuriyya*, November 23, 1954, 10.

40. Salah ‘Issa, *al-Shakhsiyyat Laha al-‘Ajab! Dhikrayyat wa Tarajim wa Dirasat wa Watha’iq* (Cairo: Nahda Misr, 2010), 99; According to al-Khalidi, Qutb had a contractual agreement with the ‘Issa Halabi Publishing House for the *Fi Zilal* series, which allowed him to be granted the official permission to write; see ‘Abd al-Fatah al-Khalidi, *Sayyid Qutb: Min al-Milad ila al-Istishhad* (Damascus: Dar al-Qalam, 2007), 367–68.

41. Calvert, *Origins of Radical Islamism*, 204; Musallam, *From Secularism to Jihad*, 150–51.

42. Maktaba Wahba and Dar al-Qalam were founded in 1946 and 1948, respectively. Established by Muhammad al-Mu‘allim, Dar al-Qalam was later renamed Dar al-Shuruq and grew into one of the biggest publishing houses in Cairo. Maktaba Wahba often served as a distributor of the books printed by Dar al-Qalam, suggesting that both publishers worked together. On the Wahba Publishing House, see Bettina Gräf, “From the Pocketbook to Facebook: Maktabat Wahba, Publishing and Political Ideas in Cairo since the 1940s,” in *Ways of Knowing Muslim Cultures and Societies: Studies in Honour of Gudrun*

Krämer, ed. Bettina Gräf, Birgit Krawietz, and Schiron Amir-Moazami (Leiden: Brill, 2018), 223–44.

43. Sayyid Qutb, *Nahwa Mujtami' Islami* (Cairo: Dar al-Shuruq, 1993), 61.

44. Sayyid Qutb, *Ma'alim fi-l-Tariq* (Cairo: Dar al-Shuruq, 1992), 26.

45. Barbara Zollner, *The Muslim Brotherhood: Hasan al-Hudaybi and Ideology* (London: Routledge, 2009), 39–43.

46. Zoller, *Muslim Brotherhood*, 43; Fatima 'Abd al-Hadi, *Rihlati ma' al-Akhawat al-Muslimat: Min al-Imam Hasan al-Bana ila Sujun 'Abd al-Nasir* (Cairo: Dar al-Shuruq, 2011), 64–65. For the Muslim Brotherhood's experience in prison, see Hannah Elsisi Ashmawi, "Mu'ataqal Machine: Power, Gender, and Identity in Egypt's Political Prisons" (PhD diss., Oxford Univ., 2019), 67–80, 281–82.

47. Zaynab al-Ghazzali, *Return of the Pharaoh: Memoir in Nasir's Prison*, trans. Mokrane Guezzou (Leicester: Islamic Foundation, 2006), 39–40.

48. Qutb, *Ma'alim*, 12.

49. Henri Lauzière, *The Making of Salafism: Islamic Reform in the Twentieth Century* (New York: Columbia Univ. Press, 2016), 217–19.

50. Lauzière, 2018.

51. Qutb, *Ma'alim*, 175.

52. Qutb, 55–56.

53. Qutb, 17–18.

54. Qutb, 19.

55. Qutb, 51.

56. Qutb, *Hadha al-Din* (Cairo: Dar al-Shuruq, 2013), 24–25.

57. Qutb, *Khasa'is al-Tasawwur al-Islami*, 6, 16; Qutb, *Ma'alim*, 37–38.

58. Sayyid Qutb, February 1951, cited in Yunis, *Sayyid Qutb*, 137.

59. Qutb, *Ma'alim*, 53,

60. Qutb, 45. He cites Mawdudi's book *Mabadi' al-Islam*, which was made available in an Arabic translation in 1957.

61. John Calvert, "Sayyid Qutb and the Power of Political Myth: Insight from Sorel," in "Islam and Modernity," special issue, *Historical Reflections* 30, no, 3. Islam and Modernity (2004): 509–28.

62. Qutb, *Ma'alim*, 69.

63. Mawdudi defined *dīn* as a system of thought and action to which a person subscribes and lives by, while *sharī'a* referred to the body of applicable rules for regulating temporal existence. As such, *dīn* was more encompassing than *sharī'a*. On these concepts in Mawdudi's thought, see Jan-Peter Hartung, *A System of Life: Mawdudi and the Ideologization of Islam* (Oxford: Oxford Univ. Press, 2014). On Qutb's usage of these terms see *Ma'alim*, 108–15 (on *sharī'a*); and *Hadha al-Din* (on *dīn*), 5–28.

64. Nadvi encountered Qutb in 1951 during his trip to the Middle East; see his memoir, *Mudhakkarat Sa'ih fi-l-Sharq al-Awsat* (Cairo: Matba'at al-Risala, 1978), 120, 149, 188.

65. For the detailed conceptual discussion on the concept of Jahiliyya in Qutb's writings, see Sayed Khatab, *The Political Thought of Sayyid Qutb: The Theory of Jahiliyya* (London: Routledge, 2006); and William E. Shepard, "Sayyid Qutb's Doctrine of "Jāhiliyya," *International Journal of Middle East Studies* 35, no. 4 (November 2003): 521–45.

66. The defining feature of Jahili systems of life, according to Mawdudi, is that they are based on "opinions," as opposed to Islam, which is based on the revealed truth. He classified communism and capitalism as Jahili systems; see Abu 'Ala al-Mawdudi, *al-Islam wa-l-Jahiliyya* (Beirut: Dar al-Fikr al-Hadith, n.d.); and Fathi Osman, "Mawdudi's Contribution to the Development of Modern Islamic Thinking in the Arabic-Speaking World," *Muslim World* 93 (July–October 2009): 476.

67. Qutb, *Ma'alim*, 77–80.

68. Qutb, 73.

69. Qutb, 64, 69, 73–74, 88.

70. Such a prioritization of the collective over the individual is visible in Qutb's treatment of non-Muslim citizens in his imagined Islamic state. In contradiction to his position that the social system had to reflect one's creed, Qutb argued that the Islamic state differed from the Jahili State in that it allowed its citizens to freely choose their religious faith. He did not anticipate the scenario of individuals falling back into Jahili practices following their emancipation from Jahiliyya, most probably because Qutb was convinced that no other religion than Islam offered a system for sociopolitical organization. See, Qutb, *Ma'alim*, 71.

71. Al-'Aqqad's late writings on Islam were collected in a posthumous five-volume encyclopedia, *Mawsu'at 'Abbas al-'Aqqad al-Islamiyya* (Beirut: Dar al-Kitab al-'Arabi, 1971).

72. 'Abbas al-'Aqqad, *al-Islam fi-l-Qarn al-'Ashrin* (Cairo: al-Hai'a al-'Amma al-Misriyya li-l- Kitab, 1993), 11–21 (*ṣumūd*), 22–33 (*shumūl*).

73. Al-'Aqqad, *al-Islam*, 11, 33. For Qutb's usage of these terms, see Qutb, *Ma'alim*, 95–98.

74. From at least 1946, al-'Aqqad actively advocated for Egypt's joining of the Islamic International Front under the Pakistani leadership. See his enthusiastic review of the Arabic translation of *al-Nizam al-'Alami al-Jadid* originally authored by Pakistani author Muhammad 'Ali, "al-Nizam al-'Alami al-Jadid," *al-Risala*, March 4, 1946, 233–34. The book was translated by Ahmad al-Sahhar, a sibling of the founder of the Misr Publishing House Sa'id al-Sahhar.

75. Nazik al-Mala'ika, "Al-Qawmiyya al-'Arabiyya wa-l-Mutashakkikun," *al-Adab* 7, July 7, 1960, 3.

6. The People against Sayyid Qutb

1. In English, the most detailed account is provided by Barbara H. E Zollner, *The Muslim Brotherhood: Hasaf al-Hudaybi and Ideology* (London: Routledge, 2009). See also

Fawaz A. Gerges, *Making the Arab World: Nasser, Qutb, and the Clash That Shaped the Middle East* (Princeton, NJ: Princeton Univ. Press, 2018), 236–83.

2. This version is provided by Muhammad Qutb. See the copy of his letter posted on a blog al-Din al-Khali: "Bara' Shaykh Sayyid Qutb," al-Din al-Khalis, April 11, 2003, http://aldeenelkhles.blogspot.com/2013/04/blog-post_11.html.

3. Walter Armbrust, *Martyrs and Tricksters: An Ethnography of the Egyptian Revolution* (Princeton, NJ: Princeton Univ. Press, 2019), 17.

4. Armbrust, *Martyrs and Tricksters*, 169–70.

5. Abu al-Hasan Al-Nadwi, *Mudhakkarat Sa'ih fi-l-Sharq al-Awsat* (Cairo: Matba'at al-Risala, 1978), 95.

6. 'Abd 'Allah al-'Aqil, *Min 'Alam al-Da'wa al-Islamiyya wa-l-Harakat al-Islamiyyat al-Mu'assara* (Jedda: Dar al-Bashir, 2008), 315–16.

7. Ahmad 'Abd al-Majid provided the list of readings given by Qutb, which included the classical scholarship of Islam and books on literature: Ahmad 'Abd al-Majid, "al-Ikhwan wa 'Abd al-Nasser: Al-Qissat al-Kamila li-Tanzim 1965," IkhwanWiki, accessed July 29, 2020, https://www.ikhwanwiki.com.

8. Wadi' Filistin, in discussion with the author, January 2014, Cairo.

9. 'Abd al-Majid, *al-Ikhwan wa 'Abd al-Nasser*. This information was also provided in the September 8, 1965, issue of *al-Jumhuriyya*.

10. 'Ashmawi was summoned to repeat his testimony on the 1965 Organization in 1982 following the assassination of Sadat, and in 2005 after the electoral victory of the Brotherhood. Serialized in *al-Musawwar* newspaper after Sadat's assassination in 1981, the memoir was published as a book in 1993 under the title *al-Ta'arikh al-Sirri li-Jama'at al-Ikhwan al-Muslimin: Mudhakkarat 'Ali 'Ashmawi Akhir Qadat al-Tanzim al-Khas*. It was republished in 2006 by Markaz Ibn Khaldun li-l-Dirasat al-Istiratijiyya.

11. One of these networks was formed by Qutb's future cellmate, Muhammad Yusuf Hawash, but was discovered early on leading to Hawash's arrest, 'Abd al-Fatah al-Khalidi, *Sayyid Qutb: Min al-Milad ila al-Istishhad* (Damascus: Dar al-Qalam, 2007), 375–76.

12. On Egypt's involvement in the war in Yemen, see Jesse Ferris, *Nasser's Gamble: How Intervention in Yemen Caused the Six-Day War and the Decline of Egyptian Power* (Princeton, NJ: Princeton Univ. Press, 2012).

13. *Al-Jumhuriyya*, December 8, 1965, 5.

14. Hazim Kandil, *Soldiers, Spies, and Statesmen: Egypt's Road to Revolt* (London: Verso, 2014), 75; Hamada Husni, *Shams Badran: Al-Rajul Aladhi Hakama Misr* (Muscat: Maktaba Bayrut, 2008), 53.

15. Ahmad Ra'if, *Al-Bawwaba al-Sawda: Safahat min Ta'arikh al-Ikhwan al-Muslimin* (Cairo: al-Zahra' li-l-'Alam al-'Arabi, 1989), 47–104.

16. "Majlis al-Wizara' . . . Fi-l Sijn! *al-Musawwar*, December 3, 1954, 16.

17. "Al-Irhabi 'Abd al-Fatah al-Sharif Ya'atarif: Hawaltu Takwin al-Tashkil al-'Alani li-Muharabat al-Tashkil al-Sirri," *al-Jumhuriyya*, October 11, 1965, 3; "al-'Itirafat al-Jadida

li-Ahad Quda al-Jihaz al-Sirri li-l-Ikhwan: al-'Itiqalat 'Ajalat al-Mu'atamirun ila-l-Qiyam bi-'Amal al-Ightiyalat wa-l-Nasf," *al-Jumhuriyya*, October 13, 1965, 3; "Mas'ul 'n al-Mutafajarat fi-l-Tashkil al-Irhabi Yaqul: Sana'tu Mutafajarat wa Qanabil Mulutuv wa Tadarabtu 'Ala al-Musara'a wa Istikhdam al-Asliha," *al-Jumhuriyya*, October 25, 5.

18. "Al-Irhabi Faruq al-Minshawi Ya'atarif: Mu'amarat al-Ikhwan Did al-Islam wa Did Maslahat al-Watan," *al-Jumhuriyya*, October 23, 1965, 10.

19. "Mas'ul 'n al-Mutafajarat fi-l-Tashkil al-Irhabi Yaqul: Mu'amarat al-Irhab La Tufid Ahadan wa Laysa fi Maslahat Ay Insan," *al-Jumnhuriyya*, October 25, 1965, 5.

20. For example, "Sibaq al-Mawt Bayn Khalaya al-Tanzim al-Irhabi wa Mabahith al-Jina'iyya al-'Askariyya," *al-Jumhuriyya*, September 9, 3; "Sayyid Qutb Yar'as al-Tanzim fi-l-Dakhil wa Sa'id Ramadan Yatawala al-Tamwil min al-Kharij," *al-Jumhuriyya*, September 8, 1965, 1; and "Dawr Sayyid Qutb fi-l Mu'amara," *al-Jumhuriyya*, October 6, 1965, 1. See also "Sayyid Qutb Abraz Muddaribin li-l Ightiyyalat," *Akhbar al-Yawm*, September 8, 1965.

21. See, for example, 'Ali Amin, "Law Lam Yahtazz Yad Mahmud 'Abd al-Latif,"in Taha Husayn, Muhammad al-Tabi'i, Ahmad Amin, Kamil al-Shinawi, Jalal Amin al-Muhamisi, *Ha'ula'u . . . Humma al-Ikhwan!!* (Cairo: n.p., 1954), 75–77.

22. The poem of Bayram al-Tunsi "Dawla al-Ikhwanjiyya," originally published in 1954 in *al-Tahrir*, and republished in al-Dustur in 2013: "Fi Dhikra Rahil Bayram al-Tunsi. Qasida Dawlat Ikhwanjiyya," *al-Dustur*, January 6, 2003, https://www.dostor.org/124316.

23. Mahmud Sa'adni, "Jama'a Hadha al-Rajul," *Sabah al-Khayr*, September 16, 1965, 17.

24. Muhammad Muhammad al-Siba'i, "Idharu min al-Ikhwan al-Shayyatin," in *Ra'i al-Din fi Ikhwan al-Shaytan* (Cairo: Majlis al-A'ala li-l-Shu'un al-Diniyya, 1965), 36–39.

25. Mustafa Bahjat Badawi, "'Yajib an Nakhud al-Dars," *al-Jumhuriyya*, October 14, 1965, 3.

26. Fathi Ghanim, "al-Irhab," *Sabah al-Khayr*, September 16, 1965, 9.

27. 'Ala' al-Dib, "al-Tafkir al-Aswad," *Sabah al-Khayr*, September 30, 1965, 26.

28. *Akhir Sa'a*, September 15, 1965, 7.

29. *Majallat al-Shubban al-Muslimin*, November 1965, 38–40.

30. "Dirasat Islamiyya," *Majallat al-Azhar*, November 8, 1954, 373. The editor in chief of Azhar's periodical was Muhibb al-Din al-Khatib, who had prefaced Qutb's *Dirasat Islamiyya*.

31. Marina Stagh, *The Limits of Freedom of Speech: Prose Literature and Prose Writers under Nasser and Sadat* (Stockholm: Almqvist & Wiksel International, 1993), 137.

32. In the Dar al-Ma'arif (1968) edition of his *Ithr al-Qur'an fi Tatawwur al-Naqd al-Adabi*, Muhammad Zaghlul Salam removed the reference to Qutb that had been included in its Maktabat al-Shabbab edition (1952).

33. A former colleague of Qutb's from Dar al-'Ulum, the poet Mahmud Hasan Isma'il, did not include in his collection a poem he had composed for the occasion of

Qutb's trip to the United States. 'Abd al-Fatah Jamal al-Dara'imi, "Dar al-'Ulum: Ma Qabla wa Ma Ba'd Hasan al-Banna wa Sayyid Qutb," *Ida'at*, September 30, 2016, https://www.ida2at.com/dar-pre-and-post-ncis-and-sayed-qutb/.

34. A 1991 edition of the collection of stories for children *Rawdat al-Tifl* omits Qutb's name, although its original 1946 edition features him alongside Yusuf Murad and Amina Sa'id. Qutb's name is similarly omitted from multiple editions of *Qassas al-Anbya'*, which was published in 1947 in collaboration with al-Sahhar.

35. Wadi' Filistin, in discussion with the author, January 2014, Cairo.

36. Ahmad Hasan al-Zayyat, "Ya Allah li-Dini al-Mazlum," *Majallat al-Azhar* 4 (October 1966): 381–84.

37. Nagib Mahfuz, *Al-Maraya* (Cairo: Dar al-Shuruq, 2007), 214–19.

38. Armbrust, *Martyrs and Tricksters*, 160.

39. Armbrust, 165–80.

40. See Giedrė Šabasevičiūtė, "Diriger L'Egypte depuis sa tombe: le retour de Sayyid Qutb, 1954, 1963, 2013," *Vacarme* 74 (2016): 44–49.

41. On the controversy, see "Markaz al-Ahram Yastu 'Ala Haqq Nashr al-A'mal al-Shi'riyya al-Kamila li-Sayyid Qutb," *al-Shuruq*, August 24, 2012, https://www.shorouknews.com/news/view.aspx?cdate=24082012&id=ebdcfa19-03b9-4dc9-b523-0baec9ba0f87.

42. On Muhammad Qutb's role in adjusting his brother's works to the Saudi Arabian political and religious climate, see Stéphane Lacroix, *Awakening Islam: The Politics of Religious Dissent in Contemporary Saudi Arabia* (Cambridge, MA: Harvard Univ. Press, 2011), 53–56.

43. One of the first to notice the importance of *waḥdat al-wujūd* in Qutb's writings was the influential Salafi shaykh Nasir al-Din al-Albani, who explained Qutb's theological clumsiness as due to him being an *adib* and not a scholar of Islam. For the debates around the reception of Qutb in Salafi milieus, see Abu 'Abdallah Ahmad bin Ibrahim bin Abu al-'Aynayn, *al-Qawl al-Badi' fi Nusuh al-Shaykh al-Rabi'* (Cairo: Dar al-Lu'lu, 2018).

44. Muhammad Qutb, "Introduction," *Muqawimat al-Tasawwur al-Islami*, by Sayyid Qutb, 8–9.

45. On the Tanwir discourse, see Mona Abaza, "The Trafficking with Tanwir (Enlightenment)," *Comparative Studies of South Asia, Africa, and the Middle East* 30, no. 1 (2010): 32–46.

Conclusion

1. Sayyid Qutb, *Ma'alim fi-l-Tariq* (Cairo: Dar al-Shuruq, 1992), 131.
2. Muhammad Qutb, *Manhaj al-Fann al-Islami* (Cairo: Dar al-Shuruq, n.d.), 45–65.

Bibliography

The Arabic article "al" is ignored in alphabetization.

1. Interviews

al-'Alam, Mahmud Amin. April 2008, Cairo.
'Abd al-Khaliq, Farid. April 2008, Cairo.
Abdel-Malek, Anouar. April 2011, Cairo.
'Azir, Shukri. March 2008, Cairo.
Blau, Joyce. July 2011, Paris.
Filistin, Wadi'. January and April 2014, Cairo.
Ghali, Gamal. April 2011, Cairo.
Grunspan, Robert. July 2011, Paris.
Habashi, Fawzi. March 2008, Cairo.
Hetata, Sherif. May 2011, Cairo.
Hijazi', Abd al-Muti'. September 2011, Cairo.
Kamal, Ahmad Hasan. April 2008, Cairo.
Ra'if, Ahmad. April 2008 and January 2011, Cairo.
al-Sharuni, Yusuf. December 2013, January and February 2014.
al-Tawil, Su'ad. March 2008, Cairo.

2. Newspapers, Magazines, and Journals

The citation of periodicals in endnotes follows the dating system of the Islamic or Gregorian calendars as used in the original periodicals.

al-Adab, 1953–60.
al-Adib, 1946–54.
Akhir Sa'a, 1954–55; 1965–66.

al-'Alam al-'Arabi, 1947.
Apollo, 1932–34.
al-Da'wa, 1951–53.
al-Fajr al-Jadid, 1945–46.
al-Fath, 1926–47.
al-Fikr al-Jadid, 1948.
al-Hadiqa, 1922–34.
al-Hilal, 1922–52.
Jaridat al-Ikhwan al-Muslimin, 1933–38.
al-Jumhuriyya, 1954–55; 1965.
al-Katib al-Misri, 1945–48.
al-Kitab, 1945–53.
Majallat al-Ikhwan al-Muslimin, 1942–48; 1954.
Majallat al-Shubban al-Muslimin, 1929–34; 1964–66.
Majallat al-Shu'un al-Ijtima'iyya, 1939–45.
al-Manar, 1898–1932.
al-Muslimun, 1951–54.
al-Nadhir, 1938.
al-Risala, 1933–53.
Ruz al-Yusuf, 1952–55.
Sabah al-Khayr, 1954–55; 1965–66.
Sahifat Dar al-'Ulum, 1934–48.
al-Thaqafa, 1939–52.
al-Zahra, 1924–28.

3. Catalogs of Publishing Houses and Official Reports

al-Nashrat al-Thaqafiyyat al-Misriyya. Cairo: Idarat al-'Amma li-l-Thaqafa, 1956–58.
al-Sijil al-Thaqafi. Cairo: Idarat al-'Amma li-l-Thaqafa, 1949–50, 1952, 1954, 1959.
Mahkamat al-Sha'b. Al-Madhbatat al-Rasmiyya li-Mahadir Jalasat Mahkamat al-Sha'b. Vol. 4. Cairo: Wizarat al-Irshad al-Qawmi, 1954.
Qa'imat al-Matbu'at al-Thaqafiyya. Cairo: Dar al-Ma'arif bi-Misr, 1957.
Qa'imat al-Matbu'at Maktaba Misr. Cairo: Dar Misr li-l-Tiba'a, 2001.
Qa'imat al-Matbu'at. Cairo: Dar Ihya al-Kutub al-'Arabiyya, 1954.
Qa'imat al-Tawzi'a. Cairo: Dar al-Ma'arif bi-Misr, 1965.

Taqrir 'n al-Idha'at al-Misriyya: al-Fatra min 23 Yuliyu 1952 ila 15 Mayu 1971. Taqrir 'n al-tilifiziyun Misri: al-Fatra min 16 Yuliyu 1960 ila 15 Mayu 1971. Cairo: Lajnat Kitaba Ta'arikh Thawra 23 Yuliyu, 1971.

4. Memoirs, Correspondence, and Literature of Tribute

'Abd al-Hadi, Fatima. *Rihlati Ma' al-Akhawat al-Muslimat.* Cairo: Dar al-Shuruq, 2011.

'Abd al-'Aziz, Ibrahim. *Rasa'il Taha Husayn.* Cairo: Mirit, 2000.

———. *Najib Mahfuz Fi Shibard.* Cairo: Battana, 2017.

———. *Taha Husayn . . . al-Watha'iq al-Sirriyya.* Cairo: Dar al-Shuruq, 2007.

'Abd al-Halim, Mahmud. *Al-Ikhwan al-Muslimun. Ahdath Sana'at al-Ta'arikh. Ru'ya min al-Dakhil.* 3 vols. Alexandria: Dar al-Da'wa, 1979.

Abu al-'Azam, Mona 'Ali. *Awda' Misr al-Sina'iyya: min 1945 Ila 1961.* Cairo: al-Hay'at al-Misriyya al-'Amma li-l-Kitab, 2020.

Abu Naja, Sayyid. *Dhikrayyat 'Ariyya.* Beirut: Dar al-Shuruq, 1979.

al-'Aqqad, 'Abbas. *Ana.* Cairo: Nahdat Misr, 1996.

———. *Rijal 'Araftuhum.* Cairo: Dar al-Hilal, 1963.

———. *Shu'ara' Misr wa Bi'atuhum fi-l-Jil al-Madi.* Cairo: Maktabat al-Nahdat al-Misriyya, 1937.

———. *Yawmiyyat.* Cairo: Nahda Misr, 1996.

Amin, Ahmad. *My Life: The Autobiography of an Egyptian Scholar, Writer and Cultural Leader.* Translated by Issa J. Boullata. Leiden: Brill, 1978.

al-'Aqil, 'Abd 'Allah. *Min 'Alam al-Da'wa al-Islamiyya wa-l-Harakat al-Islamiyyat al-Mu'assara.* Jedda: Dar al-Bashir, 2008.

al-'Aryan, Muhammad Sa'id. *Hayat al-Rafi'i.* Cairo: Maktabat al-Tijara, 1955.

'Ashur, Na'man. *Masrah Hayati.* Cairo: al-Qahira li-l-Thaqafa al-'Arabiyya, 1975.

'Assaf, Mahmud. *Ma' al-Imam al-Shahid Hasan al-Banna.* Cairo: Mu'asassa Iqra' li-l-Nashr wa-l-Tawzi' wa-l-Tarjama, 1993.

al-'Azm, Yusuf. *Ra'id al-Fikr al-Islami al-Mu'assir. Al-Shahid Sayyid Qutb.* Cairo: Dar al-Qalam, 1980.

al-Badawi, 'Abd al-Rahman. *Sira Hayati.* Beirut: Mu'asassat al-'Arabiyya li-l-Tawzi', 2000.

Bakathir, 'Ali Ahmad. *Fann al-Masrahiyya min Khilal Tajaribi al-Shakhsiyya.* Cairo: Dar al-Ma'arif, 1991.

al-Banna, Hasan. *Mudhakkarat al-Da'wa wa-l-Da'iyya*. Kuwait: Maktabat Ufaq, 2012.

Dayf, Shawqi. *Ma'i*. Cairo: Dar al-Ma'arif, 1985.

Fayad, Sulayman. *Kitab al-Namima*. Cairo: Dar Misr al-Mahrusa, 2006.

Filistin, Wadi'. *Wadi' Filistin Yatahadath 'n A'lam 'Asrihi*. 3 vols. Damascus: Dar al-Qalam, 2003.

Gharib, Ma' mun. *al-Sahhar . . . wa-l-Fikr al-Islami*. Cairo: Maktaba Misr, 1985.

al-Ghazzali, Zaynab. *Return of the Pharaoh: Memoir in Nasir's Prison*. Translated by Mokrane Guezzou. Leicester: Islamic Foundation, 2006.

Hafiz, Mahmud. *al-Ma'arik fi-l-Sahafa wa-l-Siyyasa wa-l-Fikr Bayna 1919 wa 1952*. Cairo: Dar al-Jumhuriyya, 1969.

al-Hakim, Tawfik. *Watha'iq Min Kawalis al-Udaba'*. Cairo: Mu'asassat Akhbar al-Yawm, 1977.

Hamid, Muhammad Abu Bakr. *'Ali Ahmad Bakathir fi Mira't 'Asrihi*. Cairo: Maktaba Misr, 1991.

Hamida, Qutb. *Rihla fi Ahrash al-Layl*. Cairo: Dar al-Shuruq, 1998.

Haqqi, Yahya. *Fajr al-Qissat al-Misriyya*. Cairo: Nahdat Misr, 2008.

Haykal, Muhammad Husayn. *Mudhakkarat fi-l-Siyyasa al-Misriyya*. 2 vols. Cairo: Hay'at al-'Amma li-l-Kitab, 2010.

Husayn, Taha. *The Days: His Autobiography in Three Parts*. Translated by E. H. Paxton, Hilary Wayment, and Kenneth Cragg. Cairo: American Univ. in Cairo Press, 1997.

Husayn, Taha, et al. *D. Yusuf Idris bi-Qalam Ha'ula'u*. Cairo: Maktaba Misr, 1986.

'Issa, Salah. *Al-Shakhsiyyat Laha al-'Ajab! Dhikrayyat wa Tarajim wa Dirasat wa Watha'iq*. Cairo: Nahda Misr, 2010.

Jibril, Muhammad. *Aba' al-Sittiniyyat. Jil Lajnat Nashr li-l-Jama'iyyin*. Cairo: Maktaba Misr, 1995.

———. *Al-Sahhar: Rihla ila al-Sirra al-Nabawiyya*. Cairo: Maktaba Misr, n.d.

al-Jundi, Anwar. *Al-Ma'arik al-Adabiyya fi Misr Mundhu 1914/1939*. Cairo: Maktaba Anjlu-Misriyya, 1983.

———. *Min 'Alam al-Fikr wa-l-Adab*. Cairo: Dar al-Qawmiyya, 1964.

———. *Muhakama Fikr Taha Husayn*. Cairo: Dar al-'Itisam, 1984.

———. *Taha Husayn: Hayatuhu wa Fikruhu fi Daw' al-Islam*. Cairo: Dar al-'Itisam, 1977.

Kamal, 'Adil Ahmad. *Al-Nuqat Fawqa al-Huruf: al-Ikhwan al-Muslimun wa-l-Nizam al-Khas*. Cairo: al-Zahra' li-l-'Ilam al-'Arabi, 1987.

Kazim, Safinaz. "100 'Am 'Ala Mawlid Sayyid Qutb . . . Wa 40 'Ala I'damihi." *Al-Sharq al-Awsat*, no. 10178, October 9, 2006. https://archive.aawsat.com/leader.asp?article=386673&issueno=10178#.XyK-tmQzb5s.

Khalid, Muhammad Khalid. *Qissa Hayati*. Cairo: n.p., 1993.

Khidr 'Abbas. *Ha'ula'u 'Araftuhum*. Cairo: Dar al-Ma'arif, 1998.

Mahfuz, Najib. *Al-Maraya*. Cairo: Dar al-Shuruq, 2007.

Makki, Tahir Ahmad. "Sayyid Qutb: Thalath Rasa'il Lam Tunshar Qabl." *al-Hilal*, October 1986, 124–26.

al-Malakh, Kamal. *Taha Husayn: Qahir al-Dhullam*. Cairo: Dar al-Kitab al-Jadid, 1973.

Mandur, Muhammad. *Ma'arik Adabiyya*. Cairo: Dar al-Nahda, 2009.

Mansur, Anis. *Fi Salun al-'Aqqad: Kan Lana al-Ayyam*. Cairo: Nahda Misr, 2012.

al-Mazni, Ibrahim 'Abd al-Qadir. *Qabd al-Rih*. Cairo: Mu'assasa Hindawi li-l-Ta'alim wa-l-Thaqafa, 2012.

———. *Qissa Hayat*. Cairo: Dar al-Shuruq, 2009.

———. *Sabil Hayat*. Cairo: Dar al-Shuruq, 1979.

Musa, Salama. *Tarbiyya Salama Musa*. Cairo: Mu'asassa Khanji, 1962.

al-Nadwi, Abu al-Hasan. *Mudhakkarat Sa'ih fi-l-Sharq al-Awsat*. Cairo: Matba'at al-Risala, 1978.

al-Naqqash, Raja'. *Safahat min Mudhakkarat Najib Mahfuz*. Cairo: Dar al-Shuruq, 2011.

al-Qaradawi, Yusuf. *al-Shaykh al-Ghazzali Kama 'Araftuhu: Rihla Nisf al-Qarn*. Cairo: Dar al-Shuruq, 2008.

———. *Ibn al-Qariyya wa al-Kuttab: Malamih Siruh wa-Masirah*. Cairo: Dar al-Shuruq, 2002.

Qa'ud, Ibrahim. *'Umar al-Tilmisani, Shahidan 'Ala al-'Asr: al-Ikhwan al-Muslimun fi Da'irat al-Haqiqat al-Gha'iba*. Cairo: Dar al-Mukhtar al-Islami, 1985.

Qutb, Sayyid. *A Child from the Village*. Translated by John Calvert. Syracuse, NY: Syracuse Univ. Press, 2004.

Ra'if, Ahmad. *Al-Bawwaba al-Sawda: Sahafat min Ta'arikh al-Ikhwan al-Muslimin*. Cairo: al-Zahra li-l-'Ilam al-'Arabi, 1988.

Radwan, Fathi. *72 Shahran Ma' 'Abd al-Nasir*. Cairo: Dar al-Huriyya, 1985.

Rizq, Jabir. *Madhabih al-Ikhwan fi Sujun Misr*. Cairo: Dar al-'Itisam, 1977.

al-Sahhar, 'Abd al-Hamid. *Hadhihi Hayati*. Cairo: Maktaba Misr, n.d.

———. *Suwwar wa Dhikrayyat*. Cairo: Maktaba Misr, n.d.

al-Sahhar, Sa'id. *Mawaqif fi Hayati*. Cairo: Maktaba Misr, 1991.

al-Salmawi, Muhammad. *Fi Hadra Najib Mahfuz*. Cairo: al-Dar al-Misriyyat al-Lubnaniyya, 2012.

al-Sayyid, Ahmad Lutfi. *Qissat Hayati*. Cairo: al-Hay'at al-Misriyyat al-'Amma li-l-Kitab, 1998.

Shalaq, Ahmad Zakariyya. *Awraq Taha Husayn wa Murasalatuhu*. 2 vols. Cairo: Dar al-Kutub wa-l-Watha'iq al-Qawmiyya, 2007.

al-Sharuni, Yusuf. *Rihlat al-'Umr Ma' Najib Mahfuz*. Cairo: al-Majlis al-A'ala li-l-Thaqafa, 2010.

———. *Wamadat al-Dhakira*. Cairo: al-Majlis al-A'ala li-l-Thaqafa, 2003.

al-Tantawi, 'Ali. *Dhikrayyat*. 6 vols. Jedda: Dar al-Manara li-l-Nashr, 1985.

al-Tilmisani, 'Umar. *Dhikrayyat la Mudhakkarat*. Cairo: Dar al-Tiba'a wa-l-Nashr wa-l-Tawzi', 1985.

5. General Literature

Abaza, Mona. "The Trafficking with *Tanwir* (Enlightenment)." *Comparative Studies of South Asia, Africa, and the Middle East* 30, no. 1 (2010): 32–46.

'Abd al-Hafiz, Sayyid. "Hukm Shara'i fi Jama'at al-Ikhwan al-Muslimin." *al-Jumhuriyya*, October 2, 1954, 3.

al-'Absu, 'Amr. "Al-Sha'ir al-Shaykh al-Adib Muhammad Sadiq 'Arnus." *Rabitat Udaba' al-Sham*, April 31, 2017. http://www.odabasham.net.

Abuali, Eyad. "Words Clothed in Light: Dhikr (Recollection), Colour, and Synaesthesia in Early Kubrawi Sufism." *Iran: Journal of the British Institute of Persian Studies* 58, no 2 (2020): 279–92, https://doi.org/10.1080/05786967.2019.1583046.

'Abdalla, Ahmad. *The Student Movement and National Politics in Egypt, 1923–1973*. London: Saqi, 1985.

Abdel-Hai, Muhammad. "Shelley and the Arabs: An Essay in Comparative Literature." *Journal of Arabic Literature* 3 (1972): 72–89.

Abdel-Malek, Anouar. *Egypte, Société Militaire*. Paris: Ed. du Seuil, 1962.

———. *Egypt: Military Society: The Army Regime, The Left, and Social Change under Nasser*. New York: Random House, 1968.

Abu Rabi', Ibrahim. "Al-Azhar and Islamic Rationalism in Modern Egypt: The Philosophical Contributions of Mustafa 'Abd al-Raziq and 'Abd al-Halim Mahmud." *Islamic Studies* 27, no. 2 (1988): 129–50.

Abu Salih, 'Abd al-Quddus. "Qadiyyat al-Adab al-Islami." *Aluka*, May 5, 2011. https://www.alukah.net/literature_language/0/31650/.

Abu Shadi, Ahmad Zaki. *Al-Shafaq al-Baqi*. Cairo: al-Matba'at al-Salafiyya, 1926.

Abu Wafa, Mahmud. *Anashid Dinniyya Ma' Alhaniha al-Musiqiyya*. Cairo: Maktaba Wahba, 1953.

Abu Zayd, Nasr Hamid. "The Dilemma of the Literary Approach to the Qur'an." *Alif: Journal of Comparative Poetics* 23 (2003): 8–47.

'Ajlan, Kamil Muhammad. *Sultan al-'Ulama*. Cairo: al-Matba'at al-Faruqiyyat al-Haditha, 1950.

al-'Alawina, Ahmad. *Dhil al-'Alam: Qamus al-Tarajim min al-Ashhar al-Rijal wa-l-Nisa' min al-'Arab wa-l-Musta'aribin wa-l-Mustashriqin*. Jedda: Dar al-Manara li-l-Nashr wa-l-Tawzi', 1998.

Allan, Michael. *In the Shadow of World Literature: Sites of Reading in Colonial Egypt*. Princeton, NJ: Princeton Univ. Press, 2016.

Allen, Roger. *The Arabic Literary Heritage: The Development of Its Genres and Criticisms*. Cambridge: Cambridge Univ. Press, 1998.

Amin, Ahmad. "Day'at al-Adab." *al-Thaqafa*, August 20, 1951, 6–7.

al-'Aqqad. *'Abqari al-Islah wa-l-Ta'alim: al-Imam Muhammad 'Abdu*. Cairo: Dar Nahda Misr, 1962.

———. *'Abqariyyat al-Siddiq*. Cairo: al-Hay'at al-Misriyyat al-'Amma li-l-Kitab, 2002.

———. *'Abqariyya Muhammad*. Beirut: al-Maktabat al-'Asriyya, n.d.

———. *al-Islam fi-l-Qarn al-'Ashrin*. Cairo: al-Hay'at al-Misriyyat al-'Amma li-l-Kitab, 1993.

———. *Dhu al-Nurayn. Uthman Ibn 'Affan*. Cairo: Dar Nahda Misr, 2013.

———. *Diwan 'Aqqad Arba't Ajza' fi al-Mujallad al-Wahid*. Cairo: Matba'at al-Muqtataf wa-l-Muqattam, 1928.

———. *Mawsu'at 'Abbas al-'Aqqad al-Islamiyya*. Beirut: Dar al-Kitab al-'Arabi, 1971.

———. *al-Tafkir Farida Islamiyya*. Cairo: Nahda Misr, 2007.

Armbrust, Walter. "Bourgeois Leisure and Media Fantasies." In *New Media in the Muslim World: The Emerging Public Sphere*, edited by Dale F. Eickelman and John W. Anderson, 102–28. Bloomington: Indiana Univ. Press, 2003.

———. "Egyptian Cinema on Stage and Off." In *Off Stage/On Display. Intimacy and Ethnography in the Age of Public Culture*, edited by Andrew Shryock, 69–100. Stanford, CA: Stanford Univ. Press, 2003.

———. *Martyrs and Tricksters: An Ethnography of the Egyptian Revolution*. Princeton, NJ: Princeton Univ. Press, 2019.

———. *Mass Culture and Modernism in Egypt*. Cambridge: Cambridge Univ. Press, 1996.

Arslan, Shakib. *Diwan al-Amir Shakib Arslan*. Cairo: Matba'a al-Manar, 1935.

Ashmawi, Hanna Elsisi. "Mu'ataqal Machine: Power, Gender and Identity in Egypt's Political Prisons." PhD diss., Oxford Univ., 2019.

'Atiyya, 'Ali 'Abd al-Rahman, ed. *Sayyid Qutb, al-'Amal al-Shi'riyya al-Kamila*. Vol. 1. Cairo: Markaz al-Ahram li-l-Nashr, 2012.

al-Azm, Sadiq Jalal. *Naqd al-Fikr al-Dini*. Beirut: Dar al-Tali'a li-l-Tiba'a wa-l-Nashr, 1970.

al-Badawi, Ahmad. *Sayyid Qutb*. Cairo: al-Hay'at al-Misriyyat al-'Amma li-l-Kitab, 1992.

Badawi, M. M. *A Critical Introduction to Modern Arab Poetry*. Cambridge: Cambridge Univ. Press, 1975.

Bakathir, 'Ali Ahmad. *Masrah al-Siyyasa*. Cairo: Maktaba Misr, 1952.

Behrens-Abouseif, Doris. *Beauty in Arabic Culture*. Princeton, NJ: Marcus Wiener, 1999.

Beinin, Joel, and Zachary Lockman. *Workers on the Nile: Nationalism, Communism, Islam, and the Egyptian Working Class*. London: I. B. Tauris, 1988.

Berkey, Jonathan. *The Transmission of Knowledge in Medieval Cairo: A Social History of Islamic Education*. Princeton, NJ: Princeton Univ. Press, 1992.

al-Bishri, Tariq. *al-Harakat al-Siyasiyya fi Misr (1945–1953)*. Cairo: Dar al-Shuruq, 2002.

Boullata, Issa J. "Modern Qur'an Exegesis. A Study of Bint al-Shāti's Method." *Muslim World* 64, no. 2 (1973 April): 103–13.

Bourdieu, Pierre. "L'ontologie politique de Martin Heidegger." *Actes de la recherche en sciences sociales* 5 (1975): 109–56.

Botman, Selma. *The Rise of Egyptian Communism, 1939–1970*. Syracuse, NY: Syracuse Univ. Press, 1988.

Bozarslan, Hamit. *Une histoire de la violence au Moyen-Orient: De la fin de l'Empire Ottoman à Al-Qaïda*. Paris: La Découverte, 2008.

Broucek, James. *The Controversy of Sheikh 'Ali 'Abd al-Raziq*. PhD diss., Florida State Univ., 2012.

Brugman, J. *An Introduction to the History of Modern Arab Literature*. Leiden: A. J. Brill, 1984.

Cachia, Pierre. *Taha Husayn: His Place in the Egyptian Literary Renaissance*. London: Luzac, 1956.

Calvert, John. *Sayyid Qutb and the Origins of Radical Islamism*. London: Hurst, 2010.

———. "Sayyid Qutb and the Power of Political Myth: Insight from Sorel." In "Islam and Society," special issue, *Historical Reflections* 30, no, 3 (2004): 509–28.

Olivier Carré. "L'idéologie politico-religieuse nassérienne à la lumière des manuels scolaires." *Politique étrangère* 4 (1972): 535–53.

———. "Utopies socialisantes en terre arabe d'Orient." *Tiers-Monde* 19, no. 75 (1978): 535–52.

Çayir, Kenan. *Islamic Literature in Turkey: From Epic to Novel.* New York: Palgrave Macmillan, 2017.

Cleveland, William. *Islam against the West: Shakib Arslan and the Campaign for Islamic Nationalism*. Austin: Univ. of Texas Press, 1985.

Cormack, Raphael. "Oedipus on the Nile: Translations and Adaptations of Sophocles' Oedipus Tyrannos in Egypt, 1900–1970." PhD diss., Univ. of Edinburgh, 2017.

Dakhli, Leyla. *Une génération d'intellectuels arabes: Syrie et Liban (1908–1940).* Paris: Ed. Karthala, 2009.

De Certeau, Michel. *L'invention du quotidient 1: Arts de faire*. Paris: Gallimard, 1990.

Deyoung, Terri. *Mahmud Sami al-Barudi: Reconfiguring Society and the Self.* Syracuse, NY: Syracuse Univ. Press, 2015.

Dhihni, Salah. *Fi-l-Daraja al-Thamina*. Cairo: n.p., n.d.

Di-Capua, Yoav. *Gatekeepers of the Arab Past: Historians and History Writing in Twentieth-Century Egypt*. Berkeley: Univ. of California Press, 2009.

———. "The Intellectual Revolt of the 1950s and 'The Fall of Udabā.'" In *Commitment and Beyond: Reflections on/of the Political in Arabic Literature since the 1940s*, edited by Friederike Pannewick and George Khalil, 89–104. Wiesbaden: Ludwing Reichert, 2015.

———. *No Exit: Arab Existentialism, Jean-Paul Sartre, and Decolonization*. Chicago: Univ. of Chicago Press, 2018.

Eickelman, Dale F. and Salvatore, Armando, eds. "The Public Sphere and Muslim Identities." In "Priorities of Social Justice," special issue, *Archives Européennes de Sociologie* 43, no. 1 (2002): 92–115.

El Shamsy, Ahmed. *Rediscovering the Islamic Classics: How Editors and Print Culture Transformed an Intellectual Tradition.* Princeton, NJ: Princeton Univ. Press, 2020.

El Shakry, Omnia. *The Arabic Freud: Psychoanalysis and Islam in Modern Egypt.* Princeton, NJ: Princeton Univ. Press, 2017.

———. *The Great Social Laboratory: Subjects of Knowledge in Colonial and Postcolonial Egypt.* Stanford, CA: Stanford Univ. Press, 2007.

———. "The Vexed Archives of Decolonization in the Middle East." *American Historical Review* 120 (2015): 920–34.

———. "Youth as Peril and Promise: The Emergence of Adolescent Psychology in Postwar Egypt." *International Journal of Middle Eastern Studies* 43 (2011): 591–610.

Elias, Norbert. *The Court Society.* New York: Pantheon, 1983.

———. *Mozart: A Portrait of a Genius.* Cambridge: Polity, 1993.

———. *La société des individus.* Paris: Fayard, 1991.

Elshakry, Marwa. *Reading Darwin in Arabic, 1860–1950.* Chicago: Univ. of Chicago Press, 2013.

Fahmy, Zyad. *Ordinary Egyptians: Creating the Modern Nation through Popular Culture.* Stanford, CA: Stanford Univ. Press, 2011.

Farag, Iman. "Les manuels d'histoire égyptienne: genèse et imposition d'une norme." *Genèses* 3, no. 44 (2001): 4–29.

Ferris, Jesse. *Nasser's Gamble: How Intervention in Yemen Caused the Six-Day War and the Decline of Egyptian Power.* Princeton, NJ: Princeton Univ. Press, 2012.

Frampton, Martyn. *The Muslim Brotherhood and the West: A History of Enmity and Engagement.* Cambridge, MA: Harvard Univ. Press, 2018.

Furani, Khaled. *Silencing the Sea: Secular Rhythms in Palestinian Poetry.* Stanford, CA: Stanford Univ. Press, 2012.

Gasper, Michael. *The Power of Representation: Publics, Peasants, and Islam in Egypt.* Stanford, CA: Stanford Univ. Press, 2008.

Gerges, Fawaz A. *Making the Arab World: Nasser, Qutb, and the Clash that Shaped the Middle East.* Princeton, NJ: Princeton Univ. Press, 2018.

Gershoni, Israel. "The Evolution of National Culture in Modern Egypt: Intellectual Formation and Social Diffusion, 1892–1945." *Poetics Today* 13, no. 2 (1992): 325–50.

Gershoni, Israel, and Jankowski, James. *Islam and the Arabs: The Search for Egyptian Nationhood, 1900–1930.* Oxford: Oxford Univ. Press, 1986.

———. *Redefining the Egyptian Nation, 1930–1945.* Cambridge: Cambridge Univ. Press, 1995.

Gesink, Indira Falk. *Islamic Reform and Conservatism: Al-Azhar and the Evolution of Modern Sunni Islam.* London: I. B. Tauris, 2010.

al-Ghamrawi, Muhammad. *al-Naqd al-Tahlili li-l-Kitab al-Adab al-Jahili*. Cairo: al-Matbaʿat al-Salafiyya, 1929.

Ghanim, Fathi. *Maʿaraka Bayn al-Dawla wa-l-Muthaqqafin*. Cairo: Dar Akhbar al-Yawm, 1995.

Gharib, Muhammad ʿAli. *Rajulan wa Imraʾa*. Cairo: Dar al-Maʾarif, 1945.

Ginat, Rami. *Egypt's Incomplete Revolution: Lutfi al-Khuli and Nasser's Socialism in the 1960s*. London: Frank Cass, 1997.

Giordani, Angela. "To Be an *Adib*: Sayyid Qutb's Intellectual Biography Reconsidered." Master's thesis, Columbia Univ., 2014.

Gonzales-Quijano, Yves. *Les gens du livre: Edition et champ intellectuel dans l'Égypte républicaine*. Paris: CNRS, 1998.

Gordon, Joel. *Nasser's Blessed Movement: Free Officers and the July Revolution*. Oxford: Oxford Univ. Press, 1992.

Gräf, Bettina. "From the Pocketbook to Facebook: Maktabat Wahba, Publishing and Political Ideas in Cairo since the 1940s." In *Ways of Knowing Muslim Cultures and Societies: Studies in Honour of Gudrun Krämer*, edited by Bettina Gräf, Birgit Krawietz, and Schirin Amir-Moazami, 221–45. Leiden: Brill, 2018.

Gran, Peter. *Islamic Roots of Capitalism: Egypt, 1740–1840*. Syracuse, NY: Syracuse Univ. Press, 1998.

Gunaydin, Muhammet. "The Idea of Multiple Meanings in al-Jurjani's Theory of Composition." *İstanbul Üniversitesi İlahiyat Fakültesi Dergisi*, no. 17 (2008): 127–43.

Guth, Stephan. "Islamist Belles Lettres—Bourgeois and Secular: Interesting Parallels between Ali Nar's Arilar Ülkesi (The Bees' Island, 1994) and Texts from German Enlightenment." In *Uluslararasi Karsilastirmali Edebiyatbilim Kongresi, Sakarya Üniversitesi, Adapazari, 07–08 Eylül 2006: Kongre Bildirileri*, edited by B. Baytekin and T. F. Uluc, 312–26. Serdivan: Sakarya Üniversitesi Basimevi, 2006.

Haggai, Erlich. *Students and University in Twentieth-Century Egyptian Politics*. London: Frank Cass, 1989.

al-Hakim, Tawfiq. *Muhammad*. Cairo: Maktaba Misr, n.d.

Halevi, Leor. *Modern Things on Trial: Islam's Global and Material Reformation in the Age of Rida, 1865–1935*. New York: Columbia Univ. Press, 2019.

Hammoudi, Abdellah, *Master and Disciple: The Cultural Foundations of Moroccan Authoritarianism*. Chicago: Univ. of Chicago Press, 1997.

Hamzah, Dyala, ed. *The Making of the Arab Intellectual (1880–1960: Empire, Public Sphere, and the Colonial Coordinates of Selfhood.* London: Routledge, 2013.

———. "Production des classes moyennes" et l'émergence du "social" pendant la Nahda: Et le confessionnel (al-tā'ifiyya) dans tout cela?" *Egypte-Monde Arabe*, no. 20 (February 2019): 57–78.

Hanna, Nelly. *In Praise of Books: A Cultural History of Cairo's Middle Class, Sixteenth to the Eighteenth Century.* Syracuse, NY: Syracuse Univ. Press, 2003.

Hanssen, Jens, and Weiss, Max Weiss, eds. *Arabic Thought beyond the Liberal Age: Towards an Intellectual History of the Nahda*. Cambridge: Cambridge Univ. Press, 2016.

Hatim, Muhammad 'Abd al-Qadir. "Hadhihi al-Majalla." *al-Thaqafa*, July 22, 1963, 1–2.

Haykal, Muhammad Husayn. *Fi Awqat al-Faragh.* Cairo: Maktaba al-Nahda al-Misriyya, 1968.

———. *Hayat Muhammad.* Cairo: Mu'assasa Hindawi li-l-Ta'alim wa-l-Thaqafa, 2012.

———. *Thawrat al-Adab.* Cairo: Dar al-Kutub wa-l-Watha'iq al-Qawmiyya, 2011.

Henry, Mélanie. "Le 'trésor' révolutionnaire: insurrections et militantisme à Alexandrie en 1946 et 1977." PhD diss., Aix-Marseille Univ., 2018.

Hirschkind, Charles. *The Ethical Soundscape: Cassette Sermons and Islamic Counterpublics.* New York: Columbia Univ. Press, 2006.

Holt, Elisabeth. *Fictitious Capital: Silk, Capital, and the Rise of the Arabic Novel.* New York: Fordham Univ. Press, 2017.

Hourani, Albert. *Arabic Thought in the Liberal Age, 1798–1939.* Cambridge: Cambridge Univ. Press, 1983.

Husayn, Muhammad 'Abd al-Baqi. *Diwan Sayyid Qutb.* Al-Mansurah: Dar al-Wafa' li-l-Tiba'a wa-l-Nashr wa-l-Tawzi', 1989.

Husayn, Taha. *'Ala Hamish al-Sira*. Cairo: Dar al-Ma'arif, 2004.

———. *Fi-l-Adab al-Jahili.* Cairo: Lajnat al-Ta'alif wa-l-Tarjama wa-l-Nashr, 1933.

———. *Fi-l-Shi'r al-Jahili.* Cairo: Ru'a li-l-Nashr wa-l-Tawzi', 2007.

———. *Hadith al-Arbi'a*, 3 vols. Cairo: Dar al-Ma'arif, n.d.

———. *Khisam wa Naqd.* Beirut: Dar al-'Ilm al-Malayyin, 1979.

———. *Mustaqbal al-Thaqafa fi Misr.* Cairo: Dar al-Ma'arif, 1944.

Husayn, Taha, Muhammad al-Tabi'i, Ahmad Amin, Kamil al-Shinawi, Jalal Amin al-Muhamisi. *Ha'ula'u . . . Humma al-Ikhwan!!* Cairo: n.p., n.d.

Husni, Hamada. *Shams Badran: Al-Rajul Aladhi Hakama Misr.* Muscat: Maktaba Bayrut, 2008.

Ibrahim,'Uways 'Uthman, et al. *Dumu' al-Shu'ara' 'Ala al-Rahil al-Karim Faqid al-Watan wa Za'im al-Sharq Sa'd Zaghlul Basha.* Cairo: Maktabat al-Amana, 1928.

'Izz al-Din, Yusuf. *Al-Ishtirakiyya wa-l-Qawmiyya wa Ithruha fi-l-Adab al-Hadith.* Cairo: n.p., 1976.

al-Jada', Ahmad, and Husni Adham Jarrar. *Anashid al-Da'wa al-Islamiyya.* Mansurah: Dar al-Wafa', 1992.

Jamal, 'Adil Sulayman, ed. *Jamharat Maqalat al-Ustaz Mahmud Muhammad Shakir.* Cairo: Maktabat al-Khanji, n.d.

Johnson, Amy J. *Reconstructing Rural Egypt: Ahmed Hussein and the History of Egyptian Development.* Syracuse, NY: Syracuse Univ. Press, 2003.

Kamil, 'Adil. *Milim al-Akbar.* Cairo: al-Karma li-l-Nashr wa al-Tawzi', 2014.

Kalmbach, Hilary. "Teaching Teachers How to Teach: Transnational Exchange and the Introduction to Social-Scientific Pedagogy in 1890s Egypt." In *The Long 1890s in Egypt: Colonial Quiescence, Subterranean Resistance,* edited by Marilyn Booth and Anthony Gorman, 87–116. Edinburgh: Edinburgh Univ. Press, 2014.

Kandil, Hazim. *Soldiers, Spies, and Statesmen: Egypt's Road to Revolt.* New York: Verso, 2002.

Kassab, Elisabeth Suzanne. *Contemporary Arab Thought: Cultural Critique in Contemporary Perspective.* New York: Columbia Univ. Press, 2009.

Kazziha, Walid. "The Jarida-Umma Group and Egyptian Politics." *Middle Eastern Studies* 13, no. 3 (1977): 373–85.

Kendal, Elisabeth, *Literature, Journalism, and the Avant-Garde: Intersection in Egypt.* London: Routledge, 2006.

Khalafallah, Muhammad. *al-Fann al-Qassasi fi-l-Qur'an al-Karim.* Cairo: Sina li-l-Nashr, 1999.

Khaldi, Boutheina. *Egypt Awakening in the Early Twentieth Century.* New York: Palgrave Macmillan, 2012.

al-Khalidi, 'Abd al-Fatah. *Sayyid Qutb: Min al-Milad ila al-Istishhad.* Damascus: Dar al-Qalam, 2007.

al-Kharasi, Sulayman Bin Salih, ed. *Al-Hadiqa: Majmu'at Adab Bari' wa Hikma Baligha.* Riyad: Dar al-'Asima, 2011.

Khatab, Sayed. "Citizenship Rights of Non-Muslims in the Islamic State of Hakimiyya Espoused by Sayyid Qutb." *Islam and Christian-Muslim Relations* 13, no. 2 (April 2002): 163–87.

———. *The Political Thought of Sayyid Qutb: The Theory of Jahiliyya*. London: Routledge, 2006.

———. *The Power of Sovereignty: The Political and Ideological Philosophy of Sayyid Qutb*. London: Routledge, 2006.

al-Khatib, Muhibb al-Din. *Taghur: Bi'atuhu, Tufulatuhu, Shababuhu*. Cairo: al-Matba'at al-Salafiyya, 1926.

al-Khidr, Muhammad Husayn. *Naqd Kitab Fi-l-Sh'ir al-Jahili*. Cairo: Mu'assasa Hindawi li-l-Ta'lim wa-l-Thaqafa, 2014.

Klemm, Verena. "Different Notions of Commitment (*iltizam*) and Committed Literature (*al-adab al-multazim*) in the Literary Circles in the Mashriq." *Middle Eastern Literatures* 3 (2000): 51–62.

Kreil, Aymon. "Territories of Desire: A Geography of Competing Intimacies in Cairo." *Journal of Middle East Women's Studies* 12, no. 2 (July 2016): 166–80.

Kubalek, Magdalena. "Paraenetic Character of Modern Islamic Prose." *CLEaR* 3, no. 1(2016): 1–9.

———. "Should the Culture Be Engaged? Modern Islamic Literature and Its Religious and Political Engagement." *International Journal of Culture and History* 2, no. 1 (2016): 54–58.

Lacroix, Stephan. *Awakening Islam: The Politics of Religious Dissent in Contemporary Saudi Arabia*. Cambridge, MA: Harvard Univ. Press, 2011.

Lagrange, Frédéric. "Musiciens et poètes en Egypte au temps de la Nahda." PhD diss., Paris VIII-Sorbonne, 1994.

Lahire, Bernard. *Frantz Kafka: Éléments pour une théorie de la création littéraire*. Paris: Découverte, 2018

Lauzière, Henri. "The Construction of Salafiyya: Reconsidering Salafism from the Perspective of Conceptual History." *International Journal of Middle East Studies* 42 (2010): 369–89.

———. *The Making of Salafism: Islamic Reform in the Twentieth Century*. New York: Columbia Univ. Press, 2016.

Lia, Brynjar. *The Society of the Muslim Brothers in Egypt: The Rise of an Islamic Mass Movement, 1928–1942*. Ithaca, NY: Ithaca, 1998.

Linthicum, Nancy. "The Cultural Newspaper Akhbar al-Adab and the Making of Egypt's "Nineties Generation." *Alif: Journal of Comparative Poetics* 37 (2017): 229–61.

al-Madani, Muhammad, et al. *Ra'i al-Din fi-l-Ikhwan al-Shaytan*. Cairo: al-Majlis al-A'la li-l-Shu'un al-Islamiyya, 1965.

Mahmoudi, Abdelrashid. *Tāhā Husayn's Education: From Azhar to the Sorbonne.* Richmond: Curzon, 1998.

Makarius, Raoul. *La jeunesse intellectuelle d'Égypte au lendemain de la Seconde Guerre mondiale.* La Haye: Mouton, 1960.

Massad, Joseph. *Desiring Arabs.* Chicago: Univ. of Chicago Press, 2007.

al-Mawdudi, Abu al-'Ala. *Al-Islam wa-l-Jahiliyya.* Beirut: Dar al-Fikr al-Jadid, n.d.

Mayeur-Jaouen, Catherine. "Les débuts d'une revue néo-salafiste: Muhibb al-Din al-Khatib et al-Fath de 1926 à 1928." *Revue des Mondes Musulmans et de la Méditerranée,* nos. 95–98 (2002): 227–55.

McLarney, Ellen Anne. *Soft Force: Women in Egypt's Islamic Awakening.* Princeton, NJ: Princeton Univ. Press, 2015.

Meijer, Roel. "L'élaboration d'un modernisme autoritaire: les intellectuels de gauche et la réforme de la société égyptienne dans les années 1950." *Cahiers d'histoire: Revue d'histoire critique,* nos. 105–6 (2008): 203–34.

———. *The Quest for Modernity: Secular-Liberal and Left-Wing Political Thought in Egypt, 1945–1958.* London: Routledge/Curzon, 2002.

Meisami, Julie Scott, and Starkey, Paul, eds. *Encyclopedia of Arabic Literature.* Vol. 2. London: Routledge, 1999.

Messick, Brinkley. *The Calligraphic State: Textual Domination and History in a Muslim Society.* Berkeley: Univ. of California Press, 1992.

al-Mi'ddawi, Anwar. *Kalimat fi-l-Adab.* Cairo: al-Maktabat al-'Asriyya, 1966.

Mitchell, Richard. *The Society of the Muslim Brothers.* Oxford: Oxford Univ. Press, 1993.

Mitchel, Timothy. *Colonizing Egypt.* Berkeley: Univ. of California Press, 1988.

Musallam, Adnan. *From Secularism to Jihad: Sayyid Qutb and the Foundations of Radical Islamism.* Westport, CT: Praeger, 2005.

al-Muti'i, Lama'i. *Mawsu'a Nisa' wa Rijal fi Misr.* Cairo: Dar al-Shuruq, 2003.

al-Namnam, Hilmi. *Ba'that Sayyid Qutb. Al-Watha'iq al-Rasmiyya.* Cairo: Dar al-Kutub wa al-Watha'iq al-Qawmiyya, 2017.

———. *Sayyid Qutb: Sirat al-Tahawwulat.* Cairo: al-Karma li-l-Nashr wa-l-Tawzi', 2014.

———. *Sayyid Qutb wa-l-Thawra Yulyu.* Cairo: Merit, 2010.

Nasha't Kamal. *Abu Shadi wa Harakat al-Tajdid fi Shi'r al-'Arabi al-Hadith.* Cairo: Dar al-Kitab al-'Arabi li-l-Tiba'a wa-l-Nashr, n.d.

Nelson, Kristina. *The Art of Reciting the Qur'an.* Austin: Univ. of Texas Press, 1986.

Omar, Hussein. "Arabic Thought in the Liberal Cage." In *Islam after Liberalism*, edited by Faisal Devji and Zaheer Kazmi, 17–46. London: Hurst/Oxford Univ. Press, 2017.

Osman, Fathi. "Mawdudi's Contribution to the Development of Modern Islamic Thinking in the Arabic-Speaking World." *Muslim World* 93 (July/October 2009): 465–85.

Osman, Ghada. *A Journey in Islamic Thought: The Life of Fathi Osman*. London: I.B. Tauris, 2011.

Pepe, Teresa. "Critics, Moralists, and Intellectuals: The Transformation of the Udabā of the Arab Naḥda. A Historical-Conceptual Approach." *Modern Oriente* 99 (2019): 179–202.

Picaudou, Nadine. *L'Islam entre religion et l'idéologie: Essai sur la modernité musulmane*. Paris: Gallimard, 2010.

Prakash, Gyan. *Another Reason: Science and the Imagination in Modern India*. Princeton, NJ: Princeton Univ. Press, 1999.

Qutb, Hamida. *Awba ila al-Maladh*. Damascus: Dar al-Qalam, 2011.

———. *Nida' ila al-Diffat al-Ukhra*. Cairo: Dar al-Shuruq, 2000.

Qutb, Muhammad. *Al-Insan Bayn al-Maddiyya wa-l-Islam*. Beirut: Dar al-Shuruq, 1989.

———. *Manhaj al-Fann al-Islami*. Cairo: Dar al-Shuruq, n.d.

———. *Sukhriyyat Saghira*. Beirut: Dar al-Rafidayn, 2017.

Qutb, Sayyid. *al-'Adala al-Ijtima'iyya fi-l-Islam*. Cairo: Maktaba Misr, 1951.

———. *al-'Adala al-Ijtima'iyya fi-l-Islam*. Cairo: Dar Ihya' al-Kutub al-'Arabiyya, 1958.

———. *Ashwak*. Cairo: al-Hay'at al-Misriyyat al-'Amma li-l-Kitab, 2011.

———. *Fi-l-Ta'arikh: Fikra wa Minhaj*. Beirut: Dar al-Shuruq, 2001.

———. *Hadha al-Din*. Cairo: Dar al-Shuruq, 2013.

———. *Islam wa-l-Salam al-'Alami*. Beirut: Dar al-Shuruq, 1993.

———. *Khasa'is al-Tasawwur al-Islami wa Muqawwimatuhu*. Beirut: Dar al-Shuruq, 2002.

———. *Kutub wa Shakhsiyyat*. Cairo: Dar al-Shuruq, 1983.

———. *Ma'alim fi-l-Tariq*. Cairo: Dar al-Shuruq, 1992.

———. *Ma'arakat al-Islam wa-l-Ra'smaliyya*. Cairo: Dar al-Shuruq, 1993.

———. *al-Madina al-Mashura*. Riyad: Dar al-Sa'udiyya, 1985.

———. *Mahammat al-Sha'ir fi-l-Hayat wa Shi'r al-Jil al-Hadir*. Koln: Manshurat al-Jamal, 1996.

———. *Mashahid al-Qiyama fi-l-Qur'an*. Cairo: Dar al-Shuruq, 1993.

———. *Muqawwimat al-Tasawwur al-Islami*. Cairo: Dar al-Shuruq, 1997.

———. *Mustaqbal Hadha al-Din*. Cairo: Dar al-Shuruq, 1993.

———. *Nahwa Mujtam' Islami*. Cairo: Dar al-Shuruq, 1999.

———. *al-Naqd al-Adabi: Usuluhu wa Manahijuhu*. Cairo: Dar al-Shuruq, 2006.

———. *al-Taswir al-Fanni fi-l-Qur'an*. Cairo: Dar al-Shuruq, 2002.

al-Rafi'i, Mustafa Sadiq. *'Ijaz al-Qur'an wa-l-Balaghat al-Nabawiyya*. Cairo: al-Maktabat al-Ahliyya. 1926.

———. *'Ijaz al-Qur'an wa-l-Balagha al-Nabawiyya*. Beirut: Dar al-Kitab al-'Arabi, 1973.

———. *Tahta Rayat al-Qur'an. Al-Ma'araka Bayn al-Qadim wa-l-Jadid*. Beirut: al-Maktabat al-'Asriyya, 2002.

Raineau, Thomas. "Mendiante et orgueilleuse? L'université d'al-Azhar et l'enseignement supérieur égyptien (1860–1930)." *Revue des Mondes Musulmans et de la Méditerranée* 131 (June 2012):: 111–26.

Ramadan, Yasmine. "The Emergence of the Sixties Generation in Egypt and the Anxiety over Categorization." *Journal of Arabic Literature* 43 (2012): 409–30.

Reid, Donald Malcolm. *Cairo University and the Making of Modern Egypt*. Cam bridge: Cambridge Univ. Press, 1990.

Revel, Jacques. *Jeux d'Échelles: La micro-analyse à l'expérience*. Paris: Gallimard & Le Seuil, 1996.

Reynolds, Nancy Y. *A City Consumed: Urban Commerce, the Cairo Fire, and the Politics of Decolonization in Egypt*. Stanford, CA: Stanford Univ. Press, 2012.

Richard, Jacquemond. *Entre scribes et écrivains: le champ littéraire dans l'Egypte contemporaine*. Paris: Actes Sud, 2003.

Rizvi, Sayyid Muhammad. "Muhibb al-Din al-Khatib: A Portrait of Salafist-Arabist (1886–1969)." PhD diss., Simon Fraser Univ., 1991.

Robinson, Francis. "Technology and Religious Change: Islam and the Impact of Print." In "How Social, Political and Cultural Information Is Collected, Defined, Used and Analyzed," special issue, *Modern Asian Studies* 27, no. 1 (1993): 229–51.

Roussillon, Alain. "Réforme sociale et politique en Égypte au tournant des années 1940." *Egypte/Monde Arabe*, nos. 18–19 (1994): 197–236.

———. "Republican Egypt Interpreted: Revolution and Beyond." In *The Cambridge History of Egypt*, edited by M. W. Daly, 334–93. Cambridge: Cambridge Univ. Press, 1998.

———. *al-Mujtam' al-Misri: Judhuruhu wa Ufaquhu*. Casablanca: Sina li-al-Nashr, 1993.

———. "Trajectoires réformistes: Sayyid Qutb et Sayyid 'Uways: figures modernes de l'intellectuel en Égypte." *Égypte/Monde Arabe*, no. 6 (1991): 91–139.

Russel, Mona. *Middle East in Focus (Egypt)*. Oxford: ABC-CLIO, 2013.

Ryad, Umar. "A Printed Muslim 'Lighthouse' in Cairo: al-Manar's Early Years, Religious Aspiration, and Reception (1898–1903)." *Arabica* 45 (2009): 27–60.

Ryzova, Lucie. *The Age of the Efendiya: Passages to Modernity in National-Colonial Egypt*. Oxford: Oxford Univ. Press, 2014.

———. "My Notepad Is My Friend: Efendis and the Act of Writing in Modern Egypt." *Maghreb Review* 32, no. 4 (2007): 323–48.

Šabasevičiūtė, Giedrė. "Diriger L'Egypte depuis sa tombe: le retour de Sayyid Qutb, 1954, 1965, 2013." *Vacarme* 74 (2016): 44–49.

———. "Sayyid Qutb and the Crisis of Culture in Late 1940s Egypt." *International Journal for Middle East Studies* 50 (2018): 85–101.

———. "Sociabilités et ruptures biographiques: retour sur la conversion islamiste de Sayyid Qutb." *Critique internationale* 88, no. 3 (2020): 131–50.

———. "When a Coterie Becomes a Generation: Intellectual Sociability and the Narrative of Generational Change in Sayyid Qutb's Egypt." In *Snapshots of Change: Methodological Approaches to Societies in Transformation*, edited by Yasmine Berriane, Aymon Kreil, and Annuska Derks Dorothea Lüddeckens. London: Palgrave Macmillan, 2021.

al-Sahhar, 'Abd al-Hamid, and Sayyid Qutb. *Qassas al-Anbiya'*. Cairo: Maktaba Misr, 1951.

———. *Suwwar wa Dhikrayyat*. Cairo: Maktaba Misr, n.d.

Sa'id, 'Abd al-Mughni. *Al-Islam wa l Usul al-Fikriyya: al-Ishtirakiyya al-'Arabiyya*. Cairo: Maktaba al-Anjlu-Misriyya, 1960.

al-Sa'id, Rifa't. *Al-Sahafat al-Yasariyya fi Misr, 1925–1948*. Cairo: Maktaba Madbuli, 1977.

Sapiro, Gisèle. 2009. *La Guerre des Écrivains, 1940–1953*. Paris: Fayard, 1999.

———. "Modèles d'intervention politique des intellectuels: Le cas français." *Actes de la recherche en sciences sociales* 1–2, nos. 176–77 (2009): 8–31.

Schayegh, Cyrus, and Yoav Di Capua. "Why Decolonization?" *International Journal for Middle East Studies* 52 (2020): 137–45.

Schielke, Samuli. "Is Prose Poetry a Conspiracy Against the Noble Qur'an? Poetics, Humans, and Gods in Contemporary Egypt." *Historical Social Research* 44, no. 3 (2019): 101–26.

———. "There Will Be Blood: Expectation and Ethics of Violence during Egypt's Stormy Season." *Middle East Critique* 26, no. 3 (2017): 205–20.

Selim, Samah. *Popular Fiction, Translation, and the Nahda.* Cham: Palgrave Macmillan, 2019.

al-Shahhat, Sayyid. *Umm Kulthum wa Hukkam Misr.* Cairo: Maktaba Jazira al-Ward, 2016.

Shalash, 'Ali. *Anwar al-Mi'ddawi.* Cairo: al-Maglis al-'Ala li-l-Kitab, 1990.

———. *Dalil al-Majallat al-Adabiyya fi Misr, 1939–1952: Bibliyughrafiyya 'Amma.* Cairo: al-Majlis al-A'la li-l-Kitab, 1985.

———. *al-Tamarrud 'ala al-Adab: Dirasa fi Tajribat Sayyid Qutb.* Beirut: Dar al-Shuruq, 1994.

Sharlet, Jocelyn. *Patronage and Poetry in the Islamic World: Social Mobility and Status in the Medieval Middle East and Central Asia.* London: I. B. Tauris, 2011.

Shepard, William E. "Sayyid Qutb's Doctrine of "Jahiliyya." *International Journal of Middle East Studies* 35, no. 4 (2004): 521–45.

Shumayyis, 'Abd al-Mun'am. *Suqut al-Qahira.* Dar al-Kitab al-'Arabi, 1951.

Smith, Charles D. *Islam and the Search for Social Order in Modern Egypt: A Biography of Muhammad Husayn Haykal.* Albany: State Univ. of New York Press, 1984.

Springborg, Robert. *Family, Power, and Politics in Egypt: Sayed Bey Marei—His Clan, Clients and Cohorts.* Philadelphia: Univ. of Pennsylvania Press, 1982.

Stagh, Marina. *The Limits of Freedom of Speech: Prose Literature and Prose Writers under Nasser and Sadat.* Stockholm: Almqvist & Wiksel International, 1993.

Starett, Gregory. *Putting Islam to Work: Education, Politics, and Religious Transformation in Egypt.* Berkeley: Univ. of California Press, 1998.

———. "The Varieties of Secular Experience." *Comparative Studies in Society and History* 52 (2010): 626–51.

Szyska, Christian. "Najib al-Kilani on His Career, or How to Become an Ideal Muslim Author." In *Conscious Voices*, edited by S. Guth, P. Furrer, and J. C. Bürgel, 221–35. Beirut: Orient-Institut; Stuttgart: Steiner, 1999.

———. "On Utopian Writing in Nasserist Prison and Laicist Turkey." *Die Welt des Islams* 35, no. 1 (April 1995): 95–125.

Talima, 'Issam. *Hasan al-Bana wa Tajribat al-Fann.* Cairo: Maktaba Wahba, 2008.

Temimi, Sonia. "D'un journalisme l'autre: contours d'une identité professionnelle et évolution de son rapport au pouvoir politique 1923–1970." *Égypte/Monde Arabe*, nos. 4–5 (2001): 81–101.

Toth, James. *Sayyid Qutb: The Life and Legacy of a Radical Islamic Intellectual.* New York: Oxford Univ. Press, 2013.

Vannetzel, Marie. *Les Frères musulmans égyptiens: Enquête sur un secret public.* Paris: Ed. Karthala, 2016.

Winegar, Jessica. "Culture Is the Solution: The Civilizing Mission of Egypt's Culture Palaces." *Review of Middle East Studies* 43, no. 2 (2009): 189–97.

Youssef, A. Hoda. *Composing Egypt: Reading, Writing, and the Emergence of a Modern Nation.* Stanford, CA: Stanford Univ. Press, 2016.

Yunis, Sharif. *Nida' al-Sh'ab. Ta'arikh Naqdi li-l-Idiyulujiyya al-Nasiriyya.* Cairo: Dar al-Shuruq, 2012.

———. *Sayyid Qutb wa-l-Usuliya al-Islamiyya.* Cairo: Dar Tayba li-l-Dirasa wa-l-Nashr, 1995.

Yusuf, Muhammad Khayr Ramadan. *Tatima al-A'lam li-Zarakli.* Beirut: Dar Ibn Hazm, 2002.

Yusuf, Sha'aban. *Al-Mansiyyun Yanhaduna.* Cairo: Battana, 2017.

Yvonne, Haddad. "Sayyid Qutb: Ideologue of Islamic Revival." In *Voices of Resurgent Islam*, ed. John L. Esposito, 67–98. Oxford: Oxford Univ. Press, 1983.

Zollner, Barbara H. E. *The Muslim Brotherhood: Hasan al-Hudaybi and Ideology.* London: Routledge, 2009.

al-Zayyat, Ahmad Hasan. *Difa'a 'n al-Balagha.* Cairo: 'Alam al-Kutub, 1967.

———. *Wahi al-Risala.* Cairo: Nahda Misr, 1956.

Index

Giedrė Šabasevičiūtė is a research fellow at the Oriental Institute, Czech Academy of Sciences, and an associate researcher at CEDEJ (Cairo).